While the relationship of religion and power is a perennial topic, it only continues to grow in importance and scope in our increasingly globalized and diverse world. Religion, on a global scale, has openly joined power struggles, often in support of the powers that be. But at the same time, religion has made major contributions to resistance movements. In this context, current methods in the study of religion and theology have created a deeper awareness of the issue of power: Critical theory, cultural studies, postcolonial theory, subaltern studies, feminist theory, critical race theory, and working class studies are contributing to a new quality of study in the field. This series is a place for both studies of particular problems in the relation of religion and power as well as for more general interpretations of this relation. It undergirds the growing recognition that religion can no longer be studied without the study of power.

More information about this series at
http://www.palgrave.com/gp/series/14754

Felix Wilfred

# Religious Identities and the Global South

Porous Borders and Novel Paths

Felix Wilfred
State University of Madras
Chennai, India

ISSN 2634-6079          ISSN 2634-6087  (electronic)
New Approaches to Religion and Power
ISBN 978-3-030-60737-1      ISBN 978-3-030-60738-8  (eBook)
https://doi.org/10.1007/978-3-030-60738-8

This Palgrave Macmillan imprint is published by the registered company Springer Nature Switzerland AG.
The registered company address is: Gewerbestrasse 11, 6330 Cham, Switzerland

*For my deceased Father, Mother, and Sister Prema*
*In Fond Memory*
*The passing of years has not dulled their amazing love and wisdom*
Nanos gigantum humeris insidentes

# PREFACE

To speak of religious identity is to view religion concretely and in everyday practice. This is different from considering religion merely as a system of belief, meaning, and textual engagement. The religion of the common man and woman is woven into social structures, practices, and cultural configurations. It also influences economic behavior.

Religious identities today not only play a role at the local political level but also affect international relations and politics. In the Global North, there are a plethora of theories on religion which study and interpret it mostly in co-relation (American) correlation (British) to the concept of the secular, or in conjunction with development studies, or in relation to the phenomenon of fundamentalism. The spirit of Orientalism often colors religious ethnography and studies of religious phenomena in the Global South. Globalization has introduced a new factor in theorizing of religion, and in expressions of religious identities.

The present volume is an attempt to couple religious identities and globalization and view them through the lens of the Global South. In the process, the book also reflects on the active role religious identities could play in transforming society, world, and nature, in upholding the dignity of human persons and recognizing and respecting peoples and communities.

The beginnings of this volume go back to a lecture I delivered at a conference in 2016 at the Westphalian Wilhelms University, Münster, Germany. Subsequently, when I was invited in 2017 as a visiting professor to deliver a series of lectures at the Goethe University of Frankfurt a.M., under its program of Inter-cultural Theology, I could reflect further on the theme of religious identities and globalization. Though the original lectures were delivered in German, I thought the publication in English would help global readership. The materials of the lectures were further researched and expanded for the present volume in English.

It was Prof. Thomas Schreijäck, as the chairperson of the Intercultural Theology program, who extended the kind invitation for the lecture series, provided generously office space and all necessary infrastructural facilities to work on the text of my lectures, and made every effort to turn my stay in Frankfurt a very memorable one. I wish to thank him, the faculty, students, and interested public who attended my lectures, raised questions, and made pertinent comments which helped me rethink many issues dealt in this work. In particular, the presence of emeriti professors Johannes Hoffmann, Pius Siller, Michael Raske at the lectures and interaction with them were very encouraging and stimulating.

Back home in India, I needed to work intensely to expand the thoughts of lectures to turn them into a publishable manuscript. This would not have been possible without the assistance of several people, whose help I wish to acknowledge with gratitude. Dr George Evers with whom I am bound in friendship for many decades, was very generous to go through the entire draft meticulously, checking facts, correcting flaws and pointing out missing data and orthographic errors. Dr Amirtharaj Arockiam stayed with me during two spells to go through the final draft and made several suggestions, especially regarding the flow of thought and coherence. My nephews Leo and Rudy, extremely busy as they are with management and bureaucracy, still found time to read the manuscript line by line and pointed out obscurities, made corrections, and offered suggestions to make the text up-to-date and accessible to readers from other disciplines and walks of life. Dr Mary John, my former student, helped with the identification of keywords for the creation of the index and assisted with the proofreading.

I am most grateful to Prof. Joerg Rieger for including this work in the series "New Approaches to Religion and Power," edited by him and published by Palgrave Macmillan, and above all for his encouragement and enthusiastic support in getting this work published without delay. I would also like to thank Philip Getz, Senior Editor, Palgrave Macmillan, for graciously promoting the publication of this volume, despite its unusual length.

If this work sees the light of day, I owe it in no small measure to my secretary and assistant, Ms Nirmal. Mustering her astounding power of concentration, she went through the entire manuscript over and over to double-check references and bibliography. Right from the beginning to the end she assisted me with unflagging commitment in preparing the manuscript, getting it ready for print, and doing most of the correspondence, for all of which I thank her very warmly.

I hope that this work will help readers from the Global North and South to understand and interpret more closely the religious identities in the globalized world and enter into a more in-depth and enriching dialogue and sharing of experiences.

Chennai, India                                                    Felix Wilfred

# CONTENTS

# CHAPTER 1

# Introduction

Times were when orthodoxy was considered the basis of religious identity. The heterodox were disowned. They not only lost their identity; even their life was at stake. Today we are experiencing an identity-affirmation that has less and less to do with doctrines and beliefs. The identification of one's tradition, culture, and nation with a particular religion has become today an issue of crucial importance. It explains why in Europe there is a renewed interest in the otherwise neglected Christian heritage, which one feels is threatened by those belonging to other religions and cultures.

> First, Europe's reflection and fixation on its own past and on European heritage involves a general reassessment of all that is Christian, both in the heritage and in the religious domain. Second, as a result of the rapid and widespread institutionalization of Islam throughout the transnational European community, this religion determines more and more both the religious and political debate.[1]

---

[1] Peter Jan Margry, "Memorialising Europe: Revitalising and Reframing a 'Christian' Continent," in *Anthropological Journal of European Cultures* 17, no.2 (2008): 6–33, at 13; see also Frédérique Harry, "Discourses on Religion and Identity in Norway: Right-Wing Radicalism and Anti-Immigration Parties," in *New Multicultural Identities in Europe: Religion and Ethnicity in Secular Societies*, edited by Toğuşlu Erkan, Leman Johan, and Sezgin İsmail Mesut (Leuven, Belgium: Leuven University Press, 2014), 161–70.

F. Wilfred, *Religious Identities and the Global South*, New Approaches to Religion and Power, https://doi.org/10.1007/978-3-030-60738-8_1

1

The contemporary discussions on religion and identity have turned the spotlight on such thorny issues as racism, xenophobia, ethnic antagonism, prejudice, discrimination, and Islamophobia. Those who discounted any mention of Christianity in reconstructing the European past, as happened in the attempt to draft a Constitution for the European Union,[2] are sticking their neck out to defend Christianity as their own, provoked by the presence of Muslim migrants and others.[3] Ironically, the right-wing groups like the Alternative for Germany (AfD) and other anti-migrant parties in the European Union have become defenders of Christianity. These groups have made their presence increasingly stronger in parliaments and other bodies of political representation in several countries of Europe.

European nations that not long ago bitterly fought one against the other are joined together today and have armed themselves politically and culturally against any non-European threat to their collective identity. No less ironic is the fact that in Europe, which claims to be the cradle of modernity, religion is once again viewed in an essentialist manner, evident in the widespread reactions to Islam and other religious traditions. In short, the present situation in Europe could be characterized as that of a shift from secularization to right-wing politics. If, under the influence of secularization, there came about a critique of religious establishment and its authority structures without however losing faith, what Grace Davie has called, *"believing without belonging,"*[4] today with the rise of right wing in many European states, we are assisting the phenomenon of belonging

---

[2] F. Foret, "Political Roof and Sacred Canopy? Religion and the EU Constitution," *European Journal of Social Theory* 9, no.1 (2006): 59–81; H. H. Weiler, "A Christian Europe? Europe and Christianity: Rules of Commitment," *European View* 6, no.1 (December 2007):14; Jean-Claude Eslin, *Dieu et le pouvoir: Théologie et la politique en Occident* (Paris: Éd. De Seuil, 1999); Jean-Claude Eslin, "Has France renounced its own identity?," *The Political Quarterly* 73, no.3 (2002): 266–272; Yelena Mazour-Matusevich, "(Re) Constructing the European Past: Christianity and the French Religious Memory," *Cross Currents* 60, no.4 (2010): 561–71. John D'Arcy May, "European Union, Christian Division? Christianity's Responsibility for Europe's Past and Future," *Studies: An Irish Quarterly Review* 89, no.354 (2000): 118–29.

[3] Bernhard Weidinger, "Equal before God, and God Alone: Cultural Fundamentalism, (Anti-)Egalitarianism, and Christian Rhetoric in Nativist Discourse from Austria and the United States," *Journal of Austrian-American History* 1, no.1 (2017): 40–68. Steven Woodbridge, "Christian Credentials? The Role of Religion in British National Party Ideology," *Journal for the Study of Radicalism* 4, no.1 (2010): 25–54.

[4] Grace Davie, *Religion in Britain since 1945: Believing without Belonging* (Oxford: Blackwell, 1994).

without believing. What matters to right-wing groups and individuals is ensuring their loyalty to traditional Christian religious heritage without bothering about believing in its message.

## THE WORLD OF THE SOUTH

What about postcolonial societies? Though they have a long history of religious coexistence, in the present sociopolitical situation, the relationship among the believers are strained since religion has turned into a means of *power*—political, economic, and cultural. Further, as an Asian scholar observes, "the origin and development of the study of religion have been shaped by the social and political forces of empire in Europe and the United States, and by the cultural imaginary of empire."[5] To this, we could add the fact that the study of religion in the West has been conditioned by an *evolutionary* perspective. There has not taken place any serious and sustained theorizing on the role of religion in the postcolonial situation, either. Most investigations have confined themselves to either religious ethnography or study of religion and culture in relation to the process of economic development. In the absence of any deeper theorizing, what happens is that the secularization thesis coming out of the Western academic mill gets covertly and overtly applied to postcolonial societies, resulting in a mismatch between theory and the actual ground reality.[6] At bottom, much remains to be done in terms of a postcolonial critique of the category of religion. Such an enterprise will awaken us to the woeful limits of the concept of religion in coming to terms with the experiences in postcolonial societies.

One may argue that in modern democratic societies—whether Western or postcolonial—it is necessary that religion stay away from public life and that no religion be imposed as the official one, or given preference over

---

[5] Kwok Pui-lan, "2011 Presidential Address: Empire and the Study of Religion," *Journal of the American Academy of Religion* 80, no.2 (2012): 285–303.

[6] In India, some of the well-known scholars have challenged this extrapolation of European experience in the name of secularism. See T.N. Madan, "Secularism in its Place," *Journal of Asian Studies* 46, no.4 (November 1987): 747–759; Ashish Nandy, "An Anti-secularist Manifesto," *India International Centre Quarterly* 22, no.1 (1995): 35–64. For detailed discussion, see Rajeev Bhargava, *Secularism and Its Critics* (Delhi: Oxford University Press, 1999); see also Craig Calhoun, et al., *Rethinking Secularism* (New York: Oxford University Press, 2011); Rajeev Bhargava speaks of "Rehabilitating Secularism," *Rethinking Secularism*, 92–113. For a literary approach to secularism, see Neelam Srivastava, *Secularism in the Postcolonial Indian Novel* (London: Routledge, 2007).

others. Were we to go by this simple and plain argument, we may not understand the more complex situation of religions in postcolonial societies. Should making a religion official or privileged one necessarily go against democratic principles and religious freedom? Experiences in societies of the Global South show that one need not opt for a theocratic model of the state to make room for any one religion to be the privileged or the official one. As Alfred Stepan observes, "the modern political analysis of democracy, while it absolutely requires use of such concepts as voting and relative freedom to organize, does not necessarily need the concept of secularism."[7] In other words, even in condition of modernity and globalization, many postcolonial societies adopt a different understanding of the role of religion in public life, without having to compromise democratic principles and participative mode of governance.[8]

On the other hand, it is not at all clear that in the Western societies of Europe and North America, there is a perfect separation of religion and state, and religion and public life. Theoretically, one may argue against privileging of any religious establishment in a democratic order. In many Western societies, however, one or other version of Christianity occupies a privileged place. The most obvious example is that of the UK, where Anglicanism plays a unique and privileged role. Similarly, Lutheranism still plays an important role in Denmark and in Nordic countries, not to speak of the role of Catholicism in the Mediterranean countries of Europe. The issue of separation of religion and politics/public life mostly remains at the discursive level, and as a piece of theory, whereas numerous instances in the West show that politicians as well as religious leaders often cross the imaginary boundaries to redraw them. Populist politicians exploit the religious sentiments of the masses by employing religious symbols. Matteo

---

[7] Alfred Stepan, "The Multiple Secularisms of Modern Democratic and Non-Democratic Regimes," in Craig Cahour et al., *Rethinking Secularism* (New York: Oxford University Press, 2011), 114; Rajeev Bhargava too considers a plurality of models in secularism, which avoids a univocal Eurocentric definition of this concept. A basic distinction made between the "secular," "secularization," and "secularism" by authors like José Casanova and Charles Taylor imply the possibility of a pluralist approach to the issue, taking into serious account the experiences of the South. Grace Davie indicates the importance of such a pluralist approach; see Grace Davie, *The Sociology of Religion*. South Asian edition (Delhi: Sage, 2008), 46–66.

[8] Cf. Rajeev Bhargava, "Rehabilitating Secularism," in Calhoun et al., *Rethinking Secularism* (New York: Oxford University Press, 2011), 92–113; The same is claimed also for the situation of Israel. See Aviad Rubin, "Integration of Religion in Democratizing Societies: Lessons from the Israeli Experience," *Shofar* 31, no.2 (2013): 31–54.

Salvini, a right-wing politician of Italy, appears in political campaign or on television screen holding rosary or cross in hand.[9] Further, in many parts of Europe, religion has become ambiguous: on the one hand, there is a decline in traditional religious expressions and church attendance; on the other hand, religion is increasingly present in public debate.[10]

To continue further with the role of religion in the societies of the Global South, we may need to look critically at the Western debate on the interconnection between religion and modernity. Since the times of the European Enlightenment, there is a widespread assumption that modernity is in tandem with the loss of the *sense of the sacred*. The emphasis on human agency and the confidence in the creation of a future through reason, science, technology, and other means of modernity left little room for religion. The underlying question, however, is whether modernity is to be equated with its European experience. There are "multiple modernities."[11] Given the fact that in one version of modernity (the Western, and more specifically the European) religion got progressively sidelined, does not warrant the conclusion that it is so in other modernities as well. As a matter of fact, in many parts of the South, mutual encounter and adaptation between modernity and religion have been taking place. These societies believe in a plurality of paths to modernity given the difference in their sociopolitical experiences as well as the fact that each one has followed a different historical trajectory in matters religious. There has taken place a whole process of the "secularization of the European Mind"[12] which need not coincide with the trajectories of other peoples and nations. All this has implications for the way religion and modernity are linked to each other.

Stripping religion of any public role and confining it to the private realm is not an inherent necessity flowing from the logic of secularism. One may instead need to trace back such privatization to the history of

---

[9] https://international.la-croix.com/news/matteo-salvinis-rosary-stunt-angers-italian-church/10146 [accessed on February 10, 2020].

[10] With reference to the situation in UK, cf. Grace Davie, *Religion in Britain since 1945. Believing without Belonging* (Oxford: Blackwell, 1994); Grace Davie, *Europe: The Exceptional Case. Parameters of Faith in the Modern World* (London: Darton, Longman and Todd, 2002).

[11] S. N. Eisenstadt, "Multiple Modernities," *Daedalus* 129, no.1 (Winter, 2000): 1–29; Björn Wittrock, "Modernity: One, None, or Many? European Origins and Modernity as a Global Condition," *Daedalus* 129, no.1 (Winter, 2000): 31–60.

[12] Owen Chadwick, *The Secularization of the European Mind in the Nineteenth Century* (Cambridge: Cambridge University Press, 1975).

Christendom and the claims of Christianity as the possessor of absolute truth and its religious leaders exercising all powers in heaven and on earth. Now, the instruments used to clip the wings of the church, its dogmatic posture, and its authoritarianism (of which secularism was most prominent) may not be extended to postcolonial societies to deprive them of any public role of religion. The presence of an increasing number of migrant communities in various countries of Europe attests how difficult it has been for "secularized" Europeans to accept that religion could play a significant role in the lives and communities of other peoples and that it could coexist with a life of modernity. It has been most difficult to eradicate the deep-rooted prejudice, especially among the clergy, that to be religious means to be anti-modern. A transformation of Western attitudes and approaches could occur if exposed to experiences, analyses, and views in other parts of the globalized world. It is hard to generalize the role of religion in public life today, since this has a lot to do with the history of a particular society or nation. In several instances, religious identity has been grave and consequential in the formation of national identity, both in the West and in postcolonial societies.

Religious beliefs and practices have given rise to cultural forms that characterize, and, in many instances, define the identity of a people.[13] As will be evident in the pages of this volume, far from having been something to be eschewed, religions have played a pivotal role in the national struggle for independence in many erstwhile colonized nations. Thanks to religious and cultural resources, anti-colonial struggles could be sustained. This is an integral part of the history of many peoples in the Global South.[14] No wonder that in postcolonial societies religions continue to play a wide variety of roles without violating, in principle, the functional specialization of different social systems—politics, economy, society, culture, and so on. There are efforts to maintain and respect autonomy of spheres, while not denying a public role for religions. Conflict arises when one particular religion—to the exclusion of others—is given the privilege to play a public role, whereas others are relegated to the private realm. The conflict becomes even more critical and gets exacerbated in those instances

[13] Cf. Slavica Jakelic, *Collectivistic Religions. Religion, Choice, and Identity in Late Modernity* (London: Routledge 2016).
[14] Regarding South Asia, see Peter van der Veer, "Religion in South Asia," *Annual Review of Anthropology* 31 (2002): 173–187.

where religions project themselves as defenders of the common good over against a failing state that does not discharge its role and responsibilities.

Now, all these questions, issues, and debates get reshaped and reformulated in the contemporary situation of globalization in which conventional mental and physical borders are overcome and communication and encounters unimaginable in the past are facilitated.

## "RETURN OF RELIGION" AND ITS REINVENTION

The expression "return of religion" may not represent any cutting-edge analysis of the ground reality. Nevertheless, from the perspective of secularization, one could speak in these terms. This return is not necessarily fundamentalist in nature, as is often suggested. Nor is it a rejection of modernity. Experience shows that modernity and fundamentalist expressions of religion can coexist. This is true also of globalization. For, a fundamentalist religious stream can get globalized and strategically avail the advantages of globalization for its own flourishing.

As the project of modernity was in full swing, there were three events at the global level that created a salutary interruption and set the humankind thinking. The first was the spine-chilling tragedy of the *Holocaust* and the macabre killing of millions in World War II. It raised profound and anguishing questions about the trust in human reason as the driving force of modernity. How could such senseless brutalities of war and killings take place while singing hosanna to human reason? The second salutary interruption was the Iranian Revolution. It was a challenge to the assumption of modernity that religion belongs to the private sphere and has no public consequence. The Iranian Revolution, which overthrew the regime of the Shah in 1978, led to a realization of the interventions religious forces could make in local and international politics, and in other departments of human life.[15] Third, the collapse of East European socialism in 1989 opened the eyes of the skeptics to the role religion played in different states, especially in Poland, to dismantle oppressive state-socialism and authoritarianism.

More striking than the return of religion is the fact that religions have tried to reinvent themselves in the condition of globalization. In the case

---

[15] Cf. David Menashri, *The Iranian Revolution and The Muslim World* (United Kingdom: Routledge, 2019); John L Esposito, ed., *The Iranian Revolution: Its Global Impact* (Florida: Florida International University Press, 1990).

of Europe, it is too evident that traditional churches are losing their grip on the society and the lives of people. As Grace Davie rightly observes, what has happened in Europe is a shift "from the obligation to consumption." She is referring to the way people attend church, receive sacraments, and take part in the activities of the church-community—all as a matter of obligation.[16] The declining of church attendance and participation in activities of one's religious community has to do precisely with the new mindset that looks at religion not as a matter of obligation and prescription, instead, of choice. One would be mistaken, however, to conclude that since religion is a matter of choice, it is a private affair. A religion by choice need not necessarily be equated with something private. As Grace Davie observes:

> At least some versions of secularization theory ...carry with them the notion chosen religion is necessarily privatized religion; for these commentators, religion has become simply a matter of personal preference or lifestyle. ...I am no longer convinced that this is so. Those who opt seriously for religion in European societies will want to make their views heard in public as well as private debate. It is at this point, moreover, that the forms of religion ...that have arrived more recently within Europe begin to make a practical impact: they offer positive... models to the host community—the learning process is running in both directions.[17]

Frequently cited volumes like those of Charles Taylor and José Casanova[18] on secularization and modernity are useful contributions within the Western frame of discussion. Their works rightly distinguish various strands of the secular, all of which represent different phenomena and are not to be equated with one another. For example, there is a difference between the historical experience of *secularization*, as the process by which temporal realities (politics, economy, culture, and so on) became autonomous and got liberated from religion, and *secularism* as an ideology. However, the theorizing of these scholars does not seem to reflect the

---

[16] Cf. Grace Davie, *The Sociology of Religion* (Delhi: Sage, 2008).

[17] Grace Davie, *The Sociology of Religion*, 97–98.

[18] Charles Taylor, *A Secular Age* (Cambridge MA- London: Harvard University Press, 2007); José Casanova, *Public Religions in the Modern World* (Chicago: The University of Chicago Press, 1994).

experiences from the Global South. This is true also, in large part, of the work of Peter Beyer on Religion and Globalization.[19]

## PROGRESSIVE CLARIFICATION OF KEY CONCEPTS

All the three key concepts—*identity, religion, and the global*—which the present volume attempts to relate to each other from a Southern perspective are contested territories, extremely problematic and challenging to circumscribe and define. A large amount of literature can be found on each one of these concepts from a wide variety of perspectives, from different disciplines, and from ideological positions. Should we begin to discuss and debate on them, we might end up specifying the concepts and their contours while missing out on issues of fundamental importance. Instead of defining or explicating these concepts at the very outset, as may be expected by some, I have preferred to deal with them throughout the book while considering and discussing different issues. There is also the danger of considering each of the above concepts in isolation which will not help us truly to appreciate their impact and influence. In other words, the concepts of identity, religion, and the global get progressively clarified and specified as we move on with our theme.

Exercising mass democracy in conditions of mass poverty will have its own unique characteristics which go to reconfigure the concept of democracy itself.[20] Similarly, the practice of religion in the South under manifold sociopolitical conditions is bound to have its own unique characteristics in the conceptualization of religion. Even more, the term "religion" has no equivalent in Asian languages, for example. A contemporary distinguished Western scholar readily confesses this:

> Thus, the word "religion" is not easily translated into non-European languages. This was something I discovered when, as a graduate student, I

---

[19] Peter Beyer, *Religion and Globalization* (London: Sage, 1994). The author has as case study of the Iranian Revolution and a case study of South America. Again, the basic theoretical frameworks are constructed from the Western discussions on religion and modernity.

[20] A group of international scholars in a joint project with the Center for Developing Societies, Delhi, has gone into the study of the idea of democracy as it evolved in South Asia, and have come out with new and unique specifications. Cf. *State of Democracy in South Asia. A Report* (Delhi: Oxford University Press, 2008).

went to India to do field research on the religion of Untouchables, the lowest caste in the Hindu social hierarchy.[21]

Hinduism and Buddhism speak of "*dharma*," or "*dhamma*," which is not the same thing as what a Westerner would normally understand by religion. Dharma has a few dozen meanings. It is so to say a *cohort* concept which envelops many other elements and dimensions.

As Wilfred Cantwell Smith stated decades ago, religion is a concept of clearly Western origin which got extrapolated to other parts of the globe.[22] In earlier times, one spoke of faith and tradition about what, in modern times, is referred to as religion. As Charles Taylor notes, the idea of religion got great currency in conjunction with the concept of secularism.[23] As a result, misunderstanding could arise when the experiences of peoples of other cultures and traditions are framed within this concept, reminiscent of the Procrustean bed. As many scholars of Asian religions have repeatedly pointed out, religion is not so much a set of doctrines and teachings to be believed in but something existential.[24] It is a way of life that comprises many mutually related ritual practices, beliefs, customs, injunctions, and so on. These ways and views are keys to understanding and interpreting the societies and histories of the Global South. All this cautions us on the pitfalls of the use of the word "religion." With this caveat, we shall proceed to reflect further on the concept of *identity* in relation to religion.

It cannot but sound naïve in the age of globalization were we to conjure up religion as a fixed entity to which people profess their belonging and abjure their loyalty. One of the arguments of this book is that people do not merely belong to a religious identity, but that they are active agents in constantly reshaping their religious identity and the universe they claim to belong. They negotiate through the *porous borders* and find their *novel paths*. Through the agency of believers, religion keeps changing and hence

[21] Mark Juergensmeyer, "Beyond Words and War: The Global Future of Religion," 2009 Presidential Address, *Journal of the American Academy of Religion* 78, no.4 (December 2010): 882–895, at 887.

[22] Wilfred Cantwell Smith, *The Meaning and End of Religion* (Minneapolis: Fortress Press, 1991).

[23] Cf. Charles Taylor, *The Secular Age* (Cambridge MA- London: Harvard University Press, 2007).

[24] See the contributions of scholars from across many disciplines in T.N. Madan, ed., *Religion in India* (Delhi: Oxford University Press, 1991).

becomes alive and significant. This is what is happening with globalization.

The colonial project of knowledge comprised the reification of the religions of peoples and nations. The same is true also of colonized societies. For a long time, the colonial mindset thought of colonized societies as fossilized and almost like a museum piece to be studied and researched on.[25] The assumption was that these societies do not change. One spoke, for example, of idyllic village India that is impervious to any change. Curiously but not surprisingly, change was associated only with the colonizing nations and societies.

The study of non-Western societies was done by the discipline of *anthropology*. One did not speak of sociology in India, China, or African nations. Strikingly, there was no department of sociology in India till the 1950s but only departments of anthropology. M.N. Srinivas, an Indian anthropologist, maintained that changes had been taking place in Indian society over the centuries to explain which he proposed the theory of *Sanskritization*.[26] The process of Sanskritization creates in the caste-based Indian society a movement of upward mobility: The so-called lower castes aspiring for social mobility follow the customs, traditions, and cultural practices of upper castes, thereby generating dynamism and movement within the caste-society.

This premise is essential to understand how religions in the Global South have been interpreted. Today, an increasing number of scholars focus on religious studies in the erstwhile colonized nations. They do extensive religious ethnography, apparently, for consumption in the West. Monographs in the field are growing phenomanally. As Mark Juergensmeyer noted in his presidential address at the American Academy of Religion, "the study of religion is big business. The only problem is that increasingly we are uncertain of what we are studying—what is this thing, "religion," as a subject for scholarly consideration?"[27] Though scholars distinguish between the *etic* and *the emic* approach, still, the religious world of the Global South continues to be, by and large, an *object* of research. De-historicized exercises in religious ethnography with little reference to

---

[25] Edward W. Said, *Orientalism* (London: Routledge and Kegan Paul, 1979). Postcolonial thinkers have developed further his basic insights and applied them in different fields of study.

[26] M. N. Srinivas, *The Cohesive Role of Sanskritization and Other Essays* (Delhi; Oxford: Oxford University, 1989).

[27] Mark Juergensmeyer, "Beyond Words and War: The Global Future of Religion," *Journal of the American Academy of Religion* 78, no.4 (December 2010): 882–895, at 886.

the sociopolitical context of the practice of religions make one wonder whether Orientalism has got metamorphized into the fashionable discipline of Religious Studies.

## DISTINCTION BETWEEN MODERNITY AND GLOBALIZATION

According to a broad definition by Anthony Giddens, globalization is "the intensification of worldwide social relations which link distant localities in such a way that local happenings are shaped by events occurring many miles away and vice versa."[28] Most theories of modernity were inspired by an evolutionary perspective, at least in the initial period of the use of this category. It was as if some societies had forged ahead in the race of modernity while others are lingering at different stages and not able to catch up with those ahead. Some scholars identify globalization as an advanced stage of modernization. I would rather highlight the fact that globalization does not have an evolutionary assumption as the concept of modernity. Globalization is a process in which everybody is involved in a *circular* movement and not in a *linear* movement which grades societies as for-

[28] Anthony Giddens, *The Consequences of Modernity* (Stanford, CA: Stanford University Press, 1990), 64. The difference in approaches to the understanding of globalization differs according to from where it is viewed—North or South—and also on the discipline. Well known and widely discussed in the North are the different views on globalization by Roland Robertson, John Meyer, Niklas Luhman, and Immanuel Wallerstein. For perspectives from the South, see Achin Vanaik, ed., and Academy of Third World Studies. *Globalization and South Asia: Multidimensional Perspectives* (New Delhi: Manohar, 2004); Arjun Appadurai, ed., *Globalization* (Durham; London: Duke University Press, 2001); James C Cobb, and William Whitney Stueck, eds., *Globalization and the American South* (Athens, Ga.; London: University of Georgia Press, 2005); David Ludden, ed., *Reading Subaltern Studies: Critical History, Contested Meaning and the Globalization of South Asia* (London: Anthem, 2002); William R, Thompson, and Rafael Reuveny, *Limits to Globalization: North-South Divergence* (London: Routledge, 2010). Usman A. Tar, Etham Mijah, and Mosese E. U. Tedheke, eds., *Globalization in Africa: Perspectives on Development, Security, and the Environment,* (Lanham: Lexington Books, 2016); Mahmoud Masaeli, Sanni Yaya, and Rico Sneller, eds., *African Perspectives on Global Development* (UK: Cambridge Scholars Publishing, 2018); José Antonio Ocampo, and Juan Martin, eds., and Economic Commission for Latin America the Caribbean, *Globalization and Development: A Latin American and Caribbean Perspective* (Palo Alto, Calif.: Stanford Social Sciences and the World Bank, 2003); Kema Irogbe, *The Effects of Globalization in Latin America, Africa, and Asia: A Global South Perspective* (Lanham, Maryland: Lexington Books, 2014); Francis Kok-Wah Loh, Joakim Öjendal, eds., *Southeast Asian Responses to Globalization: Restructuring Governance and Deepening Democracy* (Copenhagen S., Denmark: Singapore: NIAS Press; Institute of Southeast Asian Studies, 2005).

ward and backward, developed, developing and underdeveloped, as is the case with modernization. In that sense, globalization, I think, is more a corrective to modernity rather than an advanced stage of modernity.

Beginning from 1980s, the wider use of the term "globalization" was in effect, and may not be in design, a leveler in the sense that independent of any consideration of modern or not, a person in a remote village in Africa and a person in an urban slum in Bangladesh could be part of the globalization process in terms of what they do, what they consume, and with whom they connect and so on.

Another characteristic of globalization that distinguishes it from modernity is the fact that globalization does not revolve around the concept of rationality as is the case with modernity. Arjun Appadurai has looked at the matter from a postcolonial and postmodern perspective. He speaks of five constituent flows of globalization: ethnoscape, technoscape, mediascape, financescape, and ideoscape.[29] Globalization is not simply a single pattern of development or something leveling every field. Rather globalization comes across to people differently depending on the landscape of each situation and on the kind of various flows in a particular context. To make the picture more complete, I would add religioscape (referring to religious landscapes), which is not found in the scheme of Appadurai. Elements of the religious in terms of beliefs, practices, and rituals get de-territorialized and flow into other contexts and localities to form *new* religious configurations. All of these "scapes" connect the globe and involve everyone, groups, and communities. It is around the same period as when the discourse of globalization was gaining greater currency, and the movement in the above areas were getting accelerated, that there came about the realization to relativize spaces, especially the nation which was viewed in a fixated and essentialist manner. The present-day movement of migration challenged scholars to reimage national spaces and borders differently.

The changes and movements were not simply *physical*. The global movements were also a matter of *mind*. Globalization gave wings to people to fly in their mind far and wide and imagine different worlds, peoples, and conditions of life. Technology provided the means so that their imagination could become real and their aspirations and dreams could find realization. I think this aspect of globalization in the minds of people and groups is something momentous, and it needs to be necessarily connected

[29] Cf. Arjun Appadurai, "Disjuncture and Difference in the Global Cultural Economy," *Theory, Culture & Society* 7, no. 2–3 (1990): 295–310.

to physical movements and shifts taking place. All these flows and movements within and without along with the relativization of conventional ways of life—all making up the process of globalization—had their repercussion on traditional religions and religious identities.

The present study and reflections on religious identities are done in the fluid situation in which these different spheres crisscross and intersect, defying any tight compartmentalization. Our concern is not so much about religious identity in modernity as religious identities in the fluid condition of globalization.

## GLOBAL RELIGION OR CONVERGENCE OF RELIGIONS?

Does the process of globalization lead finally to the creation of a global religion? Anyone familiar with the endless diversity of religions and cultures will not think all of them merging into a single global religion—a new entity. If we may compare it with language, globalization has not brought to an end the plurality of languages. As symbolic systems of communication, they continue and, in many cases, get reinvigorated by new experiences calling for new linguistic expressions. Any attempt to create a super-religion for global consumption could not hope to be more successful than Esperanto.

Remarkable in the contemporary globalizing setting is the coming together of religions in defense of human dignity and the protection of nature. Globalization could contribute to the convergence of religions toward these noble goals. All the so-called world religions indeed have enshrined in their scriptures and traditions the truth that the humankind is one, and that it is to be looked at as a single family. This truth, unfortunately, has remained an abstract ideal. History attests that many conflicts, violence, and wars happened despite such lofty ideals. Globalization, as a movement of people, ideas, ways of life across the globe, has made the truth of what religions say in their books into a reality of day-to-day experience. The awakening to the unity of humankind at the global level, coupled with shocking historic experiences of brutality and violence, has given rise to an acute moral sentiment for the inviolable dignity of every human person. The discrimination and violence against the weaker sections of humankind all over the world have given birth to movements that have as their goal the upholding of human dignity and defense of human rights. The global civil, political, and cultural movements have engaged themselves to implement these ideals across the world. Religiously committed people could not be impermeable to these global developments which opened their eyes to rediscover the teachings about humanity and its oneness in their religious scriptures and traditions.

The equal dignity of all human beings, and the claims of universal human rights—civil, social, cultural, and economic—could not but also be a challenge to the religious traditions. For, most of these traditions, as history bears out, legitimized inequality through a system of sacred hierarchy of high and low. To cite an example, for millennia, in the Indian subcontinent, religiously endorsed caste inequality excluded a segment of the people, the Dalits (formerly known as "the Untouchables"), from access to the temples and debarred them from becoming temple priests.[30] This caste hierarchy did not go unchallenged. All through history, there has been opposition to caste discrimination. However, globalization has reinvigorated the challenge to the hierarchical order of things and the practice of exclusion. When globalization facilitates communication and interchange between the African American women and the Dalits women of India, it cannot but be welcomed as contributing to their solidarity and liberation.[31] It helps both groups to view very critically religious teachings, practices, laws, and customs legitimizing and supporting their discrimination. At the United Nations Durban conference of 2001, the Dalits were able to interpret their oppression in racial terms, exposing its roots in religious beliefs and traditions.

Similarly, in gender issues, thanks to global feminist awakening and women's movements across the globe, discrimination against women in religious sources and practices are openly questioned. To cite an example of recent times, in a famous Hindu shrine on the top of the hill Sabarimala, Kerala, India, pilgrims flock to visit Lord Ayyappa, who is a bachelor deity.

---

[30] Cf. Steven M. Parish, *Hierarchy and Its Discontents: Culture and the Politics of Consciousness in Caste Society* (Philadelphia: University of Pennsylvania Press, 1996); Eleanor Zelliot, *From Untouchable to Dalit: Essays on the Ambedkar Movement* (New Delhi: Manohar Publications, 1992); Gail Omvedt, *Dalits and the Democratic Revolution: Dr. Ambedkar and the Dalit Movement in Colonial India* (New Delhi; London: Sage, 1994); Sukhadeo Thorat, *Dalits in India: Search for a Common Destiny* (Los Angeles; London: SAGE, 2009); Sathianathan Clarke, Deenabandhu Manchala, and Philip Vinod Peacock, eds., *Dalit Theology in the Twenty-first Century: Discordant Voices, Discerning Pathways* (New Delhi; Oxford: Oxford University Press, 2010).

[31] Cf. Shailaja Paik, "Building Bridges: Articulating Dalit and African American Women's Solidarity," *Women's Studies Quarterly* 42, no. 3/4 (2014): 74–96.

Women in the menstrual age are forbidden to visit this temple.[32] The global struggles of women against inequality and discrimination inspired some Indian women to challenge this discrimination in the Supreme Court of India, which ruled in favor of women entering the temple.[33] This verdict provoked violent protests by right-wing religious groups who are intent on preserving the status quo. It further triggered women's rights and civil rights groups to use the verdict to appeal to the judiciary for the right of Muslim women to visit and pray at mosques.[34] It is again the impact of globalization that women in the Roman Catholic Church are networking and boldly questioning the long-held tradition of ordaining only men to priesthood.

Thanks to intercultural and interreligious encounters and greater knowledge of each other, religions could come closer and enrich themselves from their respective religious resources. Unfortunately, these openings are again sought to be blocked by groups of people in various religions who see it as a relativization of their faith. Cardinal Joseph Ratzinger (later Pope Benedict XVI), for example, spoke in his homily at the mass for the election of a new pope, about the "dictatorship of relativism that does not recognize anything as definitive."[35] It is something against which the church should defend itself, according to him. Such are efforts to arrest the new openings globalization has brought about in revising traditional doctrines and practices.

## New Experiences and Different Theorizing

This book tries to discuss the question of religious identity and globalization with special focus on the Global South. By pulling together and comparing the situations in the two hemispheres, it is possible to think of a theorizing that would overcome the prevalent prejudice that modernity

---

[32] Cf. O.B. Roopesh, "Sabarimala Protest," *Economic and Political Weekly of India* 53 no.49 (December 15, 2018): 12–15.

[33] Cf. Deepa Das Acevedo, "Pause for Thought. Supreme Court Judgment on Sabarimala," *Economic and Political Weekly of India* 53, no.43 (October 27, 2018): 12–15.

[34] https://www.newindianexpress.com/nation/2020/jan/27/scribe-moves-supreme-court-seeking-entry-of-muslim-women-for-prayers-in-mosque-2095249.html [accessed on February 24, 220]; https://www.indiatoday.in/india/story/supreme-court-plea-women-mosques-namaz-entry-1502775-2019-04-16 [accessed on February 24, 2020].

[35] http://www.vatican.va/gpII/documents/homily-pro-eligendo-pontifice_20050418_en.html [accessed on February 11, 2020].

and religion are incompatible. We need a theorizing that would account for the vibrancy of both religion and modernity in the Global South. In light of the experiences in other parts of the world, it would be possible to rethink and theorize afresh also the relationship of religion and modernity in Europe and in North America. There is today a tendency among many scholars in the Global North to extrapolate into the Global South the battles Europe waged in the past against the church and its domination. What is worse is that this trend has instilled in the minds of the ordinary European citizens the fear of a return to pre-Enlightenment times and, ultimately, a sense of threat to the Western Enlightenment heritage.

Exposure to the condition of religion in the context of globalization in the Global South could help critically revisit some of the pet theories on religion in the Global North. One thing is becoming increasingly evident from the unfolding of events in our world: *Laicité* cannot fix the highly intricate social, religious and political problems of our times. Without being judgmental on the merits or demerits of the case, let me say that experiential insights from the South would have contributed to a different approach, for example to the cartoon controversy of 2006 depicting Prophet Mohammed in the Danish newspaper *Jyllands-Posten*, or to the Charlie Hebdo cartoon issue in Paris which cost precious lives, and which continues to haunt France.[36] Is it truly an aspiration to be Voltaire's heirs of free speech? In this twenty-first century with a vastly changed situation of the world which has become ever more complex, the legitimate right to freedom of expression needs to be tempered with a fine common sense and understanding for the religious sentiments of others. This could prevent the right to freedom of expression turning into a right to trivialize and offend.

[36] Cf. Christine Agius, "Performing Identity: The Danish Cartoon Crisis and Discourses of Identity and Security," *Security Dialogue* 44, no.3 (2013): 241–58. Cécile Laborde, Anne Norton, Donald Downs, Abdulkader Sinno, and Carolyn M. Warner, "The Danish Cartoon Controversy and the Challenges of Multicultural Politics: A Discussion of 'The Cartoons That Shook the World'," *Perspectives on Politics* 9, no.3 (2011): 603–19; Nathalie Vanparys, Dirk Jacobs, and Corinne Torrekens, "The Impact of Dramatic Events on Public Debate concerning Accommodation of Islam in Europe," *Ethnicities* 13, no.2 (2013): 209–28; Geoffrey Brahm Levey, and Tariq Modood, "The Muhammad Cartoons and Multicultural Democracies," *Ethnicities* 9, no.3 (2009): 427–47; Brian Trench, "'Charlie Hebdo' Islamophobia and Freedoms of the Press," *Studies: An Irish Quarterly Review* 105, no.418 (2016): 183–91; Bakare Najimdeen, "Muslims and the Charlie Hebdo Saga," *Policy Perspectives* 12, no.2 (2015): 81–104; Neville Cox, "Understanding 'Je suis Charlie'," *Studies: An Irish Quarterly Review* 105, no.418 (2016): 148–58.

These are not isolated instances, but a pattern which we see repeated in other less known cases. To cite a more recent example, the tension between the Global South and North in Roman Catholicism was obvious in the heated discussion and bitter discord on issues of marriage, divorce, and homosexuality in the Roman Synod on Family in 2014 and 2015.[37] One could notice a sympathetic mutual understanding between those opposed to homosexuality in the West and those from the South, especially from Africa. Religious conservativism brought them together. On the other hand, the African prelates could not agree to the view of Western representatives, who meant that a sympathetic approach to homosexuals would be a sign of openness of the church to modern times. For the African bishops, instead, openness to less stringent views on polygamy would be a sign of the church's openness and understanding! This shows that more needs to be done in terms of theory and approaches than to get stuck to a position of liberalism vis-à-vis religion, which often allows no room for dialogue and encounter. Reading together both the situation in the Global North and the South could open up new avenues, strategies, and theorizing to resolve very complex and intricate issues.

Widening the discourse on religious identity and drawing from experiences of the South, especially from South Asia, this book also questions some of the favorite theories and inflexible views formulated in the West. To cite some examples, much theorizing in the West has it that modernity and any public role of religion are incongruous; or, religious fundamentalism is a resistance to modernity. Such generalized and widespread views need to be subjected to critical scrutiny in the light of a closer understanding of the complex internal dynamics of the sociopolitical and cultural conditions of a particular society in which the religious phenomena are studied. Ethno-nationalism deploys religion as a means of resistance against oppression, or manifest injustices. In such cases, there takes place obviously a spirited assertion of religious identity, which could create the impression of them becoming fundamentalist. Further, it would be highly problematic if one were to place Pentecostalism in the South along with fundamentalism. And yet, this is often done following some ideal-type definition or description of fundamentalism.[38] Such instances alert us against the danger of succumbing to certain theoretical conceptualizations on secularism and fundamentalism claiming universal validity, unmindful of widely differing experiences and histories.

---

[37] Cf. *The Tablet*, October 18, 2014.
[38] Chapter 5 in this volume goes into the various aspects of fundamentalism

## THE CONTEXT AND PURPOSE OF THE BOOK

At the academic level, we could refer to a lot of study and researches on religion in economically advanced societies like Europe and North America in the context of modernity and globalization.[39] On the other hand, we note a grave deficit of theory in the study of the religious life of the societies of the Global South. Sociology of religion mostly stops with issues like secularization and fundamentalism. Few are studies that go into the intersection of religion with political, economic, social, and cultural processes in the societies of the Global South. Still fewer are studies that investigate and try to theorize the relationship of religion and modernities in these societies. Experiences in the South would require different theorizing than the case in Europe.[40] Even North America does not fit into the theorizing for the situation in Europe. Often theoretical assertions override experiential data in the field. The asymmetry between prevalent theories of religion and ground reality call for alternatives that will be attentive to the experiences in the Global South.

I will be looking and interpreting the issue of religious identities under globalizing conditions through the lens of Asia, and of the Global South at large. I am not using North and South with any polarizing intent. I am aware of the valid postcolonial and feminist critique on binaries and dichotomies. The Global South here has a perspectival sense; namely, it refers to the position from where I look at the theme religious identities. This helps me also to focus on some of the differences between this standpoint and other perspectives. The study, analysis, and reflections making up this book are done in a spirit of dialogue among different vantage points which could be of significant common enrichment.

[39] Cf. Gregory Alles, ed., *Religious studies: A Global View* (New York: Routledge, 2010); Department of Religious Studies, *Religious Studies on the Threshold of the 21st Century: McMartin Conference: Lectures* (1994); Carl Olson, *Religious Studies: The Key Concepts* (London and New York: Routledge, 2011); Ursula King, *Turning Points in Religious Studies: Essays in Honour of Geoffrey Parrinder*. Religious Studies: Bloomsbury Academic Collections (London: Bloomsbury Academic, 2016).

[40] Cf. Peter Berger, Grace Davie and Effie Fokas, *Religious America, Secular Europe? A Theme and Variations* (Hampshire and Burlington: Ashgate Publishing Limited, 2008).

# CHAPTER 2

# Religion: A Question of Identity

It is paradoxical that the process of globalization has not signified transcending of identities; rather, we are assisting the invigorated assertion of different identities—ethnic, racial, religious linguistic, regional, and so on. All these identities play a critical role in the life of individuals and societies. The question of identity is studied from various points of view and by different disciplines such as philosophy, sociology, social-psychology, and politics.[1] Theories of identity have mostly focused on the study of self,

[1] The researches in these various fields continue to multiply, and there is a plethora of literature on the question of identity. In this chapter we will be referring to some important works. In the history of philosophy of both East and West, the issue of identity has occupied a central place. The identity of the Self and the self (Brahman and Atman) has been a core issue in Indian classical thought. The way the identity is defined here marked also the difference in philosophical orientations. It also occupied an important place in the Indic epistemology with realness of the real and the mistaken identity (the theory of maya), and in the cognitive process which implies the identity of the knower, the known and the act of knowing. Identity issue was central to some of the Hellenistic thinkers like Parmenides and Plotinus. In modern times, the issue of identity marked the thought of German idealists Fichte, Hegel, and Schelling. Going into detail into in the history of identity in East and West will take us far afield. Suffice to remember the deeper philosophical roots of the question of identity when we discuss about religious identities. Some basic philosophical works that could be helpful, S. Dasgupta, *History of Indian Philosophy*, vol.1–5 (Cambridge: Cambridge University Press, 1922); Debiprasad Chattopadhyaya, *What is living and What is Dead in Indian Philosophy*, 3rd ed. (Delhi: Peoples' Publishing House, 1993); Wilhelm Halbfass, *Tradition and Reflection. Explorations in Indian Thought* (New York:

© The Author(s), under exclusive license to Springer Nature    21
Switzerland AG 2021
F. Wilfred, *Religious Identities and the Global South*,
New Approaches to Religion and Power,
https://doi.org/10.1007/978-3-030-60738-8_2

gender, various forms of ethnicity, and class, and they generally do not refer to religion as a source of identity. But the present developments in the world force us to seriously reflect on religion as a source of identity for the formation of the self of the individual and of the self of groups. It also calls us to go deeper into the study of the role religious identity plays in our global world, its assumptions, its dynamics, and its impact on the various realms of societal life.[2] When identity is invoked for domination, for emancipation, or for negotiation of power, what follows is "identity politics."[3] Religion has

State University of New York Press, 1991); Martin Heidegger, *Identity and Difference,* translated with an Introduction by Joan Stambaugh (Chicago, Ill., London: University of Chicago Press, 2002); Eli Hirsch, *The Concept of Identity* (New York; Oxford: Oxford University Press, 1982); P. V. Zima, *Subjectivity and Identity: Between Modernity and Postmodernity* (London: Bloomsbury, 2015). For the historically minded reader, the following contribution could be of interest. Philip Gleason, "Identifying Identity: A Semantic History," *The Journal of American History,* 69, no.4 (1983): 910–31.

[2] Matt Sheedy, ed., *Identity, Politics and the Study of Islam: Current Dilemmas in the Study of Religions* (Indonesia: Equinox Publishing, 2018); Mamnun Khan and Shaykh Mohammed Nizami, "Writer of Supplementary Textual Content," in *Being British Muslims: Beyond Ethnocentric Religion and Identity Politics* (Bloomington: Author House, 2019); Claire Mitchell, *Religion, Identity and Politics in Northern Ireland: Boundaries of Belonging and Belief* (London: Routledge, 2017); Gerlachus Duijzings, *Religion and the Politics of Identity in Kosovo* (London: C. Hurst, 1999); Khalīl Al-Anānī, *Inside the Muslim Brotherhood: Religion, Identity, and Politics* (New York: Oxford University Press, 2016); Jeff Kingston, *The Politics of Religion, Nationalism, and Identity in Asia* (Lanham, Maryland: Rowman & Littlefield, 2019); William Fierman, ed., *Soviet Central Asia: The Failed Transformation* (New York: Routledge, 2019); Catherine Bliss, "The Marketization of Identity Politics," *Sociology* 47, no.5 (2013): 1011–025; Baljit Singh, "Politics of Identities: Global, South Asian and Indian Perspective," *The Indian Journal of Political Science* 67, no.2 (2006): 205–20.

[3] Cf. M. Bernstein and David S. Gutterman, "Identity Politics," *Annual Review of Sociology* 31 (2005): 47–74; Olaf Kaltmeier, Sebastian Thies and Josef Raab, eds., *The New Dynamics of Identity Politics in the Americas: Multiculturalism and beyond* (London and New York: Routledge, 2017); David S. Gutterman, and Andrew R. Murphy, *Political Religion and Religious Politics: Navigating Identities in the United States* (London: Routledge Series on Identity Politics, 2015); David Chidester, Abdulkader Tayob and Wolfram Weisse, eds., *Religion, Politics, and Identity in a Changing South Africa,* vol. 6 (Münster: Waxmann, 2004); Julia Leslie and Mary McGee, eds., *Invented Identities: The Interplay of Gender, Religion and Politics in India* (New Delhi; Oxford: Oxford University Press, 2000); Ronen A. Cohen, ed., *Identities in Crisis in Iran: Politics, Culture, and Religion* (Lanham: Lexington, 2015); Lian H Sakhong, and Nordic Institute of Asian Studies, *In Search of Chin Identity: A Study in Religion, Politics and Ethnic Identity in Burma* (Richmond: Curzon, 2002); Haldun Gülalp and *Günter Seufert,* eds., *Religion, Identity and Politics: Germany and*

become an ambiguous player to achieve certain goals in this kind of identity politics that neatly marks who is in and who is out.

## IDENTITIES AND IDEOLOGIES

Two significant ideologies tried to construct their own theoretical frameworks for the study of identity. The first is the Marxist ideology which holds that the pre-modern identities will vanish to give place to the identity of class, based on the differing economic conditions. The numerous primordial identities of race, language, culture, ethnicity, and so on, according to Marxists, deflect our attention from where our real concern should lie—the *economic* realm. The second ideology is that of the *nation*. It tried to bring under its unitary umbrella the multiplicity of ethnicities and culturally varied groups. Here, the nation as an overarching entity is projected as the primary political marker of identity. It will dissolve or accommodate other forms of identity, it is believed.

However, since the tail end of the twentieth century, increasingly serious questions have been raised regarding both these theoretical frames. They have been in gestation from 1960s and 1970s when the postcolonial societies witnessed breakout of violent conflicts among diverse ethnic, regional, and linguistic identities. This was the fruit of colonial rivalries, designs, and policies which sliced or merged territories to create nations with artificial boundary markings. Hardly did one pay attention to traditional demography and tribal identities. Analysis of the society could not anymore be done simply on the basis of class ignoring race, caste, language, and other identities. They are not transitory phenomena. The national identity perspective and the Marxist perspectives of class were in contestation in many areas.[4] Far from overcoming identities and differences, the Marxist and nationalist metanarratives were sitting on volcanos of identities that have exploded today. Religion is one such explosive identity. It does not stand isolated as a system of belief, but is embedded in culture and has been a force of robustness and vitality behind civilizations.

---

*Turkey in Interaction*, 1st ed., European Sociological Association Studies in European Societies; 18 (London: Routledge, 2013); Ulrich Schmiedel, and Graeme Smith, eds., *Religion in the European Refugee Crisis* (Switzerland: Palgrave, 2018); Jeff Kingston, *The Politics of Religion, Nationalism, and Identity in Asia* (Lanham, Maryland: Rowman & Littlefield, 2019).

[4] Susan Archer and Michael D. Grimes, "Common and Contested Ground: Marxism and Race, Gender & Class Analysis," *Race, Gender & Class* 8, no. 2 (2001): 3–22.

No wonder that Samuel Huntington could prognosticate that the future of the world is going to be characterized not by class wars or national conflicts, but by a clash of civilizational and religious identities. He enumerates six major civilizational groupings that are supposed to come into conflict with each other. They are Western, Latin American, Orthodox, Eastern World (Buddhism, Hinduism, Confucianism, Daoism), Muslim, and sub-Saharan Africa. Each one of them is shot through with a particular religious tradition and its worldview.[5] Future wars are going to be not on economic or ideological grounds, but triggered by conflicts of cultures and civilizations. The position of Huntington set off worldwide discussion and debate for about two decades. Pascal Bruckner, a French author, wonders whether the position of Huntington is not a case of warming-up across the Atlantic abandoned European theories.[6] Francis Fukuyama proclaiming the end of history with the triumph of liberal democracy seems to echo Hegel's philosophy of history.[7] In the case of Huntington, the way of looking at the world through the lens of civilizations seems to have a lot of similarity with Oswald Spengler and Arnold Toynbee and their explanations on the rise and fall of civilizations.

There are at least three underlying problems with Huntington's thesis on clash of civilizations. First, identities, whether of individuals, groups, civilizations, or religions, are not petrified entities essentialized and fixated once and for all. All kinds of identities, in fact, are in a state of constant change, flux, and movement. Persons, communities, religions, and civilizations intermittently undergo a process of transformation, thanks to factors and forces from within and without. Second, in Huntington's view, there is an overlap of civilizations and territories, just like nation and state. The process of globalization has de-territorialized nations, cultures, civilizations, and so on, and we are in the face of a new conception of space, at bottom. Globalization serves to free civilizations from their many traditional constraints and facilitates transnational and inter-civilizational dialogue and conversation. Such being the case, there is little room to speak in terms of a clash. Third, there is something like layers of identity. It means that a person or a community cannot be constricted to a single

---

[5] Cf. Samuel P. Huntington, *The Clash of Civilizations and the Remaking of World Order* (New York: Simon & Schuster, 1996).

[6] Cf. Pascal Bruckner, "Samuel Huntington ou le retour de la fatalité en histoire," *Esprit* 237, no.11 (November 1997): 53–67.

[7] Cf. Francis Fukuyama, *The End of History and the Last Man* (London: Penguin Books, 2012).

identity, but is to be regarded and treated as sharing in multiple layers of identity.[8] To be a Christian, a Muslim, or a Hindu does not define everything of a person. The same person can be an engineer with professional knowledge, networking with colleagues in the same profession, and may have a familial identity, as father, mother, son, or daughter, or an identity as a member of a local sports club interacting with football and tennis players. A person with several strata of identity may go to the church for Sunday service, or attend prayer in a local mosque, or visit a temple. Trouble begins when attempt is made to disregard and belittle multiple layers of identity and roles and view a person or a group solely through the lens of religious identity—as Christian, Hindu, or Muslim. The concentration on but one single identity, namely the religious one, creates a situation of conflict in multireligious societies. The ghettoization of identities and aggressive defense of them is one of the root causes of violence in our world.

The classification of civilizations based on religion, as is done by Samuel Huntington, flies in the face of empirical evidence and logic. The Muslim world is much larger than the religion of Islam, just like the Buddhist world is much more extensive than the religious tenets of Buddhism. We would be making the same mistake if Indic civilization were to be identified with the religion of Hinduism. Many cultures and religious traditions including Buddhism, Jainism, Islam, Sikhism, Zoroastrianism, and Christianity have been part of the larger Indic civilizational entity which cannot be equated with Hindu religious identity. In short, no civilization may be characterized by religious identity, and hence there is no need of building up a world-scenario of clash among civilizations, stripped to their bare religious identities.

It also follows that, given the embeddedness of religion in a larger whole, extremism may not be responded to by exclusively addressing doctrinal differences. The issue needs to be set in the broader social, economic, and political context. In other words, one insulated religious identity is not the answer to the extremism of another religious identity. Essentialized identities create divisions among peoples and groups, and this is true as much of religion as culture, ethnicity, and language.

---

[8] This is the chief argument Amartya Sen has fielded against the thesis of Samuel Huntington. See Amartya Sen, *Identity and Violence: The Illusion of Destiny,* 1st ed. (New York: W. W. Norton &, 2006).

## UNDERSTANDING RELIGIOUS IDENTITY-ASSERTION

Identity implies a sense of persistence and continuity; it is not anything momentary or ephemeral. There is an element of distinctness, namely there is something that differentiates it from others. Further, for a person to possess an identity means not to be dependent, but to feel confident and enjoy selfhood. It often involves a sense of belonging to a community or institution with reference to which one discovers meaning, purpose, and goals in life.[9] Belonging could be provided by a shared history, culture, experiences, and so on. The individuals share as well in the memory of the group, which binds them together.

Identity-assertion is connected with *recognition*. Individuals, as well as groups, want to be acknowledged and affirmed. In the view of Hegel, politics of recognition is a process in the journey of freedom. To be acknowledged and affirmed creates a space of freedom for individuals and communities to bring out their potential. Paradoxically, it also entails an inevitable struggle among competing identities. The need for recognition is highlighted in the West by the Canadian philosopher Charles Taylor in the context of a multiplicity of cultures, religions, and traditions coexisting. The psychologist Maslow, on his part, elaborating on the hierarchy of needs, tells us that, besides basic physical needs, human beings have needs in term of safety, love, and belonging; even more they have needs of recognition, acceptance (esteem), and self-fulfillment.[10] When a felt-need is ignored or deprived, it leads to tension and conflict. The marginalized groups claim their rights. However, the legitimacy of the claims need not always be based on their identity, but on something much broader. As Kwame Anthony Appiah points out:

> When the blacks and women in the United States campaigned for the vote, they did so very often as blacks and as women. But they weren't asking for recognition of their identity; they were asking, precisely, for the vote. Participation of this sort may presuppose a minimal sense of recognition, but it entails a good deal more. Similarly, when the lesbian and gay movement in the United States pursues recognition, it does so by asking for rights—to serve in the military, to marry—that would be worth having even

[9] Rusi Jaspal and Marco Cinnirella, "The Construction of Ethnic Identity: Insights from Identity Process Theory," *Ethnicities* 12, no.5 (October 2012): 503–530.

[10] Cf. *Abraham Maslow: The Hierarchy of Needs*. The Management Thinkers. (Corby: Institute of Management Foundation, 1998).

if they came without recognition. So not all political claims made in the name of group identity are primarily claims for recognition.[11]

In regular times, the religious identity of a group can be a matter of daily routine in a society. There are certain critical situations and circumstances, however, when religious identity gets accentuated and sharpened for achieving specific goals. This phenomenon of identity-assertion is referred to by sociologists as "*salience*." In the process of the salience of identity, one should duly recognize the role of emotions. This is particularly true of religious identities. If all identities in specific situations are vulnerable to provocation, this is doubly so in the case of religious identity, which is linked to the ultimate purpose and meaning of the life of an individual or a group.

Empirical studies show that there are three stages in the formation of religious identity.[12]

The first one is *identity by ascription*, that is to say how others perceive me and my religious belonging. I come across to others as a Muslim or a Buddhist for many external marks of identifications such as the religious places I visit and the rites I perform or participate in. The second stage of identity formation is when identity becomes *a matter of choice*. I may be born in a particular family attached to a particular religious tradition. However, when I choose to belong to the particular religious community I was born into, then, it ceases to be something given or ascribed, but becomes something that I have now consciously imbibed and made my own. Here, there is self-reflection in the process of identity-building.

In social identity theory and identity theory, the self is reflexive in that it can take itself as an object and can categorize, classify, or name itself in particular ways in relation to other social categories or classifications. This process is called *self-categorization* in social identity theory; in identity theory, it is called *identification*. Through the process of self-categorization or identification identity is formed.[13]

[11] Kwame Anthony Appiah, "The Politics of Identity," in *Daedalus* 135, no.4 (Fall 2006):15–22, at 20; see also Anthony Appiah, *The Lies That Bind: Rethinking Identity: Creed, Country, Colour, Class, Culture* (New York: Liveright Publishing Corporation, 2018).

[12] Cf. Lori Peek, "Becoming Muslim: The Development of a Religious Identity," *Sociology of Religion* 66, no.3 (Autumn, 2005): 215–242.

[13] Jan E. Stets and Peter J. Burke, "Identity Theory and Social Identity Theory," in *Social Psychology Quarterly* 63, no.3 (2000): 224–237, at 224.

The third stage is one of *declared identity*. What does that mean? At some critical situations, a person's self-identification with a particular religious group could become the sole basis of social, cultural, and political interactions in public. At the crucial juncture of political independence of South Asia, for example, the declared Muslim identity and declared Hindu identity led to the founding of two different nations—Pakistan and India. It was also the case in the aftermath of the September 11 attacks, when for many young Muslims in the USA, religion became a declared identity.[14]

We get further insight into the concept of religious identity by linking it to the active and passive voice of the word *to recognize*. In its active meaning, recognize has primarily an epistemological connotation. It could mean that I find once again what I knew, as, for example, when I meet a friend after a gap of many years. There is also another way of knowing. I recognize something because its characteristics have been already defined. I recognize an archeological object as belonging to the people of a particular culture and to a particular period, because the characteristics of the culture and times have already been established. Here, in order to recognize something, I need to apply given normative parameters. However, recognizing an object is not the same thing as recognizing a person. There is more to it than identification as an epistemic activity. In the case of persons or communities, given the self-reflexivity and self-consciousness of the subjects, it is important to understand and feel their self-perception and self-identification. To identify persons and communities by external markers and parameters would be to treat them as objects. Real recognition at the human level involves intersubjectivity and mutuality. Religion in as much as it is inherent to the subject of the person and communities requires a different approach to identity and recognition. Here, recognition is not simply understanding or grasping something by our mind, but it means, more importantly, accepting someone (individuals or communities) as true and as a value in herself or themselves.[15] This is the kind of approach most fitting to be able to understand the identity of religions. The identity of a religion is not exhausted by its doctrines, rituals, and laws; religions is identified and recognized by relating it to its believers.

---

[14] Lori Peek, "Becoming Muslim," 230.

[15] Cf. Paul Ricœur, *The Course of Recognition*, translated by David Pellauer. Vienna Lecture Series (Cambridge, Mass; London: Harvard University Press, 2005).

## FROM REIFIED TO FLUID IDENTITIES

A dynamic understanding of identity is part of a larger Weltanschaung of our times, different from the classical one. In the classical worldview, permanence and immutability are among the most cherished goals and objects of human endeavor. The traditional metaphysics of being sustained this worldview. Not subject to change was viewed as a characteristic divine attribute. Think of Aristotle's conception of ultimate reality as *"motor immobilis"*—unmoved mover. In the medieval scholastic philosophy, being, or the *"esse,"* constituted the reality, and change, or *fieri*, meant imperfection, since it meant that the being is not in a fulfilled or perfect state (*actus*) and hence in need of change (*potentia*). We could think of examples from other philosophical systems as well.

Fixing of identities has been a colonial practice all through history. Creating "stereotypes" and profiling of natives and indigenous peoples were part and parcel of Orientalism. Human societies were studied as material objects. Think of the colonial image of "village India"—an imaginary reality eternally unchanging and fixated forever. For this reason, study and critique of "stereotyping" has been a critical component in the postcolonial theory. It can also help us analyze religious stereotypes and stigmatization, and to understand how they serve as ammunitions in times of religious riots and violent conflicts. As Homi Bhabha notes, the question is not so much whether the fixed image is positive or negative. The more critical issue is the way the other is packaged, and her identity is labeled.

An important feature of colonial discourse is its dependence on the concept of 'fixity' in the ideological construction of otherness. Fixity, as the sign of cultural/historical/racial difference in the discourse of colonialism, is a paradoxical mode of representation: it connotes rigidity and an unchanging order as well as disorder, degeneracy and daemonic repetition. Likewise, the stereotype, which is its major discursive strategy, is a form of knowledge and identification that vacillates between what is lawyers 'in place', already known, and something that must be anxiously repeated.[16]

Making of stereotypes is a process of *domination* of the other. Exercising superiority of one religion over the other is not only a matter of doctrinal claims. It has a lot to do with how the other is packaged and circulated.

[16] Homi Bhabha, "The Other Question," in Padmini Mongia, ed., *Contemporary Postcolonial Theory. A Reader* (Delhi: Oxford University Press, 2000), 37–54, at 37.

This kind of profiling and stereotyping often happens because of the lack of will to get to know firsthand the religion of the other. If there are political and economic rivalries among groups, then the religion of the other is subjected to a negative stereotyping and imaging. This also can be called "ascriptive identity."[17] Such an identity conferred from without may not correspond to truth, nor to the self-perception of the other.

To cite an example, Gandhi was very concerned about the plight of the "untouchables" of India and the social discrimination and poverty they suffered. So, when he called them "*Harijan*" (people of God), he meant well; it was an effort, on his part, to confer a new dignity on them as children of God. The "Untouchables," however, found this ascription of identity by Gandhi condescending. They preferred to identify themselves by employing their subjectivity. *Dalits*, meaning a people who are crushed and ground, is how they designated themselves. It is a case of self-*acquired identity*—a matter of one's choice—in contrast to any ascriptive identity. The "Untouchables" feel proud about their collective self-identification as the Dalits.

There is another antidote to the temptation to reify or to essentialize identities, which is to unpack the concept and critically examine whether identity construction has reference to the other. This is precisely what is missing in the classical understanding of self-identity as sameness. It is self-referential and excludes anything outside itself. Post-structuralism and modern linguistics could serve as critical theoretical instruments to understand the identity of anything in its liaison to or its differentiation from the other. Identity, to express in philosophical terms, is not a matter of substance but of *relation*. Such being the case, there is no end and purpose in defining the identity of any reality. Identity keeps expanding as it could be related to or differentiated infinitely from other realities and objects. The continuous evolution of identity in relationship questions any essentializing of it as something given once and for all. This is of paramount importance in understanding religious identity, since religions tend to insulate themselves and get essentialized and reified.

Contemporary feminism and anti-racist movements have contributed even more to revisit the concept of identity. Thanks to them we understand how at the root of oppression lies the way the identity of the

---

[17] On this point see, Charles Taylor, *Sources of the Self. The making of Modern Identity* (Cambridge: Cambridge University Press, 1989); R. F. Baumeister, *Identity: Cultural Change and the Struggle for Self* (New York: Oxford University Press, 1986).

discriminated has been created and essentialized by those in power. One uses simply "women" in the abstract to define and essentialize half of humanity with no regard to history, race, context, and the subjectivity which make significant differences. Naming, classifying, and essentializing have been, as we noted, the privilege of rulers and dominators. The feminist, anti-racist, and postcolonial movements have brought to the fore in the field of both politics and academic discourses a subversive understanding of identity that functions as a trigger to overcome their alienation. They provide inspiration to rethink religious identities throughout our reflection in this volume.

Modern social psychology too has contributed significantly to clarify the concept of identity in dynamic terms. One of the distinguished exponents who saw identity as a process of growth in stages was the clinical psychologist Erik Erikson, whose contribution is widely recognized and has found applications in other fields as well.[18] The various stages and crises a child goes through in its growth process have suggested insightful elements to understand the dynamics of identity construction. The study of religious identity today could benefit a lot from his many original perspectives. Like in the personal case of Augustine and Luther, a religious group too may experience collective identity crisis which could truly be an occasion for conversion, transcendence, and self-transformation.[19] Like an adolescent, a religion could get confused about the role it is called to play and begin to doubt its own self-identity. How it overcomes and reestablishes its new identity will depend upon how it responds to the social environment where it is situated. In our case, the process of globalization and modernity, while creating a crisis in religions, could also be an opportunity to reconfigure their identity in new terms and under different circumstances.

---

[18] Erik H. Erikson, *Childhood and Society*, rev. ed. [Pelican Book. No. A754.] (New York and London: W. W. Norton & Company, 1963); see also Kenneth R. Hoover, ed., *The Future of Identity: Centennial Reflections on the Legacy of Erik Erikson* (Lanham, Md.; Oxford: Lexington Books, 2004); Robert S Wallerstein and Leo Goldberger, eds., *Ideas and Identities: The Life and Work of Erik Erikson* (Madison, Conn.: International Universities Press, 1998); R. S. Wallerstein, "Erikson's Concept of Ego Identity Reconsidered," *Journal of the American Psychoanalytic Association* 46, no.1 (1998): 229–48.

[19] Fr. Lawrence J. Daly, "St. Augustine's 'Confessions' and Erik Erikson's 'Young Man Luther': Conversion as "Identity Crisis," *Augustiniana* 31, no.3/4 (1981): 183–96.

## IDENTITY AS BASIS OF CLAIMS

Our reflections on religion and identity need to extend to another important area. While critically questioning the ascriptive or given identity, we need to, at the same time, attend to the contemporary developments in the issue of rights. The question of identity has drawn much attention since it serves as a sound basis for rights and claims. This is a very complex and engaging issue.

> Essentialism presupposes that a group or a category of objects/people share some defining features exclusive to the members of this particular group or category. This has been a highly contested idea throughout the social sciences and particularly in post-colonial as well as colonial discourse studies. Essentialism is often discussed together with the questioning of categories like race and nation. On the other hand, at a more pragmatic level, essentialist practices and modes of representation have been applied by groups and individuals in the promotion of certain minority rights or demands (as well as liberation struggles).[20]

Today, ethnic, regional, linguistic identities have become "strategic" sites to challenge the established order. One speaks, often in derogatory terms, of "identity politics." Should not the primordial identities evaporate and disappear in the age of globalization, given its universal outreach and fluidity? But the point to note is that identity in many cases has been a "weapon of the weak."[21] In political liberalism which hinges on the individual as the bearer of rights, one pays scant attention to the rights of groups, especially the marginal and discriminated ones—something that can be observed all over the world. Are we essentializing group identities? Identities, as we noted, indeed keep changing and evolving, and cannot be reified. However, in the case of those at the margins, with Gayatri Spivak, we can call for "strategic essentialism."[22] It is a provisional acceptance of essentialized identity for the purpose of attaining political goals of

[20] Elisabeth Eide, "Strategic Essentialism and Ethnification," *Nordicom Review* 31 (2010): 63–78, at 66.

[21] James C. Scott, *Weapons of the Weak: Everyday Forms of Peasant Resistance* (New Haven; London: Yale University Press, 1986).

[22] Cf. Gayatri Spivak, "Can the Subaltern Speak?," in *Colonial Discourse and Postcolonial Theory*, edited by Patrick Williams and Laura Chrisman (New York: Columbia University Press, 1993), 66–111; Gayatri Chakravorty Spivak, "Criticism, Feminism, and the Institution," an interview by Elizabeth Grosz, *Sage Journal* 10–11, no. 1 (1985): 175–187;

representation or for negotiation of power, which otherwise would not be possible. In other words, essentializing itself of a subaltern or marginal group could serve as a pragmatic strategy to safeguard its dignity and rights. While on the one hand the focus on particularity could appear as a refusal to transcend to the plane of the universal, on the other, hand the affirmation of particularity and "strategic essentialism" are important to reaching the universal human. The ultimate aim of the affirmation of the particular is not to stop there, but to foster universal solidarity. This comes out very clearly, for example, in the work of Aime Cesaire's—*The Negritude.*[23]

Religions are confronted today with the process of globalization. Through exposure to other religions and other beliefs, modes of worship, they need to get relativized instead of essentialized and absolutized. This is a great challenge globalization throws up to all religious traditions today. It provokes these religious traditions to rethink their identity in relational terms. *Without Buddha, I Could Not Be a Christian* is a thought-provoking title of a book.[24] The encounter with other religious identities shapes one's own. Little would be achieved through globalization if it were to mean only a new opportunity to bring one's religious identity to every nook and corner of the world. The real challenge is to reconceptualize one's religious identity in encounter with the other. Here is also an anthropological and sociological key for the promotion of interreligious dialogue and understanding in the globalized world.

## HETEROGENEITY IN RELIGIOUS IDENTITY

Religious identity is not monolithic or homogenous. Within the same religious group, there is plurality and diversity of perceptions, views, modes of action, and behavior patterns. While identity is something legitimate, it could become critical when a group or a community wants to impose on all its members a uniform conception of itself and its role. In such cases, religious identity would come into conflict with the rights of the

Sarah Harasym, ed., *In The Post-Colonial Critic: Interviews, Strategies, and Dialogues* (New York: Routledge, 1990), 1–16.

[23] See Doris L. Garraway, "'What Is Mine': Césairean Negritude between the Particular and the Universal," *Research in African Literatures* 41, no.1 (2010): 71–86.

[24] Paul F. Knitter, *Without Buddha I Could Not Be a Christian* (Richmond: Oneworld, 2013).

individuals. For, an individual may claim to belong to a particular religious group, however, not in terms of what is dictated by the group or its leaders.

Here, we are confronted with a dialectics between objective and normative religious structures, on the one hand, and the structures of consciousness, on the other. A reflexive process on the part of the individual leads to realize who he or she is. This is *religious self-identification* or self-categorization. An individual believer may find herself at variance with what is prescribed and her own perception of things, leading to dissent. The internal dissent within a religious group could be something creative pushing further its spiritual frontiers beyond an essentialist self-definition. To cite an example, Islamic identity may be perceived differently by the Sunnis, Shias, and the Ahmadiyyas. Again, in the case of Islam, the Sufi tradition would present a very different understanding of Islam than the Wahhabi Islamic movement that is concerned about propagating a stringent version of Islam. When Islamic religious identity is stereotyped from without, these important differences and the inner religious heterogeneity get ignored.

## FROM NORMATIVE TO NARRATIVE RELIGIOUS IDENTITY

In religious traditions, besides doctrinal characteristics, there are normative ways of defining identity. Numerous are the prescriptions that lay down what to believe, what to practice, how to conduct oneself in society, what religious rituals to participate in, and even what to eat and what not to eat. The enforcement of these prescriptions for identity may differ from religion to religion. Religious identity, as we noted, is generally equated with doctrinal or normative identity. However, besides this, there can be a narrative religious identity.[25] As Charles Taylor rightly observes, making sense of ourselves (as well as of the world and society around us) calls for us to "grasp our lives in a narrative."[26]

---

[25] Narrative identity is a very significant concept in psychology. It is defined as "a person's internalized and evolving life story, integrating the reconstructed past and imagined future to provide life with some degree of unity." Dan P. McAdams and Kate C. McLean, "Narrative Identity," *Current Directions in Psychological Science* 22, no.3 (2013): 233–38, at 233; Paul Ricoeur has gone into this concept from philosophical and hermeneutical perspective. On the concept of narrative identity, see Patrick Crowley, "Paul Ricœur: The Concept of Narrative Identity, the Trace of Autobiography," *Paragraph* 26, no.3 (2003): 1–12.

[26] As quoted in Samantha Vice, "Literature and the Narrative Self," *Philosophy* 78, no.303 (2003): 93–108, at 94; see also Peter Goldie, "Narrative Thinking, Emotion, and Planning,"

According to a currently popular view, selfhood or identity is constituted by the narratives that we tell about ourselves. More precisely, we are characters—usually the protagonists—of the stories we tell or could tell about ourselves. This claim about selfhood is usually conjoined with a transcendental claim, to the effect that we also necessarily impose a narrative structure upon the world, that narrative is the 'lens' through which our lives are experienced. Experience, in other words, is essentially narrative in form.[27]

Another way of understanding narrative identity, especially in relation to religious identity, is to distinguish, as Paul Ricoeur does, between *idem* identity and *ipse* identity. Idem refers to the sameness.[28] Something is recognized and identified because, across time, it has maintained the sameness. On the other hand, *ipse* identity is one which gives insight into the self, the subject. Very often, religious identity has been reduced to idem identity. The world of the subject and the unfolding of its story (both individual and collective) clamor for attention.

The identity of Israel, for example, was constituted through the stories the community narrated about itself and passed on from generation to generation. Given their great fluidity and flexibility, Hinduism, Buddhism, and Daoism define themselves through their narratives. We may recall here the central importance of *puranas* (religious stories and narratives) in Hinduism and the *Jataka tales* in Buddhism. This is also true of the individuals affiliated to these religious traditions. As Alsdair MacIntyre has pointed out, there is an intrinsic mutuality between life and narrative.[29] On the one hand, life is embedded in narratives and draws meaning out of

*The Journal of Aesthetics and Art Criticism* 67, no.1 (2009): 97–106. Cassie Striblen, "Collective Responsibility and the Narrative Self," *Social Theory and Practice* 39, no.1 (2013): 147–65; Simona Bonini Baldini, "Narrative Capability: Self-Recognition and Mutual Recognition in Refugees' Storytelling," *Journal of Information Policy* 9 (2019): 132–47; James L. Battersby, "Narrativity, Self, and Self-Representation," *Narrative* 14, no.1 (2006): 27–44.

[27] Samantha Vice, "Literature and the Narrative Self," 93.

[28] Cf. P. Crowley, "Paul Ricoeur: The Concept of Narrative Identity, the Trace of Autobiography," *Paragraph: The Journal of the Modern Critical Theory Group* 26, no.3 (2003): 1–12; Kim Atkins, *Narrative Identity and Moral Identity: A Practical Perspective* (London: Routledge, 2008); Mark Freeman, "From Substance to Story: Narrative, Identity, and the Reconstruction of the Self." *Narrative and Identity. Studies in Autobiography, Self and Culture*, edited by Jens Brockmeier, and Donal Carbaugh (Amsterdam: John Benjamins Publishing Company, 2001), 283–98; Pamela Anderson, "Having It Both Ways: Ricoeur's Hermeneutics of the Self," *Oxford Literary Review* 15, no.1/2 (1993): 227–52.

[29] Cf. J. B. Schneewind, "Virtue, Narrative, and Community: MacIntyre and Morality," *The Journal of Philosophy* 79, no.11 (1982): 653–63.

it; on the other hand, one tries to live one's life according to these narratives. If we apply this kind of relationship between life and narrative to the realm of religion, we get a very different picture of religious identity, different from the normative approach.

Social science theorists and historians were once dismissive of the narrative, as it does not fit into their scientific approach to knowledge. Today, increasingly disciplines in social sciences and humanities have come to realize the value of the narrative not only as an effective representation of reality but also as providing a new and different social epistemology. Unfortunately, in the study of religion and its identity, *narrative and discursive practice* have been neglected as a source of new knowledge as it (religion) remains mainly, if not solely, confined to the study of *doctrines* for defining identity. If narrativity goes to constitute our social identities, the same is true also of our religious identities, something we need to realize today more than ever in the context of the explosion of the social media and networking. By associating oneself and becoming part of the religious narratives of a particular group or community, one comes to discern one's faith identity and religious belonging.

Literature is another helpful point to understand narrative identity. For, literature is about the singular and the concrete in a definite context, like in a fiction. Literature challenges the interpretation of truth as synonymous with the universal. Religions which are prone to speak in terms of the universal imagine their own identities in this fashion. The narrative identity of a religious group and its experiences in a particular context are no less true because they are not universal or verifiable. Reading religions through the lens of literature would mean among other things to understand identity not only in terms of what *was* and *is*, but also of *what will be*, that is in terms of the future. Narrative identity gives room to define oneself through one's aspirations, dreams, and what is to come. When we apply this to religious identity, the consequences are far-reaching. It helps religions break loose of their ascriptive identity and imagine themselves in relation to the future of humanity and the entire creation in whose service every religion needs to understand itself.

## Discursive and Social Construction of Identities

The identity politics of today has given rise to a theorizing on the discursive and social construction of all kinds of identities. It is one of the most discussed contemporary epistemological issues. Thus, concepts such as culture, tradition, woman, and nation, when viewed critically, bear in themselves a lot of social construction and discursive practices,[30] which is true of religion as well. Various elements, discourses, and repetitive acts are deployed and pieced together to create a particular brand of identity. From a feminist perspective, Simone de Beauvoir expressed the social constructivism very brilliantly when she stated, "one is not born, but rather becomes a woman."[31] In the case of nationalism, Eric Hobsbawm, from a historical perspective, has shown how identity gets constructed. From a theoretical perspective, Benedict Anderson has argued on the basis of his empirical studies, how nation is a matter of creation; it is an "*imagined community.*"[32]

To unpack the interactive and relational character in religious identity-building, we may refer here usefully to the symbolic interactionism of George Herbert Mead and other scholars.[33] According to this theory, our response to and interaction with anything, person or group, is premised on the meaning we attribute to them. Where does the meaning derive from? It flows from the innumerable interactions people have with others and with their societies and which, in the course of time, have grown like a snowball. It is understandable why meanings do not remain fixed, but keep changing through an interpretative process as the social interaction and encounters keep changing and accumulating.

To give an illustration, today, what it is to be an American is not the result of a consensual identity of all the members who form part of this particular national entity. It is a result of innumerable social interactions opening the door for a variety of perceptions about national identity. Thus, depending on social interactions, there can be those who see the key American values in individual freedom and equality. With this perception of national identity, their attitude toward the issue of immigration will be

---

[30] On the concept of social construction, see Peter L. Berger and P.L. Luckmann, *The Social Construction of Reality. A Treatise in the Sociology of Knowledge* (London: Penguin Books, 1991). The numerous contributions of feminists have established how gender turns out to be a social construction.

[31] Simone de Beauvoir, *The Second Sex* (London: Vintage Book, 2011), 283.

[32] Cf. Eric Hobsbawm, *Nations and Nationalism Since 1780* (Cambridge: Cambridge University Press, 2012); Benedict Anderson, *Imagined Communities. Reflections on the Origin and Spread of Nationalism* (London-New York: Verso, 1983).

[33] George Herbert Mead, Daniel R. Huebner and Hans Joas, eds., *Mind, Self, and Society: The Definitive edition*, edited by Charles W. Morris (Chicago: University of Chicago Press, 2015).

different from someone who sees white and Christian identity as American. In this latter case, immigration will be viewed as a serious threat to offset the basic white and Christian identity and supremacy. In short, there is not only a social construction of identity but also a subjective construction of collective identity.

## CONCLUSION

It would be myopic to dismiss the issue of religions identities in the name of modernity and secularization. Anyone who realistically views the global scenario will be convinced about the increasing political role—at both national and international levels—being played by religious identities.[34] This is no more an issue of the Global South, but increasingly becoming also an issue of the Global North. With escalation of migration in the Global North and with competition and conflict for political and economic power and cultural hegemony in the Global South, the issue of religious identity has turned into a hypersensitive question with consequences for social cohesion, justice, and peace at all levels. Further, religious identities under globalizing conditions raise in fresh terms and with new urgency and vigor a host of complex issues such as religious freedom, minority, conversion, ethics, role of religion in public life, religion in diaspora, and genesis of new religious movements. We will go into these issues in the various chapters of this volume.

The present chapter has attempted an initial clarification of certain concepts and dynamics which will be important to hold in mind in treating the above themes. The religious identities could be a source of conflict and disruption if they are to be viewed from an essentialist perspective, as much as a source of claims in the context of oppression and discrimination—a fact that brings out their inherent ambiguous character. Philosophical considerations apart, global developments lead us to pass on

[34] Cf. J. Haynes, ed., *Routledge Handbook of Religion and Politics* (New York: Routledge, 2009); T. Banchoff, ed., *Religious Pluralism, Globalization, and World Politics* (New York: Oxford University Press, 2008); T. A. Byrnes & P. J. Katzenstein, eds., *Religion in an Expanding Europe* (New York: Cambridge University Press, 2006); J. Cesari, *Why the West Fears Islam: An Exploration of Muslims in Liberal Democracies* (New York: Palgrave Macmillan, 2013); J. Fox and S. Sander, *Bringing Religion into International Relations* (New York: Palgrave Macmillan, 2004); N. Sandal and J. Fox, *Religion in International Relations Theory: Interactions and Possibilities* (New York: Routledge, 2013); Nukhet Sandal and John Fox, *Religion in International Relations Theory* (London: Routledge, 2013).

to a fluid and dynamic approach to them, something that could be observed in the shift from normative to narrative forms of religious identity. A critical approach also unveils the discursive and social-constructive character of religion, like in other realms of life.

# CHAPTER 3

# Religious Identities: From the Colonial to the Global

Hailing from a remote village in India, when I began my university education at the age of seventeen in Italy and later in France, everything I experienced added to my teenage confusion. The whole world looked upside down. One of the questions people asked me quite often was an embarrassment. How many "dialects" do you speak in India? When I said there are over 200 languages, my friends were flabbergasted. I was made to feel small. For, the best response was, "we speak one language in our country." You would be made to feel proud. It was seen as a sign of advancement. I instinctively felt that something was wrong but I was too young then to articulate what it was. I knew that my mother tongue Tamil and classical language Sanskrit were over a millennium older than the language of my European friends. The Tamil language had from ancient times developed a very complex grammatical structure and syntax. The many languages of India had each developed their own scripts, unlike the European languages which, in general, do not have their own scripts but depend on the one Roman script. The Code of symbols which language is, is indeed an ingenious invention of linguistic communities.

The assumption that we overcome divisions by one single language has been proved as much wrong as the claim that unity is not achievable with a multiplicity of tongues. As a matter of fact, in my extensive travels in India, I never felt that people had difficulty in communication, though they spoke different languages. They made themselves understood.

© The Author(s), under exclusive license to Springer Nature  41
Switzerland AG 2021
F. Wilfred, *Religious Identities and the Global South*,
New Approaches to Religion and Power,
https://doi.org/10.1007/978-3-030-60738-8_3

People, even illiterate ones at the border areas of different states, spoke three to four languages and were able to get into conversation with each other with unbelievable ease and spontaneity. The richness and grandiose creation of a plurality of tongues have been, thanks to colonial representation, derided as a sign of primitivism and underdevelopment. As the flourishing of the multitude of flora and fauna on the earth is so vital for the natural environment, so is it with languages for the creation of a rich humankind. Each language is a different way of being in the world. There is a parallel between the loss of biodiversity and the extinction of many languages year after year.

What is said about languages applies also to the realm of religion.[1] For, both of them are a world of symbols and signs. Hinduism believes in the many faces of God, expressed popularly through its belief in a pantheon of thirty-three million gods and goddesses. On the other hand, colonial rule in India and the belief in the monotheism of Abrahamic religions as the highest form of belief had a very peculiar development in that country, thanks to many anthropologists, ethnologists, and colonial bureaucrats. People were made to feel religiously underdeveloped and superstitious if they had a multiplicity of gods and goddesses. This colonial assessment of their religious world led some Indians to tailor their belief and couch it in simulated monotheistic terms. The Unitarians had a role to play in all this.[2] The Father of modern India, Raj Mohan Roy (1772–1833), and the Unitarians had fruitful interaction in the nineteenth century. One was at pains to explain that the Vedas originally were monotheistic, closer to the belief in one God of Semitic religions, but the post-Vedic developments degenerated into polytheism.

---

[1] R. Brubaker, "Linguistic and Religious Pluralism: Between Difference and Inequality," *Journal of Ethnic and Migration Studies* 41, no.1 (2015): 3–32; see also Elvira Riera-Gil, "The Communicative Value of Local Languages: An Underestimated Interest in Theories of Linguistic Justice," *Ethnicities* 19 (2019): 174–99; Volker Hinnenkamp and Katharina Meng, eds., *Sprachgrenzen überspringen: Sprachliche Hybridität und Polykulturelles Selbstverständnis* (Tübingen: Narr, 2005).

[2] Cf. Spencer Lavan, *Unitarians and India. A Study in Encounter and Response* (Boston: Beacon Press, 1977).

## COLONIAL APPROACH TO RELIGION
## AND POSTCOLONIAL CONTESTATIONS

There are many colonial wounds to be healed and wrinkles to be ironed out, and theyrelate to the issue of religious identities as well. The colonial representation of religions of the subjugated people, like in many other areas, served the purpose of extolling the superiority of the colonizers, their culture, religion, and civilization. It was, obviously, not a dispassionate and objective presentation but a distorted one that served to validate and reinforce the hegemony of the colonial governance. Impressive mapping, codifying, tabulating, and surveying of the religions were done. The accumulated knowledge gave the Western scholars of the Orient like William Jones the self-assurance that they knew the Orient better than any other European scholar.[3]

However, the people practicing their religion in daily life had little role to play in this kind of accumulation of knowledge.[4] One of the colonial achievement was to impose the category of "religion" on the colonies and read through this lens the spiritual traditions, beliefs, rituals, customs, and laws of the subjugated people.[5] Moreover, colonialism essentialized religion, which made classifications easy.[6] For example, dealing with the theme of prayer, Friedrich Heiler made a scheme of prophetic and mystical religions.[7] By fitting into the mystical category the Indian and other East Asian religions, the Orientalists wanted to say that these religions were otherworldly, feminine, and passive, and not concerned about mundane realities, and they counterposed these religions to the masculine and prophetic religions of struggles, characteristic of the Abrahamic religions of the desert.[8] Such distorted representations went to the extent of attributing poverty and underdevelopment to this otherworldly nature of

---

[3] Cf. Edward Said, *Orientalism. Western Conception of the Orient* (London: Penguin Books, 1978), 78.

[4] I wonder whether this spirit of Orientalism continues with the plethora of present-day religious studies projects.

[5] Cf. Wilfred Cantwell Smith, *The Meaning and End of Religion* (Minneapolis: Fortress Press, 1991); Richard King, *Orientalism and Religion: Postcolonial Theory, India and "the Mystic East"* (London: Routledge, 1999).

[6] Cf. Edward Said, *Orientalism* (New York: Vintage Books, 1979).

[7] Cf. Williams, Rowan. "The Prophetic and the Mystical: Heiler Revisited." *New Blackfriars* 64, no. 757 (1983): 330–47.

[8] Friedrich Heiler, Das Gebet, *Eine Religionsgeschtliche und Religionspsychologische Untersuchung*, 5th edition, (Munich: Nabu Press,1923). Such a distinction was operative also in the work of other Protestant phenomenologists of religion like Nathan Söderblom.

Hinduism, Buddhism, Daoism, and similar ones. Stereotype like "caste, cow and curry" to define India had also its versions to characterize the Indic religious universe.

Colonial theology on its part saw dangers to Christian faith coming from Oriental religions. Let me cite the example of the first Lutheran missionary to India, Bartolomäus Ziegenbalg (1682–1719). Ziegenbalg immersed himself in the culture and tradition of the people, acquiring considerable mastery of Tamil to be able to translate for the first time the entire New Testament and write other works. His deep interest in local religious traditions led him to compose two major works: *Malabarian Heathenism* (1711) and *Genealogy of the Malabarian Gods*. Ziegenbalg became one of the early transmitters of knowledge about Indian society, religion, flora and fauna to the West. However, he incurred the anger of his mentor A.H. Francke, who thought that Ziegenbalg instead of extirpating heathenism as every missionary should do, was spreading "heathenish nonsense in Europe."[9] This deep-rooted colonial legacy is still alive, something evident in the warning of the Roman Congregation for the Doctrine of the Faith in 1989, against oriental meditative traditions like *yoga* and Zen as threats to Christian faith.[10]

On the other hand, religious identity-affirmation helped the native people to resist colonial forces. Generally, this is a point the theorists holding on to secularization thesis fail to understand. Politically, economically, and culturally powerless, the colonized people knew how best to make use of their religion and religious identities. Any analysis of the transition from colonialism to the independence of nations in Asia would reveal what a crucial role the religious identities played in the struggles for independence. This is true of India with Hinduism, of Sri Lanka, Myanmar, and Vietnam with Buddhism, and of Indonesia, Malaysia, not to speak of the Middle East, with Islam. In China, there has been a tradition of using popular religious resources against domination. It was a valuable means of resistance. Most glaring is the symbol of the Virgin Mary of Guadalupe in Central and South America.

---

Cf. Rowan Williams, "The Prophetic and the Mystical: Heiler Revisited," *New Blackfriars* 64, no.757 (1983): 330–47.

[9] As quoted in Stephen Neill, *A History of Christianity in India 1707–1858* (Cambridge: Cambridge University Press, 1985), 33.

[10] For the text of the document see http://www.vatican.va/roman_curia/congregations/cfaith/documents/rc_con_cfaith_doc_19891015_meditazione-cristiana_en.html

There are multiple examples of the Virgin of Guadalupe being employed as a symbol of resistance to structural oppression. In Mexico, the Virgin of Guadalupe has a long history as a symbol of revolution. Father Hidalgo evoked her name and presented her image when he gave the call for Mexico's independence from Spain.... In the Mexican Revolution beginning in 1910, revolutionary leaders used her image in their ethnic and class struggle, and today, in Chiapas, Zapatistas have done the same. In the United States, the Virgin of Guadalupe is an important symbol for Mexican immigrants and migrants, and for Chicanos and Chicanas. On banners and buttons of political protest, in artwork and murals, in tattoos, and on low-riders, the image of the Virgin of Guadalupe is frequently associated with ethnic identity and presented as a symbol of resistance to racial control.[11]

The denigration of religion and cultural values of the colonized triggered two different reactions. It led on the one hand to religious nationalism and on the other hand to reform. It also provided an occasion to critically think of their traditional religions and practices with implications for their social life. This took the form of a movement for renewal as, for example, in Hinduism in India. A classical case is that of Swami Dayananda Saraswati (1824–1883), who founded the Arya Samaj movement,[12] which was involved in the "purification" of Hinduism from its many deviations and superstitious practices. Another example would be Raja Ram Mohan Roy (1772–1833) and the movement of Brahmosamaj.[13]

[11] Deborah A. Boehm, "Our Lady of Resistance: The Virgin of Guadalupe and Contested Constructions of Community in Santa Fe, New Mexico," *Journal of the Southwest* 44, no.1 (2002): 95–104. at 102; Eric R. Wolf, "The Virgin of Guadalupe: A Mexican National Symbol," *The Journal of American Folklore* 71, no. 279 (1958): 34–39.

[12] Cf. S. R. Bakshi, *Arya Samaj: Swami Dayananda and His Ideology* (New Delhi: Anmol Publications, 1991); Suresh K. Sharma, ed., *Swami Dayananda and the Arya Samaj Movement,* First edition (Delhi: Vista International Publishing House, 2009); Kripal Chandra Yadav and Krishan Singh Arya, *Arya Samaj and the Freedom Movement* (New Delhi: Manohar Publications, 1988); Gulshan Swarup Saxena, *Arya Samaj Movement in India, 1875–1947* (New Delhi, India: Commonwealth Publishers, 1990); Lajpat Rai, *A History of the Arya Samaj,* Revised edition (Bombay: Orient Longmans, 1967); Satish Kumar Sharma, *Social Movements and Social Change: A Study of Arya Samaj and Untouchables in Punjab* (Delhi: B.R. Pub., 1985).

[13] Cf. David Kopf, *British Orientalism ad the Bengal Renaissance* (Berkeley: University of California Press, 1969); David Kopf, *The Brahmosamaj and the Shaping of the Modern Indian Mind* (Princeton: Princeton University Press, 1979); Sophie Dobson Collet, ed., *Raja Rammohan Roy* (Calcutta: Sadharan Brahmo Samaj, 1962); S. Cromwell Crawford, *Ram Mohan Roy: Social, Political, and Religious Reform in 19th Century India* (New York: Paragon House, 1987); Bruce Carlisle Robertson, *Raja Rammohan Ray: The Father of*

We need to pay attention also to how Islam came to be deployed as a weapon to challenge the economic and political domination from outside, especially the European unjust trade practices and colonization. The history of Islamic revival, reform, and fundamentalism is also a history of challenge and resistance to political domination and economic exploitation.

> Islam, in effect, became an idiom of protest against the gradual contraction of internal and external trade, brought about by the mercantile activities of European maritime nations, specifically, the Portuguese, Spanish, Dutch, British, and the French. What was contested in the name of Islam by Islamic revivalists was control over vital commodities—slaves, textiles, coffee, tea, and spices—as well as gold, all trafficked along the major trade routes from the Atlantic coast of West Africa to the Indonesian archipelago...There is no independent Muslim movement after the colonial period; all are reacting to some force or series of forces that emanate from the Western world, which is to say northern Europe and the United States.[14]

This is a legacy that lingers on, accounting for many of the problems plaguing the Islamic world today. Many liberal secularists, with little knowledge about the history of non-Western societies, seem to be unaware of the internal developments in the religious universe. The postcolonial period for many colonized people was one in which they tried to consolidate their religious and cultural identity, so very much maligned and undermined by colonial powers. There was a resurgence of religious identities which gave people a new sense of dignity and freedom. As for the Middle East, Islam served not so much for the construction of national identity as the transnational Islamic unity and brotherhood. In short, we could note movements of reappropriation of religion and forceful affirmation of religious identities in the aftermath of colonialism.

When European liberals critique religion as anti-national and anti-secular, what they may often have in mind are historical experiences like the resistance of papacy to Italian unification in the nineteenth century, or the siding of the French ecclesial establishment with the king and the

*Modern India* (Delhi: Oxford UP, 1995); see also Arvind Sharma, *Modern Hindu Thought. The Essential Texts* (Delhi: Oxford University Press, 2002).

[14] Bruce B. Lawrence, "Muslim Engagement with Injustice and Violence," in Mark Juergensmeyer—Margo Kitts and Michael Jerryson, eds., *The Oxford Handbook of Religion and Violence* (New York: Oxford, 2013), 126–152, at 142–143.

bourgeoisie. What happened with Christianity as a religion is extrapolated to all religions in the world. However, the instances we referred to show that religion far from being a force against the wellbeing of the nation was a great force of liberation from the colonial yoke, one reason why many peoples in the Global South are attached to their religious tradition and identity even today.

One of the most critical issues of religions under colonialism was the way it tried to divide communities and set the stage for endemic religious conflicts. The policies followed by the colonial dispensation disrupted relationships, for example, among Hindus and Muslims in India, among Buddhists and Hindus in Sri Lanka, among Christians and Muslims in the Philippines, and so on. One may not brand this as an anti-imperial critique, namely to ascribe responsibility to the colonial powers for the woes in the colonized societies. Surely, there were indigenous social and political factors that fostered division among religious communities. The religious policies of the colonizers could have opted to blunt and dampen these trends.[15] Instead, what happened was that their policies exacerbated the situation creating endemic conflict among religious groups.

## SHAPING OF RELIGIOUS IDENTITIES

A chemically pure religious identity is a myth. History tells us that religious identities have never been insulated from one another like watertight compartments. The evolution of the different world religions clearly exposes how each one of them has evolved by interacting with other religious identities and through absorption of alien lements into their doctrines and practices.

Christianity itself bears many traces of Judaism and early Greco-Roman religious conceptions.[16] There was a flourishing Byzantine Christianity and a very missionary Nestorian Persian Christianity. History also witnessed the "Germanization of Early Medieval Christianity"[17] with the

---

[15] Cf. Bipan Chandra, *Communalism in Modern India*, 3rd rev. ed. (New Delhi: Har-Anand Publication, 2008). The author discusses a caricatured view of colonialism as responsible for communalism in India, which is then easily demolished.

[16] Cf. Jaroslav Pelikan, *Christianity and Classical Culture: The Metamorphosis of Natural Theology in the Christian Encounter with Hellenism* (New Haven & London: Yale University Press, 1993).

[17] Cf. James C. Russell, *The Germanization of Early Medieval Christianity: A Socio-historical Approach to Religious Transformation* (New York: Oxford University Press, 1994).

absorption of many elements of indigenous religiosity and native social structures. The diversity in Christian identity right from the beginning allows us to speak of "*Christianities*" in the plural.[18] The concept of inculturation does not capture the richness of this diversity.

Most glaring is the example of Hinduism. Its identity is but the confluence of many religious streams sourced from diverse regions of South Asia and from different historical periods. "Hinduism" is a term of relatively recent origin to signify many currents of religiosity sharing among themselves a "family resemblance."[19] To change the image, the texture of Hinduism is made up of yarns of many hues and colours. Indeed, if there is a "religion" with infinite varieties and inflections, it is Hinduism. Given this diversity, it qualifies to be viewed and approached in its manifold manifestation as *Hinduisms*.[20] Buddhism, on its part, continued to evolve different forms and identities vis-à-vis the cultures, civilizations, and the religious worlds it encountered. So, we have not only the two early forms of Buddhism—*Theravāda and Mahāyāna*—but also Tibetan, Thai, Chinese, Japanese, and Sri Lankan Buddhism. Islam too, due to different historical, social, and political circumstances, has more than one single identity.

The above examples are meant to underscore that the present-day globalization is not the first time when religious identities meet, interact, and reinvent themselves. The history of religious identities is all along marked by syncretism and hybridity. Moreover, religions, like concepts, may not be defined with clear-cut boundaries and contours. In reality, what we have are the colors of the rainbow, one flowing into the other, difficult to identify which one ends where and which one starts where. What Wittgenstein said of "family-resemblance" could be rightly applied to the case of religions, and especially to Indic and East Asian religions. There is a "complicated network of similarities overlapping and criss-crossing."[21] Hinduism, as we noted, is an amalgamation of so many religious streams. One could see it as one, or as many depending upon whether one wants to underline the family resemblance or the individuality of each stream. It

[18] See Franklin Pilario, Felix Wilfred and Huang Po Ho, eds., "Asian Christianities," in *Concilium 2018/1* (London: SCM Press, 2018).

[19] Cf. Gunther D Sontheimer and Hermann Kulke, eds., *Hinduism Reconsidered* (New Delhi: Manohar Publications, 1989).

[20] Title of one of the recent works adopts this plural vocabulary. See Cf. John Zavos, Pralay Kanungo, Deepa S. Reddy, Maya Warrier, Raymond Williams, eds., *Public Hinduisms* (Delhi: Sage Publications, 2012).

[21] Cf. Ludwig Wittgenstein, *Philosophical Investigations* (Oxford: Basil Blackwell, 1976), para 66.

is like visiting a Chinese temple. One begins to wonder—as often happened to me—whether it is a Buddhist, Daoist, or Confucian temple. Speaking of identity in the previous chapter, we saw how at specific historical junctures a particular identity comes to the fore (resilience). We could adduce many such cases throughout history and from present times. Here let me illustrate the point with an example from the Indonesian history of Chinese religions. The Chinese who form a small segment of the Indonesian population are mostly people from the coastal belt of that country. One group of the Chinese settled there long ago and were at home with Indonesian culture, language, customs, and traditions. On the other hand, another group of more recent migrants continued their attachment to their mainland Chinese traditional Daoist religiosity and worship of ancestors. As a small minority, both groups of Chinese built temples for worship. There was a certain ambiguity in temples such as the Vihara Buddha Prabha in Yogyakarta. It functioned both as a Buddhist vihara and a Daoist temple. But in times when there was resentment against the Chinese community, the local rulers prevented any separate identity-building of the Chinese community. In these circumstances what the Chinese community did was to turn their temples more Buddhist than Daoist. The temple had dual identity, and which identity—Buddhist or Daoist was dominant—depended on the local political situation.[22]

Besides political factors, legal systems too contributed its part to the formation of religious identities. Chandra Mallampalli has shown how the minority Christian identity in India was forged by the creation of a legal locus for this group. According to him, the converts to Christianity were expelled from their families and the caste system. The Hindu laws of marriage, inheritance, and adoption could not be applied to them. It is in such a situation that the Christians were brought under the British Christian legal system, a measure that would help brand Christians and Christianity as "foreign."

> By the 1870's, imperial courts had come to define the Native Christian community according to European cultural standards and in opposition to the customs of indigenous caste society....Through the eyes of the law, Christian identity came to be defined as antithetical to caste identity. "Native

---

[22] Mohammad Rakib, "One House Two Temples: The Ambivalence of Local Chinese Buddhism in Yogyakarta, Indonesia, http://jurnal.uinbanten.ac.id/index.php/kwl/article/view/2043 [accessed on October 25, 2019].

Christians", along with their European co-religionists, belonged to an abstract Christian community whose laws were modeled upon English common law. This official knowledge therefore functioned as a "severance package" from Hindu society. It isolated Christians from categories of belonging that made one Indian. Estranged from the little society (*jati*) of caste, Christians would eventually find themselves estranged from the big society (*mahajati*) of the nation.[23]

Besides the political and legal developments in shaping of identities, we need to take note also of the cultural and theological developments. The period of Western propagation of Christianity in the colonized world created among the natives a discomfiture since its doctrines and practices were overly bound up with the Western cultural world. The second part of the twentieth century coinciding with the decolonization period raised the consciousness of native Christians to make their "foreign" religion truly indigenous. It led to what anthropologists call the process of "acculturation," referred to in Christian theology as inculturation.[24] Globalization accelerated the process of inculturation and the emergence of a "new Catholicity."[25] People in the Global South tried to reappropriate Christian faith and its traditional expressions in their own cultures. Those concerned with the issue of orthodoxy and heterodoxy have been debating what is proper and what is out of tune with Christian tradition in this process of inculturation. But in many cases, the Global South went farther than inculturation, to the creation of indigenous *Christianities*. Interestingly, globalization has facilitated the flow of indigenous Christianities back to the West from where the missionaries came and established churches in the Global South. With reference to the case of Africa, Olivier Roy observes:

> On the one hand, the missionary Church became indigenized and, on the other, the "African Churches" like Aladura and The Celestial Church of Christ became globalized and exported themselves to the West...These Churches gained a foothold in Europe in the 1960s, recruiting initially

---

[23] Chandra Mallampalli, *Christians and Public Life in Colonial South India, 1863–1937* (London and New York: Routledge, 2004), 2.

[24] This is pursued very earnestly in the Roman Catholic Church since the Council Vatican II.

[25] Cf. Robert Schreiter, *The New Catholicity: Theology Between Global and the Local* (Maryknoll, New York: Orbis Books, 1997).

among African immigrant communities…and then spreading into a sphere that was no longer that of immigration, either because they were reaching the second generation or those of Caribbean origin, or because they broke through among the "whites"…Today, their strategy is to recruit in non-African areas, as do the major neo-Sufi brotherhoods and the Buddhist and neo-Hindu movements.[26]

It is striking that whereas the inculturation process tried to localize or indigenize a religion, in the reverse movement, this local and ethnic aspect is overcome precisely because it intends to reach out to a wider global audience. Thus, increasingly the churches originating from Africa and Korea are drawing followers in several countries of Europe, and missionaries from the South to the North are on the increase.

It is inconceivable that Jesus, without the use of microphones, could have spoken to a crowd of more than a few thousand in his day. For an African Christian missionary to draw into a single church more than 20,000 eastern Europeans at the turn of the twenty-first century is a phenomenon that may well be interpreted best in the light of the promise of Jesus that those who listen to him and follow obediently will do "greater works." The renewal of Christianity through African initiatives suggests that in the midst of the political turbulence and other socioeconomic problems bedeviling the Continent, the revival of a Christian presence in the northern continents may turn out to be one of the areas in which Africa might make some of its greatest contributions to the global village in the new millennium.[27]

Korea has become one of the countries sending considerable number of missionaries to the West and to other parts of the globe.[28] The presence of Korean missionaries drew worldwide attention when twenty-three of them

[26] Olivier Roy, *Holy Ignorance. When Religion and Culture Part Ways* (New York: Columbia University Press, 2010), 156–157.

[27] J. Kwabena Asamoah-Gyadu, "African Initiated Christianity in Eastern Europe: Church of the "Embassy of God in Ukraine," *International Bulletin of Missionary Research* 30, no. 2 (2006): 73–75, at 75; see also Babatunde Adedibu, "Welcoming strangers! The responses of African Pentecostal Churches in London to Europe's Migration and Refugee Crisis," *Missionalia* 44, no.3 (2016): 263–283.

[28] Cf. Sebastian Kim, "Inter-Asia Mission and Global Missionary Movements from Asia," in Felix Wilfred, ed., *The Oxford Handbook of Christianity in Asia* (New York: Oxford University Press, 2014), 145–157.

in Afghanistan were kidnapped by the Taliban.[29] As for other religious groups—Hindus and Buddhists—they deculturize themselves, namely transcend the traditional association with particular ethnic groups, geographic region, or cultures and traditions. As a result, Westerners converted to these religions—Hinduism and Buddhism—go to the East to serve the believers there. As we can see from the above examples, the disjuncture between culture and religion as well as the process of deterritorialization are turning every religion a player in the global world, criss-crossing from one part to the other. Similar developments could be observed also in Islam, especially in Sufism. When religions are deculturated, deterritorialized, and exported to new places of migration, they prefer to function not so much as religion but as movements, foundations, and as nongovernmental organizations, taking on a civil form. This could be said also of many Hindu and Buddhist movements in the United States.[30]

## Religious Identities and Market Globalization

We assist at a new phase of religion trying to become increasingly global, thanks to the market. As is well known, the driving force of today's globalization is the liberal economy and market. They have pervaded all realms of life, exerting remarkable influence on every one of them. Religions under global conditions are no exceptions. They are not impervious to the influence of the market. In fact, religions have adopted some of the characteristics of the market, such as supply and demand, and deterritorialization, namely movement across nations and continents.[31] Like culture, religion also gets disembedded from its space of origin with which it has been associated in the past. In one sense, globalization has taken to a new level the *deterritorialization* resulting from colonialism. In fact, postcolonial theories and analysis tell us that colonialism has not been one-way traffic.

People were transported from one part of the world to the other to meet the requirements of the colonial powers. From India, indentured laborers were taken to South Africa, East Africa, Caribbean, Fiji in the

---

[29] Cf. Shim Ja Hoon, "Doing God's Work for the Taliban, Korean Christian Missionaries End up Bolstering the Terrorists in Afghanistan," *Yale Global* (September 4, 2007).

[30] Cf. Roy, *Holy Ignorance*, 170–173.

[31] Roy, *Holy Ignorance*, 159–185.

Pacifics, to Surinam, and Guyana in South America, Australia, Southeast Asia, and so on. A new wave of migration started from the 1960s.

For Hindu migrants, attached to the sacred geography of holy rivers and temples, and practicing caste-related customs and traditions, to become global meant disengagement from the traditional bonds.[32] In spite of that, the migrants in the diasporic situation continued to keep alive their traditions. Their efforts were assisted through movements that originated in the homeland and which started spreading their wings across the globe, winning new followers.[33] Thus, several Hindu and Buddhist movements continue to travel to the West with which the particular diasporic religious groups associate themselves. In the case of Hinduism, the Swami Lakshmi Narayana movement has firmly rooted itself in the United Kingdom. Since the 1970s, the movement of Transcendental Meditation and the movement of International Society of Krishna Consciousness (ISKON—also known as "Hare Krishna") were spreading in the USA and many Western countries, including Germany. The Rajaneesh or Osho movement had quite a significant following in many countries of the West. It attracted, besides the diasporic Indians, also those from the countercultural movement of the West during the late 1960s and 1970s.[34] The Sathya Sai Baba religious organization has over 11,000 centers across the world, doing social intervention for welfare, health, and so on. The Hare Krishna movement, which experienced a decline, is revived today and has become a rallying point for many Indians of diaspora. There is also a Krishna temple in Hamburg. Other Hindu temples in Germany are located in some of the major cities—Berlin, Bremen, Frankfurt, Munich, and Cologne. In Frankfurt, the Hindu temple has been constructed by the Hindus of Afghanistan.

Besides these movements, there are local religious organizations which perform different functions, such as maintenance of customs and traditions of the homeland. Through their social services and philanthropic activities, they come to the succor of new immigrants, and help them also with social and economic adaptation in the new environment. The

---

[32] Cf. Steven Vertovec, "Hinduism in Diaspora: The Transformation of Tradition in Trinidad," in Gunther D Sontheimer and Herman Kulke, eds., *Hinduism Reconsidered* (Delhi: Manohar, 1991),157–186.

[33] For detailed treatment of religion and diaspora, see Chap. 7.

[34] Cf. John Zavos, Pralay Kanungo, Deepa S. Reddy, Maya Warrier, Raymond Williams, eds., *Public Hinduisms* (Delhi: Sage Publications, 2012).

immigrants find a place of acceptance, encounter, and support in these religious groups and their centers.

Some years ago, during a visit to Hong Kong, I attended a *salaat*—Muslim prayer—at a big mosque in the heart of the city. I was struck by the fact that most attendees at prayer were from South Asia—India, Pakistan, and Bangladesh—and very few Chinese Muslims were to be seen. Surprised at this, I asked discreetly the Chinese Imam of the mosque. "Where are the local Muslims?" His answer was that they are all locals. He added, in a city like Hong Kong, all are locals or no one. "Tell me," he went on, "who is local in New York?" I thought there was a point in what he said. In global conditions of today of movements of people, has it not become really challenging to define who or what is "local"? Religions seem to follow today the market-movement blurring the distinction between the local and the global.

## Sacred Spaces in the Context of Globalization

Holy cities, places of hierophanies, and pilgrimage centers are common to religious traditions. The visits to and association with these sacred locations have been an integral part of traditional religious practices. Now, what is happening to the sacred topography in the context of globalization? Are they in the process of being abandoned and likely to disappear? Facts tell us that the sacred sites, far from declining, have become vibrant centers of religious activities. The exuberently cultivated sacredness of religious sites continues to occupy a significant place in the consciousness of the devotees. Holy cities like Jerusalem, Mecca, Benares, Lourdes, and Santiago of Compostela continue to be visited by millions of people whose testimonies reveal the spiritual experience and transformation they undergo in these sites. The technologically enabled modern fast travel and communication have enabled larger-than-ever groups of pilgrims flocking to sacred places. The centers of pilgrimage are not merely remnants of a past tradition. Rather the traditional practices, rituals, and healings associated with the sacred topographies get recalibrated to the needs of modern times. Analyzing the Catholic shrine of Lourdes, Kaufmann has shown in her study how it has reconfigured popular religiosity so as to respond to the needs of a modernizing society, with growing tourism and consumerism.[35] The same thing could be said also of the pilgrimage center of

---

[35] Cf. Suzanne K. Kaufman, *Consuming Visions. Mass Culture and the Lourdes Shrine* (Ithaca: Cornell University Press, 2005); see also Ruth Harri, *Lourdes: Body and Spirit in a Secular Age* (New York: Viking, 1999).

Santiago of Compostela. Apparently, tourism and consumerism have not demeaned the Christian religiosity, but have contributed, according to Kaufmann, to making Catholicism relevant and vibrant in France. Speaking of the experience of the Swedish Lutherans making pilgrimage to Santiago de Compostela (Camino), Lena Gemzöe notes:

> The Swedish female pilgrims on the Camino create rituals of their own...and the practice of pilgrimage brings new ritual forms to the Swedish Church...The pilgrimage walk as ritual borrows elements from other spiritual techniques, such as meditation, as well as from other modes of walking, as excursion into nature or fitness walking. In this way, the new practice of pilgrimage opens up a ritual creativity, drawing on various sources with no strict boundaries between aspects conventionally thought of as secular, religious or spiritual.[36]

To be able to understand the nature of space vis-à-vis religion under conditions of globalization, we need first to view the traditional distinction between sacred and profane space critically. Mircea Eliade theorized it.[37] This distinction may not serve as an adequate theoretical framework today to be able to understand the role and meaning of space in religious practices. The traditional theorizing has taken only the physical space and has seen it in association with places of hierophanies separated from other spaces. We need to be aware that there is a specific mental construction regarding space. This explains how people who are away from the original sacred places could reproduce them in their places of immigration. The new space gets constructed through the social interactions among the community of people confessing the same faith. The community then inhabits the new sacred spaces it has created.

Present-day holy cities and shrines are politically charged. Some of them have been exploited for nationalistic purposes; in other cases, there are intense contestations and vehement political conflicts around holy places. The case of the city of Jerusalem, claimed as a holy place by Jews, Christians, and Muslims, has been all along a city of contestation. To cite

---

[36] Lena Gemzöe, "Every Minute Out There: Creating Ritual among Swedish Pilgrims to Santiago De Compostela." In *Journal of Ritual Studies* 28, no. 2 (2014): 65–75, at 65.

[37] Mircea Eliade, ed., *The Sacred and the Profane: The Nature of Religion* (New York: Harcourt, Brace, 1980); see also Dominic John Farace, *The Sacred-profane Dichotomy: A Comparative Analysis of Its Use in the Work of Émile Durkheim and Mircea Eliade, as Far as Published in English* ... (California: Rijksuniversiteit, University of California, 1982).

another example, every time the prime minister of Japan visits the Yasukuni Shinto shrine, we can expect loud protests all over China. For, this shrine during the Pacific War (1942–1945) was associated with Japanese nationalism and militarism under which the Chinese suffered. The Yasukuni Shrine continues to be the national shrine commemorating those who died serving the country, including military personnel and even war criminals; it brings back in the Chinese mind the tragedies they suffered under Japanese imperialism. As for contestation, we have the typical example of the city of Jerusalem, which is, as noted, a holy place for all the three Semitic religions, each one having its own religious memorials. In India, a mosque that stood in Ayodhya for centuries was pulled down by the right-wing radical Hindu groups, who claimed that the location of a holy temple of Ram was turned into a mosque through Islamic aggression. Interestingly, a similar kind of problem exists in Bosnia-Herzegovina, where Muslims and Christians have been in conflict also concerning holy shrines and places of worship.[38]

As we saw, globalization has facilitated the relocation or multiplication of sacred spaces. Interestingly, under globalizing conditions, religiosity is also getting less and less bound to sacred spaces or territory-bound parishes and pastorates. In many Protestant Evangelical and Pentecostal churches, practice of faith is not bound to any definite location or shrine. The ubiquitous presence of the Spirit frees faith and religiosity from boundedness to any particular space. For, worship and experience of the Spirit could take place anywhere. This explains why Pentecostalism does not sacralize any space or object. One seems not to need any such thing to experience the presence and action of the Spirit. Internet and social media have spawned the rise of virtual priests and pastors with devoted online following.

## Transnationalization of Religious Practices

When a religion was moved out of its home-ground to other parts of the world, it was characterized as missionary. A missionary religion could coexist with other religious traditions as happened with Buddhism in China, Korea, Japan, and the whole of Southeast Asia. Buddhism penetrated deeply into the spiritual world of the people. But the missionary

---

[38] The 2002 Paul Hanly Furfey Lecture, "Crosses of Blood: Sacred Space, Religion, and Violence in Bosnia-Hercegovina," in *Sociology of Religion* 64, no.3 (2003): 309–331; See also a special issue of *Concilium* 2015/1 "Religion and Identity in Post-Conflict Societies".

religion could also take a negative view of other religions and present itself as a counternarrative and praxis. The denouncing of the belief of others as idolatrous has characterized, for example, the long Christian history.

Ironically, the very religions the colonizers and Christian missionaries once denounced have been brought back to the West, thanks to globalization, for a new reappropriation. I am referring to the global trend of taking on to Eastern religious ideals, spirituality, mysticism, popular religion by a new generation of people in the West. A head-shaven monk, epitomized in Dalai Lama, becomes a new ideal for today's generations who enter into a spiritual romance with oriental religions. Far from a force opposing globalization, as is generally made out, religion is becoming today a "great globalizer.". We observe a transnationalization of certain religious practices from one geographic region to the other.

Thus, we have the transnationalization of Chinese religious practices like *qigong* and *tai chi* in the Global North. The best known and perhaps the most widely spread is the movement of Falun Gong, which has found favor with a lot of Chinese immigrants, especially those who critically view the People's Republic of China and its Communist Party. This Falun Gong movement, which incorporates several elements from Daoism, Buddhism, and Chinese popular religion, has also found followers among many in Europe and America. [39]

There is a transnationalization of religion-inspired movements for liberation, philanthropy, and service to the poor. Let me refer here to the Compassion and Relief Movement called *Tzu-Chi or Ciji* that was started in Taiwan by Cheng Yen, a Buddhist nun. It has spread to different countries. Another movement that has spread around the world and is well known is the movement of socially engaged Buddhists. We have still other movements that help self-cultivation and they too have a large following.

---

[39] Benjamin Penny, *The Religion of Falun Gong* (Chicago: University of Chicago Press, 2012); Scott Lowe, "Chinese and International Contexts for the Rise of Falun Gong," *Nova Religio: The Journal of Alternative and Emergent Religions* 6, no. 2 (2003): 263–76; David Ownby, "The 'Falun Gong' In The New World," *European Journal of East Asian Studies* 2, no. 2 (2003): 303–20.

## GLOBAL RELIGIONS AND DIETARY IDENTITIES

Food not only responds to nutritional and biological needs. It has a great cultural, symbolic, religious, and social value too. No wonder that the anthropologists have delved deep into food and cooking. Mary Douglas, who studied the issue in depth, observes that food carries a lot of precoded messages.[40] In her view, food is a coded means through which social relations are given expression. Cooking and consuming food are also endowed with religious meaning and are often ritualized. Which food a person consumes and with whom he or she has commensality could be markers of religious identity. As a symbolic and religious reality, food and dietary practices signal who is in and who is out. Jainism and Buddhism advocate vegetarian food and shun meat. One stream of Hinduism is very particular about vegetarianism. There is a general impression that because some schools of Hinduism advocate vegetarianism, all of India is vegetarian. This contradicts the actual fact. The truth is that only a relatively small percentage of Indians are vegetarians.[41]

Cooking is not a matter of gastronomy; among many religious groups, it is a sacred act, and it is done with reverence as if it were a matter of worship. This is so with the Middle Eastern Jewish women preparing *kosher* food; with the Jains, Buddhists, and among some streams of Hindus, preparing different varieties of the vegetarian diet. Food is also a site of purity and impurity, marking off the higher and lower castes in India. Globalization has not radically changed food and dietary practices connected with religion. No matter where they are, devout Muslims are particular about eating *halal* (permissible) food and to avoid *haram* food (forbidden) like pork. Buddhist and Jain migrants also continue to practice vegetarianism, and traditional upper-caste Hindus continue with the vegetarian tradition, whether they are settled in the USA, the UK, Germany, or France.

In China, the Uyghur Muslims of Xinjiang province in the West care to distinguish themselves from the majority Chinese Han ethnic community. The Uyghurs are particular about eating uncontaminated *quingzhen* food, and the restaurants in this part of China make it known by displaying boards and captions that they serve quingzhen food. Though globalization may have brought about a culture of fast food and availability of a

---

[40] Cf. Mary Douglas, ed., *Food in the Social Order* (London and New York: Routledge, 1973).

[41] It may be surprising to learn that about 71% of the Indian population consume meat and are not vegetarians.

variety of cuisines across national borders, we note that those habits of food connected with religion and sacrality have hardly undergone any significant change. It is difficult to forecast if ever devout Muslims will eat other foods than halal, and committed Buddhists will eat food made up of varieties of meat. These are traditions which are likely to endure in spite of globalization. It is also confirmed by the fact that many migrants scrupulously carry on the religiously sanctioned food practices even when they settle down as migrants in other parts of the world.

## RELIGIONS, MATERIAL BLESSINGS, AND PROSPERITY

Transnational corporations and markets have created a world in which everything becomes part of a large network connectivity and communication. Thanks to globalization, religions have become, as we described above, more transnational than ever. At the same time, interestingly, the global economy driven by liberal capitalism has its impact also on the orientation adopted by various religious groups, their attitudes, and their values today. Time was when religious motives were invoked to instill the spirit of austerity and sacrifice. Today, in almost every religious group money and earthly prosperity are looked through a different lens. According to the new mantra of prosperity religion, it is not a *sin* to be rich and wealthy.

On the contrary, this new mantra suggests that God *wants* us to be successful and wealthy. Money is no more the mammon religions painted in the past. In Hindu tradition, wealth and prosperity have been a part of religious existence. Goddess Lakshmi is venerated all over India as goddess of riches and abundance. For Semitic religious traditions, reconciliation with money has been rather difficult. It is an irony that some Christian groups today justify a life of prosperity as the blessing of God, known as the "prosperity Gospel."[42] According to it, instead of speaking of poverty, we should be actually speaking about how to become rich and create wealth. The roots of the prosperity gospel can be traced to the history of Protestantism. In the Calvinist tradition, wealth was viewed as sign of God's blessing and of salvation.

---

[42] Cf. Kate Bowler, *Blessed: A History of the American Prosperity Gospel* (New York: Oxford University Press, 2013). Wilfred Asampambila Agana, *Succeed Here and in Eternity* (Bern: Peter Lang, 2016); D.L. Machado, "Capitalism, Immigration, and the Prosperity Gospel," *Anglican Theological Review* 92, no. 4 (2010): 723–30.

Today, under the aegis of liberal capitalism and individualism, this thought of prosperity and success in life has acquired a new lease of life. The prosperity gospel latches on to the existing Pentecostal movements with a new accent. If formerly healing, speaking in tongues, and prophesying were the focus of attention, there has taken place now a shift toward wealth, success, and riches. No wonder, more than any other Christian group, it is the prosperity Gospel and its message that has attracted the largest number of people in the Global South—in Africa, Latin America, and Asia. In the Philippines, the only Christian country in Asia, the dream of riches, wealth, and economic success has become the motor that drives people to charismatic and Pentecostal kind of worship and preaching. For example, El Shadai, a Catholic Charismatic movement in the Philippines which came into existence in 1981, counted already by the early 1990s about ten million followers, and it continues to grow and is certainly the largest Catholic charismatic movement in the world. Let me quote from one of its hymns which expresses the spirit of this movement. "I am rich! I am strong! Something good is going to happen to me!"[43] The prosperity Gospel not only thrives in Asia, Africa, and Latin America, but also is popular among the immigrants from these continents, especially in the US. For the 315 million sub-Saharan Africans living on less than €1a day, the cross and suffering may not be the most hopeful message; instead, as the population moves into cities and dreams of new economic opportunities, religions preaching money and wealth come across to them as a soothing message of hope that would fulfill their dreams of wellbeing and abundance.

In the present context of globalization and liberal economy, Confucianism is invoked as a valuable trigger for the flourishing of the economy in Asia, East Asia, and Southeast Asia—China, Taiwan, Korea, and Singapore. Confucianism is being made use of as an ally of capitalism to promote values of entrepreneurship and success. Some scholars like Robert Bellah and Clifford Geertz see in the correlation of religion and entrepreneurship in this eastern part of Asia, a reflection of Max Weber's thesis on the nexus between capitalism and Protestant ethics. Both Confucianism and Daoism are interpreted as promoting inner-worldly wellbeing. Southeast Asia and East Asia, which have a booming economy,

---

[43] Katharine L. Wiegele, *Investing in Miracles: El Shaddai and the Transformation of Popular Catholicism in the Philippines* (Honolulu: University of Hawai'I, 2005), 173.

are also thriving on new varieties of religious practices with ancient roots.[44] Daoist temples and Buddhist pagodas see streams of visitors who have recourse to gods and goddesses for success in business and in acquiring more wealth.

For various reasons (into which we do not enter here) Islam has not warmed up to West-induced capitalism. However, in recent times, the market has affected individual Muslims who want to prosper economically and accumulate wealth. One speaks of "*Islam de marché*"—market Islam.[45] It helps the individuals with the necessary skills in their competition in marketplace, and it advances an individual's success. Market Islam thrives, especially in Southeast Asia, adopting many elements from the American Evangelical variant of prosperity Gospel.[46]

The transition in many countries of the Global South to the market economy has led to religious revival. People struggle and compete, driven by the market economy. In addition, they seek divine blessings and interventions to become rich and prosperous. Thus, the transition from a situation of suppression of religions China experienced in the period of Cultural revolution is today followed, under the market economy, by an era of capitalism in which religions thrive in different forms.

> Praying to the supernatural is practiced not only by people pursuing wealth; poor people who have lost job security and life certainty in the market economy also turn to the spiritual for solace and fortune. Consequently, fortune-

---

[44] Seok-Choon Lew, Woo-Young Choi, and Hye Suk Wang, "Confucian Ethics and the Spirit of Capitalism in Korea: The Significance of Filial Piety," *Journal of East Asian Studies* 11, no. 2 (2011): 171–96; Timothy Brook, "Weber, Mencius, and the History of Chinese Capitalism," *Asian Perspective* 19, no. 1 (1995): 79–97; John H. Sagers, *Origins of Japanese Wealth and Power: Reconciling Confucianism and Capitalism, 1830–1885*, 1st ed. (Basingstoke: Palgrave Macmillan, 2006).

[45] Cf. Patrick Haenni, *L'Islam de marché: L'autre révolution conservatrice* (Paris: Seuil, 2005); Sarah Koenig, "Almighty God and the Almighty Dollar: The Study of Religion and Market Economies in the United States," *Religion Compass* 10 (2016): 83–97; Daromir Rudnyckyj and *Filippo Osella*, eds., *Religion and the Morality of the Market* (New York: Cambridge University Press, 2017); Gabe Johnson Ignatow and Ali Lindsey Madanipour, "Global System Theory and 'Market-friendly' Religion," *Globalizations* 11 (2014): 827–41; D. R. Loy, "The Religion of the Market," *Journal of the American Academy of Religion*, 65, no. 2 (1997): 275–90; A.J. Pace E. Blasi, "A Market Theory of Religion," *Social Compass: Revue des études Socio-, Religieuses Review of Socio-religious Studies* 56, no. 2 (2009): 263–72.

[46] Cf. Robert W. Hefner, "Religious Resurgence in Contemporary Asia: Southeast Asian Perspectives on Capitalism, the State, and the New Piety," *The Journal of Asian Studies* 69, no. 4 (November 2010):1031–1047.

telling, physiognomy (divination through analysis of facial features), glyphomancy ...fengshui and the like have become widespread. Many cities have a de facto "fortune-telling street" with dozens of fortune-tellers. There are millions of practicing shaman-doctors or spirit mediums. During the reform era, the orthodox ideology of Marxism still dictates opposition to such beliefs and practices. However, the market economy has created a thirst for spiritual imagination beyond ideological control.[47]

In India too, the market economy pursued since early 1990s has driven a higher number of people than ever to seek divine assistance for succeeding in the competitive world, and they flock sometimes in millions to shrines and *tirtha*s (the junction of rivers considered holy and auspicious) to get rich faster and enjoy material blessings. They pray especially to Lakshmi, the goddess of wealth, for a life of plenty. All this may look strange for those secularists who are not familiar with the culture and day-to-day life in the Global South. They would be surprised to find how market has become a new trigger for religiosity.

## Conclusion

The transformation religious identities are going through today is the result of the sociopolitical and economic changes taking place under globalization. Let me conclude with two observations that point to some new directions for the future.

Increasing *lay character* in religious practices is one of the things we observe in the reconfiguration of religious identities. There is a tendency to move away from the conventional religious establishment under strong clerical, monastic, and institutional hold. Many contemporary developments indicate that religion and religious traditions can be supple and malleable to be molded, remolded, and configured according to the present needs. We may call this a *religious bricolage*. It is not the same as syncretism. In today's religious bricolage, elements are culled out from many sources to serve particular purposes. It is in this context that we need to understand also the proliferation of several religious movements oriented to meditation, peace, and tranquility, which draw upon traditional religious resources and format them to the need of silence, peace, stillness of

---

[47] David Palmer, Glenn Shive and Philip Wickeri, eds., *Chinese Religious Life* (New York: Oxford University Press, 2011), 214.

mind and body in a hectic world. The meditation practices centered on monks in Buddhism, for example, are today in a way laicized and globalized thanks to a more flexible orientation of a fast-growing temple like Dhammakaya situated north of Bangkok. Far from being a remote ideal for a group of spiritual elites, Buddhism is made accessible to every man and woman in day-to-day life. Practices which were restricted to an elite or clerical group in the past are now increasingly open to everyone. This can be observed in other religions too.

A second observation concerns *the increasing participation of women* in the religious life of contemporary times. It is bound to transform traditional religious identities. It is precisely the lay and fluid character of contemporary religious expressions that creates space for women's agency in the religious sphere. We note this in as widely different movements as Pentecostalism and Theravada Buddhist movements and associations in Asia. There is an attempt to address the concerns of women, and their experiences become increasingly a part of new spirituality in the global world. Evolving new religious identities means breaking increasingly the barricades put up by essentialized religious identities to block off the liberative parade of women. Is not this a hopeful prospect for the future?

# CHAPTER 4

# Conflicting Religious Identities: The Political Turn

Most Western social scientists, political scientists, anthropologists, and psychologists—regardless of their ideologies—predicted the progressive marginalization of religion and other primordial identities, and their eventual disappearance. This was the position of Comte, Durkheim, Freud, Marx, Nietzsche, Töennies, Voltaire, and Weber. According to them, religious societies will be replaced by rational societies, thanks to industrialization, the development in science, technology, economic growth, education, and many other such modern factors. How this position—dominant for a long time—has turned out to be wrong today is there for everybody to see. World events, especially in the Global South, tell a different story from the mainline theorizing.

My intention is not to defend religion as once Schleiermacher did in his *"Defence of Religion against Its Cultured Despisers"*.[1] The purpose of this chapter is rather to look at religion dispassionately in its ambiguous roles in our times and how it is intertwined with primordial identities of race, caste, ethnicity, language, and nation resulting in many conflictual situations. We cannot but be struck by the disruption religion has introduced into the social, political, and cultural life of societies in most parts of the world. Conflicts based on ethnic and religious identities have continued to cause

---

[1] Ruth Jackson Ravenscroft, *Friedrich Schleiermacher's On Religion: Speeches to its Cultured Despisers*, 1st ed. (London; New York: The Macat Library, 2018).

© The Author(s), under exclusive license to Springer Nature Switzerland AG 2021
F. Wilfred, *Religious Identities and the Global South*,
New Approaches to Religion and Power,
https://doi.org/10.1007/978-3-030-60738-8_4

the loss of a large number of precious human lives, many of them ending in mass graves. These conflicts have resulted in many injured and maimed people, forced expulsions, genocide, ethnic cleansing, refugees, and missing and displaced people; mass rape and sexual assault; and destruction of places of worship and cultural symbols. In defense of God and religion, horrifying tragedies and war crimes against humanity were perpetrated in Bosnia and Herzegovina, Kosovo, India, Pakistan, Sri Lanka, Myanmar, Sudan, Nigeria, Armenia, Azerbaijan and so on. When I think of these tragic conflicts, what come to my mind are the three cages hanging on the spire of St. Lambert's Church in the city of Münster, Germany. During the religious war at the time of Reformation, three Anabaptists were killed and hanged on the top of the church as a warning to others. While teaching a semester in Münster, I used to pass by that church every day, and those cages made a lasting impression on me. They are reminders of the brutality of violence stemming from religious animosity.

Globalization has not put an end to religious conflicts. Instead, as many empirical studies show, in the last few decades religious violence and conflicts have been on the increase. We have simmering or open religious conflicts in most countries in West Asia (the Middle East), in Sudan and Nigeria in Africa; in the Balkan countries of Europe, and increasingly also in other parts of Europe with large immigrant populations; in Chechnya and countries of central Asia once part of the Soviet Union; in India, Pakistan, and the Philippines in Asia. In our globalized world, religion has become a crucial player in international relationships. Hence, local religious conflicts have transnational repercussions today. A Christian extremist pastor burns the Qur'an in Texas, and bombs explode in churches in Pakistan and Indonesia. ISI undergoes humiliating loss of territory in Syria, and churches in Sri Lanka are bombed on Easter Sunday.[2] Denial of religious freedom or persecution of any religious community like the Rohingyas by the Buddhist majority in Myanmar and arbitrary detention in camps, forced labor, and torture of Uighur Muslims in Xinjiang province by the Chinese Communist Party invite threat of economic sanctions. We see how even small religious conflicts bring about repercussions that are global in proportion. Many civil wars originate as religious disputes and have ripple effects. It is not always the case of one religion against the other. Inner conflicts also cause deep divisions and damage in the same religious community. For example, terrorist organization Boko Haram is

---

[2] ISI has claimed responsibility for the bomb attacks in Sri Lankan churches.

the result of inner Islamic conflict in Nigeria. These conflicts and wars cause the flow of refugees and migrants. Social harmony, economy, and education get affected deeply.

Besides the interreligious and intra-religious identity conflicts, we are experiencing today brutal religiously-motivated expressions of violence by terrorist outfits. The potential of violence they represent could be gauged, for example, by the fact that the ISI could in 2014 capture for its caliphate a territory as big as Britain, and recruit 30,000–35,000 fighters from more than eighty countries. The extent of the influence it could wield and the power it could acquire within a relatively short period of time and the chilling brutality of its methods like abducting, beheading, mass-executions, rape, and ethnic cleansing are a powerful reminder of the darkest sides of religions in conflict.[3]

At this juncture, we also need to take note of the fact that in the digital age of today there is also a religious cyberwar taking place. Large volumes of materials online spew venom and hatred to fuel emotions and incite violence.[4] It is also the power of internet and the digital world that catapults extremist leaders and movements on the world stage. There is an active transnational network of religious extremists—Christian, Hindu, Muslim, Sikh, and Jewish—in social media and in the digital world. Dozens of religiously radicalized young people from Kerala, India, moved to Syria to join the ISI. They were radicalized apparently not by preachers in mosques, madrassas, and public rallies but in the digital world of chat rooms, google groups, hangouts, and Facebook pages.[5] These youth were allegedly not inspired by extremist preachers they saw and listened to, but by the webpages they surfed, and the video clips they watched online. The digital world has made cross-border, transnational radicalization far easier and quicker than before. There are also allegations that at least some of the perpetrators of the 2019 Easter bombings in Sri Lanka had digital links with youth in south India.

---

[3] Loretta Napoleoni, *Merchants of Men: How Kidnapping, Ransom and Trafficking Funds Terrorism and ISIS,* Main ed. (London: Atlantic Books, 2017); Ahmed Al-Rawi, "Video Games, Terrorism, and ISIS's Jihad 3.0," *Terrorism and Political Violence* 30 (2018): 740–60.

[4] Cf. B. Bräuchler, "Religious Conflicts in Cyberage," *Citizenship Studies* 11, no. 4 (2007): 329–47.

[5] https://www.orfonline.org/research/the-islamic-state-in-indias-kerala-a-primer-56634/; https://www.theguardian.com/world/2016/nov/29/isis-recruiters-fertile-ground-kerala-indias-tourist-gem [accessed on February 17, 2020].

## OVERLAP OF RELIGION AND ETHNIC IDENTITIES

Religion has become for many people a symbol of national, ethnic, regional, and linguistic identity. For the modern Western society, swearing by the ideals of the Enlightenment, pursuing individualization, and cultivating an autonomous self, any discourse on collective religious identity may sound as a matter of the past. But the fact is that there are innumerable societies in our world, where religion overlaps with ethnic identity. Both are so closely intertwined as to become indistinguishable. The Serb and the Orthodox identity overlap, just as do the Croatian and the Catholic, and the Bosniak and the Islamic.[6] In Sri Lanka, the ethnic identity of the Sinhalese is Buddhist, whereas Tamil identity is Hindu. In Malaysia, to be a Malay is to be a Muslim, to be Indian is to be a Hindu, and to be a Chinese is to be a Buddhist or Confucian.[7] The state of Israel and its Muslim neighbors present cases of religion as the organizing principle of nationhood. Even today, Orthodox Christianity is a marker of Russian national identity,[8] Anglican Church of British identity,[9] and Catholicism of Bavarian and Irish identity. In central Asia, Tajiks, Uzbeks, and Kirghiz are Muslims; if they are Protestants, then it means they are Americans, Germans, or Koreans.[10]

## RELIGION AS THE BASIS OF NATIONAL IDENTITY

For many in the Global North, it may take considerable mental effort to comprehend religion as the basis of national identity, though this has been the case with their own past history, with its consequences enduring even

---

[6] Sheila Osmanovic, *Muslim Identity, 'Neo-Islam' and the 1992–95 War in Bosnia and Herzegovina* (2015). (doctoral thesis, University of East London).

[7] M. Barr and A. R. Govindasamy, "The Islamisation of Malaysia: Religious Nationalism in the Service of Ethnonationalism," *Australian Journal of International Affairs: The Journal of the Australian Institute of International Affairs* 64, no. 3 (2010), 293–311.

[8] We note how President Putin cares to attend important events of Orthodox Christianity. Cf. Benjamin Forest, Juliet Johnson, and M. T. Stepaniants, eds., *Religion and Identity in Modern Russia: The Revival of Orthodoxy and Islam* (London and New York: Routledge, 2005).

[9] Let us not forget that the British Queen is the head of the Anglican Church.

[10] S. Akiner, J. Jacobson, I. Atsuko and A. D. Smith, "Melting Pot, Salad Bowl - Cauldron? Manipulation and Mobilization of Ethnic and Religious Identities in Central Asia," *Ethnic and Racial Studies* 20, no. 2 (1997): 362–398; Kenneth R. Ross, Daniel Jeyaraj, and Todd M. Johnson, eds., *Christianity in South and Central Asia* (Edinburgh: Edinburgh Companions to Global Christianity, 2019).

today. For, in modernity, a state is based on the will of the people and on social contract going beyond primordial loyalties like religion, tribe, caste, and clan. We are in a situation in the world in which there is a mutual exclusion of secular nation-state and religious nation-state. The former *excludes* religion as the basis of national identity, whereas the latter *rejects the secular* as the rallying point for a nation. But who can really ignore the politics religions play in in our globalizing world?

Many Westerners who consider secular nationalism as the standard-setting ideal, and counterpose it to religious nationalism because of its proclivity for violence, tend to forget that secular nationalism where religion was excluded created some of the most authoritarian and violent regimes in history. Suffice it here to recall the East European socialist states of modern times. On the other hand, religious nationalism may not be branded as fundamentalism or fanaticism, since it is an attempt to highlight facets of reality ignored and rejected by secular nationalists. Juergensmyer explains why religious nationalism proves to be attractive, in the backdrop of secular nationalism that has caused disappointment in several parts of the Global South. He notes:

> The material expectations offered by secular ideologies often cause frustration because they cannot be fulfilled in one's lifetime; the expectations of religious ideologies do not disappoint in the same way because they are not expected to be fulfilled in this world.[11]

Although very often people in everyday life interact across religious borders, there are times when ethnic identities come into conflict for political, economic, and cultural reasons. At this juncture, the religious factor adds fuel to fire, providing symbols and narratives, and thus exacerbates the relationship between ethnic communities in the same nation.

In the analysis of ethno-religious conflicts, it is imperative to take note of the role played by the ambitious elites. They define the interest of the community in such a way as to coincide with their own goal of holding on to power and availing for themselves economic resources and advantages. The instrumentalization of religious extremism helps them trump up mass support. As V.P. Gagnon in his analysis of Balkan conflict observes:

---

[11] Mark Juergenmeyer, *The New Cold War? Religious Nationalism Confronts the Secular State* (Berkeley, Los Angeles, London: University of California Press, 1993), 194.

I argue that elites provoke violent conflict along ethnic cleavages in order to create a domestic political context where ethnicity is the only politically relevant identity. It thereby constructs the individual interest of the broader population in terms of the threat to the community defined in ethnic terms. Such a strategy is a response by ruling elites to shifts in the structure of domestic political and economic power: by constructing individual interest in terms of the threat to the group, endangered elites can fend off domestic challengers who seek to mobilize the population against the status quo, and can better position themselves to deal with future challenges.[12]

We also need to take into account the role played by the state. Some states are overtly or covertly religious. So, we have states that are Christian, Islamic, Buddhist, and Hindu. Though a modern state is supposed to keep equal distance from all religious groups and favor none, for reasons of political expediency it ends up, in practice, espousing the majority religion. With time, the state is overpowered by the radical religious forces. This is what happened to Pakistan, for example, and today what is happening in Indonesia. In the case of Pakistan, it started as a secular state.[13] However, political inventiveness led its rulers to side with Islamic forces which, over time, began to dictate to the state.[14] In such situations, minority religious groups have been discriminated against, with their freedom and religious expressions heavily curtailed. They also become victims of violence. In Indonesia where Islam had a different face and was known as "smiling Islam," religious radicalization has threatened the religious harmony Indonesia manifested in the past.[15] We need to attend here also to the international situation and the repercussion of local conflicts among religious groups at the global level.[16]

[12] Jr. V. P. Gagnon, "Ethnic Nationalism and International Conflict: The Case of Serbia," *International Security* 19, no. 3 (Winter, 1994–1995): 130–166, at 132.

[13] A similar development seems to have happened in Turkey. See J. Haynes, "Politics, Identity and Religious Nationalism in Turkey: From Ataturk to the AKP," *Australian Journal of International Affairs: The Journal of the Australian Institute of International Affairs* 64, no. 3 (2010): 312–27.

[14] Cf. M. Waseem, "Ethnic and Religious Nationalism in Pakistan," *Journal of South Asian and Middle Eastern Studies* 23, no. 2 (2000): 37–62.

[15] The dynamics of this transition was seen in recent times in the controversies surrounding the election of a Christian governor. See Andang L. Binawan, "The Case of a Christian Governor in Jakarta as a Sign of Times for Catholics (and Christians) in Indonesia," in *International Journal of Asian Christianity* 1, no. 1 (2018): 135–142.

[16] Cf. Elizabeth Shakman Hurd, *The Politics of Secularism in International Relations* (New Jersey: Princeton University Press, 2008).

## THE PHENOMENON OF RELIGIOUS NATIONALISM

To be able to understand the continuing religious conflicts in our world today and to respond to it, we need to go a little deeper into what is known as religious nationalism.[17] According to some political analysts, the emergence of religious nationalism is not an expression of regressive thinking, but rather result of the dereliction of duty by increasing number of the so-called modern secular states. People are disappointed with the non-performance of the secular state and its heedlessness to deliver the promises to create a society of justice, equity, and wellbeing. This is one reason for ethno-religious conflict in Nigeria, for example.[18]

Religious nationalism relates to the way a nation is defined and understood.[19] We do not want, at this juncture, to go into the numerous theories of nationalism. At least for one school of thought, nationalism has to do with a definite territory with its people sharing the same history, culture, and tradition, and thus forming a coherent group under the same political authority. If this yardstick is applied, there will be hardly any homogenous nation. In most cases, within the same nation, there is a diversity of people with distinct cultures, traditions, languages, and religions. Many nations are made up of such subnationalities. Religious nationalism makes

---

[17] No part of the world seems to be free from religious nationalism. It is to be found in the USA and Europe as well. Philip W. Barker, *Religious Nationalism in Modern Europe: If God Be for Us* (London and New York: Routledge, 2009); Sam Haselby, *The Origins of American Religious Nationalism* (New York: Oxford University Press, 2015); Peter Van Der Veer, *Religious Nationalism: Hindus and Muslims in India* (Berkeley, London: University of California Press, 1994); Mark Juergenmeyer, *The New Cold War? Religious Nationalism Confronts the Secular State* (Berkeley: Oxford University Press, 1993); David M. Bourchier, "Two Decades of Ideological Contestation in Indonesia: From Democratic Cosmopolitanism to Religious Nationalism," *Journal of Contemporary Asia*, 49 (2019): 713–33; M. Barr and A.R. Govindasamy, "The Islamisation of Malaysia: Religious Nationalism in the Service of Ethnonationalism," *Australian Journal of International Affairs: The Journal of the Australian Institute of International Affairs* 64, no. 3 (2010): 293–311.

[18] Ukoha Ukiwo, "Politics, Ethno-Religious Conflicts and Democratic Consolidation in Nigeria," *The Journal of Modern African Studies* 41, no.1 (Mar., 2003), 115–138.

[19] For an overview, see A. D. Smith, *Theories of Nationalism* (New York: Harper & Row,1971); see also Gerard Delanty and Krishan Kumar, eds., *The SAGE Handbook of Nations and Nationalism* (London, Thousand Oaks: SAGE, 2006); Anthony D. Smith, *The Nation in History: Historiographical Debates about Ethnicity and Nationalism* (Hanover, NH: University Press of New England, 2000); Romila Thapar, Abdul Gafoor Abdul Majeed Noorani, Sadanand Menon, *On Nationalism* (Delhi: Aleph, 2016); Benedict R. Anderson, *Imagined Communities: Reflections on the Origin and Spread of Nationalism*, rev. ed. (London; New York: Verso, 2016).

religion—often the religion of the majority—the rallying point for the unity of a nation. If the nation is made up of *plural* ethnic, cultural, linguistic, and religious identities, singling out one religion as the unifying whole is itself prone to create conflicts. In the context of multiple religious and ethnic identities, there arises a critical question: In whose image is the modern nation-state to be fashioned? That is ultimately an issue of power. Even at the heart of Europe, there is a right-wing undercurrent which maintains that to be European is to be Christian, and *"European Muslim"* is a strange and intolerable proposal. It would appear that at least for some time this kind of thinking was reigning during the Bosnian War.

We have a different type of religious nationalism in Japan—the most modernized country in Asia. It is not the case of religious conflicts or the religion of the majority locked in conflict with minority religious groups, as is the case in many other parts of the world. Instead, religion—in this case, Japanese Shintoism—is the legitimizing force for the nation. Here, nation and state are not simply replication of the Western models as is generally assumed. Japan has not followed the kind of separation of state and religion as in the Western secular states. Rather Japanese state formation today is very much tied to Shintoism, the divinization of the emperor, the Yasukuni Shinto shrine, and the religious rituals and symbolisms connected with it.[20] The emperor is the embodiment of the nation (*kakutai*) and genealogically is of divine descent, from the god Amaterasu. I must add, the Shinto religion bent itself to suit the political ends of the Japanese state and nation and provided the rituals for them. As such, there was hardly any chance of religion and state coming into conflict. On the contrary, the Shinto religion has served the state's objective of social control. As the Japanese sociologist Fumiko Fukase-Indergaard puts it:

> The significance of religious nationalism in Modern Japan directly correlates to the issue of how a weak state became strong. ... Influential views of dif-

---

[20] D. C. Holtom, *Modern Japan and Shinto Nationalism*, 2nd rev. ed. (S.l.: Paragon, 1963); Walter Skya, *Japan's Holy War: The Ideology of Radical Shintō Ultranationalism* (Asia-Pacific. Durham, N. C.; London: Duke University Press, 2009); Ako Inuzuka and Thomas Fuchs, "Memories of Japanese Militarism: The Yasukuni Shrine as a Commemorative Site," *The Journal of International Communication*, 20 (2014): 21–41; Mark Selden, "Japan, the United States and Yasukuni Nationalism," *Economic and Political Weekly* 43, no. 45 (2008): 71–77; James Dorsey, "Culture, Nationalism, and Sakaguchi Ango," *Journal of Japanese Studies* 27, no. 2 (2001): 347–79; Masaru Tamamoto, "A Land without Patriots: The Yasukuni Controversy and Japanese Nationalism," *World Policy Journal* 18, no. 3 (2001): 33–40.

fusion as "imitation" stress the power of Western cultural forms, implying that Meiji state formation was powered by Western culture. Such an explanation minimizes the role of the Japanese state and culture. It also relegates religion to the sidelines. …[T]he unique nature of Japanese religion and the creative maneuvering of the Meiji state effected a different path to modernity—one where nationalism and religion became entwined with modified Western institutions.[21]

Let me illustrate the point of religious nationalism with another recent example. The Orthodox Church of Russia with its patriarchate in Moscow has been the point of reference for all the Orthodox Churches in the former Soviet Union.[22] However, the fragmentation of the Soviet Union and the ensuing conflict with Ukraine had its impact on the relationship among the churches too. The Ukrainian Orthodox Church resented its continued dependence on the Patriarchate of Moscow. It led the Ukraine Orthodox Church to declare itself an autocephalous church which has caused severe conflicts between these two churches. As if to complicate the matter and strain relationships further, the Patriarch of Istanbul Bartholomew granted recognition to Ukrainian Orthodox Church as an autocephalous community. This move threatens to cause a split in the Eastern Orthodox Church. The political tension between Moscow and Kiev is played out in the religious field by Kiev's assertion of independence from the patriarchate of Moscow.[23]

## STRATEGIES IN RELIGIOUS CONFLICTS

Christopher Jaffrelot, who studied in depth the Hindu religious nationalism, the ideology which was forged during 1870–1920, analyzes the strategies it has been using to cause religious conflicts.[24] What he says in the case of India applies in general to many other societies under religious

---

[21] Fumiko Fukase-Indergaard and Michael Indergaard, "Religious Nationalism and the Making of the Modern Japanese State," *Theory and Society* 37, no. 4 (2008): 343–374.

[22] Anastasia Mitrofanova, "Russian Ethnic Nationalism and Religion Today," in *The New Russian Nationalism: Imperialism, Ethnicity and Authoritarianism 2000–2015*, edited by Pål Kolstø, 104–31 (Edinburgh University Press, 2016).

[23] Cf. *The New York Times* (January 6, 2019). See also https://www.europarl.europa.eu/RegData/etudes/BRIE/2019/635525/EPRS_BRI(2019)635525_EN.pdf [accessed on October 31, 2019].

[24] Cf. Christophe Jaffrelot, *The Hindu Nationalist Movement in India* (New York: Columbia University Press, 1996).

conflicts. The strategies are *stigmatization, emulation,* and *mobilization.* To create conflicts, Hindu religious nationalists brand and caricature the other—Muslims mainly and Christians too. Stereotype profiling of Muslims is made, and it is circulated, and the masses of people consume these stereotypes. It is very similar to National Socialist ideology which did the profiling of the Jews in the twentieth century.

One of these stereotypes is a demographic one: The Muslims are said to beget a lot of children, which, if left unchecked, could be a threat eventually to the Hindu population, currently the majority religious community in the country. There is a deep-rooted fear that with the growth of Muslim population, India will not be any more Hindu but a Muslim nation. Why should the Hindus—who will remain a majority for decades to come—still fear the Muslims, who will be a minority? The point is that the Hindu religious nationalists do not fear the rise of Muslims in India alone. They see the larger South Asian threat posed by collective South Asian Muslim population in Pakistan, Afghanistan, Bangladesh, and Sri Lanka. The Hindutva brigade fears a consolidated Muslim "majority" in the region, and therefore preemptively wish to create and consolidate a stronger Hindu Rashtra (Hindu nation), on the one hand, and alienate and scatter the Muslims, on the other. Thus, the Muslims will continue to remain a minority in the South Asian region. There are many other stigmatizations. For example, the Hindu religious nationalists believe that the Muslims in India (second largest Muslim population in the world) in the event of war will support Pakistan rather than being loyal to the Indian nation. Muslims will rape Hindu women is yet another stereotype. These images of the inimical *other* and heightened sense of threat are exploited to whip up the emotions of the Hindu masses and turn them against the Muslim community.

Christianity is stigmatized as a "foreign" religion, and it has the malicious intent, according to Hindu religious nationalists, of converting all Hindus to Christianity with the help of money and political support from the "Christian countries" of the West. The charitable and social work Christians do out of compassion for the poor is construed as a ruse to do the same old work of converting the poor to Christianity. In short, the history of Christian mission and the activities of the missionaries are viewed through the lens of proselytization. More about this in chapter 10 on the politics of conversion.

The second strategy is called *emulation.* Though in religious conflicts, the religion of the other is turned into an object of detraction and disparagement, paradoxically there is also the emulation of the hostile other religion. For example, millions of gods and goddesses populate the Hindu religious world. But in opposition to Islam, the right-wing Hindu groups feel that it is a weakness. So, they try to interpret Hinduism as if it were a monotheistic religion. Following the model of one prophet in Islam, they project Rama, the epic hero as the functional equivalent of the prophet in Islam. As for sacred writings, Hinduism has no one single book like the Bible or Qur'an. However, the right-wing Hindutva movement elevates Bhagavad Gita as the sacred book of Hindus. Transforming Hinduism this way by emulating the rival religion, the Hindutva nationalist religious movement considers itself in the best position to fight against Islam and Christianity.

A third strategy is that of *mobilization*. Here religion gets highly politicized. It whips up the sentiments of the Hindus and incites them to violence against the Muslims, their places of worship, property, and business interests. At this point, I must mention the vicious role played by *rumors* in mobilizing the people for violence. Sometimes rumors are deliberately floated to make people believe falsehood about Muslims and their conspiracy which have no basis in reality at all. It conjures up the fake-news circulated throug social media today. These rumors play a strategic role of consolidating the Hindu religious majority and stir them up for violence. All these three strategies help to gain political mileage and bring the Hindu religious right-wing party to power.

In the post 9/11 world of today, Muslims are stereotyped as a source of terror and violence. However, one should not forget that Islamophobia commits the same kind of violence that Muslims are accused of. In India, though a minority, the number of Muslims who died in religious conflicts are larger than the Hindus. In Myanmar, the Rohingya Muslims have been rendered stateless and have become the object of persecution by the Buddhist majority. In the southern part of the Philippines, the violent struggle of Muslims (the Moros) has a lot to do with the policies of discrimination by the majority of Christians and with the fear of their (Muslim) traditional territories being encroached by the Christians.

## SOME THEORETICAL PERSPECTIVES FOR INTERPRETING RELIGIOUS CONFLICTS

There are numerous theoretical explanations for religious conflicts worked out by sociologists and scholars in related disciplines.[25] From a theoretical point of view, the question of religious identity gets illuminated when it is viewed and interpreted in the frame of the social theory of recognition and politics of difference. As Charles Taylor rightly observes:

> The thesis is that recognition or its absence partly shapes our identity often by *mis* recognition of others, and so a person or group of people can suffer real damage, real distortion, if the people or society around them mirror back to them a confining or demeaning or contemptible picture of themselves. Non-recognition or misrecognition can inflict harm, can be a form of oppression, imprisoning someone in a false, distorted, and reduced mode of being.[26]

In the same vein, Pierre Bourdieu reminds us about the paramount importance of recognition when he points out that "there is no worse deprivation, no worse privation, perhaps, than that of losers in the symbolic struggle for recognition, for access to socially recognized social being, in a word humanity."[27]

Democratic functioning in multicultural, multiethnic, and multireligious societies and nations is possible when the identities of various groups and communities are recognized and respected, as this matters a lot to them. Further, the identity of an individual is enmeshed in the web of the community of one's belonging. Through the community's manifold expressive forms (including religious ones), an individual actualizes herself. The religious community also provides meaning-making schemes in one's life. Respect for the individual and respect for the community should go hand in hand.

---

[25] Cf. Jonathan Fox, "Religion and State Failure: An Examination of the Extent and Magnitude of Religious Conflict from 1950 to 1996," *International Political Science Review / Revue Internationale de Science Politique* 25, no. 1 (2004): 55–76.

[26] Charles Taylor, "The Politics of Recognition," in *Multiculturalism: Examining the Politics of Recognition* (Princeton: Princeton University Press, 1994), 25; see also Axel Honneth, *The Struggle for Recognition: The Moral Grammar of Social Conflicts* (Cambridge: Polity Press, 1995).

[27] As quoted in Zygmunt Bauman, *Consuming Life* (Cambridge: Polity, 2007), 1.

The link between identity and recognition applies particularly in the case of religion. If in the larger world the emergence of equal recognition of identity has taken place as a result of the decline of hierarchy and hierarchical thinking, the same should be applicable also in the case of religious identities. It would be unfair and undemocratic to maintain a hierarchy in religious identities theologically, whereas global thinking and culture call for a more democratic approach in treating all religions equally independent of their private beliefs and claims.

In the context of inequality and discrimination, we also begin to understand the story of religious conflicts, violence, and wars in a new light. The problem can get exacerbated when religion becomes a player in the conflict of power among groups and communities divided on majority–minority lines. The struggle the discriminated and excluded minorities and marginal groups—ethnic and religious—wage is moral. In his *Leviathan*, Thomas Hobbes, while analyzing reasons for conflict in human societies, identified three roots: *competition, diffidence*, and *glory*.[28] Remarkably, religion is involved in all the three. For example, economic competition and business rivalries in India takes on the form of Hindu-Muslim conflict. By "diffidence," Hobbes meant the feeling of insecurity in which case religion is invoked for the cause of protection. Furthermore, when groups and communities fight for their dominance, religion serves as an instrument of "glory."

Religion becomes for the discriminated and oppressed minorities the site for their moral *claims of dignity and rights*. The question is deeper than an equitable distribution of material goods in a polity made up of many ethnicities and communities. The negation of equity and justice is interpreted by the discriminated communities as a sign of something more profound, namely the denial of dignity and recognition. We observe this in the situation of migrants and refugees. Surrounded by a culture, tradition, language, and way of life very different from their own, the migrants and refugees find a haven in their religious identity and community. This understandable insecurity and estrangement could escalate into an explosive situation of violence and terrorism when they feel stigmatized, humiliated, and are deprived of opportunities. In this context, we may not interpret violence as proceeding directly from religious extremism. One

[28] Thomas Hobbes and Marshall Missner, eds., *Thomas Hobbes: Leviathan* (London and New York: Routledge, 2016), chapter 13. See also, Pärtel Piirimäe, "The Explanation of Conflict in Hobbes's *Leviathan*," *Trames* 10, no. 60/55 ((2006): 3–21.

has to take into account the environment in which the migrants live and the discrimination and insecurity they experience. As psychologists say, the feeling of threat and anxiety are at the root of violence; on the contrary, where there is an atmosphere of security and trust, violence gets reduced or disappears.[29] To stigmatize a particular religion as a source of violence without attending to the external environment that provokes violence would be a distortion of truth.

Another theoretical issue concerns how the past is reconstructed. How history is reviewed and written depends on the positionality of the historian.[30] No serious historiographer would hold the widespread view that history recounts the past *as it happened*. The truth is that the accounts of the past get shaped in the light of present-day interests, desires, struggles, dreams, projects, and experiences in the fields of politics, economy, culture, and so on. This is true of contending groups harking back to the past. Structuralism led to the awareness of the construal element in the representation of the past, and post-structuralism has enlightened us that the narration of history as a linear sequence is more imaginary than real, as it is full of silences, gaps, omissions, and erasures, and hence the need for deconstructing many of the conventional historical accounts.[31]

All of the above help us evolve a critical and analytical approach to the conflicting claims about history by contending religious groups. The perceived injustice suffered in the hands of an inimical religious group in the past becomes a breeding ground for continuing conflicts today. For example, the Tamil narrative of the past in Sri Lanka is entirely different from the Sinhalese one.

> Whatever "facts" are known of the past are intermingled with myth and fantasy, and a new perception is created of a past that is glorious, pure and exclusive. New customs, traditions, festivities, rituals and so forth are invented in keeping with these perceptions. These are then accorded historical status and imagined to have existed from immemorial times. The Sinhalese and Tamil identities of Sri Lanka, now embroiled in a tragic con-

---

[29] Cf. James Gilligan, *Violence: Reflection on a National Epidemic* (New York: Vintage Books, 1997).

[30] Cf. Sumit Sarkar, *Writing Social History* (Delhi: Oxford University Press, 1999).

[31] Cf. John Sturrock, *Structuralism*, 2nd edition with an Introduction by Jean-Michel Rabaté (Oxford: Blackwell, 2002); John Sturrock, ed., *Structuralism and since: From Lévi-Strauss to Derrida* (Oxford: Oxford University Press, 1979); Nancy Armstrong and Leonard Tennenhouse, "History, Poststructuralism, and the Question of Narrative," *Narrative* 1, no.1 (1993): 45–58.

flict, illustrate this process. Both have created images of the past based on their respective contemporary predicaments.[32]

How the past is reconstructed by Jews, Christian, and Muslims in West Asia (Middle East) conditions the mutual relationships of the three religious bodies today. It may be recalled here that conflicting narratives of the past among Muslims and Orthodox Christians played a role in the war in Bosnia-Herzegovina.

## ECONOMIC JUSTICE AND EQUAL OPPORTUNITIES

A crucial aspect of conflict is that it often arises from unequal economic development among particular groups and ethnicities, causing a strong perception of injustice and deprivation. Hence, where religious identities are locked in conflict, to come out of the tangle, one would need to address the issue of *economic* justice and equal opportunities. For, in many societies, competition for scarce resources pits different groups against each other. Identity becomes a weapon for claims. As many analyses show, if the *economy* weakens, submerged ethnic passions take wings and tensions flare up. The situation could turn for the worse when there is inequality among the identities in sharing economic benefits. Hence, economic development needs to take place for all, irrespective of ethnic or religious belonging. Moreover, the structural causes of inequality also need to be analyzed and addressed. In short, the conditions for long-lasting peace among multiethnic, multireligious, and linguistic groups are created when appropriate ways and means for equitable development are put in place. Lack of employment and opportunities, low-wages, and corruption are common issues to grapple with across ethnic and religious divides.[33]

[32] H.L. Seneviratne, ed., *Identity, Consciousness and the Past* (Delhi: Oxford University Press, 1999).

[33] By way of illustration, it may be pointed out here that the relatively poorer-illiterate north Indian states are more prone to Hindu-Muslim tensions than the relatively prosperous-educated south Indian states.

## RECOGNITION OF DIFFERENCE: A NEW
## EDUCATIONAL PRAXIS

Religion could be a catalyst to promote education for the recognition of *difference*. There is a temptation to find secure solutions by steamrolling the different identities in favor of a misconceived model of unity and peace. The practice of the exhortation to "love one's neighbor as oneself" might have been relatively straightforward when the neighbor was someone belonging to one's tribe, ethnicity, or of one's religious, national, cultural, caste or linguistic group. Today, we are in a situation in which our neighbor is someone of a different race, religion, language, interests, or of different religious belief, way of life, history, and aspirations for the future. The acid test of one's conviction in human dignity and rights is in the respect he or she gives to the difference the new type of neighbor represents. Recognition of difference needs to be an essential component in overall educational praxis. I mean it should be an important component in formal, nonformal, and informal modes of education. It is something more fundamental than interreligious understanding. What is at stake is not merely the sacredness of religions and their beliefs as the respect for the other and the difference of the other.

## HEALING OF MEMORIES AND REWRITING OF HISTORY

In post-conflict conditions like in Sri Lanka, or in Bosnia-Herzegovina, should we recall the past, or rather bury it in order to be able to move ahead?[34] Forgetting the past is a pragmatic approach that can be attractive. On the other hand, unredeemed memory can be the cause for the breakout of new conflicts, and therefore needs to be tackled. Traumatic memories and feelings, like a festering wound, continue to afflict societal life. History needs to be addressed for proper healing.

Healing of memories is a positive role religion could play in conflict and post-conflict situations. By helping to remove the sting of revenge and hatred, it could contribute to social harmony and cohesion.[35] Of course,

---

[34] Jude Lal Fernando, "The Politics of Representations of Mass Atrocity in Sri Lanka and Human Rights Discourse: Challenge to justice and Recovery," in *Loss and Hope,* edited by Peter Admirand, 19–49 (London-New York: Bloomsbury, 2014).

[35] Cf. Rajmohan Gandhi, *Revenge and Reconciliation* (New Delhi; London: Penguin, 1999).

justice needs to be done, and truth should come out in the open as a pre-requisite for peace and harmony in any wounded society. However, any amount of restorative justice cannot reestablish the status quo ante—the situation before violence and destruction were unleashed. "What's done cannot be undone," to express with Shakespeare.[36] Any effort at restorative justice needs to take into account the incontrovertible truth fact that there will always remain a deficit. It can be addressed only through a process of reconciliation which remains, to speak in Christian terms, "a matter of grace."[37] It is an extremely delicate situation of bringing together forgiveness and atonement.

> Like most places recovering from violent conflict, Norther Ireland is divided on the question of whether past wrongs should be forgiven or atoned for. Forgiveness may help a peace process, but leave justice undone. Atonement may satisfy the wronged, but punishing wrongdoers risks reviving conflict.[38]

Since conflicts and violence among the identities often stem, as we noted, from fear, insecurity and a sense of threat, creation of trust in the other is something religion, and religious agents could foster for the construction of peace and for a future unencumbered by the weight of the past.

History narrated and written through the lens of ethnic and religious identity invariably turns out to be partisan, especially in conflict and post-conflict situations. Such a history veils the facts and strays away from the truth. Curiously, the current interests, concerns, and aspirations of religious identities condition the narrative of the past. The suffering and injustice one's group has undergone gets highlighted while the suffering of the other is conveniently forgotten or made light of. Hence, history also needs to be redeemed by a rewriting in the light of truth and reconciliation. This is, indeed, a very challenging task.

---

[36] William Shakespeare, *Lady Macbeth* Act III, Scene 2.
[37] Cf. Jacques Haers, Felix Wilfred, Kristien Justaert and Yves De Maeseneer, "Reconciliation: Empowering Grace," in *Concilium 2013/1*(London: SCM Press, 2013).
[38] *The Economist*, February 15–21 (2020): 46.

## RELIGIONS AS CATALYSTS OF PEACE

Not unlike technology and science, religions too are double-edged and ambiguous. They have as much potential for destruction as for construction of peace, harmony, and concord. Unfortunately, religious and cultural resources are not availed enough for the project of peace. In modern times, it was Pope John XXIII who brought peace to the fore as a common issue of humanity that the church needs to address. His encyclical *Pacem in Terris* (1963) set a new direction for the Catholic Church and its theology, opening them up to the larger concerns of humankind. It was the first time that the world was to hear from the Catholic church something addressed to the entire human family. Highlighting the significance of this encyclical, Joseph Gremillion comments:

> It was *Pacem in Terris* (Peace on Earth) which won for John and his aggiornamento a universal hearing. Millions who had never paid the least attention to popes and their jaw-breaker encyclicals suddenly sat up and listened. Here for the first time, a pope was addressing himself "to all men of good will". And his message responded to a deep longing shared by all.[39]

Bringing about peace in a world of religious conflicts cannot be achieved by the religious leaders alone. And yet, their role matters immensely for the impact it can have on the followers of their religion as well as those of other religious traditions.[40] Leaders like Dalai Lama of Tibet, Bishop Desmond Tutu of South Africa, Bishop Carlos Belo of East Timor, and Swami Agnivesh of India have set great example for the pursuit of peace.

History and experience attest that peace may not be achieved without justice. It means then that while speaking of the contribution of religions to peace, in the same breath we need to speak of justice. The Roman Catholic Church, thanks to the trigger of Vatican II, was brought to this realization in one of its synods. It formulated its theological conviction, stating:

[39] Joseph Gremillion, *The Gospel of Peace and Justice. Catholic Social Teaching Since Pope John* (Maryknoll: Orbis, 1976), 68.

[40] Philip Broadhead and Damien Keown, eds., *Can Faiths Make Peace? Holy Wars and the Resolution of Religious Conflicts* (London; New York: International Library of War Studies, 2007).

Action on behalf of justice and participation in the transformation of the world fully appears to us as a constitutive dimension of the preaching of the gospel or, in other words, of the church's mission for the redemption of the human race and its liberation from every oppressive situation.[41]

All this means that peace and justice in the world are not an afterthought for the believers or an ethical application of Christian beliefs, but form part of the very stuff of faith and salvation. The program "Justice, Peace and Integrity of Creation" of the World Council of Churches stirred among Christian communities worldwide a renewed commitment to peace as fruit of justice.

What the religious leaders and agents could contribute more specifically is to undergird the project of peace with mystical dimension. Let me explain the point with reference to a thinker of early modernity, Nicholas of Cusa, who was deeply concerned about the concord among religions. In his work *De Pace Fidei* (1401–1464), he tells us that his conviction about the harmony of religions was the fruit of a vision. It is remarkable that in a provocative situation such as the fall of Constantinople (1453)—a cultural earthquake that shook the very foundations of Europe's identity—he was able to relate the warring religions of Christianity and Islam from a mystical perspective and see their ultimate unity. He proposed reconciliation, harmony, dialogue, and peace rather than aggression and revenge. Narrating his experience, Nicholas of Cusa says:

> It came to pass that after a number of days—perhaps because of his prolonged incessant meditation—a vision was shown to this same zealous man. Therefore he educed the following: the few wise men who are rich in the experiential knowledge of all such differences as are observed throughout the world in the (different) religions can find a single readily available harmony; and through this harmony there can be constituted, by a suitable and true means, perpetual peace within (the domain of) religion.[42]

---

[41] *Justice in the World, Synod of Bishops Second General Assembly* (1971), no. 6. For the text see, J. Gremillion, *The Gospel of Peace and Justice* (Maryknoll: Orbis Books, 1976), 514.

[42] Nicholas of Cusa, *De Pace Fidei*, trans. Jasper Hopkins (Minneapolis: Arthur J. Banning, 1994), chapter I. See also Inigo Bocken, ed., *Conflict and Reconciliation Perspectives on Nicholas of Cusa* (Leiden and Boston: Brill, 2004).

## CONCLUSION

Some years ago, while visiting the concentration camp in Dachau, Germany, one thing struck me in particular. I saw in front of the gas chamber the statue of an emaciated prisoner representing the thousands of innocent people who underwent senseless suffering and death at this spot. It read: *Ehre den Toten und Mahnung den Lebenden*—Honor to the dead, and a warning to the living. Humankind needs to remember all the people who died in ethnic and religious wars and conflicts, especially in the recent history. Religions have been, unfortunately, an accomplice in ethnic and religious wars, if not always by their sins of commission, but certainly by omissions, especially their *failure to do enough* to prevent conflicts and to contribute to the process of peace and harmony.

Religions have failed to come out of their ambiguities. The wars in Kosovo and Bosnia, the endemic violence in West Asia, and the conflicts in Sudan and Nigeria and in India and Indonesia hold important lessons to the whole of humankind on what should never be repeated. In Srebrenica, not far from Sarajevo which I visited, 8000 people were massacred in a day to eliminate a rival religious group.[43] It is a perpetual reminder, and indeed a warning to the religions and theologies, that they cannot sit idle when the house is burning, but need to engage themselves on a priority basis to quench the fire and take measures to build bridges of peace and harmony, in cooperation with all women and men of goodwill.

[43] Cf. Noreen Herzfeld, "The Dangers of Religious Nationalism: Lessons from Srebrenica," *Dialog: A Journal of Theology*, 58 (2019): 16–21.

# CHAPTER 5

# Religious Fundamentalism in the Age of Globalization

In the last chapter, we dwelt on the issue of religious conflicts. The present one proposes to explore one of the underlying reasons for religions taking a violent turn. This has to do with a fundamentalist approach to one's faith which breeds in particular sociopolitical environments. We will also examine how fundamentalism operates under globalizing conditions.

"Fundamentalism" is a very loosely used term. The use of it is often ambiguous since its connotation depends on the perspective of the one who employs it.[1] That tells us about the danger of generalizing the concept of fundamentalism. Fundamentalism refers to such a wide variety of situations and contexts that as a concept it is hardly generalizable.

---

[1] The use of this term goes back to the nineteenth- and early twentieth-century Protestant conservative movement in the US. More directly the term "fundamentalism" is connected to a series of pamphlets brought out during 1910–1915 by this movement under the title "The Fundamentals: A Testimony of the Truth." The scope of this series was to lay down in clear terms the nonnegotiable Christian truths as perceived by the followers of this conservative movement. Martin Riesebrodt and Don Reneau, "Protestant Fundamentalism in the United States, 1910–1928," in *Pious Passion: The Emergence of Modern Fundamentalism in the United States and Iran*, 33–99 (Berkeley; Los Angeles; London: University of California Press, 1993). For the results of a significant contemporary research project on fundamentalism, see Martin E. Marty and R. Scott Appleby, eds., *Fundamentalism Observed* (Chicago: University of Chicago Press, 1991). This volume, bringing together the fruits of worldwide research, was followed by a series of publications on the various aspects of fundamentalism.

© The Author(s), under exclusive license to Springer Nature Switzerland AG 2021
F. Wilfred, *Religious Identities and the Global South*,
New Approaches to Religion and Power,
https://doi.org/10.1007/978-3-030-60738-8_5

Though fundamentalism is used mostly with reference to religion, it is not exclusive to religious phenomena. Fundamentalism could be spoken of also about different kinds of ideologies. Some versions of secularism, for example, could be characterized as "xenophobic secularism" in the sense that it does not tolerate anything outside its purview.[2] There could also be a Marxist fundamentalism, for example, when its tenets and explanations fail to respond to new social, economic, and political situations. Such a failure seems to have caused the collapse of the socialist states in Eastern Europe. In some of these countries where the Marxist ideological structure caved in, there has been a tendency to restore it, leading to resurgence of political extremism. Another example would be market fundamentalism, which claims that the laissez-faire economy, when put into effect, can solve all social, political, and economic problems of our planet. The faith in "the invisible hands" of the market is held and venerated with religious fervor and dogmatic certainty. Anyone who opposes the creeds of the market economy is not considered an economist. Today, one also speaks about "eco-fundamentalism," meaning a project readied in the Global North and imposed on the Global South with little regard to the lifeworld of the local people and their millennial harmonious relationship to nature and the environment.[3] All kinds of fundamentalisms operate so to say a priori, namely out of a fixed scheme of things with its ready-made solutions, without having to study and analyze the developing situations on the ground—a posteriori. In this sense, fundamentalism is a way of thinking, a mindset.

There is a widespread impression that fundamentalism is something exotic and an issue of the Global South, and it is too difficult to understand. Commenting critically upon the massive project on fundamentalism led by Martin Marty, on the assumption that fundamentalism is regressive thinking and hard to understand, Peter Berger, with a tinge of humor commented thus: "The difficult to understand phenomenon is not

---

[2] Cf. Daniel O. Conkle, "Secular Fundamentalism, Religious Fundamentalism, and the Search for Truth in Contemporary America," *Journal of Law and Religion* 12, no. 2 (1995): 337–70; Paul F. Campos, "Secular Fundamentalism," *Columbia Law Review* 94, no. 6 (1994): 1814–827; Vegard Skirbekk, Eric Kaufmann and Anne Goujon, "Secularism, Fundamentalism, or Catholicism? The Religious Composition of the United States to 2043," *Journal for the Scientific Study of Religion* 49, no. 2 (2010): 293–310.

[3] Deepak Lal, "Eco-Fundamentalism," *International Affairs* 71, no.3 (1995): 515–28.

Iranian mullahs but American university professors—it might be worth a multi-million dollar project to try to explain that!"[4] It is no more a secular West which has the burden of grappling with the religious fundamentalism of less advanced peoples and societies in the South. Religious and other kinds of fundamentalism and religious identity politics are today a stark reality in the countries of Europe and in the USA.[5]

We could observe different forms of religious fundamentalism in the Middle East, South Asia, Southeast Asia, Africa, Latin America, and North America. If we analyze the conditions in each of these geographical regions, we will also realize that fundamentalism may not be univocally applied to every situation. Protestant fundamentalism of the USA and Protestant fundamentalism in Latin America are markedly different, because of different histories and sociopolitical contexts. Moreover, each religious group has its form of fundamentalism. As a result, the fundamentalist character of Islam, Judaism, Christianity, Hinduism, Buddhism, and Sikhism in many respects differ from each other, despite many commonalities. The religious conflicts in the Balkan states in Europe (the Bosnian war) are different from the ones we find in Bangladesh, Malaysia, or Indonesia.

In the first part of this chapter, I intend to highlight how material forces are enmeshed in the emergence and growth of religious fundamentalism. In the second part, we shall look at fundamentalism as a theological category.

## PART I: ANALYZING FUNDAMENTALISM AND ITS DYNAMICS

### Globalization, Deterritorialization, and Fundamentalism

Let us begin with the question: How does fundamentalism relate to globalization? The spontaneous response could be that globalization with all its modern means of communication and mobility of people make it possible that fundamentalism could move fast and reach different parts of the world; that the fundamentalists could have global links and networking.

---

[4] Peter Berger, "The Desecularization of the World: A Global Overview," in Peter Berger, ed., *The Desecularization of the World: Resurgent Religions and World Politics* (Washington, DC: Ethics and Public Policy Center, 1999), 1–18, at 2.

[5] George Marsden, "Fundamentalism as an American Phenomenon, A Comparison with English Evangelicalism," *Church History* 46, no. 2 (1977): 215–32; Doebler Stefanie, "Relationships Between Religion and Intolerance Toward Muslims and Immigrants in Europe: A Multilevel Analysis," *Review of Religious Research* 56, no. 1 (2014): 61–86.

We see this happening in the way violence is planned and executed globally. However, we need to dig deeper and try to understand the correlation between globalization and fundamentalism through another analytical approach.

In an earlier chapter, I referred to the process of deterritorialization of religion which makes it possible to have global reach more easily. The same process of deterritorialization could explain also the birth and growth of fundamentalism. Religion, abstracted from territory-bound sociopolitical and cultural conditions, gets decontextualized, deculturated, and dehistoricized. In the words of Olivier Roy:

> Two factors play a key part in the transformation of religion today: deterritorialization and deculturation. Deterritorialization is not only associated with the movement of people ...but also with the circulation of ideas, cultural objects, information and modes of consumption generally in a nonterritorial space. However, in order to circulate, the religious object must appear universal, disconnected from a specific culture that has to be understood in order for the message to be grasped. Religion, therefore, circulates outside knowledge.[6]

This dynamics of decoupling of religion and culture leads to the creation of "religious purity"—free from any cultural specificity—which fundamentalists seek to establish by any means, even with most violent ones, and become defenders of its purity against any threat, be it from within or without. Any adoption of elements from other religious traditions are viewed as syncretism and hybridity and branded as heretical. The example of Yezidis in Iraq shows how there is a flow of different religious streams in forming specific religious configurations. The religion of Yezidis incorporates elements from ancient Mesopotamian religions, from Islam, Christianity, and Judaism. Precisely because the Yezidis represent a merging of different religious traditions, they are viewed as heretical, and have been target of attack and persecution. They experienced discrimination in the hands of the Iraqi state and the Sunni Muslims, and then by ISIS—a radical Islamist group.[7]

---

[6] Olivier Roy, *Holy Ignorance: When Religion and Culture Diverge* (London: C. Hurst & Publishers, 2010), 6.

[7] Cf. Paul S. Rowe, ed., *The Routledge Handbook of Minorities in the Middle East* (London: Routledge, 2018). J. D. Freilich and W. A. Pridemore, "Politics, Culture, and Political Crime: Covariates of Abortion Clinic Attacks in the United States," *Journal of Criminal*

Social, political, economic, and cultural situations condition the emergence and growth of fundamentalism. However, religious fundamentalism may not be reduced to these material causes and factors. If one set of analysis of the phenomenon of fundamentalism tends to see it as nothing but a particular configuration of sociopolitical conditions in which religion is instrumentalized for acquiring power, there is another set of analysis which sees it exclusively in terms of religious beliefs, convictions, and theologies, with no reference to context. A more complete picture of fundamentalism emerges when both these sets of analyses are in dialogue with each other.

### Global Rise of Religious Fundamentalism

We observe an increasing influence of religious fundamentalism in determining the politics of several countries in the global world. We have the examples of Egyptian Muslim Brotherhood; the right-wing Jewish fundamentalism in Israel; the religious fundamentalist movements causing civil wars in Sudan, Nigeria, Kenya, Mali, Somalia, and in other parts of the African continent; and the surge of politically active fundamentalist groups in many countries of South America. It would be naïve to think that fundamentalism is a phenomenon of the Global South. Suffice here to recall the influence of the Christian Right in the US elections of the past two decades or so. With the electoral gains of right-wing parties in many countries of Europe, religious fundamentalism seems to be back in "secular" Europe today.[8] It is further sharpened by the flow of migrants from other religious worlds.

*Justice: An International Journal* 35, no. 3 (2007): 323–36; Cathy Otten, *With Ash on Their Faces: Yezidi Women and the Islamic State* (New York and London: OR Books, 2017); Philip G. Kreyenbroek, *Yezidism: Its Background, Observances and Textual Tradition*, vol. 62 (Lewiston, N.Y.; Lampeter: Edwin Mellen, 1995); Eszter Spät, "Yezidi Identity Politics and Political Ambitions in the Wake of the ISIS Attack," *Journal of Balkan and Near Eastern Studies*, vol.20 (2018): 420–38.

[8] Natalia Eremina, *Right Radicalism in Party and Political Systems in the Present-day European States* (Newcastle upon Tyne, United Kingdom: Cambridge Scholars Publishing, 2015); Andrea Mammone, Emmanuel Godin, and Brian Jenkins, eds., *Mapping the Extreme Right in Contemporary Europe: From Local to Transnational* (London and New York: Routledge, 2012); Michael Minkenberg, ed., *Transforming the Transformation? The East European Radical Right in the Political Process* (London and New York: Routledge, 2015).

## *Misconstrued Theories and New Awakening*

In the face of contemporary forms of religious fundamentalism, Western academia was quick in providing theoretical frames of interpretation. Religious fundamentalism was viewed as resistance to modernity, and to the process of secularization it set in motion. Closer analysis of the phenomenon of religious fundamentalism has led us to critically question the standard thesis of the Northern academia that religious fundamentalism is a reaction to the threat represented by modernity and secularization.

This kind of analysis reminds us of the insecurity felt by the religious establishment at the time of the European Enlightenment, which responded to it with a fundamentalist mindset. A nineteen-year-old French boy Jean Francois Léfebvre Chevalier de la Barre was tortured and executed publicly for "blasphemy," and the blasphemy was nothing else but that he did not take off his hat as the Eucharistic procession was passing by! Moreover, he was found in possession of a work of Voltaire.[9] Could we view fundamentalism of today as a reaction to modernity, similar to the fundamentalism reacting to the spirit of Enlightenment? I surmise that such European experiences of the past has its influence on theorizing the origins of today's fundamentalism as resistance to modernity.

Max Weber saw the ever-shrinking role of religion resulting from disenchantment and demystification.[10] In this perspective, the fundamentalists would be misguided fanatics wedded to pre-modern values who want to take us back to the dark ages of the past. They are the ones who confound the social and political order by their obscurantist religious beliefs, intolerance, and patriarchal practices out of step with the modern world, and pose a challenge to the stability of our societies and the world, they pose a danger. For those who view fundamentalism this way, the pursuit of secularization is the solution. It was projected that with the rise of the sun of secularization, the dark force of religious fundamentalism would vanish into thin air.

However, the resurgence of fundamentalist religious forces from the late 1970s led to revising this line of thought. Iranian Islamic revolution of 1979 was a wake-up call for those who underestimated the power of religion and had even written its obituary. As Peter Berger has pointed

---

[9] Olivier Roy, *Holy Ignorance*, 112. During a journey to Malta in 2019, I visited the Inquisitor's Palace in Birgu (Citta Vittoriosa) with its prisons and the gears of punishment for those suspected of heresy. Among them were two British Quaker women—Katherine Evans and Sarah Cheevers.

[10] Cf. Max Weber, *The Sociology of Religion* (Boston, MA: Beacon Press, 1993).

out, the secularization thesis explaining religious fundamentalism failed to anticipate two interrelated developments: First, secularization carried within itself the seeds of a remystification of the world; second, there would be resistance to demystification.[11] Those who were involved in the remystification of religions and resisted demystification came to be labeled fundamentalists. This religious process did not take place in a vacuum but in particular sociocultural contexts and environments in which groups of people were involved in power conflicts. The religious process only aggravated further the sociopolitical conflicts.

There is a failure to take into account and analyze the underlying forces that foment fundamentalism and fanatic violence. The experience of injustice—real or perceived—discrimination, exclusion, and denial of recognition are some of the factors that lead to terrorism and violence. When there are gross economic disparities among groups, or when economic opportunities are denied, religion becomes a player in the conflicts among communities. To cite an example from history, while the Hindu elites of India took to English education, the Muslim elites of the nineteenth century felt that the changeover to English affected their opportunities. For, the Mughal court had employed them in its administration which was done in Urdu. The switching over to English meant the advancement of the Hindu elites while the Muslim elites felt left behind with denial of opportunities.[12] In more recent times, the privileging of the Tamils in Sri Lanka by the British in their administration and bureaucracy was resented by the Sinhalese majority, who turned their Buddhism into a fundamentalist and extremist force to suppress the Tamils and dislodge them from their privileged position in the postindependent period. In the case of Nigeria, the economic development of the South populated by Christians vis-à-vis the poverty-stricken North, the traditional homeland of the country's Muslim population, has been an enduring source of conflicts in that country. As an analyst observes;

> The pressure for Wahabi and Salafi ideas to evolve into aggressive violence
> has in Nigeria come from Muslim's experience of corrupt government,
> gross inequalities in wealth and persistent youth unemployment, as well as

[11] Cf. Peter L. Berger, *A Far Glory: The Quest for Faith in the Age of Credulity* (New York: Free Press, 1992); see also Peter L. Berger, ed., *Desacralization of the World: Resurgent Religion and World Politics* (Grand Rapids: William B. Eerdmans Publishing Company, 1999).

[12] See Asghar Ali Engineer, "Remaking Indian Muslim Identity," in *Economic and Political Weekly* (April 20, 1991), 1036–1038.

rote learning and rudimentary level of Islamic education... Boko Haram became many things to many people: from a sponsor of criminality and banditry to a channel for alienated, unemployed and angry youth to earn a living through the barrel of a gun.[13]

Fundamentalism is also associated with identity assertion of different kinds. Both the powerful and the powerless resort to religious fundamentalism as a means for their identity assertion. We have cases of a commanding majority making use of fundamentalism to assert itself, like the Hindutva in India. However, we have also instances where a situation of powerlessness and marginalization could drive a discriminated minority to have recourse to religious fundamentalism in support of its cause. Such is the case of radicalized Indian Muslims.

### Intra-Religious Fundamentalism

Fundamentalism operates not only vis-à-vis those *outside* one's religious fold but is at work also among those inside—intra-religious fundamentalism. In fact, in its early use, fundamentalism referred to the Protestant conservative movement of early twentieth century in the USA. It connoted the kind of attitude and practice directed against the modernizing and liberal stream among the Protestant groups.[14] In Islam, for instance, Wahhabism represents a constricted and fundamentalist trend; the Sufi stream, on the other hand, is more open and flexible. Hence, there are conflicts within Islam between those attached to Wahhabism and those inspired by Sufi mysticism. This could be seen all over the Islamic world. In nineteenth-century India, the Wahhabists invoking the authority of Ibn Taymiyyah of Damascus turned their critique against those who, in their view, were trying to accommodate Islam to the Hindu surroundings. In the Roman Catholic Church, some movements challenge the renewal of Vatican II and consider it as a degeneration of Christian faith and dogma. They find orthodoxy in the Council of Trent and Vatican I. They do not even spare Pope Francis, whose orthodoxy of faith is brought under a

---

[13] Ian Linden and Thomas Thorp, "Religious Conflicts and Peace Building in Nigeria," *Journal of Religion and Violence* 4, no.1 (2016): 85–100, at 94.

[14] This group sidelined and even ridiculed by the liberal stream of Protestantism eventually isolated itself from the rest and built parallel structures and strategies of action. The global resurgence of religion in the 1970s offered the occasion for the Christian fundamentalist group to reemerge with great vigor to influence public life and become politically active.

cloud of suspicion. For example, in September 2016, four cardinals—Raymond Burke, Carlo Caffarra, Walter Brandmüller, and Joachim Meisner—wrote a letter to Pope Francis in which they raised "doubts" (*dubia*) about the open and pastorally inspired views of Pope Francis on issues of family and marriage in his *Amoris Laetitia*.[15]

### *Fundamentalism and Escalation of Global Violence*

History amply testifies to a close link between religion and violence. In the Christian tradition, the practice of the Inquisition stands out as an illustration of how violence was used to create religious conformity. It was often applied also to those who did not belong to the Christian fold. The Inquisition created a general mindset of punishing and even liquidating the dissenters and those suspected of holding "unorthodox" positions.

Today, the impact of fundamentalism is most intensely felt in its capacity for brutal violence—suicide bombs, beheading, attacks on peoples of other faiths, demolition of their places of worship, and so on. Hardly a day passes without some form of religiously motivated violence on people taking place, and the number of such events and victims keep growing. Mark Juergensmeyer in his work *Terror in the Mind of God* tried to study and analyze through personal interviews with those involved in terror activities and their friends and relatives, to understand what motivates them to do such things in the name of religion.[16] One of the revealing things that has come out from these interviews is that there are not only religious motives that cause damage and destruction to the life and property of others, but that there is also a *performative or symbolic* aspect to violence. By their dramatic performance, the perpetrators of violence want to shock the society and draw attention to their cause. The goal is to create a *spectacle* that will have enduring global impact.

The very adjective used to describe acts of religious terrorism—symbolic, dramatic, theatrical—suggest that we look at them not as tactics but as *performance violence*. In speaking of terrorism as "performance", I am not suggesting that such acts are undertaken lightly or capriciously. Rather, like a

---

[15] For the text of the letter, see https://catholicherald.co.uk/news/2016/11/14/full-text-cardinals-letter-to-pope-francis-on-amoris-laetitia/ [accessed on November 7, 2019].

[16] Mark Juergensmeyer, *Terror in the Mind of God: The Global Rise of Religious Violence* (Berkeley: University of California Press, 2000).

religious ritual or street theatre, they are dramas designed to have an impact on the several audiences they affect.[17]

These acts of violence are directed not only against the religiously "other" but also against those *within* one's religious fold if they are found to vent different views or do not act in orthodox ways. Those transgressing are viewed as traitors deserving violent treatment. On the other hand, we also need to point out that, in general perception, there is a conflation of violence and fundamentalism. However, the fact is that most fundamentalist groups are not violent, as borne out by the numerous evangelically conservative Protestant groups in the so-called Bible Belt states in the USA.

Often critical analysts try to show the inextricable connection of religion with violence, and this is illustrated from history as well as through empirical analysis. From a theological point of view, the nexus of religion and violence is substantiated by René Girard, who held that religions vicariously try to overcome the human tendency to violence by symbolically doing violence to the sacrificial animal—the "scapegoat" theory.[18] This reminds us of the thesis of Sigmund Freud for whom the birth of civilization needs the repression of instincts through superego, without which there will be only chaos.[19] Religious fundamentalism explodes violently also when religious rights are curtailed, or religious convictions idealized and made absolute are challenged. For this reason too religion and violence remain theologically connected, and the spiral of violence continues.

Religions, cultures, and communities live not on bread alone but by sacred memories. People try to shore up their identity by memorializing sacred places, monuments, and religious heritage sites. Fundamentalism tries to strike at these symbols significant for the hostile other. The victims feel most hit when the sacred spaces, monuments, and symbols they hold dear are attacked by rival groups or by state intervention. Such a

---

[17] Juergensmeyer, *Terror in the Mind of God*, 124.

[18] René Girard, *Violence and the Sacred* (London and New York: Continuum, 2005); see also Chris Fleming, *René Girard: Violence and Mimesis* (Cambridge: Polity, 2004); Jean Baptiste Fages, *Comprendre René Girard* (Toulouse: Privat, 1982); Stéphane Vinolo, *René Girard: Du Mimétisme À L'hominisation: la Violence Différante* (Paris: Harmattan, 2005); Michael Kirwan and Sheelah Treflé Hidden, eds., "Mimesis and Atonement: René Girard and the Doctrine of Salvation," *Violence, Desire, and the Sacred*, vol. 5 (New York and London: Bloomsbury, 2017).

[19] Cf. Sigmund Freud, *Civilization and Its Discontents* (New York: W.W. Norton & Company, 2010).

violence can be attested in history as well as in present times.[20] In India, one of the most strident religious controversies is about the demolition in 1992 of a sixteenth-century mosque (built in 1528), which the right-wing Hindutva claims to have been earlier a temple that was destroyed by the Muslim "invaders."[21] A holy place like the Gurudwara (temple) of Sikh people in Amritsar, India, witnessed armed conflicts. The Shiite Golden Mosque at Samara, Iraq was bombed in 2006, severely damaging its beautiful dome. About a decade later, there took place the bombing in the Christ Church mosque in New Zealand. Extreme iconoclastic ideology led to the unfortunate destruction of the renowned Buddha statues in Bamiyan in 2001. The same kind of mindset has been at work in 9/11 destruction of Trade Towers, which, though is not in itself a religious site, is a symbol of Western economic power.

The performative nature of religious violence gets heightened when directed against religious sites and works of art. Speaking of the Islamic case in this regard, Kristy Campion notes:

> Findings suggest that jihadists are engaging in a subconscious reconquest of the contemporary Salafi identity, through opportunistic (yet deliberate) dominance performances. These performances take advantage of the strategic appeal of heritage sites while sending symbolically loaded messages to target audiences. Through re-enacting the Abrahamic rejection of idols, jihadists reimagine and propagate themselves as heirs to ancient conquest traditions. This tradition–involving the rejection, defacement, and destruction of works of art and antiquities–is rooted in a chaotic attempt at reconstructing identity. To that end, artworks and antiquities are being targeted by jihadists.[22]

[20] D. H. Davis, "Editorial: Destruction and Desecration of Sacred Sites during Wars and Conflicts: A Neglected Travesty," *A Journal of Church and State* 44, no. 3 (2002), 417–24; Nicholas Stanley Price, ed., *Cultural Heritage in Postwar Recovery* (Rome: ICCROM Conservative Studies, 2005).

[21] Cf. A. G. Noorani, "The Babri Masjid-Ram Janmabhoomi Question," *Economic and Political Weekly* 24, no. 44/45 (1989): 2461–466. This dispute is believed to have ended with the supreme court ruling of November 9, 2019, which allowed the construction of the Ram Temple in Ayodhya at the disputed site, while directing the government to allot land for the construction of a mosque in the same city.

[22] Kristy Campion, "Blast through the Past: Terrorist Attacks on Art and Antiquities as a Reconquest of the Modern Jihadi Identity," *Perspectives on Terrorism* 11, no. 1 (2017): 26–39.

## PART II: FUNDAMENTALISM AS A THEOLOGICAL STANCE

In this second part, we shall focus our attention on fundamentalism from a theological perspective, and shall examine briefly some of the underlying convictions and assumptions behind this phenomenon. Fundamentalism is characterized by its belief in the immutability and inerrancy of one's scriptures and faith tradition; resistance to the deployment of critical hermeneutics; dualistic worldview (good/bad; holy/profane, etc.); chosenness and exclusionary identity construction with attendant attitudes and practices; and millenarianist and messianic mindset. We shall go into some of these theological questions as treated by the fundamentalists.

### Immutability and Inerrancy

Given the preoccupation of the fundamentalists to protect faith, they become resistant to anything that could compromise its inviolable sacredness and certainty. Faith offers a haven of certitude in a world full of uncertainties; an anchor in the turbulent sea of views and opinions; a fortress against the onslaught of attacks; and a guarantee against attempts to dilute or compromise faith. In the perspective of the fundamentalists, it is not their religious doctrines and faith which have to change; rather what is to change are the world and society, and they should indeed change according to the immutable truth of faith.

### Insulated from Critical Hermeneutics

Given the belief in the immutability of their faith, the fundamentalists more often than not adhere to the literal meaning of texts and believe in the absolute inerrancy of sacred writings—Bible, Qur'an, Bhagavad Gita, Bhagavata Purana, Tripitaka, Adi Granth, and so on. They resist any historical and contextual interpretation of the sacred writings. The texts are placed on a dehistoricized universal plane.[23] These sacred writings, according to them, are the foundations, and they should not be shaken by employing any critical hermeneutics. The sacred books are not subjected

---

[23] Benjamin E. Zeller, "Extraterrestrial Biblical Hermeneutics and the Making of the Heaven's Gate," in *Nova Religio: The Journal of Alternative and Emergent Religions* 14, no. 2 (November 2010): 34–60; John Bartkowski, "Beyond Biblical Literalism and Inerrancy: Conservative Protestants and the Hermeneutic Interpretation of Scripture," *Sociology of Religion* 57, no. 3 (1996): 259–72.

to changing times and ephemeral opinions. This explains why the historic-critical method in biblical interpretation has been anathema to Christian fundamentalist groups. There is no room for allegoric, moral, and ana-gogic interpretation of the Christian scriptures, nor for *sensus plenior* (fuller sense).[24] All that matters is the literal meaning of the texts. No distinction is made between the author, the text, and the reader. Sacred writings are considered as the repository of revelation. They are to be safeguarded from any momentary whims and fancies.

### Chosenness and Exclusive Identity

The fundamentalists feel passionately a sense of divine destiny and con-sider themselves as chosen instruments to fulfill the will of God. From here flows their commitment even to the point of sacrificing their life for the cause of God as they perceive and interpret it. The theology of election leads them to think of themselves in terms of exclusionary identity and create a "we" versus "they"—those outside of the fold of election. It is in the nature of fundamentalism to demarcate clear religious boundaries. It lays down in unambiguous terms who is *in* and who is *out* and establishes criteria for religious belonging. Whereas in reality, as a result of encounters and exchanges, fluidity has characterized the life of religions and their practices, fundamentalist movements aim at purity of identity, which they believe is safeguarded by erecting borders. Such a view suffers from an essentialist conception of religion and an exclusionary theological concep-tion. Moreover, defining religious identity in the fundamentalist move-ments has political implications, as, for instance, in the case of constructing Sikh identity, which has been a significant issue since the nineteenth century.[25]

---

[24] Tibor Fabiny, "The Literal Sense and the 'Sensus Plenior' Revisited," *Hermathena*, no. 151 (1991): 9–23. James M. Robinson, "Scripture and Theological Method: A Protestant Study in 'Sensus Plenior'," *The Catholic Biblical Quarterly* 27, no. 1 (1965): 6–27; Pierre Benoit, "La Planitude De Sens Des Livres Saints," *Revue Biblique (1946-)* 67, no. 2 (1960): 161–96.

[25] See Pashaura Singh and Louis E. Fenech, eds., *The Oxford Handbook of Sikh Studies* (New Delhi: Oxford University Press, 2014).

## *Dualism, Cosmic War, and Apocalypticism*

Fundamentalists describe the situation of the world in terms of a struggle between the forces of good and evil. True believers must throw out of power the political forces that support in any way questionable policies and immoral practices. Some go even farther and see themselves facing a cosmic war and urge the need to be prepared to combat the evil one—the Satan—and overthrow its kingdom and power.[26] In the imagination of the fundamentalists, the satanic force is represented by communism, which should be combated to establish the Kingdom of God.

The idea of a God of War is not something totally new. Some of the Christian fundamentalists refer to the Old Testament and see how God avenges God's enemies.[27] The Islamic interpretation of the concept of *jihad* is well known. At one extreme is the interpretation of it as a spiritual struggle a person needs to undertake to become a true believer. On the other extreme is the use of it as justification for aggression and brutal violence against the "infidels." In Hindu extreme fundamentalism, the epics Ramayana and Mahabharata are invoked for war against enemies. Such an use of Hindu epics leads to violence against minorities, justification of caste structure, and patriarchal practices. It is also used against those who oppose the Hindutva ideology.

The motive of war gets heightened when it is couched in apocalyptical terms. Some of the fundamentalists see the ultimate struggle between God and God's enemies as a veritable Armageddon of cosmic proportions. The Japanese Aum Shinrikyo fundamentalist movement—which attained notoriety through the chemical gas killings in the Tokyo subway in 1995—was gripped by this impending doom. The apocalyptic hold on the consciousness of the fundamentalists and the sense of urgency they feel allow little room for any accommodation, negotiation, or compromise. The believers become the *soldiers of God*, and they have to take a definite stand *with* God in the battle *against* the evil forces. All this explains why there is some "spiritualization of violence." Violence and terror become a means to attain the "spiritual goods" in the apocalyptic imagination of the

---

[26] Cf. Adela Yarbor Collins, *Cosmology and Eschatology in Jewish and Christian Apocalypticism* (Leiden: Brill, 1996); John J. Collins, "The Mythology of Holy War in Daniel and the Qumran War Scroll: A Point of Transition in Jewish Apocalyptic," *Vetus Testamentum* 25, no. 3 (1975): 596–612.

[27] Frances L. Flannery, *Apocalyptic Terrorism Countering the Radical Mindset* (London: Routledge, 2016).

fundamentalists. The apocalyptic and messianic traits of fundamentalism could go to the extent of collective suicide as was the case with members of Peoples Temple in Jonestown in 1978, and with the members of Solar Temple in Switzerland and Quebec between 1994 and 1997. The leaders of these apocalyptic and millenarian sects convinced their followers that they should drink poison in order to attain eternal bliss in the world after.[28]

### *Intransigent Theological Views on Gender and Morals*

The fundamentalists take a rigorous view of the moral situation of society and the world. They deplore the moral decline in society as use of drugs, abortion, promiscuity, homosexuality, and same-sex marriage, and other forms of depravity, according to them, become rampant. Not seldom is this attitude related to the flag-waving and muscular nationalism. An example of this type of fundamentalism would be the Christian Right fundamentalists in the USA, who want to save their country from decline and from losing its privileged leadership position in the world. For, the Christian fundamentalists believe that America is the chosen instrument of God to achieve God's purpose in the world. We see them quoting from the Holy Scriptures to judge the present immoral situation and fighting against all those who they think are the cause for it. Jerry Falwell of Moral Majority became a rallying point for the Christian Right as he justified his position based on Christian scriptural passages. We are witnessing similar developments in India with the religious right-wing activists who do moral policing in the name of cultural and religious purity, and this is closely associated with their brand of nationalism. The strident moral stance also justifies their violence against all those who, in their view, are perpetrators of immorality or anti-national.

Most fundamentalist groups target women and seek to control their *bodies* by intervening in issues of reproduction, and suppress their *minds* by imposing severe restrictions on their critical thinking and free expression.[29] These groups flaunt patriarchal values to subjugate women and seek to stunt women's free development as human persons. There is little

---

[28] We deal with this subject matter in detail in another chapter in this volume on new religious movements. See Chap. 6.

[29] Betty A. DeBerg, *Ungodly Women. Gender and the First Wave of American Fundamentalism* (Micon: Mercer University Press, 2000); Carolina S Ruiz Austria, "The Church, the State and Women's Bodies in the Context of Religious Fundamentalism in the Philippines," *Reproductive Health Matters* 12, no.24 (2004): 96–103.

difference in this among Islamic, Christian, or Hindu fundamentalist movements. Hindutva fundamentalists, for example, would call for Hindu women to produce more children so as to counter the threat represented by the Muslims and their fast population growth. We could observe similar kind of polemics between the Croatian Catholic fundamentalists and Orthodox Serbian fundamentalists in the Balkans—both of them instigating their women to produce more children in their fight against the enemy. Women are at the receiving end with no voice and agency of their own. During the anti-colonial struggle, the Hindu fundamentalists wanted to show that the colonizers could not conquer India's culture, and, in this context, women were forced to take on the role of the guardians of tradition. Women came to symbolize the purity and honor of one's tradition.[30] Their autonomy is viewed suspiciously by fundamentalists as it could, in their estimation, upset the social order. The most insidious manner in which Hindutva fundamentalism operates is to turn women as foot soldiers of fundamentalism. This is visible in Hindu-Muslim communal riots.

> Women led mobs and dragged Muslim women and children into the streets, applauded their gang rapes and joined men in stoning Muslim women and setting them on fire. ... Nationally, women engaged in the front ranks of the Hindu fascists have increased dramatically in recent years. At demonstrations, remnants of the feudal aristocracy from metropolitan centers march shoulder to shoulder with upwardly mobile women from district towns. Female religious preachers, draped in saffron robes, defy the judiciary and police and hold forth on why the temple to Rama must be built, 'even if the waters of the Saryu (local river) turn red with our blood'."[31]

Not surprisingly, feminism and feminist struggles for liberation have not been successful among these women trapped in patriarchal values.

---

[30] Cf. Partha Chatterjee, *The Nation and Its Fragments: Colonial and Postcolonial Histories* (Princeton: Princeton University Press, 1993).

[31] Sucheta Mazumdar, "Women on the March: Right-Wing Mobilization in Contemporary India," *Feminist Review*, no. 49 (1995): 1–28, at p. 2. Similar trends could also be observed in Christianity and Islam. Cf. Shahin Gerami, *Women and Fundamentalism. Islam and Christianity* (New York: Routledge, 1996).

## *Fundamentalism and Restoration*

It is in the nature of fundamentalism that it finds the golden age in *the past*. Hence, it endeavors to restore what was there before. This restorative mindset could be found in fundamentalists of all religions. If we apply this yardstick, the Pentecostals are not fundamentalists. For, they focus attention on the direct and unmediated present action of God, of the Spirit. They speak of the experience of the salvation of body and soul, here and now.

This characteristic also distinguishes the revolutionaries from fundamentalists. Whereas the revolutionaries intend to change and transform the existing order, fundamentalists seek to reestablish the past glory, *the status quo ante*. Contrary to the general impression, the Zealots and Sicarii of the New Testament times were not revolutionaries, but a group intent on restoration of the past.[32] Jesus's movement of the time departed from such restorative movements, as it was focused on the present and future of the coming of God's Kingdom. It was a forward-looking movement of hope.

Right-wing Hindutva is a restorative movement of fundamentalism since in its efforts to construct a world of past glory, it turns myths into history. Indian history is converted into Indology. The Hindutva claims through pseudo-scientific "evidence" that the ancient India had already invented the modern developments in science and technology. In the Roman Catholic Church, the resistance to the spirit of innovation came from right-wing groups of different hues and colors. There was an outright rejection of Vatican II and its renewal, and a call to go back to the Council of Trent and to reestablish the Tridentine liturgy as was the case with the Society of Saint Pius X, founded by Archbishop Marcel Lefebvre. A milder version of this restorative tendency is to be found in the various movements inspired by Catholic fundamentalism, especially in the USA. Wahabism is another example of restoration; so are all those Islamic movements calling for the reestablishment of the Caliphate.

[32] M. Smith, *Zealots and Sicarii, Their Origins and Relation* (Leiden, The Netherlands: Brill, 1995).

## CONCLUSION

Religious fundamentalist movements present the same kind of threat to humanity as political totalitarianism, and both are a severe menace to human dignity, rights, and freedom. Despite the efforts of past many years in the field of interreligious dialogue, we are far from creating a world of peace and religious harmony. The interreligious dialogue could sometimes give the impression of conversing with and preaching to the converted. Further, one of the weaknesses of the interreligious dialogical practice is that it is not sufficiently based on social, political, and cultural analysis of religious identity and belonging. Interreligious dialogue is not able to take on religious fundamentalism with its stubborn theological positions.

Fundamentalism is a complex phenomenon, the addressing of which calls for multipronged approaches—social, cultural, and political. Since there is a theological component to fundamentalism in terms of religious doctrine and faith convictions, it needs to be addressed at that level too. This should be done with the humble acknowledgment that theological antidote is not the panacea to fundamentalism. However, it can make a small but significant difference. In this sense, the *kenosis* (the practice of self-emptying) that is embedded in Christian Scriptures could be of service. The conviction that one's faith has the fullness (of truth, revelation, etc.) and claims connected with it do not tolerate the religiously "other." *Kenosis*, on the other hand, calls for acknowledgment of human vulnerability even when we speak of things divine. It is a call to come down from the height of triumphalism and exclusion.

While proposing kenosis as a counter-theology to fundamentalism, we need to attend to two things: First, *kenosis* needs to be set in a concrete context. An abstract discourse on kenosis may not have any sociocultural impact. Second, we need to take kenosis to its radical conclusions. For, incarnation as kenosis of God in the Christian scriptures is not a dogma to be defended and hold on to, but rather it is an opening up of a new path (*odos*) to be followed in freedom to its ultimate consequences. Incarnation is not a closure of history, but a disclosure to the future course of history. The way of kenosis is the path to truth and life. It is by walking on the path that one discovers both truth and life. To think in these terms is to move in a completely different direction from fundamentalism.

Religions by their very nature are defenders of the universality of their truth, namely the truth they hold is not only theirs but is universally valid for all. The theological program of the fullness of truth needs to be critically challenged. Kenosis is the espousal of nonviolence. For the sense of obligation to defend the truth of one's religion not only gives birth to moral violence but leads almost inevitably to physical harm, torture, inquisition, death, and all-round destruction. The kenotic act is a matter of giving up the claim of the infinite and universal as positions of power; it is God's espousal of finitude, symbolized by flesh and by the tent pitched among us (*kai o logos sarx egeneto kai eskēnōsen en ēmin*), as we read in the Gospel of John (Jn 1:14). Incarnation means to become one with the vulnerability and relativity of the particular, and indeed we could say, incarnation is the immanence of the divine and end to the alienating transcendence religions foster.

In other words, there will not be any trace of fundamentalism—theological or scriptural in Christianity—because there are no truths to defend, but only a sublime divine vocation to move ahead in history and respond to its ever-new challenges. The sense of call to something yet to come will override the pathology of defense of one's truth which is at the bottom of every fundamentalism. Interpretation of scriptures will foster this call and contribute to the overcoming of fundamentalism. I have cited the case of the Christian concept of kenosis as an example. Other religious traditions have within their scriptures and traditions critical conceptions and motives which could help address the problem of fundamentalism at the local and global levels.

CHAPTER 6

# Novel Ways of Being Religious

The world of globalization is also becoming increasingly a world of post-modernity. The postmodern conditions in which we live today have an impact on our ways of being religious. The collapse of grand narratives is also applicable to the religious sphere.[1] The overarching mega identity of religions with strong institutionalization has got weakened and in its place we find several mini-narratives that are fragmentary, contingent, and relative. From institutional belonging, there is a shift toward new ways of being religious within one's tradition, and often beyond it.

Those who are familiar with life in Asia will note that what is described as an effect of the postmodern condition has been for centuries and millennia the way religion has been practiced, namely in a fragmentary way through symbols and rituals relating to particular contexts and circumstances. At any given time or a particular juncture of one's life, one is not concerned about the totality a religion represents in terms of doctrines,

---

[1] Ernest Gellner, *Postmodernism, Reason and Religion* (London: Routledge, 1992); Philippa Berry, and Andrew Wernick, eds., *Shadow of Spirit: Postmodernism and Religion* (London: Routledge, 1993); David Ray Griffin, *God and Religion in the Postmodern World* (New York: State University of New York Press, 1989); Robert P. Scharlemann, ed., *Theology at the End of the Century: A Dialogue on the Postmodern* (Charlottesville: University Press of Virginia, 1990); Graham Ward, ed., *The Blackwell Companion to Postmodern Theology* (Malden: Blackwell, 2001); Justin Thacker, *Postmodernism and the Ethics of Theological Knowledge* (New York and London: Routledge, 2016).

© The Author(s), under exclusive license to Springer Nature Switzerland AG 2021
F. Wilfred, *Religious Identities and the Global South*,
New Approaches to Religion and Power,
https://doi.org/10.1007/978-3-030-60738-8_6

laws, modes of worship, but with the concrete situation one is faced with and how to make sense of it. In this chapter, we shall go into the consideration of the new ways religion is practiced, mirroring particular situations in one's life or in the life of one's community.

## RELIGION WITHOUT AFFILIATION AND AFFILIATION WITHOUT BELIEF

Globalization has led to a critical questioning of established hierarchy (including the religious ones), normativity, and identity dictated by foundationalism and essentialism. Further, the process of individualization characteristic of modernity has grown, facilitated by the process of globalization. As a result, for many people, the traditional institutional belonging to a particular religious group with its hierarchy, doctrines, and morals has become problematic. These individuals, however, would not relinquish the spiritual core of their respective religious traditions. This is what Grace Davie has called "*believing without belonging.*"[2] People explore their spiritual path in freedom availing the spiritual resources of their tradition without declaring, for example, their ecclesial membership and the obligations deriving thereof.[3] Another variant of this trend is when people say that they are not religious (meaning that they do not belong to any religion as an institutionalized entity with which often the word "religion" is identified) but claim to be in pursuit of spirituality.[4]

On the other hand, we witness today also the phenomenon of *belonging without believing.* This is illustrated by the case of many Jews who, though they do not profess any Jewish faith at all, or believe in any religion, yet

[2] Grace Davie, *Religion in Britain since 1945: Believing without Belonging* (Oxford: Blackwell, 1994).

[3] The study of Grace Davie is based on empirical researches in various regions of the UK. The hypothesis of Grace Davie, which undermines the secularization explanation, is challenged by other scholars and researches. Olav Aarts, Ariana Need, Manfred Te Grotenhuis and Nan Dirk De Graaf, "Does Belonging Accompany Believing? Correlations and Trends in Western Europe and North America between 1981 and 2000," *Review of Religious Research* 50, no. 1 (September 2008): 16–34.

[4] Robert C. Fuller, *Spiritual, But Not Religious: Understanding Unchurched America* (New York: Oxford University Press, 2012).

declare themselves belonging to the Jewish heritage.[5] Here is the case of an ethnic identity reversing its identification with a religion, but confining only to ethnicity. In other words, it tells us that even a Jewish identity which generally is associated with religion could coexist with the profession of atheism. According to the results of a Pew Research Foundation study, one-third of American Jews under thirty years of age declare themselves as having no religion.[6] There are any number of Europeans who profess no Christian faith, but see themselves as part of the Western Christian legacy.

Another important marker of religiosity today is personal experience. Institutional religions and their significance are subjected to critique from this angle of personal experience. Religious experience, like many other forms of experiences in the globalized society, becomes a constituent of the individual self. The validity of traditional religious establishments is judged to the extent they contribute to the self-formation or self-cultivation of personal identity. The self-help movements and "do-it-yourself" modes of practices characteristic of the developing global culture get reflected also in religion. The mobility and fluidity of modern life have led to a thin form of functional religious associational life, rather than the thick religious identity of institutional belonging of organized religions. Believing becomes a matter of the construction of the self and not something flowing out of one's institutional belonging to a religious group or identity.

## TRANSFORMATION OF ACTUAL RELIGION INTO VIRTUAL IDENTITY

To be able to understand the transformation of identity religions are going through in our global world, we need to be aware of the changes in the mode of and conditions for social interactions. In former times, social interactions were bound to physical space and time. The process of globalization has created disembodiment of physical space and time. Hence, for religious practices and communications to take place, there is no need for a

---

[5] David Ibry, *Exodus to Humanism: Jewish Identity without Religion* (Amherst, NY: Prometheus Books, 1999); B. A. Phillips, "Accounting for Jewish Secularism: Is a New Cultural Identity Emerging?," *Contemporary Jewry* 30, no. 1 (2010): 63–85.

[6] See http://reformjudaism.org/secular Jew Spinoza was the inspiration for forging a secular Jewish identity. The question of religion and secularity is hotly debated in Israel relating to its identity.

concretely located community assembled in a particular place and at a particular time. As the process of deterritorialization grows, there is also a "disembodiment" of interhuman and societal interactions.

In his well-known, The Consequences of Modernity, Anthony Giddens (1990) speaks of the disembodiment of social interaction from temporal and spatial conditions as a distinguishing feature of modernity. With the beginning of the modern era, he says, social space becomes increasingly independent of real places. Social interaction involves partners who do not share the same geographical space and whose communication is realized over spatial distances.[7]

As a result, a new religious identity has come into existence known as "virtual religion" or "online religion" or "cyber-religion."[8] This is different from the institutional use of modern media to offer religious services like worship, pastoral counselling, and so on; to impart religious doctrines and beliefs; and to carry out mission through tele-evangelism. Whereas the former is a digital or virtual religion with its unique characteristics, the latter is a question of religious presence in the digital world by reproducing the traditional religion in the digital world. Saied Reza Ameli expresses the difference by distinguishing between "religion online" and "online religion."

'Religion online' suggests a kind of religion in virtual space, which provides a set of information about religion in the virtual space in order to be used by users. But 'online religion' suggests a condition in which an individual performs his or her religious rites in virtual space. It is about being with the

[7] Oliver Krueger, "The Internet as Distributor and Mirror of Religious and Ritual Knowledge," *Asian Journal of Social Science* 32, no. 2 (2004): 183–197, at 183.

[8] Morten T. Hojsgaard and Maargit Warburg, eds., *Religion and Cyberspace* (London: Routledge, 2005); Rachel Wagner, *Godwired: Religion, Ritual, and Virtual Reality* (Abingdon, Oxon; New York: Routledge, 2012); C. Helland, D. E. Cowan, "Online-Religion/Religion-Online and Virtual Communities," *Religion and the Social Order* 8 (2000): 205–24; M. T. Hojsgaard, and M. Warburg, "Cyber-religion: On the Cutting Edge between the Virtual and the Real," in *Religion and Cyberspace* edited by M. T. Hojsgaard and Maargit Warburg (London: Routledge, 2005), 50–64; Mohammed El-Nawawy, and Sahar Khamis, *Islam Dot Com: Contemporary Islamic Discourses in Cyberspace* (New York; Basingstoke: Palgrave Macmillan, 2009); F. Foltz, "Religion on the Internet: Community and Virtual Existence," *Bulletin of Science, Technology & Society* 23, no. 4 (2003): 321–30; Mark Grimshaw, ed., *The Oxford Handbook of Virtuality* (Oxford; New York: Oxford University Press, 2014).

masses without getting involved in face-to-face contact. This is a new experience of individualism without the isolation of society, and socialism without an interruption of individualism.[9]

Whereas the traditional use of media for communication of religious content was so to say a one-way path, the virtual or internet religion is very much interactive.[10] It creates large spaces for the expression of religion and religious experiences through mutual exchange among the participants. There comes into existence a kind of virtual religious community around this exchange and communication.[11] Virtual religion allows room for the expressions of the differing perceptions and experiences of consumers of religions and religious goods. In keeping with the general digital mediation of our global world, virtual religion allows the experience of virtual communities, pilgrimages, conversions, and so on. Further, unlike the physical space, the virtual space offers immense opportunities to shape freely one's religious identities without the constraint of tradition or religious authority. Moreover, it provides religious alternatives to the traditional ones.

What has been said bears significant social implications. Whereas through exclusionary practices religious hierarchy creates normativity regarding the sacred spaces and access to them, the virtual religion seems to rip them open. For example, in India, where caste is connected with ritual purity-pollution, and the "untouchables" are victims of exclusionary practices, virtual religion could bring about a sense of freedom and openness. Similarly, the proscriptions of women entering sacred spaces in almost all religions stand challenged by virtual religion where women

[9] Saied Reza Ameli, "Virtual Religion and Duality of Religious Spaces," *Asian Journal of Social Science* 37, no. 2, (2009): 208–231, at 217.

[10] Whereas religious traditions with strong hierarchical structure do not have an interactive structure in their presence on the internet, the religious traditions with less or no real hierarchy seem to be open to interaction. One author compares the Vatican website with no possibility for feedback but only providing the institutional services and pieces of information, with small religious groups like Zoroastrianism and new Afro-American religious movements are open to an interactive mode of religion. Cf. Oliver Krueger, "The Internet as Distributor and Mirror of Religious and Ritual Knowledge," *Asian Journal of Social Science* 32, no. 2 (2004): 183–197.

[11] Gregory Price Grieve, *Cyber Zen: Imagining Authentic Buddhist Identity, Community, and Practices in the Virtual World of Second Life* (New York: Routledge, 2016). The online means are also used to create fundamentalist virtual communities. Neil Krishan Aggarwal, *The Taliban's Virtual Emirate: The Culture and Psychology of an Online Militant Community* (New York: Columbia University Press, 2016).

could feel liberated from traditional religious practices. In the cyberspace, to be religious is an interactive exercise.

> The internet may enrich the process of identity construction through providing new possibilities of creating and acquiring the tools, skills and knowledge needed for handling the increased insecurity and ambivalence of late modern society. Thus, the Internet might expand the possibilities of the individual in his or her project of constructing a meaningful, integrated self-identity that might also be communicated in social interaction.[12]

In the digital space or world, what we have is a new religious mediation, different from the traditional ones, and this new mediation goes to reshape religious identities. Historically, significant changes in religion and religious identity took place with the advent of new media. A significant contribution of the digital world is to have made visible and audible the plural forms of religious expressions. Thanks to the digital mode of religion, plurality has become something normal, and new possibilities of dialogue and understanding among religions are expanding.[13]

Digital religions are not without their ambiguities and limitations. I do not want to enter into them at this juncture as it would take us afar from our main point of consideration. All that I want is to highlight virtual religion as a new mode of being religious in our globalized world. The virtual religion has also contributed to a reappraisal of the interconnection between religion and space. Henri Lefebvre distinguishes three kinds of spaces—physical, mental, and social.[14] In virtual religion, the association of physical sacred places get transformed into mental space and digital social space of encounter. If space is not neutral and is produced culturally,

---

[12] Morten T. Hojsgaard and Maargit Warburg, eds., *Religion and Cyberspace* (London: Routledge, 2005), 125. See also Lorne L. Dawson, and Douglas E. Cowan, eds., *Religion Online: Finding Faith on the Internet* (New York; London: Routledge, 2004).

[13] The online religion is also full of bigotry, hate-inciting materials, and it also helps to build up insulated and aggressive communities prone for violence and terrorism. See Morten T. Hojsgaard and Maargit Warburg, eds., *Religion and Cyberspace* (London: Routledge, 2005); Further, internet has also become a source of cyber-conflict among the religions, especially with radical religious groups venting all kinds of queer views and opinions. Concerning Hinduism, see, R. Robinson, "Virtual warfare: The internet as the new site for global religious conflict," *Asian Journal of Social Science* 32, no.2 (2004): 198–215.

[14] Cf. Henri Lefebvre, *The Production of Space* (Oxford: Blackwell, 1991). See also R. Janzen, "Reconsidering the Politics of Nature: Henri Lefebvre and The Production of Space," *Capitalism, Nature, Socialism* 13, no. 2 (2002): 96–116.

religiously, and socially (think of Jerusalem, Rome, Mecca, or Varanasi), so are the religious spaces of the digital world.

Further, online religion brings into the virtual sphere the good and the bad of both religion and online. For example, the perceived anonymity that the virtual world gives otherwise sensible people the license to be intolerant and more fundamentalist. Fundamentalist beliefs held in check in the physical world have no lid in the virtual world. Open-minded religious viewpoints are virtually assassinated online. Fundamentalists spew venom at the people involved, and intimidate them with threats of violence and bodily harm. Some women who have voiced progressive religious views have often had their home addresses posted online with the not-so-subtle message to "shut up or else."

## BODILY PRACTICES AND FESTIVE RELIGIONS

Body has become a new site of religious celebration. Till recent times, there has not taken place much theorizing on the body. It was a neglected issue, and was mostly relegated to biological sciences. However, recent developments in the field of cultural studies, feminist studies, and sociology of knowledge have brought to the fore the importance of proper theorizing on body.[15] For the body is the window to the understanding of many cultural expressions and social interactions. Since social categories get inscribed on to the body, the body is a crucial site for the study of social interactions. The body is also the site of exercise of power, control, and surveillance as Michael Foucault has shown through empirical studies. He has popularized the concept of bio-power. As it plays a significant role in the acquisition, dissemination, and transmission of knowledge, the body has an important epistemological role and significance as well.

---

[15] Margaret Lock, "Cultivating the Body: Anthropology and Epistemologies of Bodily Practice and Knowledge," *Annual Review of Anthropology* 22 (1993): 133–155. In contemporary times, the French thinker Michel Foucault highlighted the body as a site for the exercise of power (bio-power) and went to trace the genealogy of corporal punishment, and the technology for repression and control of human bodies. See Jean-Jacques Courtine, *Déchiffrer Le Corps: Penser Avec Foucault* (Grenoble: Milon, 2011); Jean-François Bert, *Michel Foucault: Regards Croisés Sur Le Corps: Histoire, Ethnologie, Sociologie [sous La Direction De Jean-François Bert]* (Strasbourg: Portique, 2007); Hubert L. Dreyfus and Paul Rainbow, *Michel Foucault. Beyond Structuralism and Hermeneutics* (Chicago: The University of Chicago Press, 1983); Colin Jones, and Roy Porter, eds., *Reassessing Foucault: Power, Medicine and the Body* (London: Routledge, 1998).

In most mainline religious traditions, body, sensuality and sexuality have been viewed in negative terms, and ultimate bliss has been interpreted as a liberation from the body binding one to this-worldly concerns. However, in marginal religious traditions and in popular and indigenous religious cults, body and physiological practices have always found a prominent place. This is true of almost all religious traditions in the world. These neglected past traditions have found a new lease of life under the present conditions of modernity and globalization. These somatic practices are reimagined to suit the present-day needs of a global society.

Well-known is the fact that bodily practices play an essential role in the religious life of the overwhelming majority of people in the globe—peoples of Asia, Africa, Oceania, and Latin America. These bodily practices are part of the *cultivation of the self* in Asian traditions, which are intrinsically related to religious and spiritual existence. There is no need to elaborate on the role of dance and corporeal movements in the religious worship of the African, Caribbean, and Latin American peoples. They have a cosmology of their own into which these religious practices, spirituality, and worship harmoniously get integrated. Unfortunately, most classical anthropologists and sociologists of religion have looked at them as ritual practices and interpreted them from the framework of a ritual theory which itself was based on mind-body dichotomy. In this frame, the bodily rituals are empty unless they are invested with meaning from the belief system. Instead of discussing the cosmology into which these bodily religious practices fit, which may not be easy for the readers in the Global North to grasp, let me present two Western authors whose insights, fortunately, help understand the role of bodily practices.[16] Both Pierre Bourdieu and Michel de Certeau have argued against an epistemology that makes a dualism of body and mind, and against the assumption that mental structures and operations precede body and its operations. Adopting the anthropologist Mau's term *habitus*, Bourdieu draws our attention to the repetition of bodily practices of everyday life and their internalization through the socialization process.

To revert to religious practices, we note a trend nowadays to attain spiritual maturity through bodily ones, and this is spreading widely among all sections of people and religious traditions. Even in Islam which associates spiritual practice chiefly with prayer, today greater accent is placed on various forms of sensual and aesthetic practices. As Jonathan Shannon notes:

---

[16] More about this in the next chapter.

According to the great twelfth-century Muslim scholar, al-Ghazali (1058–1111), the spiritual life of the devout Muslim is formed not only through prayer but also aesthetic practices. Among these is the art of 'sanma' (audition), which denotes acts of listening and bodily practices associated with the achievement of ecstatic states.[17]

The well-known scholar of Chinese religions C.K. Yang tells us that the mainline religious traditions in China were as concerned about philosophy, doctrine, and ethical precepts like any other religion. It has all those ingredients generally associated with established religion.[18] At the same time, however, there have been diffused forms of religion that fused with many spheres of life.[19] These religious traditions were embodied in the materiality of life—prosperity, defense and safety, fortune and success, health, and healing. Many of the bodily, medical, and martial practices have to do with this type of religiosity.[20] As David Palmer and others note:

In the Chinese tradition, the body is the site for the battle against ghosts and demons whose attacks are made manifest through illness; it is also a site for physical fights against "bad guys", national enemies or oppressive rulers, such as in the martial arts tradition. The priests, exorcists, immortals, emperors, and errant warriors…all have one thing in common: it is through their bodies selected through the discipline of virtue, that the battle against the forces of chaos and corruption are waged. At the same time, their bodies are sites for refinement toward ever-higher levels of spirituality, nurturing health through harmony with cosmic forces and processes, and even tending to transcendence.[21]

In India, like in China, bodily exercises are not merely a technical means to keep it fit. Instead, they are ingredients of self-cultivation, self-discipline, cosmic energy, interconnectedness, spirituality, and mysticism. In this

[17] Jonathan Shannon, "The Aesthetics of Spiritual Practice and the Creation of Moral and Musical Subjectivities in Aleppo, Syria," *Ethnology* 43, no. 4 (Autumn, 2004): 381–391, at 381.
[18] Cf. C.K. Yang, *Religion in Chinese Society* (Berkeley; Los Angeles: University of California Press, 1961).
[19] Jonathan H. Shannon, "The Aesthetics of Spiritual Practice and the Creation," 381–391.
[20] Cf. David Palmer, Glenn Shive, Philip Wickeri, eds., *Chinese Religious Life* (Oxford; New York: 2011); Cf. also Avron Boretz, *Gods, Ghosts, and Gangsters: Ritual Violence, Martial Arts, and Masculinity on the Margins of Chinese Society* (Hawai'i: University of Hawai'i Press, 2011).
[21] David Palmer, *Chinese Religious Life*, p. 105.

sense, the practice of *yoga* in India, and the practice of *Zen*, *tai chi*, and *qigong* in East Asian traditions have a religious and spiritual anchorage.[22] Confucianism, Taoism, as well as Buddhism in China developed different forms of bodily exercises. They all saw the mind–body flow as part of their cosmological vision.

In the West, the eastern bodily practices were found to be esoteric even as they provided an avenue for escape from the anomie of modern life. The journey of the Beatles, Steve Jobs, Richard Gere, and such celebrities to India, Tibet, and other places in the Global South is an illustration of this trend. Instead of getting discarded as practices of a bygone age, Asian bodily practices are packaged in new formats and made available to a broader audience in the urban and rural societies. These practices help to free oneself from cultural and social constraints, as well as from the control of state and its power.

The fascination with these practices could be explained from the fact that they serve also as *a site of protest and resistance*. Empirical studies show, for example, how the Chinese peasants are making use of these traditional corporeal practices to resist the alienation of their lands by the state authorities and their bureaucracy.[23] *Falun Gong* religious movement which absorbed within itself *qigong* (popular Chinese religious bodily practices of breathing and meditation) was formed in 1992, and within a few years it has become a formidable religious and spiritual movement challenging the centralized Chinese state.[24] The Falun Gong protests have such a great mass appeal as they are based on the Chinese spiritual tradition that the Chinese Communist Party sees them as a great threat and has tried to control and suppress the movement, but without success. The movement has spread throughout the country and also in different parts of the world, galvanizing the protest against the Chinese state.

---

[22] Cf. Mircea Eliade, *Yoga: Immortality and Freedom*. Translated from the French by Willard R. Trask. 2nd edition (Routledge & Kegan Paul, 1982); Paul Tucker, and Don Last, *Tai Chi: For Inner Harmony and Balance* (London: Southwater, 2000); Caitlin C. Finlayson, "Performativity and the Art of Tai Chi: Understanding the Body as Transformative," *Southeastern Geographer* 55, no. 3 (2015): 362–76.

[23] Interestingly, this kind of use of religious resources for protest not only for political but also economic reasons is made by the ethnic and religious minorities in China. For a fascinating case study, see Qiangqiang Luo* and Joel Andreas, "Using Religion to Resist Rural Dispossession: A Case Study of a Hui Muslim Community in North-west China," *The China Quarterly* 226 (June 2016): 477–498.

[24] Benjamin Penny, *The Religion of Falun Gong* (Chicago: Chicago University Press, 2012).

There is a deeper reason for the revival of these religiously and cultur-ally inspired somatic practices which one can understand better against the background of Chinese history. In Maoist China, individuals were made to surrender their bodies to the nation, which made use of it for labor and for the promotion of its communist ideology. It resulted in an unprece-dented massification turning individuals into cogs in the body machine of the party. The post–cultural revolution period and the new economic openings have created some space for the regaining of one's own body and selfhood. In this context, the traditional bodily practices like *qigong* have become a new means to take possession of one's self, liberated from external controls.[25]

## BODY, RELIGION, AND CONTEMPORARY CULTURE

In the practice of religion, never before has the role of the body been rec-ognized as it is today. Contemporary culture has raised to a new level the body in the sphere of religion and religious experiences. What globaliza-tion has done is to catapult to the center stage the marginalized traditions of the body. It is not a mere reproduction of old forms; rather, many new bodily expressions of being religious are created and followed in different parts of the world. We see it today, for example, in the globalization of Pentecostal experience in the shaking of bodies, rhythmic clapping con-joined with vociferation of prayers and outcry of confessions. Its sensorial and embodied religious experience proves attractive to an ever larger num-ber of people all over the world.[26] We see this also in movements like Hare Krishna where religiosity is expressed in public spaces and thoroughfares

[25] Qigong Jian Xu, "Body, Discourse, and the Cultural Politics of Contemporary Chinese," *The Journal of Asian Studies* 58, no. 4 (November 1999): 961–991.
[26] Cf. Jonathan R. Baer, "Redeemed Bodies: The Functions of Divine Healing in Incipient Pentecostalism," *Church History* 70, no. 4 (December 2001): 735–771; Mariaconcetta Costantini, "Reconfiguring the Gothic Body in Postmodern Times: Angela Carter's Exposure of Flesh-Inscribed Stereotypes," in *Gothic Studies* 4, no. 1 (2002): 14–27. Miranda Klaver, and Linda van de Kamp, "Embodied Temporalities in Global Pentecostal Conversion," *Ethnos* 76, no. 4 (2011): 421–425; A.F. Droogers, "Globalization and Pentecostal Success," in A. Corten; R. Marshall-Fratani, eds., *Between Bale and Pentecost: Transnational Pentecostalism in Africa and Latin America* (London: Hurst, 2001), 41–61. John Brahinsky, "Pentecostal Body-Logics: Cultivating a Modern Sensorium," in *Cultural Anthropology* 27, no. 2 (2012): 215–238.

through dances to the accompaniment of drums.[27] What were once local experiences of bodily religious experience today have travelled across the world and have become global.

The experiences of the Global South with body-inscribed religiosity seems to echo also in the postmodern thought. In postmodern thought, the very formation of individuality takes place through public presentation of the body, and in feminist theorizing the body is in a way constructed through discourses and everyday practices which get then internalized.[28] The psychosomatic unity also gets reflected in the type of postmodern religiosity, experienced as a corporal as well as a spiritual reality. No wonder then that the experience-based global and postmodern religiosity emphasizes healing.[29]

## DANCE, RELIGION, AND BODY

When Chung Hyun Kyun, a Korean woman theologian danced at the WCC General Assembly in Canberra (1991) and invoked the spirit of ancestors, it electrified the participants and shook Christians of numerous denominations. This could not be otherwise. For those engrossed in the world of words and enthralled by rituals, witnessing religion in exotic and ecstatic dance form appeared scandelous. And yet, dance represents a very

[27] Angela Burr, and International Society for Krishna Consciousness, *I Am Not My Body: A Study of the International Hare Krishna Sect* (New Delhi: Vikas, 1984); E. Burke Rochford, *Hare Krishna in America* (New Brunswick, N.J.: Rutgers University Press, 1985); Edwin F, Bryant, and Maria Ekstrand, eds., *The Hare Krishna Movement: The Postcharismatic Fate of a Religious Transplant* (New York; Chichester: Columbia University Press, 2004); J. Isamu Yamamoto, *Hinduism, TM, and Hare Krishna*. Zondervan Guide to Cults & Religious Movements. (Grand Rapids, Michigan: Zondervan Publishing House, 2016).

[28] I Varga, "The Body—The New Sacred? The Body in Hypermodernity," *Current Sociology* 53, no. 2 (2005): 209–235; Judith Butler, *Gender Trouble: Feminism and the Subversion of Identity* (New York; London: Routledge, 1989); Philip A. Mellor and Chris Shilling, *Re-forming the Body. Religion, Community and Modernity* (London: Sage Publications, 1997).

[29] We could observe many similarities of global Pentecostalism to some characteristics of postmodernity. To cite some examples, the attention to the present, here, and now without bothering overly about the past—something characteristic of postmodernity—could be identified in Pentecostal and similar forms of contemporary religious experiences. Among other characteristics would be freedom from attachment to any hierarchical conception of life and society, the attention to narratives rather than to doctrines, and greater emphasis on community and community experience of religion rather than religion viewed and experienced by atomistic individuals as a private matter.

significant bodily practice in religion which deserves greater attention than it has been accorded.

As is well known, most influential Western thinkers have viewed religion primarily as a matter of belief and have interpreted its various expressions in terms of their meaning. This dominant perspective got universalized and has become a standard approach to the study of religion. The intellectual and textual engagement with religion led to hot debates on the relationship between the cognitive regimes of belief and reason. For these thinkers, the process of cognition and formulation of thought are the gateways to truth, including religious truths whose objectivity depends upon its meaning structure. This kind of approach led Kant, the chief European Enlightenment figure, to consider "Religion within the Limits of Reason." Such a knowledge-centered and text-driven approach to religion, prevalent even today, led to the eclipse of the body in the practice of religion. If at all, bodily expressions are valued for the *meaning* supposed to be lurking in them. For example, in ritual performances, one is attentive to the meaning behind the gestures and symbols. The anthropological studies of ritual generally suffer from a separation of meaning from actions. In fact,

> The effect of the British and American semiotic traditions has been to maintain an analytical separation between religious meanings, found in myths and sacred texts, and bodily experiences, understood as a neutral template upon which mythical and sacred meanings are inscribed.[30]

In theological explanations of sacramental rituals, the meaning behind those practices are explained and highlighted. In this general environment, dance too gets interpreted as a medium to represent religious truths, and hence as a means in religious communication. The classical work by Catherine Bell on rituals bears out such a tendency. As Kimerer LaMothe observes:

> Only when we assume that religious phenomena are like texts can we assume that in the process of learning languages, deciphering texts (whether written or enacted), and translating meaning from a foreign context to our own will produce objective scholarship, a rational perspective on "religion" .... In relation to dancing, for example, when scholars approach it as symbolic action of dancing itself, they assume that interpreting the dance entails

---

[30] Jonathan Shannon, "The Aesthetics of Spiritual Practice and the Creation of Moral and Musical Subjectivities in Aleppo, Syria," *Ethnology* 43, no. 4 (Autumn, 2004): 381–391, at 382.

*reading* the gestures as expressions of stories or states of consciousness and translating this body language into rationally-defensible motivations.[31]

In organized religious rituals, physical and kinesthetic sensations too get textualized and interpreted, as, for example, the gestures of the priest in the Roman Catholic mass. Now, the introduction of dance into Roman Catholic liturgy, in the name of inculturation, was supposed to be an innovation.[32] But then it remains a peripheral element at the fringes to an already-well-defined, structured, and norm-bound liturgy according to the standardized Roman Missal. Dance is viewed as contributing to the meaning of liturgical performance. Dance becomes a "form of knowing."[33] The weight of Catholic tradition is so overwhelming that it may not be easy for its many believers to accept dance and bodily movement as a way of experiencing faith *valid in itself*, and not in terms of the meaning it is expected to convey. Here is an opening to the global transformation of religion. That said, when the Africans dance in the liturgy, it would be quite absurd to look for meaning.[34] Dance is so innate in the African ethos and tradition that the very performance of it turns into a valuable worship.

Globalization and postmodernity invite religions to rethink the dance performance closer to the nature of religion and everyday life. If the study of religion and theories about it were woven in the past around reason, development of thought, and doctrines, today, under conditions of globalization, the human body presents a very crucial resource and arena to understand religion and interpret it. In other words, human bodies are not merely a medium and representation of religion (viewed mainly in the realm of thought) but form part of the reality of religion itself.

The disregard in Christian history for dance has several causes. Dance was associated with diversion, entertainment. Hence, it was disentangled from the realm of the sacred with which religion has to do. Some considered dance as something associated with the realm of the nonreasonable,

---

[31] Kimerer L. LaMothe, "Why Dance? Toward a Theory of Religion as Practice and Performance," *Method and Theory in the Study of Religion* 17, no. 2 (2005): 101–133, at 111.

[32] Cf. Francis Peter Barboza, *Christianity in Indian Dance Forms* (Delhi, India: Sri Satguru Publications, 1990).

[33] Martin Blogg, *Dance and the Christian Faith: Dance: A Form of Knowing* (London: Hodder & Stoughton, 1985).

[34] M. Huet, *The Dance, Art and Ritual of Africa* (S.l.: Collins, 1978); Michel Huet, and Claude Savary, *Africa Dances* (London: Thames & Hudson, 1995); Peter Larlham, *Black Theater, Dance, and Ritual in South Africa* (Ann Arbor, Mich.: UMI Research Press, 1985).

feminine in its value, and cultivated by the leisured class. Though there is a wealth of material about dance in the Christian scriptures, to most theologians and Christian thinkers it did not occur to be something that could be an integral part of religious experience. However, there are some laudable exceptions in the Global North like Isadora Duncan and Gerard van der Leeuw, who, going against the grain, tried to highlight the role of body and dance in the practice of religion. What made Duncan unique was that she saw dance as a force that reinvigorates religion and confers it a unique dimension.

> For Duncan, dance renews "religion" by generating new ideals of the human relation to the constitutive forces of the universe—ideals of good, beauty, and love; and it does so when a dancer moves from an awakened soul... Supported by her family, she nurtured her passion for dancing into a conviction that dancing is the art capable of overcoming western Christian antipathy to the body she believed that dance could generate new ideals of bodily being as "holy"... She envisioned a future where what counts as "dance" would be practiced and performed as "religion", and where ideas and actions recognized as "religion" would be accountable to the practice of dancing.[35]

When religion was looked at quintessentially as a matter of belief and reason, one could hardly expect a different view of dance as affirming the sensual in the experience of faith. Further, if a religion views the body *in opposition to* divinity conceived as disembodied, then it is difficult to reconcile this belief with the practice of dance, much less to experience the divine *through* the body. However, there are religions like Christianity which do affirm that the divine has become flesh (Jn 1: 14), and yet have shown reluctance and even fierce resistance at times to any bodily manifestation of religious experience. Certain moralist orientations saw the flesh as weakness and a force restraining the believers from the experience of the divine. In other religious traditions such as Hinduism and many indigenous religions, the body is positively valued and has a significant place in religious existence. The classic *natya* śā*stra* affirms the value of the body in the religious realm.[36] Dance is viewed as expressing love and devotion to divinity. It is also a partaking in the creation of the world which takes place

---

[35] L. LaMothe, "Why Dance?," 116–118.

[36] Cf. Anupa Pande, *A Historical and Cultural Study of the Nāṭyaśāstra of Bharata* (Jodhpur: Kusumanjali, 1991); Radhavallabh Tripathi, *Lectures on the Nāṭyaśāstra* Publication

through divine cosmic dance (the dance of Shiva). To dance is to get united with the divine and share in its cosmic play. In India, there has been a long tradition of dance associated with temples where the *devadasis*—women symbolically married to gods—perform dances as an integral part of temple worship.[37] Unlike verbal expressions which often fail to transform, dance through its rhythmic movement creates vibration, change and transformation. The exterior movement could have a profound transforming effect on the consciousness of the performer and on the audience of believers.

In a dance of trance, the persona of the dancer is taken hold of by god or goddess, and it becomes in reality a divine dance. Here dance is not merely a vehicle or a means to the divine, but itself becomes an encounter with god or goddess; the devotee becomes an empty vessel for the divine and its action. Further, in Vajrayana Buddhism, body plays a crucial role in the enlightenment. In Islam too there is a whole tradition of ecstasy-inducing dances which one finds in the mystical tradition of Mevlana Jalal ad-Din Rumi. The body is viewed as a microcosm. All these examples tell us about the deep transformative potential somatic movements and dance have in the realm of religious experience

## RELIGION ON WHEELS

From time immemorial pilgrimage to sacred spaces and sites has been a form of popular religiosity.[38] A pilgrim undertakes a sacred journey for various religious motives. In the Hindu tradition, sacred spaces—particular mountains, particular landscape, the junction where rivers meet (called *tirtha*)—are replete with salvific power in themselves, even at times independent of any association with a deity. However, these sacred spaces are mostly associated with particular gods or goddesses whose *darshan* (vision)

---

of the Center of Advanced Study in Sanskrit. Class F; no. 1. (Pune: Center of Advanced Study in Sanskrit, University of Poona, 1991).

[37] S. Jeevanandam, and Rekha Pande, *Devadasis in South India: A Journey from Sacred to Profane Spaces* (New Delhi: Kalpaz Publications, 2017).

[38] Surinder Mohan Bhardwaj, G. Rinschede, eds., *Pilgrimage in World Religions: Presented to Prof. Dr. Angelika Sievers on the Occasion of her 75th Birthday* (Berlin: Dietrich Reimer Verlag, 1988); Simon Coleman, and John Elsner, *Pilgrimage: Past and Present: Sacred Travel and Sacred Space in the World Religions* (London: British Museum Press, 1995); Ellen Badone, and Sharon R. Roseman, eds., *Intersecting Journeys: The Anthropology of Pilgrimage and Tourism* (Urbana-Champaign, Ill.: University of Illinois Press, 2004).

the pilgrims seek by undertaking pilgrimages.[39] People go on pilgrimage also to fulfill religious obligations as the Hajj pilgrimage to Mecca and Medina; to attain illumination such as Buddhist pilgrimages to Kyoto in Japan; to cleanse oneself from evil as in the case of pilgrimage to Lhasa in Tibet and to river Ganges in Hinduism; to do penance and get remission of sins as in Catholicism by visiting shrines and basilicas privileged with indulgences; and to get healed in mind and body as in the case of pilgrimage to Lourdes.

The age of globalization, through its fast modes of transportation, has made access to pilgrim centers easier and faster. In southern India, the abode of deity Ayyappa on the Western Ghats attracts hundreds of thousands of pilgrims who often reach his sanctum, stretching hundreds of miles, traveling on foot. Today, many pilgrims not only travel by bus and trains but increasingly also by air. In India, the pilgrimage to Haridwar and the meeting point of three sacred rivers (*Triveni Sangam*) in Allahabad have been among the most popular ones. The *Kumba mehla* witnesses a record gathering of humans in one place—over twenty million. The traditional pilgrimage centers are also becoming increasingly international. We hear about apparitions and miracles of gods and goddesses which attract more and more devotees. One more recent example is the Marian pilgrim shrine of Medjugorje. In Japan, we may refer to the Gion Matsuri Festival of Kyoto, which brings together a large gathering of people.

If pilgrimage seems to be a perennial trope with its enduring appeal even today in modern conditions of globalization,[40] it has been also a mixed bag. It is a mixture of disparate elements—dimensions of penance, restraint, and control of the body and at the same time relaxation and enjoyment of the company of others, the discovery of new places and lands, contemplation of nature and so on.[41] There is an interstitial border between pilgrimage and tourism. Today this has become increasingly evident. One speaks in the same breath of pilgrimage and tourism.[42] Rightly

---

[39] Cf. *Brill's Encyclopedia of Hinduism*, vol. I (Leiden: Brill, 2009), 381–410.

[40] Cf. Jill Dubisch, and Michael Winkelman, eds., *Pilgrimage and Healing*, 1st edition (Tucson, AZ: University of Arizona Press, 2005).

[41] John Eade and Michael Sallnow, eds., *In Contesting the Sacred: The Anthropology of Christian Pilgrimage* (Eugene, Oregon: Wipf& Stock, 1977), 1–29.

[42] William H. Swatos, Jr. eds., *On the Road to Being There: Studies in Pilgrimage and Tourism in Late Modernity* (Leiden and Boston: Brill Publishers, 2006); see also Ellen Badone, and Sharon R. Roseman, eds., "Approaches to the Anthropology of Pilgrimage and Tourism," in *Intersecting Journeys: The Anthropology of Pilgrimage and Tourism* (Urbana-

then it is characterized as "intersecting journeys." Hyphenated pilgrim-tourist is becoming a standard pattern.

No doubt, there is a commodification of pilgrimage in the way it is organized and in the way pilgrim centers function. There is often an over-lap of motivations too. It would be utopian in this age of globalization to expect a scheme of pilgrimage devoid of economy and commodification. Besides technical facilitation, globalization has woven around pilgrimage a whole new kind of spirituality and quest for the divine closely connected with the materiality of life. In an environment of competition and scarcity of resources, people seek the blessings from gods and goddesses for suc-cess in their enterprises. This is especially so in regions of the Global South.

On the other hand, in the Global North too where the so-called secu-larization has been taking place, we note the revival of pilgrimages. We could observe this in several parts of Europe. Traditional centers of pil-grimage like the Camino de Santiago (Santiago Way) in Spain have cast a spell on the youth in quest of spirituality and self-understanding. The experience of peregrination seems to have a lasting impact on the young pilgrims. Even in a modernized society as Sweden, we note the rediscov-ery of the traditional pilgrimage to Santiago. New rituals are created as young pilgrims perambulate together long stretches. In the process of walking, the pilgrims true to the spirit of religious cosmopolitanism, adopt spiritual techniques from other religious traditions. For example, there is a shift in accent in the understanding of walking. In the past, often the challenging physical aspect of exertion in long pilgrimage-walk got emphasized. The influence of Eastern religions has given to the physicality of walking a new dimension. Every step the pilgrim takes is transformed into an exercise in mindfulness about which Buddhism speaks abundantly. Walking becomes a spiritual journey of discovery, transformation, self-reflection and meditation. Aspects of leisure, like forays into the world of nature are integrated into this pilgrimage. "In this way," as Lena Gemzöe notes,

> the new practice of pilgrimage opens up ritual creativity, drawing on various sources with no strict boundaries between aspects conventionally thought of

Champaign, Ill: University of Illinois Press, 2004), 1–23; Simon Coleman, and John Eisner, *Pilgrimage Past and Present in the World Religions* (Cambridge, Mass: Harvard University Press, 1995); E. Alan, *Pilgrimage in the Hindu Tradition: A Case Study of West Bengal* (New York: Oxford University Press, 1984). There is also available an *International Journal of Religious Tourism and Pilgrimage* with inter-disciplinary approach and covering many reli-gious traditions.

as secular, religious or spirituality ... The Camino exists as a liminoid space outside both the social structures of everyday life and the realm of institutionalized religion, thus offering renewal through ritual, to participants with widely varying needs and backgrounds.[43]

There are other pilgrim centers which have found reconfiguration under the conditions of globalization: the Shrine of Saint Mary Magdalene in France, the Marian shrine in Częstochowa in Poland, and Medjugorje in former Yugoslavia. These shrines attract a lot of pilgrims—young and old. The new quest of spirituality among the youth is drawing them to Taizé in France.[44] It has become a rallying point of vibrant youth spirituality in an environment of music, meditation, informality, intercultural encounters, narration, and exchanges of experiences. The atmosphere of freedom to question religious traditions and institutions and the absence of any spiritual imposition from above create the right milieu for the youth to discover responses to their problems, quests, and aspirations. Thousands of young people flocking to Taizé are enchanted by the lively community of the brothers there, enraptured by the liturgy, lured by the life of simplicity, and enthralled by the sense of beauty exuding all around. The cultivation of art there seems to elevate them to new contemplative and mystical experiences. Striking is the fact that these are not an outcome of teaching and learning, but the result of spiritual discovery. In the general environment of silence, prayer, chanting and singing, the young people, who otherwise do not heed visiting churches or attending services, get immersed in the environment of Taizé. In Taizé, the youth could feel that they are praying and living spirituality with all their sensorial experiences of art and pure beauty. For many European youth, Taizé presents a contrast experience to the baroque churches back home with the traditional liturgy of frozen words and gestures. If globalization brings mobility of the young people from Europe and other parts of the world, the sense of postmodernity of our times lets them live and express religious faiths in new ways and expressions. It is interesting to note that art and music have

---

[43] Lena Gemzöe, "Ritual Creativity, Emotions and the Body," *Journal of Ritual Studies* 28, no. 2 (2014): 65–75, at 65 & 73.

[44] Frère Roger, *Communauté De Taizé* (Taizé: Les Presses De Taizé, 1980); Vladimir Sichov, and Brother Roger, *The Taizé Experience* (London: Geoffrey Chapman Mowbray, 1990); Kathryn Spink, *A Universal Heart: The Life and Vision of Brother Roger of Taizé*, 3rd ed. Centenary ed. (London: SPCK, 2015).

not remained in Taizé but have travelled all over the world evoking spiritual experience even among the youth who are not able to visit this place.

In short, Taizé is an example of the traditional trope of pilgrimage reconfigured in response to the challenges of modernity and globalization. In the reinvented modern pilgrimage, we will note the blurring of many boundaries. As Coleman and Esner observe:

> It may be that conventionally secular forms of pilgrimage, from tourism to museum visiting, are no more than distant analogies for the phenomenon of sacred travel, despite their close structural resemblances and historical links with pilgrimage in the world religions. Yet it is a mark of the power of pilgrimage as a ritual structure in human experience that so many of its qualities should have taken contemporary forms. Despite revolutions in communication technology and cultural identity, pilgrimage has proved remarkably persistent in adapting to and even appropriating the innovations of secular modernity.[45]

The new religious and spiritual experiences centered around sacred localities have facilitated both bonding and bridging. The confluence of people from different parts of a country or from the world inspired by religious and spiritual motives creates a sense of community and togetherness. There is a bonding among those affiliated to a particular religious tradition to which a sacred shrine or space belongs. But increasingly today we observe, especially in Asia, that pilgrim centers are visited by people of other religious traditions too, in a spirit of universality and openness transcending the conventional religious boundaries. There is a shrine of Mary in the southern part of India on the east coast, known as Vailankanni, where Catholic pilgrims throng all through the year, but Hindu and Muslim pilgrims routinely outnumber them.[46] There are other Muslim sacred places which are visited regularly by Hindus. Many shrines have become centers of religious cosmopolitanism. More on religious cosmopolitanism in Chap. 13.

---

[45] Simon Coleman and John Eisner, *Pilgrimage Past and Present in the World Religions* (Cambridge, Mass: Harvard University Press, 1995), 220.

[46] Brigitte Sébastia, *Caste et christianisme à Vailankanni* (Pondicherry: CIDIF, 2008); A. Arokianathan, "Vailankanni as Tourist and Pilgrimage Centre," Unpublished doctoral dissertation (Tiruchirapalli: Bharathidhasan University, 2013). See also Alexander Henn, "Crossroads of Religions: Shrines, Mobility and Urban Space in Goa," *International Journal of Urban and Regional Research* 32 no. 3 (2008): 658–670.

## CONCLUSION

We observe two markedly different trends of religion and spirituality in the contemporary age of globalization. One trend finds new ways and channels of religious expression for our present times. This involves reforming and renewing traditional religion and interpreting its sources in new ways. However, there is another trend which, despite all these changes, is not convinced about religion at all. Spirituality *without* deity and religion seems to be the in-thing for many people today. People who follow this trend at the same time manifest a lot of spiritual depth and sense of compassion and solidarity in day-to-day life. Their attitude and behavior may not be explained by secularization either in which one seeks to privatize religion based on some past historical experiences. I am referring here to a large number of people who seek to live a spirituality which they are not ready to equate with religiosity identified in practice with institutionalized religion.[47]

This new trend of spirituality without religion is not new to the present age of globalization. It has its antecedents in the ancient civilizations of India, China, and the Greco-Roman world. The spiritual traditions of Buddhism and Jainism have as their foundational belief the nonexistence of God. They are ways of being in the world deeply committed to the transformation of the self and the world. In the Chinese civilization, Confucianism is a *way of life* rather than a *religion*, which prepared people to transform themselves and adopt an ethical and socially transformative behavior. Daoism showed the way to live in harmony with nature. Stoics and Epicureans did not busy themselves to placate gods or entreat their favors. Instead, they focused on a life of serenity and peace and heightening the quality of human life.[48] Spirituality without religion and community is not any marginal trend. It exercised probably no less influence than the theistic religious traditions in ancient civilizations.

Interestingly, at the present historical juncture of globalization, this pattern of *spirituality without religion* is gaining ground. This trend is especially pronounced among those attached to an established religion with strong authority structure as the Roman Catholic Church. For this reason, this orientation could also be called as *unchurched* spirituality.

[47] Sven Erlandson, *Spiritual but Not Religious: A Call to Religious Revolution in America* (Bloomington: Iuniverse, 2000).

[48] See Peter Heehs, *Spirituality without God. A Global History of Thought and Practice* (London: Bloomsbury, 2018).

Particularly the baby boomer generation of the West has exhibited a dissociation with established forms of societal relationship which also includes the religious ones.

The spiritual trends of a period reflect the social and cultural environment of the times. The general decline in the sense of community and civic life led to what figuratively Joseph Putnam called "Bowling alone."[49] A similar trend could be observed in the religious practice in which far from an interpretation of religion with reference to the sacredness of community (Durkheim), one undertakes a spiritual journey of one's own without requiring the support of institutional religion or community. It is very much in line with contemporary cultural trends shaped by new means of communication. The immense possibilities opened up through communication media create opportunities to become also the kind of spiritual person one chooses to be. According to Peter van der Veer, "the spiritual and the secular are produced simultaneously as two connected alternatives to institutionalized religion in Euro-American Modernity."[50]

On the other hand, spirituality without religion is not solely a phenomenon associated with the Christian West and its process of secularization. We find it in other religious traditions too, which seek to deterritorialize themselves and want to be universal and inclusive. An illustrative example is the transnational movements of spirituality and gurus who, though having their roots and religious practices in Hinduism, dissociate themselves from being identified as Hindu. The spirituality they proclaim could stand alone and does not require any institutional affiliation to Hinduism. There may be many reasons for this dissociation. One reason could be because globalization of a spirituality in order *to have universal appeal* cannot appear bound to a particular *brand* of religion or a particular *region* of the globe. The transnational spirituality the gurus advocate is often related to the Advaita philosophy with its universalism. Here is the case of a spirituality that is dissociated from its religious origin and roots.

---

[49] Robert D. Putnam, *Bowling Alone: The Collapse and Revival of American Community* (New York: Simon & Schuster, 2000).

[50] Peter van der Veer, "Spirituality in Modern Society," in *Social Research* 76, no. 4 (Winter 2009): 1097–1120, at 1097; see also Amanda J. Huffer, "Hinduism Without Religion: Amma's Movement in America," *Cross Currents* 61, no. 3 (2011): 374–98.

CHAPTER 7

# Globalization and New Religious Movements

Hindus follow Sunday worship in temples in the UK and the USA. In doing so, they do two things different from home. First, in their tradition there is no fixed sacred day of the week to attend the temple. Back home, they follow a different calendar of festivities according to the movement of celestial bodies. Second, there is no tradition of community worship. Worship is done as individuals, as families. To celebrate and worship as a community and that too regularly every Sunday is something quite alien to Hindu religious tradition. What the Hindus do in the UK and America is an adaptation to new conditions in an alien land and culture.[1]

To recall some historical antecedents, the missionary expansion of Christianity in the sixteenth century started with an antipathetic and hostile view of other religions and cultures. In due course, however, a new realization dawned, of which the Jesuit missionaries De Nobili in India[2]

---

[1] We will discuss this in detail in Chap. 8.

[2] Cf. S. Rajamanickam, ed., *Roberto De Nobili on Indian Customs* (Palayamkottai: De Nobili Research Institute, 1972); S. Rajamanickam, *The First Oriental Scholar* (Tirunelveli: De Nobili Research Institute, 1972); Vincent Cronin, *A Pearl to India. The Life of Roberto De Nobili. [With Plates, including a Portrait, and a Map]*. (London: Darton, Longman and Todd, 1966); Peter R. Bachmann, *Roberto Nobili 1577–1656: Ein Missionsgeschichtlicher Beitrag Zum Christlichen Dialog Mit Hinduismus* (Roma: Institutum Historicum S.I., 1972).

© The Author(s), under exclusive license to Springer Nature Switzerland AG 2021
F. Wilfred, *Religious Identities and the Global South*,
New Approaches to Religion and Power,
https://doi.org/10.1007/978-3-030-60738-8_7

and Matteo Ricci in China[3] were illustrious representatives. After negation of the religions and cultures of the people, the new strategy honed was that of *adaptation* or *accommodation* and more recently called *inculturation*. Inculturation accompanies the preaching of the gospel in different parts of the world. To cite another example, the *Tenrikyo* movement in Japan, which came into existence already in the nineteenth century, was found studying language and traditions of other continents to be able to have global reach out, even before the recent wave of globalization was set in motion.[4]

What we are attempting here in this chapter is to study new religious movements in the context of globalization,[5] which is something different from the project of adaptation or inculturation of mainline religions in particular cultural contexts as they expand globally. Our concern here is whether and how the conditions of modernity and globalization have been instrumental in the emergence of new religious expressions responding to the aspirations of a different period. At the same time, they also have triggered fierce controversies on different scores.[6]

[3] Cf. Jacques Gernet, *Chine et Christianisme: Action et Réaction* (Bibliothèque Des Histoires, 1982). Jonathan D. Spence, *The Memory Palace of Matteo Ricci* (New York: Viking, 1984); Mary Laven, *Mission to China: Matteo Ricci and the Jesuit Encounter with the East* (London: Faber & Faber, Bloomsbury, 2011); Vincent Cronin, *The Wise Man from the West. Matteo Ricci and his Mission to China* [An Account of the Missionary Service in China of Father Matteo Ricci. With Maps and Plates, including a Portrait.] (London: Harvill Press, 1955); R. Po-chia Hsia, *A Jesuit in the Forbidden City: Matteo Ricci 1552–1610* (Oxford: Oxford University Press, 2010).

[4] Masanobu Yamada, "Tenrikyo in Brazil from the Perspective of Globalization," *Revista de Estudos da Religião março* (2010): 29–49; Henry Van Straelen, "The Religion of Divine Wisdom: Japan's Most Powerful Religious Movement," *Folklore Studies* 13 (1954): 1–166.

[5] The literature on new religious movements is on the increase. Here are some works that could throw light on certain critical aspects of this phenomenon. Irving Hexham, and Karla O. Poewe, *New Religions as Global Cultures: Making the Human Sacred*, 1st ed. (London: Routledge, 2018); Irving Hexham, and Karla O. Poewe, *Understanding Cults and New Religions* (Grand Rapids: Eerdmans, 1986).

[6] James R. Lewis, and Jesper Aa Petersen, *Controversial New Religions*, 2nd ed. (New York: Oxford University Press, 2014).

## New Religious Movements, Cults, and Sects:
## The Question of Boundaries

Three phenomena, namely *new religious movements, cults,* and *sects,* are clubbed together not only in popular parlance but also in scholarly discourses. The three have this in common: They are very difficult to define and have gray borderlines. Despite the fogginess surrounding these three categories, still, some sort of differentiation is possible.

"Cults" are not a new phenomenon. In early religious history, the expression "cult" was used to refer to forms of worship directed to a particular deity or to a religious performance or ritual followed by a particular group of people. The concept of "cult" is so elastic today that it has acquired significantly different connotations. To illustrate with an extreme example, the Italian journalist Paolo Pontoniere designates Al Qaeda as a cult, and not merely as an extremist religious group.[7] There is a call for a new definition of cult.[8]

Some of the characteristics of a cult in modern sense would be the following: a centralized leader who holds authority over a group of people who live in a closed community situation of "we" versus "they"—the inimical ones; a process of brainwashing which robs people of their freedom and truns them into members of the cult. The cult groups have destructive practices inflicting harm on themselves (collective ritual suicides) and others through physical violence. Some of the cults gained notoriety as, for example, "Heaven's Gate,"[9] Aum Shinrikyo cult.[10] Cults, which have a long history, are also looked at as something threatening the orthodoxy of one's religious identity. There is also an undertone that cults are something secretive, to be counted among occult activities. Further, as Eugene Gallagher rightly notes, "the marking of difference through the

---

[7] Cf. Paolo Pontoniere, "Al Qaeda—Call it a Cult," in *Asia Week* (November 22, 2001).

[8] Geoffrey K. Nelson, "The spiritualist movement and the need for a redefinition of 'cult'," *Journal for the Scientific Study of Religion* 8, no. 1(spring 1969): 152–160.

[9] Cf. Winston Davis, "Heaven's Gate: A Study of Religious Obedience," *Nova Religio: The Journal of Alternative and Emergent Religions* 3, no. 2 (2000): 241–67.

[10] Cf. Ian Reader, "Imagined Persecution: Aum Shinrikyo, "Millennialism and the Legitimation of Violence," in *Millennialiam, Persecution, and Violence: Historical Cases,* edited by Catherine Wessinger (Syracuse: Syracuse University Press, 2000), 138–152; John R. Hall, Philip D. Schuyler and Sylvaine Trinh, *Apocalypse Observed: Religious Movements and Violence in North America, Europe and Japan* (London and New York: Routledge, 2000).

use of the term 'cult' is a very political matter indeed."[11] It is clear that, given all these implications, it is mistaken to equate and assume cults within the range of the new religious movements. We also need to highlight the fact that in contemporary times cults have become hugely controversial. They require a separate treatment.[12] In our considerations in this chapter we do not include cults under new religious movements. We shall maintain the distinction between the two.[13]

What about sects? From a Christian apologetic perspective, sects have been viewed as exclusive Christian groups dangerous to the orthodoxy of faith.[14] Some authors like van Baalen viewed the sects negatively from a theological perspective. Nevertheless, they saw in them an opportunity to learn as they are "the unpaid bills of the church."[15] From a sociological point of view, it is good to recall here the classical typology of church-sect by Max Weber[16] and Ernst Troeltsch[17] which generated a lot of discussion and critique in the study of religion. According to them, while church has inclusive membership and is accommodative to the society, sects are exclusive and define themselves against the values of the society and are in

[11] Eugene Gallagher, "'Cults' and 'New Religious Movements'," in *History of Religions* 47, no 2/3 (2007–2008): 205–220, at 218.

[12] Cf. James R. Lewis, *Cults: A Reference and Guide* (London: Routledge, 2014).

[13] Philip Jenkins, *Mystics and Messiahs: Cults and New Religions in American History* (New York: Oxford University Press, 2000); Douglas E. Cowan, and David G. Bromley, *Cults and New Religions: A Brief History,* 2nd ed. (Chichester: John Wiley & Sons, 2015).

[14] Cf. Walter Martin, *The Kingdom of the Cults. An Analysis of the Major Cult Systems in the Present Christian Era,* 1st British ed. (London, Edinburgh: Marshall, Morgan & Scott, 1967); Walter Martin, Jill Martin Rische, and Kurt Van Gorden, *The Kingdom of the Occult* (Nashville, Tenn.: Thomas Nelson, 2008).

[15] Jan Karel van Baalen, *The Chaos of Cults* (Grand Rapids: Eerdmans, 1956), 14.

[16] Introduced the distinction between "Church" and "Sect" in his well-known work, Max Weber, and Stephen Kalberg, *The Protestant Ethic and the Spirit of Capitalism,* New Introduction and Translation by Stephen Kalberg (Chicago; London: Fitzroy Dearborn, 2001); See also William H. Swatos, and Lutz Kaelber, eds., *The Protestant Ethic Turns 100: Essays on the Centenary of the Weber Thesis* (Colorado, USA; London: Paradigm, 2005).

[17] Ernst Troeltsch, *The Social Teachings of the Christian Churches* (London: Allen & Unwin, 1931); Benton Johnson, "A Critical Appraisal of the Church-Sect Typology," *American Sociological Review* 22 (February 1957): 88–92; See also William W. Mayrl, "Marx' Theory of Social Movements and The Church-Sect Typology," *Sociological Analysis* 37, no. 1 (1976): 19–31; John A. Coleman, S. J., "Church-Sect Typology and Organizational Precariousness," *Sociological Analysis* 29, no. 2 (1968): 55–66; William H. Swatos, "Weber or Troeltsch?: Methodology, Syndrome, and the Development of Church-Sect Theory," *Journal for the Scientific Study of Religion* 15, no. 2 (1976): 129–44.

tension with it. The concept of the denomination was introduced as a third polarity to indicate an advanced form of sect.

Could the new religious movements be characterized as "sects"? Though often presented as a neutral universal category, a sect is something that is best understood with reference to Christian history. The splinter groups from a mainline Christian church get qualified as "sects." It is a concept corelated to the concept of church: any rupture in the mainline church leads to the formation of sects. The applicability of "sects" concerning other religions is questionable, since it only reads into other religions what have been developments within Christian history.

"Neopaganism" is yet another nomenclature used to refer to new religious groups. Again, it would make sense only against the background of Christianity and Western Christian history. Christianity spread in the early centuries in cities first, and the people of the countryside remained bound to their traditional religions. The very fact of living in the countryside (*pagus* meaning countryside in Latin, and hence *pagani*—those from the countryside) was equal to be a non-Christian. The word "pagan," employed for long centuries in the Christian tradition acquired a very pejorative connotation. It was used to refer to peoples in the South who did not convert to Christianity, and hence considered inferior and not enlightened. Unfortunately, this spiteful term has found a new lease of life when it was used to refer to a new religious phenomenon. The expression neopaganism is fraught with prejudices, and it will not be used in our reflections.

Some would reserve the expression "New Religious Movements" only to those movements that have their origin outside Christianity. However, here we employ the expression to include all kinds of movements also originating from Protestant Christianity such as Pentecostalism, millennial groups, and so on.

Another question is whether fundamentalist movements of contemporary times are to be included under new religious movements. In a certain sense, yes. We have dedicated a whole chapter to the question of fundamentalism in a world of globalization.[18] In the present chapter we do not go into them either.

We have made some necessary distinctions which would help us see the circumscribed field of new religious movements more clearly. Now, instead of laying down a strict definition of new religious movements, I have

---

[18] See Chap. 5.

allowed this clarity to emerge while treating the issue. The analysis and comments made in treating this subject matter will throw more light on the boundaries or liminal spaces between different movements. The religious nature of some movements is self-evident, whereas this is not so in other cases which are often characterized as "quasi religions."

There is a difference in how a movement is looked at from the outside and by those inside. In some cases, the followers refuse to be identified as belonging to a religion or religious group. They shun the category of religion, preferring to define themselves with reference to spirituality, or integral wellbeing which also includes the wellbeing of the body through *yoga* or similar bodily practices. There are other movements that reject the attribute of "religious" to themselves as they claim to operate along secular and scientific lines as the Transcendental Meditation or offer self-help, psychotherapeutic means for realization of the full potential of the self. Under the rubric of "quasi-religious movements," one would include the "New Age" movement and other apocalyptically oriented groups. In our treatment, we include all these complexes of movements under the very generic name of "new religious movements."

Another way to make sense of new religious movements is to see them from the broader framework of the hierarchy of needs, a typology proposed by the psychologist Abraham Maslow,[19] to which we referred in another context in this volume when we spoke of identity-building.[20]

> The typology classifies new religions into five groups or levels according to the needs and values of their members: survival; safety; esteem; belongingness and love; self-actualization...These five levels [can be combined] into two broad groupings: traditionalism (levels 1–2) and personal development (levels 3–5).The traditionalist movements share a focus on conservative or traditional values, whereas those in levels 3–5 may be understood in terms of a spectrum of personal development from simple self-improvement to spirituality.[21]

[19] *Abraham Maslow: The Hierarchy of Needs* (Corby: Institute of Management Foundation, 1998).

[20] See Chap. 2.

[21] Cf. Lorne L. Dawson, ed., *Cults and New Religious Movements. A Reader* (Oxford: Blackwell Publishing, 2003), at 242.

In this scheme, the new religious movements would be responding to the needs at the level of personal development.

## AT THE ORIGINS OF THE NEW RELIGIOUS MOVEMENTS

When secularization theory was at its apogee, social scientists could not see in the new religious movements, anything but the remnants of the past religious world trying to come out in bits and pieces in new avatars. For example, Bryan Wilson and others, at the height of the theory of secularization reigning supreme in Europe and America, interpreted the new religious movements as attempts by religions which have been marginalized by secularization, to save themselves from falling into insignificance.[22] They were viewed as the last gasps of religion at the point of death.

Another theoretical explanation for the origin of these movements speaks of dislocation and disjuncture created by modernity and industrial society. The traditional religions could not cope up with the new situation, nor integrate within its architecture the evolving different spheres of life. New religions are viewed as a spiritual mechanism to grapple with the modern experience of alienation. In the context of the general cultural and social dislocation, there appeared gurus to support the new generation in their quest and help them resocialize themselves in new ways. This integrating function was crucial in the case of dropouts, drug users, and others.

These movements resemble, at the religious level, the other countercultural and anti-establishment movements of the young generation in Europe and America in the 1960s and 1970s when conventional behavioral modes, social relationships, and philosophy of conformity to the system were all challenged, bringing into life novel fashioning of the self and community. The countercultural movement, went hand in hand with the loss of credibility in traditional social and religious structures. The emergence of new religious movements would then be explained in terms of an attempt at an alternative free community open to the individual without any constraint and imposition. With the loosening of primordial ties of

---

[22] Cf. Bryan R Wilson, Jamie Cresswell, eds., and Institute of Oriental Philosophy European Center, *New Religions Movements: Challenge and Response* (London; New York: Routledge, 1999); Bryan R. Wilson, *The Social Dimensions of Sectarianism: Sects and New Religious Movements in Contemporary Society* (Oxford: New York: Clarendon Press; Oxford University Press, 1992); Bryan R. Wilson, *Religious Sects: A Sociological Study* [World University Library] (London: Weidenfeld & Nicolson, 1970).

family and neighborhood, the youth went in search of new forms of community where they could be at home.

Speaking of the new global religious movements, we could characterize them as reinventing of religion in response to the aspirations and exigencies of contemporary times often through a process of *bricolage*. The French word "bricolage" expresses the process by which something new is created as per need out of the fragments and materials already available. Here it is a matter of reassembling of existing religious bits and pieces into a new religious product.

Further, the modern technological developments and functional differentiation of the social systems, each one with its own inner dynamic, logic, and autonomy have led to the loss of the sense of community. New religious movements offer an opportunity to be part of a community/group of one's own choice to be able to fulfill spiritual and religious needs, instead of being constrained to an established religious community.

Most analysis of the origins of new religious movements is Eurocentric. They depart from the situation of an established religion like Christianity as the mainstream and view from this situation the origin and nature of new religious movements. In this perspective, some authors like Rodney Stark and William Bainbridge see in the new religious movements a new impetus for revitalizing the traditional mainline religion of Christianity. According to them, these movements complete and fill what have been lacking in the Christian tradition.[23] A slightly variant approach is to see in them a kind of synthesis between traditional Christian and eastern religious traditions.[24]

---

[23] These authors are critical of the typology of "Church-Sect," and try to define more precisely the concepts. For these authors, church would refer to the established religious organization, whereas sect is defined as deviance in beliefs and practices, however without departing from the mainstream. In contrast, they see in cults new beliefs and practices not compatible with the mainline religious belief system. Cf. Rodney Stark, and William Sims Bainbridge, *The Future of Religion: Secularization, Revival and Cult Formation* (Berkeley: University of California Press, 1984); Rodney Stark, and William Sims Bainbridge, *A Theory of Religion* [with a New Foreword by Jeffrey K. Hadden] (New Brunswick, N.J.: Rutgers University Press, 1996); Rodney Stark, and William Sims Bainbridge, *Religion, Deviance, and Social Control* (London: Routledge, 1996).

[24] Cf. Steven M. Tipton, *Getting Saved from the Sixties: Moral Meaning in Conversion and Cultural Change* [Foreword by Robert N. Bellah] (Berkeley, [Calif.]; London: University of California Press, 1982).

## INTERPRETING THE NEW RELIGIOUS MOVEMENTS

The new religious movements are so diverse that they seem to defy any common framework of interpretation. However, in order to gain greater conceptual clarity on their nature and traits, we could identify these movements from different points of view. To begin with, as to their being "new," Martin Marty distinguishes between "Old New Religions" and "New Old Religions."[25] What he means by "old new religions" are religious movements that have their roots in ancient religions in other parts of the world, especially Asia, but have emerged in new forms and expression in response to contemporary needs in the West. In their esoteric form, these movements appear to the Westerners as strikingly new, which may not be the case in regions of their origin. We could think of the Hare Krishna movement and other movements around any number of Hindu gurus offering spiritual remedies to European and American followers and disciples. On the other hand, by "New Old Religions" is meant mainly movements from the old religion of Europe and America—Christianity—in its new avatars in the form of many Christian groups like "born-again," Pentecostals, and so on. These do not lay emphasis on newness as on the revitalization of an old religion. As such, most Christian renewal or revitalization movements may not draw on different sources and are exclusively focused on its own tradition. However, a few other Christian movements indeed integrate within themselves striking new elements from other traditions and create a religious bricolage. One such example would be the Unification Church, which has incorporated in itself elements of the Christian tradition, aspects of Korean religious legacy, and contemporary science.[26] Such religions movements, as we noted, are different from the ones which have their root in one single religion which they want to innovate and make available in a renewed form to men and women of our times. Some authors like Hexham and Poewe would char-

---

[25] Cf. Thomas Robbins, "'Quo Vadis' the Scientific Study of New Religious Movements?," *Journal for the Scientific Study of Religion* 39, no. 4 (2000): 515–23, at 518.

[26] Cf. Ian Reader, "Imagined Persecution: Aum Shinrikyo, millennialism and the legitimation of violence," 138–152. Michael L. Mickler, and James R. Lewis, eds., *The Unification Church (Cults and New Religions)* (New York: London: Garland, 1990), 15–17; Herbert Richardson, ed., *Ten Theologians Respond to the Unification Church*, 1st ed. (Barrytown, New York: Rose of Sharon Press, 1981); George D. Chryssides, *The Advent of Sun Myung Moon: The Origins, Beliefs and Practices of the Unification Church* (London: Palgrave Macmillan, 1991).

acterize as new religions the ones that are syncretic in nature, drawing from different religious and cultural traditions. Only these, according to them, would qualify as new religions.[27]

According to another view held, for example, by Reender Kranenborg, to be counted as a new religion,[28] there should be a break with an old religious tradition. Obviously, it is so generic about what is to be treated as a break. We are thrown back to old questions like whether Christianity is a new religion or whether it is a renewal movement from within Judaism. We are also made aware of the contemporary discussion as to whether Christianity is to be interpreted as in continuity with Judaism, or as a break because of its new doctrinal content and way life.

From the perspective of body-soul, one could speak of movements that focus on the interfusion and immingling of body and soul and cultivate a religiosity and spirituality to promote this integration through practical strategies. Some movements concentrate on the body and its healing to such an extent that questions could be raised about whether they qualifiy to be classified under "religion" at all. Generally, many movements of thaumaturgical character promising healing, welfare, and wholeness pass for new religious movements, even though there are sufficient reasons not to include them under religious movements.

The new religious movements go along with the modern developments in that they do not seem to advocate the *restoring* of religions back to their earlier public position of power and centrality, but instead go along the *privatization* of religion providing the members opportunities to avail what suits their needs and inclinations most. In other words, restructuring in religion and religious practices happens when it follows patterns of the modern economy of market and consumption. In the global conditions of the economy, religion also becomes a global marketable good. This may be the case with some of the new religious movements. Religious needs are identified. Either the old religions are revitalized, or new religious identities are created in order to fulfill the needs of the self and groups.

---

[27] Cf. Irving Hexham, and Karla Poewe, *New Religions as Global Cultures: Making the Human Sacred,* chapter 3 (New York, London: Routledge, 2018).

[28] Here is perhaps the difference between "cults" and sects. If cult represents a rupture from a mainstream religious tradition, the sect would be a subdivision of the main religious traditions. Thus, one could speak of Hindu, Buddhist, or Christian sects. Cf. R. Kranenborg, and Mikael Rothstein, eds., *New Religions in a Postmodern World* (Aarhus; Oxford: Aarhus University Press, 2003).

Wendy Smith and others have studied the globalizing of new Asian religious movements from the perspective of market and management.[29] The analogy with marketing in the economic field has certain limits when applied to religion. For one thing, the goal of religion is not solely or primarily profit-making. As so many management gurus tell us, the purpose of business is not so much profit as the *creation of customers* who will be loyal to the product. Here we could draw a parallel to the spread of new religious movements. They seek new followers or customers across the globe from among different regions, ethnicities, and old religious traditions. Some of them like Unification Church, Falun Gong, have adopted certain aspects of the style of functioning and management of multinational corporations. Falun Gong has its headquarters in New York from where it reaches out to the global audience as well as to the Chinese diaspora. There has been a gradual transformation of what appeared in the beginning as a new religious movement. Increasingly, it took on the characters of a transnational enterprise. For the new religious movements, the adoption of management approaches and techniques are meant not only for the efficiency and easy global reach out; what is striking is that some new religious movements integrate themselves with international enterprises to be able to transmit their religious message. One such example is that of *Al-Arquam*, which originated in Malaysia as an Islamic religious movement but, due to suppression by the state, reinvented itself as a business enterprise called *Rufaqa*, which, while marketing *halal*-related items, spreads its religious message in Southeast Asia and other parts of the world.

Many studies on new religious movements have focused their investigation on whether and to what extent they are agents of modernization and globalization. In order to gain an understanding of the cultural significance of new religious movements in the broader sense, it is essential to look at them as responding to some of the primary humanistic and religious concerns the process of globalization has raised. In this sense, globalization is distinctly different from the theory of secularization. While the latter *undermines* religion and questions its scope of survival, globalization brings the religious question *to the fore in new ways*. Globalization helps to relativize the identity of the self and of communities or groups in as much as it challenges them to redefine themselves in the light of a broader global context of social relationships and interconnections. The

[29] Manderson Lenore, and Wendy Smith, and Matt Tomlinson, eds., of Compilation, *Flows of Faith: Religious Reach and Community in Asia and the Pacific* (Dordrecht: Springer, 2012).

identities which have been approached from a local and often absolutist perspective, and issues and questions formulated in a particular context, get reformulated under the conditions of globalization. The locally defined self and community now could be relativized vis-à-vis what happens to humankind at large. The consciousness of a shared global humanity and its destiny helps to redraw the religious agenda for our world today, going beyond conventional patterns of religious affiliation, rituals, and practices. It is precisely here that new religious movements become meaningful and culturally significant.[30]

There is another conventional interpretation of new religious movements, especially of fundamentalist orientation. According to it, these movements are but a counter or a backlash to modernity and globalization. To put it concretely, the destruction of the World Trade Center, some would interpret, as a religious act of opposition to globalization. But the fact is that there are contrasting views on globalization—some new religious movements favoring it and others opposing it. Those against it are mostly the ones which think that globalization is westernization in new guise, and can threaten, for example, Islamic identity and culture. According to Ahmet T. Kuru, who studied some cases of Turkish Islamic religious movements, the stance of religious movements vis-à-vis globalization is dependent on two factors. First, wherever globalization was perceived as offering an opportunity at the international level, it was viewed positively by these movements which became supporters of globalization. Second, wherever the normative structures of a religious movement manifest openness, tolerance, and interreligious understanding, it ended up in supporting the process of globalization.[31] In the absence of these two factors, a religious movement turned against globalization as a threat to Islam and to Turkish Islamic identity. This kind of approach is nuanced and it challenges any homogenous stance vis-à-vis globalization on the part of Islamic movements. Closer empirical study of many new religious movements would show that they are players in globalization rather than a force against globalization.

---

[30] Cf. Lorne L. Dawson, "Significance of New Religious Movements and Globalization: A Theoretical Prolegomenon," in *Journal for the Scientific Study of Religion* 37, no. 4 (1998): 580–595.

[31] Ahmet T. Kuru, "Globalization and Diversification of Islamic Movements: Three Turkish Cases,"
*Political Science Quarterly* 120, no. 1(Summer 2005): 253–274.

The striking thing about many of these New Religious Movements (NRMs) is that they constitute themselves as global entities from the outset and they unify their followers globally, transcending their cultures of origin by replacing many of their day-to-day cultural practices with the ones practised within the movement. As is the case of long-established religions such as Islam, in NRMs such as Brahma Kumaris and Sūkyō Mahikari, when followers meet each other at the pilgrimage place, a truly global culture is experienced, in which individual members' race, ethnicity and native language become less important than the common fact of membership in the organization.[32]

The fact that a new religious movement has spread globally does not imply that it is managed from a global center of diffusion and control. There are many local routes to globalization these religious movements take, though they may not all systematically be planned or networked. For example, Sekai Kyusei Kyo (SKK), which addressed initially the diaspora Japanese in Brazil, builds upon local interactions and reaches out to non-ethnic Japanese and then to other Portuguese colonies like Angola and Mozambique.

There is another form of transnationalization of religious movements which have fundamentalist traits. There is an attempt to reproduce only one's religious beliefs, practices, and ideology in a transnational location. One such example would be Vishwa Hindu Parishad (VHP). With nationalist ideological tone, this movement is attentive to safeguard the religious culture and belief of Hindus in other countries. We also have a compelling case of Hinduism transmuting itself, not so much due to globalization per se, but by the political forces surrounding it in a new transnational situation. I am referring here to the unique example of Hinduism in Bali, known as Agama Hindu Dharma.[33] In Indonesia, to be accepted as an official religion, one should profess the nationalistic philosophy of monotheism. It forced Hinduism to reshape itself as a monotheistic religion by drawing from its resources those aspects and elements that foster this belief. It is a tailored Hinduism to fit into the Islamic monotheistic belief and state religious policy and for public consumption. This "public Hinduism" for the Hindu followers is a foil and what happens is that

[32] In Wendy Smith, Hirochika Nakamaki, Louella Matsunaga, and Tamasin Ramsay, eds., *Globalizing Asian Religions. Management and Marketing* (Amsterdam: Amsterdam University Press, 2019), 18.

[33] Cf. June McDaniel, "Agama Hindu Dharma Indonesia as a New Religious Movement," in *Nova Religio* (2010): 93–111.

privately they have recourse to their gods and goddesses in their daily lives.[34] Though Agama Hinduism is in a way artificially shaped from ancient roots of Hinduism, June McDaniel considers that it could be classified among the new religious movements. It appears to be a unique case. There are other movements or practices like *yoga* or Transcendental Meditation, which are on the borderline or in the gray zone in many respects to be assuredly categorized under new religious movements.

## POSTMODERNISM AND NEW RELIGIOUS MOVEMENTS

The postmodern framework could help us see more clearly some of the characteristics of the new religious movements and also partly explain the why of their emergence. Though one may have started to theorize on globalization in more recent times, as a matter of fact, the process had already begun in the 1960s with fast means of transportation, communication, and movements of goods, commodities, and services. All this opened up immense possibilities of encounter and exchange with different worldviews, cultures, ways of life, and so on. This could not but make people look at their old certainties with new eyes and observe the relativity of many things that they held as absolute. This sweeping change of mood with globalization let people explore new possibilities and alternatives. In this sense, globalization and the pluralist environment it created were conducive to the birth and growth of new religious movements.

These movements also share some other characteristics of globalization and postmodern pluralism. It has been observed that some of these movements experienced phenomenal growth and expansion, but their fading and, in some cases, even disappearance was also equally fast. It is reflective of a postmodern characteristic, namely the transient nature of everything. Changes and transformations have always been there in human history and every sphere of life. However, some spheres like religion resisted changes. Religion is expected to be an anchor of stability amid changes—something it has been doing through its meta-narratives and comprehensive explanations and worldviews. The new religious movements, on the other hand, by their immense variety, plurality, and diffusion have relativized the traditional approach to religion and attitudes connected with it. I would say that the new religious movemens are experiments in faith. Whereas the conventional understanding associates religion with certainty,

---

[34] Cf. McDaniel, "Agama Hindu Dharma Indonesia as a New Religious Movement."

solidity, and permanence, the experimental character of new religious movements introduces something different from the classical approach and understanding to religion. The new religious movements claim no infallibility or perpetuity, but are ready to offer here and now new insights for the vexing questions and problems being faced, and provide some kind of new opening to the search of individuals and communities.

The attitude to and perspective on human sexuality, reflective of post-modernity, could explain the attraction toward some of the religious movements. The revolutionary sexual turn of the 1960s in the West also meant a break with an oppressive taboo-like sexual morality reminiscent of the Victorian times in England. An open and nonconventional approach could be characterized as sex revolution. A movement like that of Rajaneesh, or Osho (1931–1990), proved to be very attractive for the naturalness and spontaneity with which it treated sex as an integral dimension of being human and even as part of spirituality. It appeared to liberate the seekers of spirituality from moral rigidity of the past and made them feel comfortable with themselves not by evading or suppressing sexuality but integrating it within the ambit of spiritual growth. No wonder that the media termed Osho as "sex-guru."[35]

The general crisis of culture and a new attitude to sex and gender led to a situation of cohabiting without formal marriage. Between the 1960s and 1970s, the percentage of people cohabiting increased by 700%.[36] Communes, inspired by religious beliefs and ideology, created an environment of legitimacy and acceptability of something which conventional morality condemned. It removed the sense of anxiety and ambiguity caused by traditional sexual morality. Sexual permissiveness would be an old way of characterizing a new phenomenon and cultural change. In fact, many communes were self-regulatory in matters of sex, with some following celibacy as a rule and others making it voluntary, and still others following married life. There are less known new religious movements which draw upon Tantric tradition, which, it is claimed, helps many people, espe-

---

[35] Hugh B. Urban, *Zorba the Buddha: Sex, Spirituality, and Capitalism in the Global Osho Movement* (Oakland: University of California Press, 2015); Alan Jacobs, ed., *Osho: Living Dangerously: Ordinary Enlightenment for Extraordinary times* (Watkins Masters of Wisdom. London: Watkins, 2011); Osho, *Returning to the Source*, 2nd ed. (Shaftesbury: Element, 1995); Rām Chandra Prasāda, *Rajaneesh, the Mystic of Feeling: A Study in Rajaneesh's Religion of Experience*, 2nd rev. ed. (Delhi: Motilal Banarsidass, 1978).

[36] Cf. Angela A. Aidala, "Social Change, Gender Roles, and New Religious Movements," *Sociological Analysis* 46, no.3 (1985): 287–314.

cially the youth, to liberate themselves from sexual inhibition and scrupulosity imposed by traditional puritan morality.

## BEYOND EUROCENTRIC ANALYSIS AND FRAMES OF INTERPRETATION

We need to investigate in each case the cause and circumstances of the emergence of religious movements in the Global South, the local impact they create, and how the movement reconfigures in transnational situations where it tries to strike root.

Let us start with the case of Hinduism by way of illustration. Unlike most other world religions, it has no founder, no canonical book, and no official membership. As is well known, Hinduism is a new nomenclature employed by the British colonizers, who were awed at the immense variety of religious streams and expressions. They could not make sense out of them, and yet needed some kind of classification for governance, administration, census, for conducting the election, and so on. The simple way was to club together all and sundry religious movements represented by a baffling variety of peoples and groups and call them by the generic name of "Hinduism."[37] It is an umbrella concept under which diverse religious streams found a common point of reference. Unlike established religions with their rigid frames of orthodoxy, Hinduism has no idea of "deviance" or apostasy. Hence, new religious streams were not looked at as anything strange or esoteric as it might appear to a Western observer. After all, as noted, Hinduism itself is an amalgamation of many religious streams originating at different periods of history and from diverse sources. When new ones come up, they are viewed not with any feeling of threat or strangeness but as an enrichment to the already-existing religious legacy. This open-endedness is such that the new religious movements could inhabit under the roof of Hinduism without encountering any serious problem of hostility and rejection.

---

[37] Cf. Heinrich von Stietencron, "Hinduism: On the Proper Use of a Deceptive Term," in Gunther D. Sontheimer—Herman Kule, eds., *Hinduism Reconsidered* (Delhi: Manohar, 1991), 11–27; Robert E. Frykenberg, "The Emergence of Modern 'Hinduism' as a Concept and as an Institution: A Reappraisal with Special Reference to South India," In Gunther Sontheimer, and Hemann Kulke, eds., *Hinduism Reconsidered* (Delhi: Manohar, 1989), 29–49.

The trait of Hinduism to add on new religious movements could be compared to a snowball that becomes bigger and bigger as it rolls down the slope of history. This may not be said of Christianity or Islam, where religious borders are well marked and defined and whatever is outside of its pale calls for explanation and justification. They are no snowball religions. Besides Hinduism, some other Asian religious traditions like Buddhism and Daoism also share the snowball character. Given that Hinduism is a vast reservoir of beliefs, narratives, symbols, and rituals, it often happens that a particular group of people in terms of their caste identity or regional identity or in order to create solidarity in their struggle against oppressive powers fashion a religious variety of their own by drawing from the extensive repertoire of Hinduism. Every new religious movement is but an "add-on" so to say.[38]

I think modern linguistics could be of help to explain the emergence of new religious movements of Asia. We could compare religion to a language, namely a symbolic system of signs and codes. Language is not the possession of anyone. It can never be created or founded by one person. It is the heritage of a particular linguistic community. As the linguistic heritage opens itself to new terms and expressions to convey new experiences, so too Hinduism and other similar religious traditions lend themselves for ever new religious expressions and movements.

Hinduism, Buddhism, Jainism, Confucianism, and Daoism do have, historically speaking, external social and cultural circumstances and factors that account for their emergence. One such factor is identity. The same could be said of some of the new religious movements. They are attempts, at the symbolic level, by marginalized groups and communities to stake claim for power in the society where they have been oppressed and marginalized. This is something which we find through the history of Asian societies, namely marginalized groups and peoples create their religious movements. That some of these movements coming from Asia bespeak to the current condition of globalization is something new and a variation on a pattern in Asian religious history. For example, it is difficult to classify and interpret *Falun Gong*, to which we referred in an earlier chapter,

---

[38] However, it needs to be remarked that some transnational movements, which others may designate as having Hindu religious background, do not wish to be identified as "Hindu." They find it limiting. What they are aiming at is spirituality and transcendence beyond all religious borders and boundaries. We could cite the case of Amma Movement in America. So also, the Sri Sai Baba cult.

through Western theorizing. The movement stands out against the back-drop of the political centralization and repression by the Chinese state and its bureaucracy. It is a genre of folk religion functioning as a force of resistance to oppressive powers.

Then there are movements in the South with a strong belief in all kinds of spirits. Members are transported to another world of ecstatic experience. With the dimming of consciousness, a believer becomes the medium to the spirit world and interpreter of the divine will. Many times, through possession they themselves become the spirits. As is well known, in many regions of the Global South, psychology, psychiatry, and counselling are not common practices. One seeks remedy for mental vexation or derangement caused by conflicts, social rejection, oppression, and so on, through the medium of new religious practices. These keep proliferating in the South, also because of their thaumaturgical effects. They draw their inspiration and resources from shamanism and incorporate them into new religious practices.

> [A shaman is] an inspired prophet and healer, a charismatic religious figure with the power to control the spirit, usually by incarnating them. If spirits speak through him, he is also likely to have the capacity to engage in mystical flight and other out of the body experiences.[39]

We could find this shamanistic character in many new religious movements hailing from Korea and Japan.[40] They are strongly present as well in religious movements from Africa, from the Caribbean, and other parts of the world. Such ecstatic movements in the South offer avenues for freedom of mind and physical healing. Being a source of a different kind of knowledge and as a healing system, shamanism offers much attraction to a lot of people in the South.[41]

> During the 1970s and '80s, aspects of shamanism have been introduced into the eclectic mix of practices, beliefs and dogmas that constitute emerging new religions. Some new religions recognize the spirit world that in shamanistic religion is understood to be mastered by shamans. Other new reli-

---

[39] M. Lewis, *Religion in Context: Cults and Charism* (Cambridge: Cambridge University Press, 1986), 88.

[40] Clark Chilson, and Peter Knecht, eds., *Shamans in Asia* (London: Routledge, 2003); Adam J. Rock, and Stanley Krippner, *Demystifying Shamans and Their World: A Multidisciplinary Study* (Exeter: Andrews UK Ltd., 2011).

[41] Sudhir Kakar, *Shamans, Mystics, and Doctors: A Psychological Inquiry into India and Its Healing Traditions,* 1st ed. (New York: Knopf, 1982).

gions simply practice the ecstatic expressions of shamanism—shaking, dancing, rolling, aggression, group drama, and so on.[42]

For an oppressed woman, to be possessed by a goddess is a moment of freedom both at home and in society. For, at the moment of possession, she becomes the goddess herself and her words become that of the goddess, and therefore she is respected, feared, and listened to with rapt attention. Moreover, a possessed woman exhibits exceptional power and vitality in marked contrast to the submissiveness and acquiescence she is subjected to in daily life.[43] In the state of possession, these women often have visual and auditory hallucinations. Here is a religious experience where oppressed women regain their dignity and freedom—even if momentarily. In Japan, the *kami* (gods) take possession of people who were considered mentally deranged, and once they are possessed, the whole perception changes about them, and they become respectable persons as the medium for the revelation of the divine. This is similar in other regions of South and Southeast Asia. Religious experience becomes a way to regain their human dignity and freedom. As we can see new religious movements in the South with roots in tradition—like Shamanism—have other cultural and social significance than the religious movements in the context of modernity in Europe and the USA.

> It was the new religions that attempted, albeit not indiscriminately, to preserve cultural capital, a term that includes religious culture, while the so-called historical or mission churches, and mainstream Islam, attempted to transform the local religious landscape. The adoption of the role of defenders of cultural capital accounts in great measure,…for the success of many African NRMs [New Religious Movements], including African Independent Churches (AICs), new Islamic movements such as the Murid brotherhood of Senegal, and neo-traditional movements, such as the Mungiki movement in present-day Kenya.[44]

[42] Irving Hexham and Karla Poewe, *Understanding Cults and New Age Religions* (Vancouver: Regent College Publishing, 2000), 145.

[43] A recent research shows how even in the popular religious practices of the Catholic Church in South India such a shamanistic aspect is present. The three ladies in the case study who are possessed are not only medium for communication with the Virgin Mary, but they themselves become the persona of the Virgin. Their words and gestures are taken to be as that of Mary herself. See Kristin C. Bloomer, *Possessed by the Virgin: Hinduism, Roman Catholicism, and Marian Possession in South India* (Oxford: Oxford University Press, 2018).

[44] Peter B. Clarke, "New Religious Movements in Sub-Saharan Africa," in Olav Hammer, and Mikael Rothstein, eds., *New Religious Movements* (Cambridge: Cambridge University Press, 2012), 303–320.

Elements originating from shamanism and other traditional religious resources are fused with modern religious movements when they do transnational migration. Hare Krishna movement, though not a thaumaturgical movement per se, however, has absorbed many ecstatic elements. The mystical dance, chanting, and singing transports the Western disciples of the movement to another world of experience where they probably get relieved from the tensions and conflicts of a pell-mell and overhasty style of everyday life. This is the world where one has to prove his or her competitive prowess to be respected and to enjoy power and wealth.

The many movements associated with gurus, meditations, and shamanistic practices appear differently in America or Europe than in Asia and in the Global South at large. However, when they appear in Europe or America, the new religions with Asian roots are constrained to adapt to postmodern conditions. One such factor is the kind of image they project of themselves in public. In contemporary global cultural environment, it is important *how* they appear than *what* they really are. In fact, in the postmodern condition, there is often an overlap of reality and appearance or image. The new religious movements, to appear relevant and significant in the public realm and be attractive to its recruits, need to continually revise their self-image. There being no absolute and timeless truth claims for its beliefs, the new movements can accommodate themselves to modern cultural conditions and needs of individuals and groups. That explains their magnetic charm.

These various religious movements have created enthusiastic followers and disciples not only in Europe and America but also in other parts of the South. Some years ago, on landing in Rio de Janeiro, Brazil, I hired a taxi at the airport. On hearing that I was from India, the taxi driver's first question was whether I visited Sathya Sai Baba in Puttaparthi.[45] When I told him, unfortunately not yet, he was amazed. He could not comprehend that someone from India had not yet visited the transnational guru and saint Sathya Sai Baba!

Some of the gurus and leaders of these new movements would not like to be identified as "Hindu." For it could be restrictive and construed as

---

[45] Cf. On this movement, see Tulasi Srinivas, "The Sathya Sai Baba Movement," in Ola Hammaer—Mikael Rothstein, *New Religious Movements*, 184–197; Chad Bauman, "Sathya Sai Baba: At Home Abroad in Midwestern America," in John Zavos, Pralay Kanungo, Deepa S. Reddy, Maya Warrier, Raymond Williams, eds., *Public Hinduism* (Delhi: Sage, 2012), 141–159.

an ethno-nationalistic connotation. Distancing themselves from the ambiguous Hindu identity, they present themselves as universalistic offering spirituality for the contemporary world. There could also be a practical reason for this dissociation from Hinduism. For the foreign followers of Christian background, it may be easier to migrate to a religious identity that transcends religious boundaries, than to shift to another religion like Hinduism which was denigrated and shown in poor light since the colonial times. Some of the movements are based on *Advaita-Vedanta*, which could pass for philosophy, and not necessarily as part of Hindu religion. The Advaita-Vedanta offers a broader perspective and greater scope than any claim of affiliation to Hinduism that could be viewed somewhat narrowly. The universalistic intuitions, experiences, and perspectives the Advaita-Vedanta-inspired movements offer are not something new to the American audience, for example. Already at the time of the first World Parliament of Religions (1893), an Indian participant, Pratap Chandra Muzumdar, made a distinction between religion and spirituality. The attractiveness of the latter, coupled with universalism, found great resonance among the American Unitarians. There was a perceptible change in America regarding Hinduism in the final decades of the nineteenth century and early decades of the twentieth century. Until then, the general American perception of Hinduism was on the same page with the British colonial Raj, which found Hinduism to be the fountainhead of all social evils in India and the cause for its poverty and backwardness.

In a vastly changed religious scenario of today, the "spirituality" movements with Hindu background seem to offer something responding to the personal quest and freedom from institutionalized religions from which many American and European seekers wish to dissociate themselves ("spiritual but not religious"). These movements propose the idea of *Sanatana Dharma*—universal religion and spirituality, not bound to any establishment. Hence, becoming disciples of any one of these movements and pursuing the goal of spirituality and self-realization are viewed *not in opposition* to one's affiliation to a particular religious tradition. Hence, the question of being *converted* from ones' original religion to a new religious group does not arise.

Movements promoting bodily practices as yoga too try to distance themselves from Hinduism and project themselves as universal. There is some tension between Hindu roots and the aspiration to be something more universal than being a Hindu. This could be clearly seen in the case of a woman guru movement—Amritānandamayī, known popularly as

Amma. Other examples would be the "Art of Living" movement by the guru Sri Ravishankar or Jaggi Vasudev (Sadhguru). All have drawn several disciples both in India and abroad. In India, there is an effort to "mainstreaming" of discipleship through educational and "commercial" endeavors. As examples let me refer here to Amma's massive network of academic and professional colleges, Sri Ravishankar and Jaggi Vasudev's "subscription-based" meditation or wellness, mindfulness courses, workshops, and lectures, and Baba Ramdev's massive network of Patanjali products and franchisees (herbal, ayurvedic, etc.) which all seem to blur the line between Indian and Hindu nationalism.

## JUDAISM AND NEW RELIGIOUS MOVEMENTS

In modern times, according to the changing sociopolitical situation of the Jews, there has come about new religious expressions of Judaism. Neo-Hasidism, Sephardic movement, and Chabad are examples of a reworking of Jewish religious heritage for greater reach out to modernity and globalization. In Israel, like in the case of Europe, in the 1960s, the new generation went through a dramatic change, and this had its influence in the way they looked at their traditional religious heritage. The Jewish interest was not only with renewal movements within its tradition. Beginning from the 1970s, many Jews took an active part in new religious movements hailing from other parts of the world and other religions. So, it should not be a surprise if one finds Jews among the followers of Hare Krishna movement or neo-Buddhist or Zen movements, for example. In fact, the Jews count among the founders and leaders of the Hare Krishna movement at New Goloka Temple in Hillsborough, North Carolina.

There has been a steady increase in the following of new religious movements, and today they are an integral part of the cultural and religious landscape of Israel.[46] Some of these movements fuse Jewish tradition with traditions and practices from other religions such as Buddhism. Not few find that they could be Jews and, at the same time, practitioners of Buddhism, and they are referred to as JuBus. Given the deep monotheistic belief in Judaism as a core element, for many Jews to feel at home in movements from a religion like Hinduism with any number of gods and goddesses have been difficult. Instead, movements centered on

---

[46] Cf. Yaakov Ariel, "Jews and New Religious Movements: An Introductory Essay," in *Nova Religio* 15, no.1 (2011): 5–21.

self-improvement or those focused on meditation and techniques of concentration like the Transcendental Meditation have huge appeal and following among the Jews, especially in Israel.

There is also an exciting new religious movement that combines Jewish
identity and evangelical Christianity and is known as Messianic Judaism.[47]
Like in the case of anti-cult movements in America, Israel too experienced
stiff opposition to new religious movements which were looked at suspiciously for enticing Jews into their fold. The opposition is both from the
Orthodox Judaism and from those following secularism. However, most
strident is the opposition in the name of religious identity whose roots and
symbols overlap with the identity of the state of Israel. One is very appre-
hensive of the threat these movements represent. It would seem that
orthodox Judaism has no serious difficulty with the Jews even if they are
atheists who do not abide by traditional religious laws and injunctions, as
long as they do not betray their ethno-national and religious identity by
becoming a member of a religious group which has little connection with
Judaism and Jewish identity. The opposition to new religious movements
in Israel is an extreme illustration of a general pattern. Wherever religion
and state, due to history, tradition, and heritage, have been tied together,
we will find opposition to the new religious movements. The degree of
opposition is dependent upon how close this connection is, for example,
in diferent countries of Europe and America.[48]

## MOVEMENTS IN CONTEXT

The religious movements in the South need to be related, as I noted earlier, to the history and context of their provenance. Viewing the matter
thus, in regard to Hinduism, the modern religious movements have a
certain continuity with new religious movements of earlier times—in the
pre-Independence era. Some common patterns could be identified. Some
of the pre-Independence movements came as an attempt to renew
Hinduism and make it more rational, or make it modern, or transform it
with an explicit social agenda and so on. On the other hand, the new

---

[47] Mark S. Kinzer, "Twenty-First Century Messianic Judaism: Evangelical and Post-
Evangelical Trajectories," *Hebrew Studies* 57 (2016): 359–66.

[48] Cf. James Beckford, "The 'Cult Problems' in Five Countries. The Social Construction
of Religious Controversy," in *of Gods and Men: New Religious Movements in the West*, edited
by E. Barker (Macon GA: Mercer Unity Press, 1983), 198–214; ID., *Cult Controversies*
(London: Tavistock Publications, 1985).

religious movements originating from India in the post-Independence period are attempts to respond to the needs of the times, especially in the West. I think we need to analyze the colonial cliché branding the West as *materialist* and the East as *spiritual*, internalized by Hindu thinkers and reformers. A classic example is Vivekananda, in whose tone of speech, at the World Parliament of Religions in Chicago 1893, we could hear the echo of such an attitude and orientation.

> I am anxiously waiting for the day when mighty minds will arise, gigantic spiritual minds who will be ready to go forth from India to the ends of the world to teach spirituality and renunciation, those ideas which come from the forests of India and belong to the Indian soil only.[49]

With such an attitude and the belief that Hinduism had the resources for the spiritual renewal of the world, several movements adopted ways and means to make themselves attractive to the Western audience.

The reformative spirit of Neo-Hinduism as represented in the Ramakrishna Mission[50] and numerous such initiatives instilled a more direct and more organized involvement for the service of society, very much like the Social Gospel movement of the nineteenth-century America. The socially conscious new streams merged with the undercurrent of spirituality in many traditional Hindu religious movements, which made them attractive even more. This is reflected today in movements like "The Art of Living" founded by Sri Ravishankar, to which I referred earlier.[51] It is a movement that tries to relate spirituality to new conditions of life, especially fostering altruism and spirit of service. The many and diverse kinds of social activities the movement is engaged in gives it legitimacy and social acceptance.[52]

If we look at the origins of many religious movements—old and new— we could identify great charismatic personalities as their founders or

---

[49] As quoted in Klaus Klostermeier, *Hinduism. A Short History* (Oxford: OUP 2000), 271.

[50] Cf. Swami Ranganathananda, *The Ramakrishna Mission, Its Ideals and Activities*, 6th rev. ed. (Madras: Sri Ramakrishna Math, 1963); Gwilym Beckerlegge, *The Ramakrishna Mission: The Making of a Modern Hindu Movement* (New Delhi: Oxford University Press, 2000).

[51] Stephen Jacobs, *The Art of Living Foundation: Spirituality and Wellbeing in the Global Context* (London: Routledge, 2016); François Gautier, *The Guru of Joy: Sri Sri Ravi Shankar & the Art of Living* (New Delhi: Books Today, 2001).

[52] Samta P. Pandya, "New Strategies of New Religious Movements," *Sociological Bulletin* 64, no.3 (2015): 287–304.

inspirers. In the case of Hinduism, what is called a charismatic person is represented by the figure of *guru*. In Hinduism, a guru is more than a charismatic religious personality. The guru becomes the medium of communication with divinity, and not in few cases becomes the *avatar* (embodiment) of the divinity, and hence held in very high esteem and venerated sanctimoniously by the disciples. The archetypal figure of the guru is essential to explain the global movement of Hinduism. The guru is the central figure around whom many new religious movements are organized.

The alienation in Western society and loosening of traditional bonds could also be found in the South in a related but different way. In India, the loosening of traditional joint family, the weakening of other support systems, and isolation in the urban milieu especially among the middle class created an ambience of uncertainty, estrangement, and anxiety the remedy for which was sought in the new religious movements. In this general environment, the traditional figure of guru got a fresh lease of life in modern conditions. What is striking is the fact that the gurus in modern India have been rhapsodically sought after by the politicians who visit them, fall prostrate at their feet seeking blessings, especially before elections. This bond with a guru is considered essential to be politically successful. The middle-class urban Indian, no wonder, took to similar practices to succeed in their enterprises. In fact, the different religious campaigns started by various gurus enjoy the patronage of politicians and entrepreneurs.

## NEW RELIGIOUS MOVEMENTS IN JAPAN

Japan is a fertile ground for the study of new religious movements under globalizing conditions. The flourishing new religious movements in Japan grabbed the attention of the world with the notorious case of Aum Shinrikyo sarin subway gas attack on March 20, 1995. It caused the death of thirteen people and injured a few hundred. Japan shares with Europe and America many of the conditions of modernity. It shares even more many aspects of life with Asian peoples relating to religion and spirituality. The hard-core theorists of secularization would be disappointed that their thesis of religion being marginalized in the process of modernization was not vindicated in Japan. Shinto is being restored after the imperial "secularization" program.[53]

According to the classical secularization thesis, the functional specialization of different areas of life and the process of individualization in modernity lead inevitably to the decline of traditional religions. If one is insistent on using the category of secularization for interpreting the developments in religion in Japan, it has to be turned and twisted in such a way, that one would end up asking whether such a process could be named secularization at all. In the postwar period, and especially since 1970s, Japan saw a unique development of refashioning of religions—Buddhism, Shinto, Christianity, and so on—to suit the needs of a modernizing society with technological dominance.[54] What is even more interesting is, as the commodities of industrial production was made in Japan for the needs of other parts of the world, so too Japanese religion was, in many cases, redesigned to respond to global needs. These were religions meant both for domestic consumption and equally for export to other parts of the world.

The "secular" in Japan is understood and interpreted not in relation to modernity, as done in the West (with the decline of religion), but rather in relation to the process of globalization. Religions are shaped in such a way that they lose a lot of their aura and traditional attributes and resemble in their structure, presentation, and leadership to the secular organization and even multinational enterprises. The symbols, teachings, rituals, and internal organization of religions are transformed to be able to attract international market. The Japanese take care that their new religions have a global character by establishing branches in the West and in other parts of the world. To cite an example, *Kagamikyo* is a new religious movement in which leaders are not called, "pastors" "priests," "gurus," or by any such names associated with religion. Kagamikyo resembles a modern corporate and its head is called chairman, and other cadres are referred to as chief, managers, branch leaders, and similar designations used in the business world. Members of Kagamikyo identify themselves as belonging to

---

[53] Cf. Mark R. Mullins, "Japanese Response to Imperialist Secularization: The Postwar Movement to Restore Shinto in the Public Sphere," in *Multiple Secularities Beyond the West: Religion and Modernity in the Global Age*, edited by Marian Burchardt, et al. (Boston-Berlin-Munich: De Gruyter, 2015), 141–167.

[54] Cf. Ugo Dessì, *Japanese Religions and Globalization* (London and New York: Routledge, 2013); Inken Prohl, and John Nelson, eds., *Handbook of Contemporary Japanese Religions* (Leiden: BRILL, 2012); Hirochika Nakamaki, *Japanese Religions at Home and Abroad: Anthropological Perspectives* (London: Routledge, 2003).

"The Paradise on Earth Research Institute"—a highly secular sounding expression for a global religious body!

In short, in Japan new religious movements are packaged in the form of modern commodities in a business enterprise. The global standing of the new religions is significant because, through this global criterion, it can gain more local followers. In his study of Kagamikyo, Isaac Gagne speaks about the efforts of new religious movements in Japan to make "super-religion" which would surpass religious boundaries in the traditional sense.

> Analyzing the formation of the secular in Japan within the context of contemporary globalization is thus instructive in demonstrating one way in which certain groups attempt to find a way out of the secular/religious cul-de-sac. In a modern society without invoking simplistic teleological argument about a religious past versus secular modernity. Like Kagamikyo many groups in Japan make claims to one form or another of a "superreligious" organization, eschewing classifications of the conventionally religious or conventionally secular. Rather than presenting themselves as either religious or non-religious, these organizations are skillfully able to claim *both* without clashing with other secular or religious institutions.[55]

## Ambiguities and Bright Spots in New Religious Movements

Many new religious movements have been accused of "brainwashing" its members, and particularly when young people are drawn into these religious groups. It is said that by controlling their minds through indoctrination, the youth are made to lose their freedom of choice.[56] Not in a few cases, parents have approached courts to free their wards from the grip of the new religious movements, mainly when they are confined to their closed "enclaves."

It would be simply an exaggeration to claim that new religious movements are radically different from mainline religious traditions regarding discrimination against women and their marginalization in leadership roles. Most groups function under the influence of patriarchy characteristic of all religious traditions. However, there are some laudable exceptions.

---

[55] Isaac Gagné, "Religious Globalization and Reflexive Secularization in Japan," *Japan Review*, no. 30 (2017): 153–177, at 170–171.

[56] Marc Galanter, *Cults: Faith, healing, and coercion*, 2nd ed. (New York: Oxford, 1999).

One striking case is that of *Brahma Kumaris*.[57] This movement believes not only in the equality of men and women, but goes even a step further and claims the spiritual superiority of women. Women are looked at as teachers, gurus, and masters.[58] This is not only a matter of belief. The predominance of women could be observed in the way this religious group is organized and roles are assigned. Another movement that accepted the equality of women and even their priority was the Rajaneesh, or Osho, movement. Barring such exceptions, most of the new religious movements do not have anything that could be strikingly distinct from the habits of traditional religious attitude and practices vis-à-vis women. This is strange since many women leave behind their religions which they found misogynic and turn to new religious movements in the hope of being able to play an active role. But the fact is that most new religious movements too do not fulfill their aspirations and hopes.

On the other hand, in the Western history of Christianity one could note that it was in sectarian groups that a more significant role for women was recognized and practiced as in the case of Shakers in America and Seventh Day Adventism, and in more recent times in the church Universal and Triumphant, founded and led by Elizabeth Clare Prophet (1939–2009), who was also recognized as teacher and guru.[59] Mā

[57] Cf. John Wallis, *The Brahma Kumaris as a 'Reflexive Tradition': Responding to Late Modernity*, 1st ed. (London: Routledge, 2017); Stephan Nagel, *Brahmas Geheime Schöpfung: Die Indische Reformbewegung Der "Brahma Kumaris": Quellen, Lehre, Raja Yoga*, Theion, Bd. 11. (Frankfurt Am Main; New York: P. Lang, 1999); J. Day Howell, P. L. Nelson, "Structural Adaptation and 'Success' in the Transplantation of an Asian New Religious Movement: The Brahma Kumaris in the Western World, Part I," *Research in the Social Scientific Study of Religion: A Research Annual* 8 (1997): 1–34.

[58] Cf. Sister Sudesh, "Women as Spiritual Leaders in the Brahma Kumaris," in Elizabeth Puttick, and Peter B. Clarke, eds., *Women as Teachers and Disciples in Traditional and New Religions. Studies in Women and Religion* 32 (Lewiston: The Edwin Mellen Press, 1993), 39–46; Vieda Skultans, "The Brahma Kumaris and the Role of Women," in Elizabeth Puttick, and Peter B. Clarke, eds., *Women as Teachers and Disciples in Traditional and New Religions. Studies in Women and Religion* 32 (Lewiston: The Edwin Mellen Press, 1993): 47–62.

[59] Cf. Stephen J. Stein, *The Shaker Experience in America: A History of the United Society of Believers* (New Haven; London: Yale University Press, 1992); William C. Ketchum, *Simple Beauty: The Shakers in America (Art Movements)* (New York, Great Britain: Todtri, 1996); Stephen C. Taysom, *Shakers, Mormons, and Religious Worlds: Conflicting Visions, Contested Boundaries* (Bloomington and Chesham: Indiana University Press, 2010); Bradley Whitsel, *The Church Universal and Triumphant: Elizabeth Clare Prophet's Apocalyptic Movement* (Syracuse, NY: London: Syracuse University Press; Eurospan, 2003).

Ānandamayī (1896–1982) is, perhaps, the most acclaimed woman saint and guru of twentieth-century India who had huge following all over the world and continues to be worshipped as a divine avatar in ashrams across the world.[60] Mataji Nirmala Devi (1923–2011), a disciple of Rajaneesh (Osho), became herself a guru with many disciples. Helena Blavatsky (1831–1891) was much instrumental in founding the Theosophical Society in Chennai, India, and promoting Theosophy. Yet another movement founded by a woman that has the transnational following is that of Māta Amritānandamayī (1953–). She is a guru with followers in every part of the world. By and large, the new religious movements have created slightly more space of freedom for women to give expression to their spiritual leadership.[61]

Unlike traditional mainline religions where the role of a mediator—priest—is central, in many new religious movements what counts most is discipleship. It is correlated to the other concept of guru or teacher. The members are bound in an intimate relationship of loyalty and surrender to the guru. The teachings and injunctions of the guru become the reference point for the devotee and of the community of disciples. In the Indic Bhakti tradition, there is a belief that women with their devotion, loyalty, and commitment to the deity or guru excel in discipleship, surpassing the discipleship of men. In the Bhakti tradition, men sometimes impersonate themselves as women to express their utmost devotion to the Lord.

The phenomenal success stories of many new religious movements are dampened by scandals of money, wealth, and sexual abuses connected with its leaders and gurus. To cite some examples of movements from India thriving in the West: Rajaneesh, or Osho, is known for the enormous wealth he commanded and the luxurious fleet of Rolls-Royce cars he owned; Sri Sathya Sai Baba before his death was entangled in allegations of sexual abuse.[62] Another case is that of Swami Rama (1925–1996) of the Himalayan Institute of Honesdale, Pennsylvania, and Yogi Amrit Desai,

[60] Cf. Orianne Aymard, *When a Goddess Dies. Worshipping Ma Anandmayi after her Death* (New York: Oxford University Press, 2014)

[61] Cf. Elizabeth Puttick, "Women in New Religious Movements," In *Cults and New Religious Movements: A Reader,* edited by Dawson, Lorne L. (Oxford: Wiley-Blackwell, 2003), 230–244; Laura Lee Vance, *Women in New Religions* (N.Y.: New York University Press, 2015).

[62] https://www.indiatoday.in/magazine/cover-story/story/20001204-allegations-of-sexual-molestation-continue-to-dog-sai-baba-778528-2000-12-04 [accessed on February 19, 2020].

head of the Kripalu Center, Lenox, Massachusetts. Some of these and other movements have gone through a deep crisis. Among these are the International Society of Krishna Consciousness, founded by Swami Bhaktivedanta, and the Transcendental Meditation movement, founded by Swami Maharishi Mahesh Yogi. Ironically, many new movements which sprouted to provide spiritual guidance in a world of abundance and materiality were themselves found to be affected by the very things they wanted to free the people from.

Besides these scandals, there are issues of collective suicide and homicidal violence connected with one or other movement. Following are some of the most knowns cases: the collective suicide of fifty-three members of the apocalyptic movement—Order of the Solar Temple in Switzerland and in Quebec in 1994; the tragic death of thirty-nine members of Heaven's Gate at Rancho, Santa Fe, California in 1997; the disastrous conflagration of Peoples Temple in Jonestown, Branch Davidians' Mount Carmel compound near Waco, Texas, which consumed seventy-six persons including children.[63]

## THE LIFESPAN OF NEW RELIGIOUS MOVEMENTS

Hundreds of religious groups, big and small, have emerged in the past few decades; more are likely to germinate in the future. An important point to consider is their longevity. Are they all crowned with success? Will they continue to attract disciples and followers? The fact is that many of them flourish and then fade away with little trace, with a handful of followers in the end. Some others continue with success for a longer period and sustain the momentum adding new followers. How come that there is such a difference? Rodney Stark has gone into this question and has come out with ten factors that are responsible for determining the relative success or failure of a new religious movement. We need not go into all of them. I would like to highlight the very first factor, which seems to be also the most important one. According to him, if a new religious group shows some cultural continuity with an existing mainstream religion, then it is likely that the new group succeeds.[64] For example, if its followers can iden-

---

[63] Cf. Hall, Schuyler and Trinh, "The Apocalypse at Jonestown," 186–207.

[64] Cf. Rodney Stark, "New Religious Movements Succeed or Fail: A Revised General Model," in Lorne L. Dawson ed., *Cults and New Religious Movements. A Reader* (Oxford: Wiley-Blackwell, 2003), 259–270.

tify a new religious group as a variant or improvement upon the existing forms of Christianity, then it is likely to have a longer life. The author refers to the case of Mormons as an example who share a lot of cultural continuity. I think this argument is valid to some extent but may not apply to every case. The dancing, singing, and reciting mantras by Hare Krishna movement was a common sight in European and American cities. It had numerous disciples from India and in the West, which is not the case today. The same may be said of Transcendental Meditation. Now, both these movements have cultural continuity with Hinduism, its symbols, its practices, and so on. And yet they have not been able to sustain themselves for too long.

I think the explanation is to be sought instead in the transformed post-modern cultural environment in the West. Like in other areas of life where any permanent commitment is shunned (think of the revised conception of marriage and family), so too one may not stick to any one religious group based on a firm commitment to its teachings and practices. This is a cultural trait in these times of globalization and postmodernity. As long as a movement resonates with one's aspirations and responds to the problems at hand, a follower maybe with a group. It could be a short spell. Depending on the needs, one may look for another group, or not at all; all left to one's perception, mood, and motivations.

## NEW RELIGIOUS MOVEMENTS AND THEIR FUTURE

We have been able to view from different angles and perspectives the how of the emergence of new religious movements. How about the continuity of this phenomenon? Are we to expect more and more of them appearing and responding to the quest of people in our times? We may need to distinguish between the situation in the Global North and the Global South. In the North, one striking thing is that there is not today the kind of proliferation of movements that was there a few decades ago. Even the movements that exist today do not have, probably, the same kind of pull they once had. One reason could be that today we do not find the kind of quest that was there in an earlier period. In former times, there was a challenge to the established religions, their morality, worship, and so on, which went in the direction of looking for alternative ways of being religious and being spiritual. I think today the conception about life, society, and the world have changed so very much that more and more people do not raise the kind of primordial questions about the meaning of life and death as was done in the past. They are made to feel that even God is a "delusion."[65] At bottom, one is not looking anymore for solutions to problems of life in religion. The possibility of any opening to a transcendental horizon of meaning for self, society, and the world is now being sucked into the black hole of consumerism. Once into this world, there takes place a whole transmutation of values, visions, and conception about life. Consumer goods and commodities as fetishes become ends in themselves and less and less as means for something else. The fetish world of consumerism anaesthetizes any thought and opening to those concerns and values with which religions were busy. Commodities and consumption define one's social stand and condition all interhuman relationships.[66] The consumer world does not think of permanence, immortality, and eternity.

In the classical worldview, the phenomenal world was viewed as something transient, and one was directed to look for the nontransient, eternal, and abiding things. However, today, that horizon is closed. It is a world which one knows is not permanent but transient and fleeting. The difference is that, unlike in the past, the transient nature of things does not become a motive to relativize them, or subordinate them to what are permanent. Instead, as in the Tamil conception of the secular ideal, the transient character of life and the mundane world is not a reason to renounce them, but a motive to enjoy them and savor the pleasures they offer. Precisely because they may not be available anymore, or not to be expected in an uncertain future, they need to be consumed and enjoyed. The symbolic value of commodities also marks the social standing of consumers.

Against the above background, the likelihood of new religious movements thriving in our world of globalization and postmodernity becomes less and less. The chances of new religious movements growing as they did in the 1960s–1980s are dim for the reasons we saw above. Many of them have had ephemeral existence, and even among those that survived, one may not find the same vibrant discipleship as in the years immediately following their emergence. These movements have social and cultural significance in that they give us the pulse of the society and the developments and processes taking place in it. In many cases, the new religious movements seem to be "single generation phenomena."[67]

---

[65] Cf. Richard Dawkins, *The God Delusion* (London: Black Swan, 2007).

[66] Cf. Felix Wilfred, "Consumerism as Play of Signs and the Project of Liberation," chapter 9, in Felix Wilfred, *Theology for an Inclusive World* (Delhi: ISPCK, 2019), 174–200.

[67] Irving Hexham, and Karla Poewe, *Understanding Cults and New Age Religions*, 116.

## Conclusion

The case of religious movements migrating from one region of the world to the other and adapting to local condition is not something new. What is remarkable is that some of them are born global in the sense that they are independent of their place of origin and culture. They succeed to create a global identity in such a way that people across the globe and ethnic and cultural identities could feel at home in these movement and share many commonalities. The process of deterritorialization inherent in globalization confers these movements an existence of their own as they strike root in the local soil and assume the characters of the environment.

Some of the new religious movements may appear exotic and bizarre, but I think they have succeeded by their very presence to challenge the anthropocentrism in the Western culture and religion by projecting a more mystical view of things attuned to integration and wholeness rather than fragmentation and excessive reliance on human ingenuity. They sometimes present the darker side of reality, not visible to the conventional cognitive and epistemological means.

The centuries-old prejudices and negative attitudes toward other religious traditions, other than Christianity, made Europe and America religiously insulated. The explosion of religious pluralism we experience today, thanks to globalization, came about through the new religious movements. Even before Hinduism, Buddhism, and Daoism could become part of the Western religious landscape, the New Religious Movements had arrived. As a matter of fact, for many Westerners, knowledge about other world religions was brought through these new religious movements. Despite their many ambiguities and contradictions, one significant contribution of new religious movements is to broaden the religious horizons offering immense possibilities for individuals and communities to seek and discover what would suit their spiritual aspirations and hopes.

# CHAPTER 8

# Religions in Diaspora: The Case of South Asian Migrants

By the rivers of Babylon—there we sat down and there we wept
When we remembered Zion
On the willows there
We hung up our harps…
How could we sing the Lord's song
In a foreign land?
If I forget you, O Jerusalem,
Let my right hand whither!. (Ps. 137: 1–2, 4–5)

This is the impassioned lament of the Jews who found themselves in exile in Babylon. Their longing for homeland was so movingly captured by the Italian composer Giuseppe Verdi in a chorus—*Va penisero*—in his immortal opera *Nabucco* (1842). The experience of being away weighed heavily on them, and their hearts were yearning to get back to Zion, to their roots. Would these words echo the sentiments of South Asians who find themselves dispersed in many countries in East and West, North and South?

The term "diaspora" referred initially to the Greeks who were dispersed in different parts of the Mediterranean world. However, the term got wider currency because of its association with Jewish history.[1] It referred

---

[1] Howard Wettstein, ed., *Diasporas and Exiles: Varieties of Jewish Identity* (Berkley, London: University of California Press, 2002).

© The Author(s), under exclusive license to Springer Nature Switzerland AG 2021
F. Wilfred, *Religious Identities and the Global South*,
New Approaches to Religion and Power,
https://doi.org/10.1007/978-3-030-60738-8_8

to the Jews in exile living often under oppressive conditions among the gentiles, nurturing, however, the hope of returning one day to their promised homeland. In this sense, the term is hardly applicable to the situation of South Asians and other migrants today.

As Susan Koshy notes:

> Contrary to the tenets of diaspora theory which held that a strong and active myth of return is a precondition of a strong diaspora, in the South Asian case, the opposite can be just as real—a weak myth of return can coexist with and, indeed, foster a strong diaspora. Historically, the terms under which South Asians have entered into diaspora have made the issue of return an undecidable one, a question rather than a certainty, subject to deferral and continuous renegotiation. ...[T]he decision to leave, to stay, to return, or to move to yet another location is fraught, ambiguous, and inflected by myriad factors like religion, class, education, and concerns about children.[2]

These words show the limits of the applicability of diaspora in its original sense to peoples of South Asian origin. The semantic potential of the word "diaspora" is being debated among scholars, and the word is acquiring new layers of meaning.[3] It has become a widely used expression since the 1980s.[4]

What about the religions of the migrants outside their homelands? The question assumes great relevance today in the context of globalization.[5]

---

[2] Susan Koshy, and R. Radhakrishnan, eds., *Transnational South Asians. The Meaning of a Neo-Diaspora* (Delhi: OUP, 2008), 7–8.

[3] For a critical approach to the concept of diaspora, see Aoileann Ní Éigeartaigh, et al., eds., *Rethinking Diasporas: Hidden Narratives and Imagined Borders* (Cambridge: Cambridge Scholars Publisher, 2007); Stephane Dufoix, *Diasporas* (Berkeley: University of California Press, 2008); Gabriel Sheffer, *Diaspora Politics: At Home Abroad* (Cambridge: Cambridge University Press, 2003); Kim Nott, and Seán McLaughlin, eds., *Diasporas: Concepts, Intersections, Identities* (London and New York: Zed Books, 2010); See also Rajesh Rai, and Peter Reeves, eds., *The South Asian Diaspora. Transnational Networks and Changing Identities* (London and New York: Routledge, 2009).

[4] Cf. Gijsbert Oonk, ed., *Global Indian Diasporas: Exploring Trajectories of Migration and Theory* (Amsterdam: Amsterdam University Press, 2007), 16: "It was in the period from the late 1980s to the early 1990s that the term 'diaspora' became fashionable. The Jewish diaspora no longer monopolized its connotations. The question was raised whether other groups of migrants could be labelled as a diaspora. Politicians and representatives of overseas communities started using the term 'diaspora'. Africans, Armenians, and indeed Indians and Chinese migrants began to refer to themselves as being part of a 'diaspora'."

[5] Carolin Alfonso, Waltraud Kokot, and Khachig Tölölyan, eds., *Diaspora, Identity and Religion: New Directions in Theory and Research* (London: Routledge, 2004); Robert

Fast means of travel and communication makes it easy for the migrants to keep abreast of the religious developments in their homelands, and at the same time nurture it in their new lands of migration. One could observe the process of hybridity characterizing the phenomenon of migration at work also in the religious sphere.[6]

This chapter will be in the form of a case study, namely enquiring into the religious identities of South Asians in diasporic condition. We will focus particular attention on Christian migrants and their religious identity.

## PART I: MIGRANTS AND THEIR RELIGIONS

### The Wider Context

We need to place the diasporic religious condition of South Asians in the larger frame of migration. Time and space are fundamental features that define human existence. Displacement, whether voluntary or forced, is a change that profoundly affects individuals and groups in several ways. We may think of the transatlantic slave trade in which millions from Africa were forced into slavery and transported to the new world of the Americas. More recent statistical studies show that there took place 34,808 voyages to transport African slaves. A few million perished on the way. For every European in the Americas, there were four African slaves.[7] It was not a marginal phenomenon, but a colossal forced movement of people in human history.

The Europeans migrated to different parts of the world in search of greener pastures, wealth, and then colonies. It is estimated that within the span of about one hundred years from the middle of the eighteenth century to the middle of the nineteenth century, about eighty million

W. Hefner, John Hutchinson, Sara Mels, Christine Timmerman, eds., *Religions in Movement: The Local and the Global in Contemporary Faith Traditions* (London: Routledge, 2013).

[6] Cf. Marwan Kraidy, *Hybridity, or the Cultural Logic of Globalization: The Cultural Logic of Globalization* (New Delhi: Temple University Press, 2005); Anjali Prabhu, *Hybridity: Limits, Transformations, Prospects* (Albany: State University of New York Press, 2007); Iyall Keri E. Smith, ed., *Hybrid Identities: Theoretical and Empirical Examinations* (Leiden: BRILL, 2008).

[7] Cf. David Eltis, and David Richardson, eds., *Extending the Frontiers: Essays on the New Transatlantic Slave Trade Database* (New Haven: Yale University Press, 2008); James Walvin, *Crossings: Africa, the Americas and the Atlantic Slave Trade* (London: Reaktion Books, Limited, 2013); Mariana Candido, *An African Slaving Port and the Atlantic World: Benguela and its Hinterland* (Cambridge and New York: Cambridge University Press, 2013).

Europeans migrated to different parts of the earth. Then came the migration of East Asian peoples—China and Japan. South Asian migration
forms part of these movements. They were simple plantation workers,
unskilled laborers, professionals, service providers in educational and
health-care sectors, or traders.[8] Though small in number, in many ways,
they were significant in terms of their contribution to the economy and
culture of the countries of migration.

### Different Waves of Migration

There have been several waves of South Asian migrations—from what are
the present-day nation-states of India, Sri Lanka, Pakistan, and Bangladesh.
When one speaks of migration and diaspora, one refers mostly to the latest
phase that began in the 1960s. It may be a surprise to many that as far back
as seventeenth century, South Asians had traveled to Europe, especially
England and had settled down there.[9] It is almost contemporaneous to the
British East India Company moving to India for commerce. Some of these
migrants distinguished themselves in public life of the countries of their
migration. However, the crucial factor in migration was colonialism.
Gandhi himself was a migrant in South Africa, where he lived for over two
decades, and it was the plight of Indian minorities that triggered his life-
long struggle against colonialism and for Indian independence.[10] The
Dutch and the British colonial modes of production dispersed in different
parts of the world, in order to maintain the profitability of colonies, called
for cheap labor. Therefore, people from the Indian subcontinent were
transported to South Africa, Kenya, Tanzania, Uganda, Malaysia, Surinam,

---

[8] Cf. Crispin Bates, ed., and the University of Edinburgh, Center for South Asian Studies,
*Community, Empire and Migration: South Asians in Diaspora* (Basingstoke: Palgrave, 2001);
Amy Bhatt, and Nalini Iyer, "South Asian Oral History Project, and University of Washington
Libraries," in *Roots & Reflections: South Asians in the Pacific Northwest,* foreword by Deepa
Banerjee (Seattle, USA: University of Washing ton Press, 2013); David Yoo, and Eiichiro
Azuma, eds., *The Oxford Handbook of Asian American History* (New York: Oxford University
Press, 2016); N. Jayaram, ed., *Themes in Indian Sociology, The Indian Diaspora Dynamics of
Migration* (New Delhi: Sage Publications, 2004).

[9] Cf. M. Fisher, *Counterflows to Colonialism. Indian Travellers and Settlers in Britain
1600–1857* (Delhi: Permanent Black, 2003).

[10] Cf. Goolam Vahed, "'An Evil Thing': Gandhi and Indian Indentured Labour in South
Africa, 1893–1914," *South Asia: Journal of South Asian Studies* 42 (2019): 654–74;
V. Pathak, "Indian Diaspora in South Africa," *Africa Quarterly* 43, no. 1 (2003): 72–85.

Fiji, Trinidad, and so on.[11] The decolonization of these countries had serious adverse effects on the South Asian migrants, who were looked at as the leftover of the colonial regime and economy. Hence, there have been cases of severe restriction, discrimination, and even expulsion, as was the case during Idi Amin's regime in Uganda.

In some countries like Malaysia, the South Asian population is about 10%, whereas in Trinidad they form 40% of the population and in Fiji over 50%, exceeding even the local population. As for the West, the presence of South Asian migrants is significant in the UK—constituting almost 45% of all migrants in that country. Since 1960s, the number and proportion of South Asian migrants in the USA and Canada have increased steadily.

The situation of South Asians is varied and conditioned by such factors as the historical time of their migration, geographic location, gender, economic condition, the nature of the occupation, and so on. In this chapter, after profiling the South Asian diaspora, we will interpret their condition at a theoretical level, and then go on to focus on how their religious traditions define their identity and practices.

In terms of social and economic conditions, the diaspora situation is varied. It spans from indentured laborers of the past to present-day highly professional and technically skilled persons. In between are skilled, semi-skilled, and unskilled laborers migrating mostly to the Middle East countries. Many South Asians have distinguished themselves in their profession. Indian migrants are the community with the highest income in the USA.[12] Lakshmi is the goddess of wealth in the Hindu tradition, and her temples are found among migrant communities in the USA and other parts of the West.

### Typological Value of South Asian Diaspora for Religious Studies and Migration Studies

South Asia, in a way, is a laboratory of the world. Here, experiments in secularism, democracy, intercultural, and interreligious relationships take

---

[11] Cf. Crispin Bates, "Some Thoughts on the Representation and Misrepresentation of the Colonial South Asian Labour Diaspora," *South Asian Studies* 33, no.1 (2017): 7–22; Reshaad Durgahee, "'Native' Villages, 'Coolie' Lines, and 'Free' Indian Settlements: The Geography of Indenture in Fiji," *South Asian Studies: Journal of the Society for South Asian Studies* 33 (2017): 68–84.

[12] Sabeen Sandhu, *Asian Indian Professionals: The Culture of Success* (El Paso: LFB Scholarly Publishing LLC, 2012).

place. This is true also of South Asian migration and the diaspora. They represent something new. In general understanding, migration is inextricably related to well-defined territories in terms of nations and their boundaries. The South Asian migrants navigate through more than one territory and their being a community is often precisely in this negotiation in more than one society, one culture, one territory.[13] There is an extensive global network with different locations in the diaspora.[14] Think of the Indian community in Uganda who made a second migration to the UK, but are in touch with India, Uganda, USA, Canada, and so on. Digital technological means have facilitated these connections enormously.[15] It is not a simple relationship between the country of origin and country of migration. The point is well explained by the concept of transnationalism.

The South Asian diaspora foreshadows things to come when the idea of the nation will get further weakened and diluted. And what may come, indeed, will supersede the categories of hybridity and hyphenated identity. Moreover, the South Asian diaspora helps us redefine the problematic concept of nation, ethnicity, the idea of boundaries, identities, communities, as well as the ideas of belonging and allegiance. The more significant implications of globalization, in short, are reflected in the case of South Asian diaspora. Reversely, the South Asian diaspora offers us a vantage point to study and interpret globalization itself. For example, looking from the perspective of the diaspora, one would realize how globalization creates an environment for *multiple layers of identity* in the present world.

### Transformation of Ethnicity through Migration

To be able to understand the diaspora, we need to pay close attention to the way ethnicity is transformed in new contexts. It is no more a case of exporting lock, stock, and barrel the ethnic identity to a new location. The multiple layers of identity stands out clearly in diaspora when migrants

---

[13] Jackie Assayag, and Veronique Benei, eds., *At Home in Diaspora. South Asian Scholars and the West* (Bloomington: Indiana University Press, 2003). This is an exciting volume written by migrant South Asian scholars narrating their personal experiences of crossing the boundaries.

[14] Cf. Gita Rajan, and Shailja Sharma, eds., *New Cosmopolitanisms: South Asians in the US* (Stanford, California: Stanford University Press, 2006).

[15] Cf. Ajaya Kumar Sahoo, and Johannes G. de Kruijf, *Indian Transnationalism Online: New Perspectives on Diaspora* (London and New York: Routledge, 2014).

relate at different levels and with different groups—linguistic, regional, religious, and so on. There is some decomposition of identity and a creative configuration of a new identity. Moreover, this diaspora formation of identity is conditioned by the different contexts of diaspora—whether it is in Ireland, the UK, the USA, Canada, and so on.

Today, with the media and transnational communication, the former forms of identity manifestation of South Asians in the diaspora is giving way to new ones. A large amount of literature—novels, poems, narratives, autobiographies—produced by diaspora Indians bring out sharply the experiences of ambivalence felt by this group. One could sense it in the writings of V.S. Naipaul, Salman Rushdie, and many others. The analysis of this growing disaporic literature itself will make an interesting study as it unravels many hidden dimensions in the experience of the South Asian diaspora.[16]

Ethnicity is not like a cache of treasure transmitted from one generation to another unaltered. It is rather chameleon-like. It takes on different colors in different contexts and at historical junctures and among different generations. Ethnicity is hidden when the drive of pragmatism and success is up, and shows itself openly when discrimination happens, and rights are violated. In other cases, the ethnic is connected with the realm of the private, whereas one's citizenship or affiliation as British, Irish, German or American identity is for the public sphere.

### Religion in Diaspora

One major issue of the South Asian diaspora, especially in the West, is that they live in an environment in which religion is increasingly relegated to the private sphere, whereas for the migrant South Asian communities religion is vital on many counts. First of all, it is an important marker of identity.[17] The role of religion may not always be so apparent as the situation keeps changing. However, "there are times in which it is quite significant

---

[16] Cf. Chandrima Karmakar, "The Conundrum of 'Home' in the Literature of the Indian Diaspora: An Interpretive Analysis," *Sociological Bulletin* 64, no. 1 (2015): 77–90; Sandhya Rao Mehta, ed., *Exploring Gender in the Literature of the Indian Diaspora* (Newcastle upon Tyne: Cambridge Scholars Publisher, 2015).

[17] Cf. K.A. Jacobsen and P. P. Kumar, eds., *South Asians in the Diaspora. Histories and Religious Traditions* (Leiden and Boston: Brill, 2004), xiii–xiv.

and must be taken into consideration."[18] Another aspect of religion is that it helps the migrants to cope with various crises of life. More immediately, the transcendent religious base supports them in the profound changes and transformation the migrants experience. This seems to be one of the reasons why America as a nation of many immigrant groups is more religious—understood in terms of external observance—than Europe.[19]

The influence of Hinduism in the case of the diaspora needs to be analyzed from two angles, namely the influence of it on the societies where they live, and its influence on India and the Hinduism there. There was a time when some Hindu movements like the International Society of Krishna Consciousness (Hare Krishna movement) and Vedanta Society found great appeal in the UK, the USA, Canada, and elsewhere. However, in the last couple of decades, this influence has waned. Be that as it may, the diaspora communities have succeeded to make Hinduism global. It is not merely a religion of a minority ethnic group. Its presence in different societies, especially today in the West, has contributed to making the traditionally Christian societies into really multireligious societies.

Once upon a time, Hinduism was the preserve of some Oriental scholars of Europe who knew the Indic classical languages, religious texts, and traditions. For the rest of the people, it remained an outlandish and exotic religion of a people at the end of the world. Now Hinduism has come nearer home for the Westerners, who could see its visible presence and manifestations concretely. Hinduism has become part of European and American societies, so too in many other societies across the world.

Studies are showing the connection between Hindu diaspora and the right-wing religious movement of Hindutva, which is politically very active. Hindutva is an ideology of religious nationalism. According to scholarly studies, some of the right-wing movements like Vishwa Hindu Parishad are active in promoting in the diaspora a *standardized* form of Hinduism. It may appear strange but true that migrants who are exposed to liberal and secular way of life in Europe and America become supporters of extremist religious forces and movements back home. This phenomenon is hard to explain.

---

[18] Cf. Carolin Alfonso, Waltraud Kokot, and Khachig Tölölyan, eds., *Diaspora, Identity and Religion: New Directions in Theory and Research*, 170.

[19] Cf. John Hinnells, ed., *Religious Reconstruction in the South Asian Diaspora*, 144.

However, if we look at a deeper level, we begin to see that it is a problem of identity construction. To cultivate self-consciously ethnic identity, religion could be used since it is a puissant marker of identity. In fact, it is used all over to cultivate ethnic consciousness. Thus, a tradition-bound transmission of Hinduism has become in several instances, a way of fomenting Indian identity abroad and Indian nationalism back home. One ignores the fact that no one can be Indian, Sri Lankan, Pakistani, or Bangladeshi in the diaspora as at home. The relationship to the country of origin in the diaspora is in many ways a construct or creation of an "imaginary homeland." The changes in one's experience of diaspora conditions their imaging of the homeland.

We need to pay attention also to the internal developments in religion in the diaspora communities. One thing that has become evident is that, in general, there is a tendency to overlook regional, linguistic, and other local differences prevailing at home in order to make room for a unified Hinduism. In this connection, some institutions and movements have claimed to represent the entirety of Hinduism. Such is the case, for example, of the Swaminarayan Movement, which is well rooted in different countries, with its mandir, or temple, in Britain proving an attraction.[20] But such claims of representing Hinduism do not go unchallenged. Regional, linguistic, and sectarian differences prop up as points of convergence and basis for formation of group identities in the diaspora. The internal differentiation gets pronounced as the different communities become financially more resourceful, build distinct temples, and engage in religious activities according to one or other stream of Hinduism.

It is true that religious fundamentalism, whether Hindu or Muslim, is reflected also in the diaspora communities.[21] This is clearly seen in the influence Hindutva wields among a section of the Indian migrants. Many in the diaspora have also become staunch supporters in carrying out the extremist Hindutva agenda in the home country. However, there is another side to the phenomenon. In periods of crisis or discrimination, often religious identity was subsumed under the cultural one. For example, South Africa in the apartheid period saw greater unity among Hindu and Muslim migrants from India who redefined the we versus they when

---

[20] Cf. R. Dwyer, "The Swaminarayan Movement," in Jacobsen K. A. and Kumar P.P. eds., *South Asians in the Diaspora. Histories and Religious Traditions* (Leiden-Boston: Brill, 2004), 180–199.

[21] Cf. Walter K. Andersen, and Shridhar D. Damle, "The RSS Overseas," chapter 3, in *The RSS. A view to the Inside* (Delhi: Penguin-Viking, 2018), 43–62.

faced with a common experience of discrimination. They were first Indians fighting the White man; they were first colored opposing racial discrimination before they were Hindus or Muslims. This tendency repeats itself today when crises threaten the South Asian community who tend to bond together transcending their religious identity temporarily. The bad news of course is that as the crisis wanes, old religious identities spring back to the fore and enmities resume.

## *Places of Worship*

The South Asian diaspora has always carried their gods and goddesses with them, no matter to which part of the world they migrated. This is true of the indentured laborers in Malaysia, Trinidad, and Surinam of the past. This applies as well to the economic migrants in the West in contemporary times. Unskilled laborers of earlier times, coming from rural areas, continued to practice their folk religions and festivals in the diaspora. These were often centered around the temples which they constructed in the new homeland. Temple constructions got intensified with new waves of migration in the West. So, we have in Great Britain about 400 Hindu temples, 200 Gurudwaras, and 500 mosques. In the USA, there are about 400 Hindu temples. In Germany, the relatively few professionals who migrated were not keen on building temples. However, as in other countries in the West, the Vishwa Hindu Parishad constructed the first temple in Frankfurt in 1989. The Hindu temples began to increase with the arrival of Sri Lankan Tamil refugees and Hindus fleeing persecution in Afghanistan. There are about 100,000 Hindu migrants in Germany, of whom 45,000 hail from Sri Lanka.[22]

In earlier periods, in constructing these temples, one forgot the local differences in terms of the *sampradaya* (tradition) to which one belonged in the country of origin. Temples came into existence through joint efforts. But then with increased economic prosperity, there were more temples built, and each one of them was to underline the regional identity or the different streams of Hinduism—Saiva temples, Vishnu temples, and so on. Many times, there is what Diana Eck calls transportation of "*sacred*

---

[22] Cf. Annette Wilke, "Tamil Hindu Life in Germany. Competing and Complementary Modes in Reproducing Cultural Identity, Globalized Ethnicity, and Expansion of Religious Markets," in P. Pratap Kumar, ed., *Religious Pluralism in the Diaspora* (Leiden: Brill Academic Publishers, 2005), 235–268.

*topography.*" It means that the migrants replicate in their diaspora temples and churches dedicated to particular deities or saints back home. Thus, we have temples which represent India's renowned Tirupati dedicated to Lord Venkateswara, or Balaji.

Temples and places of worship in the diaspora are invested with new meanings. They are not merely functional or serving as places of worship. In the diaspora, they mean a visible sign of the particular religious group's presence and identity. Hence, the migrants care, when their financial conditions permit, to adorn the temples and gurudwaras, and other places of worship with a lot of intricate ornamentations and conduct from time to time religious processions.

> The Swaminarayan temple in north London, completed in 1955 at the cost of £ 12 million, is one of the latest in this creation of very public Hindu sacred space. It is the largest Hindu temple outside India, modelled to one near Ahmedabad, Gujarat, a glittering edifice in white stone, for which much of the carving was done by over a thousand craftsmen imported from India. In America too Hindus have built temples in many traditions...They are demonstrations both of devotion and increasing levels of disposable income, as well as symbols that Hindus are 'at home' in the new diaspora location.[23]

Construction of places of worship and maintenance activities bring the devotees together in mutual interactions, in ways that are not to be seen in the countries of origin. Moreover, temples get transformed into a new environment. Let me explain it through an example. In India, the temples are not constructed for *community* worship, since this is not a Hindu practice. Hindus visit temples to worship as *individuals* and *families.* On the other hand, in many Western countries where Christianity is the dominant religion, as in the USA, the Hindu diaspora has turned temples also into places of *community* worship similar to Christian churches. Even more, the temples also organize religious instruction, similar to Sunday catechism, on their premises. They also serve as centers for works of charity for the needy in the community.

Another exciting aspect of temple-building is the process of negotiation of identity. While building places of worship in a distant country, far away from the environment of the countries of origin, the diaspora

---

[23] Judith M. Brown, *Global South Asians. Introducing the Modern Diaspora* (Cambridge: Cambridge University Press, 2007), 103.

community enters into a negotiation with the land of their migration. They adopt local ways in temple-management. The way Hinduism has negotiated its identity through temple-building is highlighted by Diana Eck. She observes:

> Tocqueville pointed to what American religious historians have called the spirit of "voluntarism" distinctive American religious life. With no government support and the freedom to flourish, religious communities have had to compete for and gather adherents, building religious institutions by the voluntary contributions and energies of their constituents. This has lent a distinctive shape to religious life in the United States...Thus Hindu communities constitute themselves for the purpose of building temples, they too develop a pattern of participation that few are likely to have encountered in India. They must incorporate, elect officers, solicit members, keep records, and garner volunteers for temple activities.[24]

This democratic spirit in temple construction and management in the diaspora is very different from how temples are built and managed in India where it is heavily centered on the priestly class of Brahmins.

### Public Manifestation of Religion Through Processions

Like temples, processions are very important in the religious expression of South Asians. Any procession is a claim of public space and the manifestation of identity. As for Hinduism, in South Asia, the unity of the community is not created through collective worship, but through other manifestations. Procession is one of those expressions of unity as it involves the cooperation of different segments and strata of society acting *in unison*. They are united through the visit of the deity taken in procession and received by the crowds waiting to have the *darshan* or vision of it. Everyone in the village or the city where procession takes place becomes the host of the deity. It is the occasion in which the divine image carried around showers its blessings on the people and the society.

In the diaspora too we note a replication of procession, though not all components of the procession in the home country come to play. These processions have expanded the presence of the temple and made more

---

[24] Diana Eck, "The South Asian Religious Diaspora in Britain, Canada, and the United States," in Harold Coward, John R. Hinnells, and Raymond Brady Williams, eds., *The South Asian Religious Diaspora in Britain, Canada, and the United States* (Albany: State University of New York Press, 2000), 26.

visible the deity. No wonder that they are on the increase.[25] For example, it is reported that the procession of Sri Kamadchi Ampal Temple in Hamm, Germany, when it was started counted 200–300 devotees, whereas already by 2007 it had grown to 20,000,[26] which shows the popularity of procession among the immigrants. Such processions are done in other temples in Berlin, Hanover, and other cities. Such religious processions of Sikhs take place annually in Norway.

## Transmission of Religious Tradition

In South Asia, one paid little attention to what may be called transmission of religious traditions to the next generations. People did not need any organized efforts because religious practices, myths, symbols, and tenets were absorbed informally from the environment, from frequent rituals celebrated at home, and festivals in the village temples. On the other hand, new generations in the diaspora do not have any such experience. Hence, there is a concern regarding how to transmit the religious tradition to younger generations. The problem is not only that of teaching. It is compounded by the fact that children being brought up in the diaspora and in interaction with another world of life and system of values do not seem to resonate with religious myths, symbols, and stories reflecting a world that has become quite alien to them. Of course, there are efforts, as I noted, to teach Hindu religious tradition in temples similar to Christian catechism or Sunday Schools. It is not yet clear in what ways the young generation of Hindus would relate to the religious tradition of their parents and grand-parents. We could expect some exciting developments and turning points in this field.

## Reinterpretation of Sacred Texts, Narratives, and Myths

Indic intellectual traditions had a long history of hermeneutics. In the ancient period and in Medieval times, semiotics and semantics were objects of study, and well-framed rules were in vogue for structuring the classical languages and for elucidating the meaning of texts. The accessible mode

---

[25] Cf. Knut A. Jacobsen, "Hindu Processions, Diaspora, and Religious Pluralism," in *Religious Pluralism in the Diaspora*, edited by P. Pratap Kumar (Leiden: Brill Academic Publishers, 2005), 163–174.

[26] Knut A. Jacobsen, ed., *South Asian Religions on Display. Religious Processions in South Asia and in the Diaspora* (London and New York: Routledge, 2008), 181.

of interpretation of religious texts and narratives was generally done in temple discourses or in a domestic environment in connection with some celebration or festival.

Life in a new setting and environment has led the diaspora to spontaneously see and read the traditional texts with news eyes and in different ways. For example, the story of Rama narrated in the grand epic of Ramayana has been endowed with a new meaning. Many diaspora Hindu devotees identify themselves with the plight of Rama who was deposed from his throne and sent into the forest, where he continued to practice righteousness and maintained his virtue and nobility until his reenthronement after years of travails. Here is an attempt to see the text (the epic) as open-ended and capable of yielding new meanings in new contexts. Such a hermeneutical orientation of the autonomy of text could lead to distinct forms of Hinduism in the diaspora with its own characteristics—American Hinduism, British Hinduism, German Hinduism, and so on. But, unfortunately, there is so much dependence on South Asia, its tradition, and its gurus that autonomous Hindu streams have not yet emerged in the diaspora. However, this is possible given the fluidity of Hinduism and its ability to grow with new cultures and traditions. For, as Peter van der Veer notes,

> To be a Hindu is neither an unchanging, primordial identity nor an infinitely flexible one which one can adopt or shed at will, depending on circumstances. It is an identity acquired through social practice and, as such, negotiated constantly in changing contexts.[27]

### Facing Some Thorny Issues

The South Asian diaspora and the multireligious Western societies have to face jointly also some thorny issues. We need to remember that India has a population of about 14% Muslims, and Pakistan and Bangladesh are overwhelmingly Muslim. This religious demography is also represented in migration, making, for example, the South Asians the largest Muslim group in Britain among its over four million Muslims. Let me highlight at least three thorny issues here.

First of all, there is the most obvious question of *violence and terrorism*. It was very shocking for many that the London subway bombing of July

---

[27] Peter van der Veer, and Steven Vertovec, eds., *Aspects of South Asian Diaspora* (Delhi: OUP, 1991).

2005 was done by South Asian Muslims born and brought up in the UK.[28] The imams serving the South Asian community are not familiar with local realities and situations and are, unfortunately, not equipped to help the Muslim communities adequately to forge relationships with peoples of other religious traditions. Such being the case, these religious leaders could also fan communal passion and cause radicalization of Islam.

That said, the discontent within the diaspora Muslim community and especially among its youth needs to be addressed. It could be traced to unfulfilled aspirations, dwindling educational opportunities, lack of employment, alienation, and so on. We should remember that diaspora Muslims are connected with international issues and questions. It is too evident today that religion plays a very significant role in international politics. The war in Iraq and Afghanistan, the lack of understanding for the Palestinian cause, the attitude toward Iran, and the show of military prowess against Islamic countries, may have created the feeling of threat among the diaspora and especially its youth. Sure, every case of violence and terrorism is to be severely condemned. However, more needs to be done. Deeper causes are to be sought in contemporary international politics. The nexus between, diaspora and terrorism may not be analyzed solely with reference to nation but have to be studied as a transnational phenomomenon going beyond the analytical category of nation.

The second question concerns *the perceived offence or insult by the migrant religious groups*. This could come about from other religious groups or from secularist quarters. There were Muslims who were vociferous against Salman Rushdie and his work. Through their protests, burning of his work, and so on, they wanted his book *The Satanic Verses* to be withdrawn from circulation. There was a serious grievance that the Western states did not take action against the perceived offence to the Islamic community. The point here to note is that in such controversial issues one may not assume that the entire Muslim community would be of the same view. There are different views and opinions in the same religious community, which is important to take into account in conducting fruitful dialogue in contested issues.

---

[28] Cf. Ron Geaves, "A Reassessment of Identity Strategies Amongst British South Asian Muslims," in John R. Hinnells, ed., *Religious Reconstruction in the South Asian Diaspora* (London: Palgrave Macmillan, 2007), 13–28.

The third issue is that of *knowledge of other religious traditions.* Knowledge can contribute to dispelling a lot of prejudices and misconceptions regarding religions. It can also help understand and reconcile with memories of the past. The people of the countries of immigration require greater familiarity with other religious traditions. Despite Western societies becoming factually multireligious, at the level of attitudes the traditional negative attitude to other religions and ignorance of them still persists, especially among right-wing Christian groups. I am reminded of the strange proposal of Cardinal Carlo Caffarra of Bologna, who said at the height of migrant crisis that Italy should welcome Christian migrants instead of non-Christians! We may recall here that the first person who was killed in response to the attacks of September 11, 2001, was a Sikh. It was simply because he wore a beard and a turban. For the attacker, there was no difference between a Muslim and a Sikh.

## The Issue of Representing Religion

One of the striking facts is the reaction of the diaspora community to the academic representation of their religion in the West. From colonial times, the religions of the colonized people were an integral part of the so-called Oriental scholarship. Western scholars went into the study and dissecting of the religions of the colonized people as if they were frozen objects. The world of the subject of the believers was not taken into account. Many of those studies, though claimed to be *objective,* were *ideologically colored.* No care was taken to check whether the Orientalist studies of religion mirrored the experience of the people who practiced it. The postcolonial critique of the study in the diasporic situation has accentuated the view that most often Western studies of religion are distorted, by ignorance or by design.[29] This controversy has led to a methodological enquiry into whether and to what extent Hinduism, Buddhism, or Islam could be represented academically by a person who is not an insider or a practitioner of that particular religion. The question has political overtones. In a minority situation, when academics of the majority religious group want to represent the other, it could easily become a cause of contention and conflict. On the other hand, practical experience seems to show that in diasporic situation when a person actually professing Islam or Hinduism (and not a

---

[29] In order to counter the Western efforts, new initiatives have come up from the diaspora religious communities, such as Infinity Foundation in the USA.

mere academic) teaches members of these religious traditions he or she is accepted favorably by the student body.[30]

How much room could one give to sentiments of religious identity in the context of the academia? Like any other field, religion also needs to be approached from a scientific point of view. This means that if there is one place where the taboos and some of the socially harmful practices are to be critically questioned, it is the academia. If there is refusal to subject to a critical study one's religion, then the best thing is not to bring it into the academic sphere. If the study of religion is to be treated as an academic exercise—conceding that religion is undoubtedly much more than academic study—then it should be open to an enquiry by all those who are interested in the subject matter. This is meaningful also given the need for interaction and exchange among scholars of comparative religion and comparative theology. That *only* a Hindu can be a teacher of Hinduism or a Muslim a teacher of Islam does not reflect the spirit of interreligious understanding required today for peace and harmony in society, nor does this seem to respect the canons of academic study and research. It may be recalled here that a huge controversy erupted in the state of California, in the USA, in 2006, regarding the way Hinduism and Indian history were represented in the school textbooks.[31] Some Hindu organizations in the diaspora objected to a textbook that spoke of Aryan invasion, and, according to them, misrepresented caste and the role of Indian women in society. The Education Department of California state was taken to court for perceived misrepresentation.

---

[30] Cf. Arti Dhand, "Hinduism to Hindus in the Western Diaspora," *Method and Theory in the Study of Religion* 17, no. 3 (2005): 274–286.

[31] Cf. Purnima Bose, "Hindutva Abroad: The California Textbook Controversy," *The Global South* 2, no. 1 (2008): 11–34; Jakob De Roover, "Courting Controversy in the West," *Economic and Political Weekly* 41, no. 18 (2006): 1764–765; Sangeeta Kamat, and Biju Mathew, "Religion, Education and the Politics of Recognition: A Critique and a Counter-proposal," *Comparative Education* 46, no. 3 (2010): 359–76; Sudarsan Padmanabhan, "Debate on Indian History: Revising Textbooks in California," *Economic and Political Weekly* 41, no. 18 (2006): 1761–763; Kamala Visweswaran, Michael Witzel, Nandini Manjrekar, Dipta Bhog, and Uma Chakravarti, "The Hindutva View of History: Rewriting Textbooks in India and the United States," *Georgetown Journal of International Affairs* 10, no. 1 (2009): 101–12.

## Pedagogy for Religious Understanding

The study of religions as an integral part of educational curriculum is highly important in our contemporary times. This project started already in some countries like Britain, but it needs to be intensified and constantly revised in light of new experiences. The syllabus needs to reflect the nature of these religious traditions. For, there is the danger of treating other religious traditions in the same way as Christianity. Commenting on the British curriculum of religious education, John Hinnells cautions against what he calls "protestantizing of non-European religions." He observes:

> Apart from the fact that this [school syllabus] may inculcate Christian values, even where Asian religions are part of the syllabus the image and emphasis that are conveyed can determine the self-perception of young Hindus, Muslims, and so on. The obvious example is the priority given to doctrine and "scriptural" texts, rather than to family practices and values. ...The goal, clearly, is to spread understanding and thereby tolerance, but the "emphasis on "faith" as in the common phrase "the faith communities", gives a particular Christian slant to what is seen to be the essence of religion. The widespread assumption that to be effective, prayers must be understood, the stress on congregational worship, all result,...in the protestantizing of non-European religions.[32]

At the level of higher education, the establishment of Hindu or Islamic studies similar to Christian theology would provide a forum for promoting more excellent knowledge of them. In this regard, it may be recalled here that the German government, on the recommendation of German Council of Science and Humanities, took the initiative of establishing departments and centers for Islamic theology in German universities. The idea was that the Imams and other Islamic teachers be trained in a scientific and academic approach to the study of faith, similar to Christian theology. One of the more recently founded institutions is the Center of Islamic Studies at Goethe University of Frankfurt a.M., which offers courses in Islamic theology. Since 2011 other centers for Islamic Studies have been established in Tübingen, Münster, and Erlangen.

---

[32] John Hinnells, "South Asian Religions in Migration," in *The South Asian Religious Diaspora in Britain, Canada, and the United States,* edited by Harold Coward, John R. Hinnells, and Raymond Brady Williams (Albany: State University of New York Press, 2000), 7.

## PART II: THE CASE OF INDIAN CHRISTIAN DIASPORA
## AN ILLUSTRATION

After general reflections on South Asian religious diaspora in the age of globalization, in this second part of the chapter, we will focus on the case of Indian Christian diaspora as an illustration. The case study is interesting because we deal with a religious group which experiences diaspora-like situation already in their countries of origin, because of their minority status. In the eyes of many South Asians, Christians do not belong to India, Pakistan, Bangladesh, or Sri Lanka, but in a way are "foreigners." Whether a religion comes from outside ones' cultural and civilizational sphere is not essential; most important is how it has interacted with the new society and cultural environment.[33] Buddhism has been an Indic religion which spread to most of East and Southeast Asia—China, Japan, Korea, Vietnam, Cambodia, and Indonesia. But Buddhism was not viewed as alien or foreign.

If Christians have been viewed as in diaspora in their own home of South Asia, this is mainly due to the long period of colonization of the subcontinent by the colonial powers from traditionally Christian countries. For many, the loyalty of the Christians to the country is suspect. Indian Christians did not migrate from anywhere else but are sons and daughters of the land like the rest of the population. There has been a gross misrepresentation of the connection between colonialism and Christianity in India. One of the widespread prejudices is that the Indian Christians sided with the foreign Christian rulers. History is more complex than that. Very often, it is the consideration of power, influence, position, and economy that conditioned the relationship of the colonized with their colonizers. If there were Christians who supported the colonial powers, so were also Hindus and peoples of other religious traditions. Neither were all Christians *for* colonial power nor were all Hindus *against* it. In her very significant contribution to Indian feminism through a historical reconstruction of the life of Pandita Ramabai—a convert from Hinduism to Christianity—Uma Chakravarti has this to remark:

> There has been an easy conflation not only of nationalism with Hinduism but more importantly of Christianity with colonialism. There is a latent

---

[33] Cf. Felix Wilfred, ed., *Oxford Handbook of Asian Christianity* (New York: Oxford University Press, 2014).

assumption that in opting for Christianity Ramabai and others had accepted the religion of the rulers and had therefore become 'compradors' and were complicit with the colonial presence. Such an assumption is both simplistic and motivated. The mere existence of a relationship between Christianity and colonialism is not enough to treat Christianity automatically as the handmaiden of colonialism. ...There were also major moments and points of tension between the colonial administration and the Christian missionaries.[34]

Moreover, there were numerous ways in which Christianity and South Asian culture interacted. As Robert Frykenberg has rightly pointed out, there were various forms of cultural communication and interaction of Christianity with Indian society all along which speaks about the Indianness of Christianity as well as the plurality of Indian Christianity.[35]

But we need to even go back further in history. Even before the modern period of inculturation and contextualization of Christianity began, there have been many forms of interaction between Christianity and South Asian societies at different levels. The result is that Christianity became fully Indian in its culture, tradition, celebrations, art, and architecture.[36] This has been most evident among the community of Thomas Christians, who remained almost indistinguishable from the rest of the people by their identification with the surrounding cultural world. It was a matter of course and not result of any pre-planned project of inculturation.[37] The interaction and influence were mutual.[38] There has been an influence of Christian faith in some of the streams of Hinduism. This is an area where we have little materials and which awaits more in-depth research.

[34] Cf. Uma Chakravarti, *Rewriting History. The Life and Times of Pandita Ramabai* (Delhi: Kali for Women, 2000), ix–x.

[35] Cf. Robert Frykenberg, ed., *Christians and Missionaries in India. Cross-Cultural Communication Since 1500* (Grand Rapids: William B. Eerdmans, 2003).

[36] Cf. Felix Wilfred, "Christianity in Hindu Polytheistic Structural Mould. Converts in Southern Tamilnadu Respond to an Alien Religion during 'the Vasco Da Gama Epoch'," *Archives de sciences sociales des Religions* 43, no. 103 (1998): 67–86.

[37] Cf. Placid J. Podipara, *The Thomas Christians* (London: Darton, Longman & Todd, 1966).

[38] A. Mathias Mundadan, "Cultural Communication Encounter of the St. Thomas Christians with the Hindus in Kerala," *Journal of Dharma* 24, no. 3 (1999): 244–54.

## Profile of Christian Immigrants

The migrant Indian and South Asian Christian communities are not a homogenous group. For, Christianity in the subcontinent is marked by diversity. At one level, this diversity derives from the mission history and the denominational divisions. Thus, in the subcontinent, various church-traditions are represented—Catholic, Protestant, Orthodox, Pentecostal, and many independent churches. But the diversity of South Asian Christianities also derives from many cultural, linguistic, and regional factors. Thus, there are Tamil, Andhra, Tribal, and Dalit Christians. This diversity is reflected also in the profile of the Christian diaspora.[39]

The Christian immigrants hail from three major groups: the Christians from Kerala, especially those belonging to the Eastern rites; those from Goa, which was once the principal colony of Portugal and the gateway of their expansion in the East; those from Punjab, where there took place mass conversion to Christianity in the nineteenth century. To these three groups, we need to add also a significant number of Tamil Christians from Sri Lanka who were displaced through protracted war and had migrated to different countries in the West. The Goan Christians have a long history of migration to countries of the European Union, not only from India but also from other countries where they had settled down, for example Kenya. There is yet another group of South Asians who when migrating were not Christians, but converted to Christianity in the diaspora, occasioned by marriage alliances or through the efforts of evangelistic and Pentecostal initiatives of South Asian groups.

It is difficult to estimate the relative number of South Asian Christians in different countries. According to one estimate, in the UK, there are about 45,000 South Asian Christians.[40] In terms of class and profession, Christian immigrants belong to different categories like the rest of immigrants from the subcontinent. One speaks of "invisible diaspora" referring to the South Asian Christian migrants. This is so because people associate South Asia with Hinduism, Buddhism, Jainism, Islam, and Sikhism. A South Asian Christian is for many people in the West a strange category since they take Indians to be Hindus. Moreover, the Christian immigrants of South Asia were rarely the object of research as is the case, for example, with Hindus, Muslims, and Sikhs. One reason is the fact that other

---

[39] Cf. Knut A. Jacobsen, and Selva J. Raj, eds., *South Asian Christian Diaspora: Invisible Diaspora in Europe and North America* (Farnham: Ashgate, 2016).
[40] Cf. Jacobsen, and Selva, *South Asian Christian Diaspora*, 18.

religious traditions represent something new, not to say exotic, evoking the spirit of enquiry, which is not so in the case of Christian migrants whose religion is well known in the West.

There is a difference in the pattern of migration in the UK and North America. In Britain, the earlier generation of Christian migrants were mostly those who went there as students and subsequently settled down as professionals. In France, there is a sizable number of Christians from Pondicherry, a former French colony, now part of India.[41] Some of the Catholics of Indian origin from Pondicherry have been earlier in Vietnam—then a French colony—from where later they migrated to France. This once again goes to show the transnational character of the South Asian migration. The Pondicherrians with French nationality number around 45,000–50,000, most of whom are Catholics.[42] Probably, this is one of the highest concentrations of South Asian Christians in the West.

Health care is a profession in which the Christian migrants have acquired greater visibility. In the early 1960s, when there was a dearth of nurses in many European countries, nurses from India, along with those from Korea and the Philippines, were welcomed by Germany, Italy, and later also by Ireland, the USA, Canada, and the Gulf states.[43] In Germany, the beginnings of South Asian Christian presence go back to the arrival of Indian nurses in the 1960s. The acceptance of nurses as professionals in the USA since 1965 facilitated their immigration in large numbers. The number of female migrants to the Gulf States from the state of Kerala, which makes up almost half of the four million Indian migrants in the Middle East, has risen to 16%, and those from Sri Lanka are at an even

---

[41] Cf. Sebastie-Gille Brigitte, "Inculturation ou ethnicisation. Les pratiques religieuses des Pondichériens catholiques en Île-de-france," *Archives de sciences sociales des Religions* 111 (2002): 99–126.

[42] Knut Jacobsen, and Selva Raja, *South Asian Christian Diaspora*, 4.

[43] Cf. Nikki Dunne, Lynn Jamieson, Degree Supervisor, and the University of Edinburgh, Degree Granting Institution, *Who Cares?: Indian Nurses 'on the Move' and How Their Transnational Migration for Care Work Shapes Their Multigenerational Relationships of Familial Care over Time*, 2018 (Ph.D. Thesis, Edinburgh: University of Edinburgh 2018); Alessandro Stievano, Douglas Olsen, Tolentino Diaz, Sabatino, Laura Ymelda, and Gennaro Rocco, "Indian Nurses in Italy: A Qualitative Study of Their Professional and Social Integration," *Journal of Clinical Nursing* 26 (2017): 4234–245; P. Thomas, "The International Migration of Indian Nurses:," *International Nursing Review: Official Journal of the International Council of Nurses* 53, no. 4 (2006): 277–83.

higher percentage.[44] The Christian nurses in the Gulf are among the 32% of female migrants from Kerala.

> Female emigrants are much more educated than their male counterparts. As many as 45 per cent of the female emigrants are degree holders compared with only 15 per cent among the male emigrants. About 80 per cent of female emigrants have a secondary level education or higher, while the corresponding percentage among male emigrants is only 45 per cent. Thus, female emigrants from Kerala are educationally highly qualified, not only relative to the general population of the state, but also in comparison with male migrants.[45]

Another profile of the Christian women is the fact that often their migrations precede the male ones. This is explainable because as nurses women got employed first, and, subsequently, they brought their husbands to the country of migration. Further, the policy of allowing reunification of families in the USA brought in more people to that country. On the other hand, in cases like Canada, where the law of the country does not allow the reunification of families, the number of Christian immigrants is small.

Why do nurses come from Christian communities? This is explainable by the fact that from the times of Christian missionary work there was a long association of Christianity with health care, when hospitals, dispensaries, and clinics were established. Young women, mainly from Kerala where Christians are a sizable population, were encouraged by priests and nuns to take up this profession and were given opportunity to work in Western countries, where, as I noted, there was a dearth of young women taking to the nursing profession.

The migrant Christians forming linguistic and ethnic communities are ministered by priests and pastors coming from India on their own, or sent by the respective churches in India. There are also many priests and pastors serving in the already-established churches of the country. They do

---

[44] For detailed statistics, see Marie Percot, and S. Irudaya Rajan, "Female Emigration from India: Case Study of Nurses," *Economic and Political Weekly* 42, no. 4 (2007): 318–325; See also Prakash C. Jain, and Ginu Zacharia Oommen, eds., *South Asian Migration to Gulf Countries: History, Policies, Development* (New York: Routledge, 2017); Mehdi Chowdhury, and S. Irudaya Rajan, eds., *South Asian Migration in the Gulf: Causes and Consequences* (London: Palgrave Macmillan, 2018).

[45] Marei Percot and S. Irudaya Rajan, "Female Emigration from India," 319.

these services temporarily and in a subsidiary manner without holding leadership positions. One significant exception has been the appointment of Bishop Michael Nazir Ali of Pakistan, who was chosen in 1995 and served as Bishop of Rochester in the UK till 2009. He was a convert from Islam.

## *The Gender Issue*

A critical issue regarding the migration of South Asians is the question of gender. This is true irrespective of religion. There is practically no difference between Hindus, Christians, and Muslims. South Asia is still a *highly patriarchal* society in which women, their life, and their movements are rigorously controlled. Notwithstanding, a significant percentage of women have made an impact by their professional competence in the host countries.

I must also add here another type of migration—the Catholic women religious in Europe, in Italy, Spain, Germany, and so on. At a time when due to secularization and other factors, vocation fell drastically in the many religious orders of Europe, these orders found a fertile soil of vocation in India, especially in the state of Kerala. Thus, young girls were recruited and sent to European countries, where they worked in institutions managed by these religious orders, in hospitals and nursing homes. However, this has been a sad story of both oppression of women and racial discrimination. Many of these girls had to live in prisonlike conditions under the panopticon of the white religious superiors. They experienced humiliation and ostracization. Some of them dared to leave to find a life for themselves, and few others had no other choice than to become sex workers. The issue was made known to the general public in India through the media as "nun-running business," and the matter was discussed in the Indian parliament, and stringent regulations were imposed for the migration of women religious to Europe and America.

Urmila Goel brings out the experience of patriarchy and ethnic discrimination experienced by the female migrants—the nurses and the nuns:

> The racism they faced was not direct and violent but rather institutional, subtle and exoticizing. So, for example, the nurses were portrayed as ever-smiling 'Indian angels' who were naturally kind and caring, thus reproducing 'white' German stereotypes about 'Asian' women. Most of their names were changed in their pronunciation to fit German articulation. The full

force of institutional racism hit when in the late 1970s, unemployment rates in West Germany had risen, and there were enough 'white' nurses who wanted to work in the health sector. The authorities, especially those in the federal states where conservative parties formed the government, refused to extend the work and residence permit of the 'Indian nurses'.[46]

On the other hand, with time, the women religious from India and other countries of South Asia have also shown their leadership abilities, and increasingly candidates from the Indian subcontinent are being elected or appointed in high administrative positions in these religious congregations with their headquarters in Europe.

### Marriages in Diaspora

Like other immigrants from the subcontinent, for the Christian diaspora too marriage serves as a means of maintaining their tradition—caste, religion, and language, which also have become deciding factors in the choice of spouse in arranged marriages or semi-arranged marriages. As a result, intermarriages are rare occurrences in the South Asian diaspora community. Influenced by the traditional Christian morality as well as the Indic culture, the migrant community feels threatened by what they see as promiscuity in the Western society, and arranged marriage comes in handy, in the view of parents, against such dangers as dating, premarital sex to which their children are exposed. Marriage by free choice is not objected as long as it is of the same *religion* and even more, in some cases, of the same *caste*. Given the centrality of families in the social fabric of South Asian societies, this is viewed as necessary for proper understanding and familial harmony.

Here again, the situation is changing with new generations. It is striking, as some fields studies have ascertained, that the second generation women of immigrant parents do not opt for Indian males as their partners since they feel that Indian men are patriarchal and domineering. Having been brought up in a liberal environment, they tend to go for interracial marriages.

---

[46] Urmila Goel, "The Seventieth Anniversary of 'John Mathew': 'Indian' Christian in Germany," in Knut Jacobsen, and Selva J Raj, *South Asian Christian Diaspora: Invisible Diaspora in Europe and North America* (Farnham: Ashgate publishing Limited, 2008), 62–63.

### *Negative and Critical Attitude toward Hinduism*

Contrary to what one may expect from the Christian community from South Asia, its attitude toward people of other religions in the diaspora is generally negative, and in this they are not different from most Christians. Coming from a very strongly multireligious region like South Asia, the Christian community would be expected to be an example of forging interreligious relationships and understanding. But this does not seem to happen. The reasons could be numerous. The immigrants had the upbringing in traditional Christian homes, and have not been exposed to new developments in mainline Christianity toward other religious traditions. Further, given the general invisibility of South Asian Christian diaspora, the small Christian groups would like to distinguish themselves from the larger group of migrants such as Hindus, Muslims, and Sikhs, and this requires that they maintain the traditional and conservative expressions of Christianity.

Moreover, in the case of Dalit Christians in the diaspora, there is an added reason for the negative attitude. It has been the contention of the Dalit community that the ideology of *caste* sanctioned and legitimized by Hinduism has been the cause of their oppression and humiliation. In the great epic of Ramayana, the much-venerated Hindu God Rama kills Shambuka, who was an "Untouchable," for daring to take up a life of renunciation. Many Dalits would not like to associate themselves with the practices and tenets of Hinduism. In fact, when among Indian Catholics a great movement of inculturation started by adopting a lot of symbols and signs from the Hindu tradition, the Dalits vehemently opposed it. Making a study of the Catholics of Pondicherry origin in France, most of whom hail from the community of the "untouchables," Brigitte Sebastia notes:

> For Catholic Untouchables, affirming a Christian identity means the rejection of everything that symbolizes Hinduism. Although their behaviours and their habits indicate a strong interiorization of Hindu customs, they condemn the hierarchical model that stigmatizes them and the Hindu rites that were defined in the past as "superstitions". It is a manner of priding themselves on belonging to a more advanced, equalitarian and fraternal religion. They have little interest in works on inculturation, which they find too intellectual or too abstract.[47]

---

[47] Brigitte Sebastia, in "Religion as an Arena for the Expression of Identity: Roman Catholic Pondicherrians in France," *South Asian Christian Diaspora: Invisible Diaspora in*

Some evangelical groups of South Asia extend their mission work among the Hindus in the migrant communities and distribute tracts and other literature in English and other South Asian languages. Many of them are not happy that Hindus are allowed to build temples in what they believe are Christian countries. Besides, their conservative theological reasons for this stand, there is also a more immediate motive. They know that in recent times in communal violence, Hindu radical groups have burnt down churches and Christian institutions and have harassed Christian priests, pastors, and nuns. So, they do not see it proper that the same Hindus are welcomed and given space to build temples in the USA, Canada, the UK, and other European countries.

The reaction of migrant Dalits and in particular Christian Dalits has to be understood against the background of caste discrimination. The high castes carry with them all the trappings of caste and exercise it vis-à-vis the lower castes in the host country where they find themselves together. There are many stories of severe caste discrimination that a law prohibiting the practice of caste was mooted in the UK. But it was fiercely opposed by the Hindu Council UK and the National Council of Hindu Temples.[48]

### Enclave Churches

Immigration opens up new possibilities regarding how a person continues with his or her Christian faith and practice. Some of them have joined with the established churches in the countries of immigration, as is the case of students who went to the UK to study and then settled down there. Such cases are rather rare. The earlier strategy on the part of the Mar Thoma Church and Church of South India was to encourage Christians to join local congregations—in Britain, for example, the Anglican parishes. However, with the increasing number of immigrants, the situation changed.

How the ethnic, cultural, and linguistic factors dominate over religious affiliation is best illustrated by the South Asian Christian diaspora. It is natural to expect that being Christians the immigrants would relate closely with the Christians of the country of diaspora. Instead of any such rapport

*Europe and North America,* edited by Knut A. Jacobsen, and Selva J. Raj (Farnham: Ashgate publishing Limited, 2008), 53.

[48] Cf.    https://thediplomat.com/2017/12/has-caste-discrimination-followed-indians-overseas/ [accessed on December 12, 2019].

with the local Christian community, the diaspora South Asians have generally tended to create their own enclave churches which is maintained by South Asian pastors and leaders and where services are conducted in local languages—Tamil, Malayalam, Telugu, and so on. These churches understand themselves in practice as an extension of Christianity from the Indian subcontinent.

This model of enclave churches is most clearly manifest in the case of Indian Oriental churches—the Syrian Orthodox churches and the Catholic Syro-Malankara and Syro-Malabar churches. In the case of Catholic Oriental churches, this trend is the consequence of the mutual relationship among the three rites in India—Latin, Syro-Malabar, and Syro-Malankara, which got aggravated since the 1980s.[49] There was strong resistance to what the Orientals felt as Latinization of their tradition, and they lamented the loss of their identity and theological and liturgical heritage. The claim that they are different and that their Oriental church needs to be present in all places wherever its members migrate prompted the expansion and establishment of these churches in America and other parts of the West. The Mar Thoma Church also started establishing its own parishes and centers, and even bishops have been appointed. This is, perhaps, the church from India that has grown more than any other and has firmly established itself in the West.[50] To this we should add the proliferation of many independent and Pentecostal Churches initiated by South Asians themselves in the countries of immigration. All these churches could be called "enclave churches."

### Problems Faced

The enclave churches face serious problems which are realized but are not adequately responded to. One of the important questions is that of the new generations whose schooling and experience is part of the country of immigration. A striking difference between generations among Indian immigrants is in what concerns the family. No one would understand the Indian culture without the central role family plays. This is a point which

---

[49] Cf. Felix Wilfred, "Catholics," in Kenneth R. Ross et., eds., *Christianity in South and Central Asia* (Edinburgh: Edinburgh University Press, 2019), 211–222.

[50] Clara A. B. Joseph, "Rethinking Hybridity: The Syro-Malabar Church in North America," in Jacobsen K.A. and Kumar P.P., *South Asians in the Diaspora. Histories and Religious Traditions* (Leiden and Boston: Brill, 2004), 220–239.

Sudhir and Katharina Kakar have made in their insightful work *Indians: The Portrait of a People*.[51] The value system and practices of the older generation center around *family*. On the other hand, the new generation of South Asians born in immigrant countries absorb from the environment and through the socialization process the spirit of *individualism*. So, there is often a clash of vision and values among the generations which get also reflected in the religious practices. The new generation needs to negotiate ethnicity, culture, and religion too.[52] The youth of the new generation exhibit little interest in the church services in Indian languages—which they know less and less—and find themselves odd in the enclaves of tradition cherished by their parents and grandparents. And yet the general pastoral praxis has tended in these enclave churches on finding ways and means to keep the new generation committed to the religious tradition of parents and grandparents. The conflict is expressed thus by Raymond Brady Williams:

> Structures developed to administer congregations in a small area or region of India are expanding, sometimes enduring great stress, to reach around the world. Disciplines developed to lead farmers in villages of Kerala toward Christian maturity are made available to (or imposed on, depending on one's perspective) young professionals and second-generation children in Houston, London, and Toronto. Symbols shaped by centuries of use in India are truncated and reinterpreted to be meaningful throughout a transnational church.[53]

There seem to be practically no efforts to help the new generation to relate themselves with the multireligious society around or to get sensitized to the broader sociopolitical issues or issues of justice and human rights. The pastors and priests in charge of the enclave churches do not exhibit the skill and training required to understand and guide the young generation growing up in a different social and cultural environment. We need to also take note of different variations in the church communities of South Asian immigrants. Some tend to be strongly ethnic and

---

[51] Sudhir Kakar, and Katharina Kakar, *Indians: Portrait of a People* (Delhi: Penguin, 2009), 233.

[52] Cf. Bandana Purkayastha, *Negotiating Ethnicity: Second-Generation South Asians Traverse a Transnational World* (New Jersey: Rutgers University Press, 2005).

[53] Raymond Brady Williams, "South Asian Diaspora in Britain, Canada and in the United States," in Harold Coward et al., eds., *The South Asian Religious Diaspora*, 13–30.

tradition-bound, whereas other communities seem to follow a middle course—namely, neither assimilation to the existing churches in the countries of immigration nor a total closure. Taking the context into account, they try to adapt their religious symbols and practices to the new environment.

After a detailed study of facts and conducting interviews with the pastors and laity of Syro-Malabar communities in the USA, Selva Raj observes:

> These facts suggest that while the church serves as the locus and agent of transmission of culture and tradition, it also fosters—some might say self-consciously—a climate of cultural insulation helping to create an insular community, isolated and removed from the fears and ambiguities of the mainstream American culture. Its insular character is evident in the pastor's self-admission. He said: 'Though I have been here for two years, I never felt I have been in America...The language I speak, the food I eat, and the homes I visit are all from Kerala...I am living in Kerala in America'.[54]

## Self-Isolation or Organized Isolation?

The formation of enclave churches is to be also explained partly by the experience of immigrants in the Christian communities of the host countries. Whereas the immigrants generally hail from traditional Christian backgrounds, in Europe and America they find a Christianity attuned to a secularist society, and therefore are not able to adapt themselves to this new situation. There are still more in-depth reasons. Most of the immigrants do not feel at home with these communities, though one would think that sharing the same faith they would naturally get integrated into these communities. There are many instances of discrimination experienced by South Asian immigrants who find that in the Christian communities of host countries there is no atmosphere for their participation as full church members. Jonathan Tan explains the point about the general tendency of maintaining separate identity of churches by the Asian immigrants in America.

> It appears that assimilation into existing American congregations is not a viable option for many Asian American Christians not because of differences

---

[54] Selva J. Raj, "New Land, New Challenges: The Role of Religion in the Acculturation of Syro-Malabar Catholics in Chicago," in Knut A. Jacobsen and Selva J. Raj, eds., *South Asian Christian Diaspora*, 192.

of language, or theological or doctrinal positions, but primarily because of discrimination and stereotyping arising from their physical inability to blend in with the dominant white American society in the same manner as nineteenth-century and early twentieth-century European Catholic and Jewish immigrants to the United States were able to do.[55]

In this connection, Jonathan Tan refers to the distinction between "cultural assimilation" and "structural assimilation" employed by sociologists in migration studies.[56] Cultural assimilation is the way immigrants adapt in their life and expressions the culture of the surrounding society. Structural assimilation is one in which the immigrant is accepted as "one of us" and have equal chances and opportunities. Since structural assimilation does not happen as in the case of European immigrants, the South Asians and other Asian communities tend to maintain a separate identity also in the church. The discrimination and the sense of exclusion they experience push them to form and nurture ethnic and language-based church groups.

In short, assimilation is a good strategy, but the experiences of migrants—Christians and others—tell that, despite their best efforts at this, they still experience discrimination. Here is a hurdle that limits the horizons of individual migrants. Therefore, the cultural assimilation on the part of migrants needs to go hand in hand with the agency of the citizens of the host country on whose disposition and positive attitude the structural assimilation of the migrants depends.

If external factors force immigrants to construct their identity and express their tradition by forming enclave communities, there are also instances where the land of immigration has endeavored to facilitate structural assimilation. One such instance would be the interrelationship between the Catholic Sri Lankan immigrant community and the local churches and society in Norway. The already-existing connections from the 1960s between the Tamil region of Sri Lanka and Norway facilitated the migration of Catholics to that country.[57] The positive role Norway tried to play in the efforts of the peace process in war-torn Sri Lanka was

---

[55] Cf. Jonathan Tan, *Introducing Asian American Theologies* (New York: Orbis Books, 2009), 60.

[56] Cf. Jonathan Tan, *Introducing Asian American Theologies*, 41–42.

[57] Cf. https://www.catholicsandcultures.org/norway/migration-immigration [accessed on December 12, 2019].

an expression of the acceptance of the Tamil migrants in that country, in the initial period for labor and later as refugees.

## The Future of South Asian Christian Communities

The South Asian Christian communities do have much potential to make a significant change in the religious scenario of the Western countries of their migration, which at the moment does not seem to be used in any appreciable manner.

First of all, they could present *new* facets and models of Christianities. In fact, today, the profile and difference in forms of Christianity are not based on the past denominational divisions. For, new forms of Christianities are emerging through cultural encounters in new contexts in the Global South. Therefore, there is no need for these communities to be part of the various traditional denominational Churches—Catholic, Protestant, Orthodox, Pentecostal, and so on. Rather, they would be making a distinct contribution if they highlight in the lands of migration the face of the Christianity of South Asia, and of the Global South, at large. The enclave churches, because of their lack of broader vision and failure to reach out, may not be in a position to make this contribution. So, this remains a challenge.

A second challenge would be that these churches in diaspora open up to more significant issues and questions of the society, both at the local and the global level. The ecclesiological vision behind these churches does not seem to allow any earnest social, ethical, and political involvement as the Christian faith would require. This is because these communities are so engrossed in internal matters and issues of worship and doctrinal orthodoxy that they fail to involve themselves in issues of the society in which they live and operate. From a sociological perspective, these groups of churches fulfill only a limited function of offering security to the immigrant groups and space for their cultural expressions. Other aspects of religion concerning society need to develop in these communities which would also help break their relative isolation.

A third challenge is that of *interculturality*. Harmony and understanding among diverse peoples, races, and cultures is one of the high ideals of Christianity that understands itself as universal. South Asian Christians find themselves betwixt between cultures—of the homeland and of the land they have made their new home. Their liminal position of sharing in two different cultural worlds could make them the best agents to foster communication and understanding among peoples and nations.

Yet another challenge is that of developing a South Asian theology in the diaspora that would reflect the new context while drawing from the rich resources of South Asian cultures, traditions, and civilization. This seems to be indispensable to face the first two challenges we mentioned earlier. A south Asian theology in context—in the context of America, Canada, UK, Germany, and so on—would help the communities to develop their faith into a commitment to society at large and empower them in this task. This theology would, at the same time, reflect experiences of the migrant groups, their struggles, anxieties, suffering, and hopes. In this, the theology of the African Americans or the Hispanic theology that focused on the mestizo identity could be of inspiration. These are theologies emanating from particular ethnic communities but their significance is polyvalent and far-reaching.

As for other Asian regions, I must add, there has taken place something more positive in this direction. There are, for example, Asian American theologies developed by Chinese, Korean, Vietnamese communities in the USA. One could cite the examples of C.S. Song, Peter Phan, Jonathan Tan, Kosuke Koyama, and others. They have also developed methodologies and hermeneutics that should sustain the Asian American theological reflections.[58] How would a South Asian-American theology or South Asian-European theology look like? There are a lot of prospects. We need to await their exploration and fulfillment.

## CONCLUSION

On February 5, 2011, the then British prime minister David Cameron, at the Munich Security Council, announced that multiculturalism as state policy has failed and that migrants need to conform to British ways, something France was already trying to do.[59] The statement of David Cameron responds to the popular perception of migrants as destabilizing the established order, a clear departure from the vision of multiculturalism as a clear marker of a tolerant society. Understandable though his reaction against the background of terror attacks and the pressure from conservative political and Christian groups about the leniency of the state toward would-be

---

[58] Cf. Peter Phan, *Christianity with an Asian Face. Asian American Theology in the Making* (Maryknoll: Orbis Books, 2003).

[59] Cf. Pathik Pathak, *The Future of Multicultural Britain: Confronting the Progressive Dilemma* (Edinburgh: Edinburgh University Press, 2008).

immigrants, it nevertheless is a short-sighted view. In particular, reactions of this type show how migration and diaspora are seen very closely in relation to the nation and nation-state. In contrast, migration and diaspora are realities of *transnational order* and a phenomenon that needs a more sophisticated analysis and response regarding other factors such as capitalism and globalization.

Second, the statement reveals a static understanding of what the British ways are. These ways have never been static, and society keeps changing. In fact, these societies have changed considerably and continue to change with the presence of migrants from South Asia and elsewhere. Third, the reaction of the Prime Minister also ignores the history of colonialism which, like the capitalism of today, was the primary reason for migration and displacement of people at a large scale. Colonialism, as the Indian theory of karma, would say, has to face the consequences of its own deeds. During a protest march by South Asians in London against discrimination, one Indian woman was holding a placard that read: "*We are here because you were there!*."

I think when one is weary of tolerance, the response is not intolerance of tolerance which does not lead anywhere but produces only a spiral of intolerance. A breakthrough of the vicious circle is possible only if we are imaginative and invent new ways and means. By projecting an imaginary, static national identity and calling for all immigrants to conform to that identity would only complicate problems, especially in areas of religious sensitivity. The realpolitik of pragmatism needs to give place to imagining other ways to approach the relationship of diversity and constitutionalism. All this would call for active engagement of civil society, since the state and its apparatus may not be able to solve alone.

The debate between multiculturalism and assimilation has its repercussions also in the religious realm. For example, one speaks not only of Muslims in Europe or America but also of European Muslim (Tariq Ramadhan), American Muslim, and so on. Similarly, one could think of European Hindu or European Sikh. What would that really mean? We cannot have *made to order* new religious models; they cannot be cultivated like hothouse plants. They have their own dynamic and modes of development. Indeed, it is not to be expected that Hinduism, Islam, and Sikhism of South Asian diaspora have the same profile in the diaspora as in the lands of origin. But the transformation of these religious identities and practices need to involve the agency of the practitioners.

Finally, let us not forget the positive values that have come about through the creation of multireligious societies in the Global North, thanks mainly to the presence of the South Asian diaspora. When everything is said and done, the interaction between migrants from South Asia and people of the West contributes to mutual enrichment and understanding in a measure that was never there before. Diaspora and multiculturalism and multireligious experiences are a prelude to significant transformations that await humankind. The axial period to which Karl Jaspers and others referred happened spontaneously without interaction. From different parts of the earth—from Greece, India, and China,—a new civilizational vision came forth. What we could project as a new axial period will come about through harmony of civilizations, cultures, and religions, far from the "clash of civilizations" model projected by Samuel Huntington. We are at the birth of a new era, and the migrants and diaspora communities with their diverse religious traditions are catalysts of the new.

Let me conclude with the words of Octavio Paz:

> What sets worlds in motion is the interplay of differences, their attractions and repulsions. Life is plurality, death is uniformity. By suppressing differences and peculiarities, by eliminating different civilizations and cultures, progress weakens life and favors death. The ideal of a single civilization for everyone, implicit in the cult of progress of technique, impoverishes and mutilates us. Every view of the world that becomes extinct, every culture that disappears, diminishes a possibility.[60]

---

[60] As quoted in Jamake Highwater, *The Primal Mind: Vision and Reality in Indian America* (New York: Harper and Row, 1981), x.

# CHAPTER 9

# Religious Freedom: Beyond the Liberal Paradigm

Viewed from the Global North, religious freedom is primarily a matter of conscience of the individual; it is an integral part of human rights, a touchstone of modernity, and a benchmark of good democratic governance. As "first freedom," it is also a mark of civilization and the ground for political legitimacy today. The United Nations' declaration of religious freedom (1981) envisages the freedom of the individual to profess the belief of his or her choice.[1] In international law, the upholding of religious freedom follows the recognition of human dignity. We could analyze the global religious scenario through the extent of religious freedom people enjoy in different parts of the world. However, the analytical instrument of

---

[1] Declaration on the Elimination of All Forms of Intolerance and of Discrimination Based on Religion or Belief. Article 1: "Everyone shall have the right to freedom of thought, conscience and religion. This right shall include freedom to have a religion or whatever belief of his choice, and freedom, either individually or in community with others and in public or private, to manifest his religion or belief in worship, observance, practice and teaching." Article 2: "No-one shall be subject to coercion which would impair his freedom to have a religion or belief of his choice." Cf. Kevin Boyle, and Juliet Sheen, eds., *Freedom of Religion and Belief: A World Report* (London, New York: Routledge, 1997); See also Heiner Bielefeldt, and International Institute for Religious Freedom, *Freedom of Religion or Belief: Thematic Reports of the UN Special Rapporteur 2010–2013* (Bonn: Verlag fuer Kultur und Wissenschaft, 2014).

© The Author(s), under exclusive license to Springer Nature Switzerland AG 2021
F. Wilfred, *Religious Identities and the Global South*,
New Approaches to Religion and Power,
https://doi.org/10.1007/978-3-030-60738-8_9

individual religious freedom may not help us see the many intricacies that characterize the ground reality of the Global South.

In many parts of the South, religious freedom is inextricably linked to the political management of groups and communities. For, religion is a social phenomenon that may not be relegated to the private sphere, meant to be achieved through the complete separation of religion and state. The denial of freedom to minority communities results in persecution as is amply attested by the many instances today.[2] Further, the separation of *state* and *religion*, which is taken for granted in the North, is not something that fits into the tradition or current situation in the Global South. Upholding the religious freedom of minorities today calls for a community-based approach. Even in an economically advanced country like Japan, the separation of religion and state is not clear. Both in prewar and postwar times, there have been many instances of the state exercise of power over religion.[3] Hence, we may arrive at some wrong conclusions were we to apply certain parameters of judgment that do not do justice to the complexity of the actual communitarian situations on the ground. This chapter intends to throw light on this by studying, especially the case of Asian religious situation.

To understand religious freedom in the multiethnic and multireligious societies of the South, especially Asia, is to break the conventional liberal framework. Religious freedom has to do not only with *individuals* and their choice of religion but with the legitimate self-expression of *communities* marked by their religious identities and often locked in conflict with each other on social, political, cultural, and economic grounds. Increasingly in our global world, the situation of the South is also becoming the situation in the North where the expanding multireligious situation has brought about new issues to the fore, and these can no more be resolved within the framework of individual religious liberty or as an issue of conscience. It is now compounded with the rise of right-wing political and religious forces in the North. Further, there are several moral issues like abortion, euthanasia, contraception, same-sex marriage, and issues of bioethics in all of which the question of religious freedom of communities are

[2] Cf. Brian J. Grim, and Roger Finke, *The Price of Freedom Denied: Religious Persecution and Conflict in the Twenty-First Century* (New York; Cambridge University Press, 2010).

[3] Cf. Tokihisa Sumimoto, "Religious Freedom Problems in Japan: Background and Current Prospects," *International Journal of Peace Studies* 5, no. 2 (2000): 77–86; David M. O'Brien, and Yasuo Ohkoshi, *To Dream of Dreams: Religious Freedom and Constitutional Politics in Postwar Japan* (Honolulu: University of Hawaii Press, 1996).

also implicated; so too the relationship between religion and state.[4] Today, with the growth of faith-based organizations involved in the public sphere, the question of religious liberty is required to cover a broader range of issues, namely the extent of freedom these organizations are to enjoy to be able to realize their mission.[5]

In the following, I shall present three different paradigmatic situations in Asia and analyze the interplay of religious freedom with other factors and forces in each of those situations. I shall also highlight some of the thorny, intriguing, and ambiguous issues caught in the dialectics of religious freedom and its negation. I shall also refer to the long history of religious intolerance and denial of religious freedom in the West, and reflect on how some of the Asian struggles for religious freedom could be of help to the West in encountering the new challenges connected with increasing migration of people from other religious traditions.

As we noted, the Asian situation breaks conventional frameworks and assumptions on religious freedom.[6] Multiethnic and multicultural as Asian societies are, freedom of religion has to do with a host of issues: with recognition and identity of different religious communities, with power relationships between majority and minority groups[7]; with the relationship of state and religion; with the creation of a harmonious environment to achieve national objectives and goals; with political expediency and stratagems; and, most importantly, with the practice of human rights.[8] Further, religious freedom concerns not only the legitimacy of a plurality of belief

---

[4] James Hitchcock, *Abortion, Religious Freedom, and Catholic Politics* (London and New York: Routledge, 2017); see also Douglas Laycock, et al., eds., *Same-Sex Marriage and Religious Liberty: Emerging Conflicts* (Lanham Maryland: Rowman & Littlefield Publishers, 2008).

[5] Cf. Stephen V. Monsma, *Pluralism and Freedom: Faith-Based Organizations in a Democratic Society* (Lanham Maryland: Rowman & Littlefield Publishers, 2011).

[6] Given the unique and intricate situation of the Middle East, which calls for treatment all by itself, this chapter does not cover that part of Asia.

[7] The term "minority" is often used in a fluid way. It needs to be more precisely defined. The following definition of Neera Chandhoke would also apply to religious minorities: "A minority is a group that is numerically smaller in relation to the rest of the population, it is non-dominant or not represented in the public sphere or in the constitution of social norms, it has characteristics which differ from the majority group and more importantly it wishes to preserve these characteristics." Neera Chandhoke, *Beyond Secularism: The Rights of Religious Minorities* (Delhi: Oxford University Press, 1999), 26.

[8] Cf. Kenneth Christie, and Denny Roy, *The Politics of Human Rights in East Asia* (London: Pluto Press, 2001).

systems but openness to a cluster of practices, behavior patterns, symbols, insignia, rituals, institutions, and so on, different from one's own. In short, religious freedom has to do with the *freedom of a community* as such whose way of life and meaning-making scheme an individual shares. These are essential tools and perspectives to analyze and understand Asian approaches to religious freedom.

## TYPOLOGIES OF RELIGIOUS FREEDOM

Even at the risk of oversimplification, let me highlight three different situations in Asia with corresponding approaches to religious freedom.

### *Religious Freedom through the Lens of Race and Ethnicity*

The first one is a situation in which religious identity overlaps with race and ethnic identity. For example, in Sri Lanka, Thailand, and Myanmar, the majority of the people are Buddhists, whereas Pakistan, Indonesia, Bangladesh, and Malaysia have an overwhelmingly Muslim population.[9] In all these cases, the national identity is viewed *as one* with cultural and religious identity.[10] To be a true Malay means to be a Muslim, and to be an authentic Thai is to be a Buddhist. Reinforcing this overlap, several of these countries have at the political level, the religion of the majority either as official state religion or religion enjoying sponsorship and special status guaranteed in the Constitution.[11] As for other religions, they are *allowed* to exist with different degrees of autonomy and freedom. At one end of the spectrum, the minority religious groups are permitted to have their places of worship, ownership of lands, religious education, and even freedom to

[9] Cf. Hui Yew-Foong, ed., and Institute of Southeast Asian Studies, *Encountering Islam: The Politics of Religious Identities in Southeast Asia* (2012); Jajat Burhanudin, and Kees Van Dijk, eds., *Islam in Indonesia: Contrasting Images and Interpretations* (Amsterdam: Amsterdam University Press, 2013); Arskal Salim, *Challenging the Secular State: The Islamization of Law in Modern Indonesia* (Hawai'i: University of Hawaii Press, 2008).

[10] This model would correspond to the establishment model in the Western tradition. For example, in England, the Anglican Church is the established church with the Queen as its head. In Italy, Spain, Portugal, Austria and Belgium, Catholicism enjoyed, and to some extent continues to enjoy a privileged position. Cf. Erich Kolig et al., eds., *Identity in Crossroad Civilisations: Ethnicity, Nationalism and Globalism in Asia* (Amsterdam: Amsterdam University Press, 2009).

[11] For the Japanese too, certain Shinto religious practices related to the Emperor and some festivals are a matter of national identity.

run educational and charitable institutions, without, however, infringing the rights and privileges of the majority religious community. At the other end is a situation in which the minority religious groups are *deprived* of many fundamental rights, oppressed, harassed, and discriminated against.[12] They are to function in the private sphere with practically no space allowed for any public manifestation of their religious belief. In some cases, running for public office is restricted to individuals from the majority religion which is also often economically privileged.[13] Such discrimination is to be explained also from the fact that in many instances minority religious groups are ethnically and linguistically different from the group espousing the majority religion. Thus, in Myanmar where religion and majority ethnic identity of Burmese overlap, the tribal peoples—Karen, Chin, Kachin, and Liu—who are *Christians*, are oppressed; and the Rohingyas, who are racially different from the Burmese and are *Muslims*, suffer many forms of discrimination and oppression.[14]

The restriction of religious freedom relates not only to other religions; it applies as well to internal minorities or sects. These are viewed as *unorthodox*, hence discriminated against and disowned. Such is the case, for instance, with the Ahmadiyyas—an Islamic sect—in Pakistan and Indonesia. Ahmadiyyas are not recognized as Muslims.[15] Moreover, members of the minority religious communities by and large do not have the right to convert, especially from the majority community, and any attempt to do so becomes a severely punishable offence. There are numerous laws and injunctions that restrict the freedom of ethnic, religious minorities, and internal minorities.

---

[12] Cf. David M. Kirkham, ed., *State Responses to Minority Religions* (London and New York: Taylor & Francis Group, 2013).

[13] Cf. Jeroen Temperman, *State-religion Relationships and Human Rights Law: Toward a Right to Religiously Neutral Governance* (Leiden: BRILL, 2010).

[14] Cf. Lowell Dittmer, ed., *Burma or Myanmar? The Struggle for National Identity* (New York, Singapore: World Scientific Publishing Co. Pte. Ltd., 2010).

[15] Cf. Surendra Nath Kaushik, *Ahmadiyya Community in Pakistan: Discrimination, Travail and Alienation* (New Delhi: South Asian Publishers, 1996); Zakaria M. Virke, *The Qur'an and the Ahmadiyya Movement: The Services of the Ahmadiyya Movement in the Propagation of the Qur'an, 1800–1978* (Toronto: Zakaria M. Virke, 1978).

## Religious Freedom under Centralized State

A second situation is one of *control* of all religions by the centralized state. The most glaring example is China, where there has been a continuous tradition of religion under political power from the Imperial Times through the Republican Period to the present Communist Period. It is striking that unlike the Indo-European tradition where there have been two power centers—altar and throne, priest (*Brahmin*) and ruler (*Kshatriya*)—in China there has been no instance of any religious or priestly power center. It is the emperor who, besides exercising political power, also mediates heaven and earth, abolishing thus any intermediaries of the religious realm. This means absolute power is vested with the political authority, which also controls the sphere of religion. History attests that the political power center—whether the emperor or the Communist Party—does not tolerate any challenge or threat to it.[16] This is true of China as much as of Vietnam.

In the modern period at the beginning of the Communist takeover of China by Mao Zedong (1949), religions were despised as unproductive and as superstitious forces. They were allowed to function only under very restrictive conditions. Things changed to the worse with the Cultural Revolution (1966–1976) when religious leaders and followers were persecuted, imprisoned, and tortured; properties owned by religious institutions were confiscated; and places of worship were either destroyed or turned into barracks, theaters, and so on. The period beginning from 1978, coinciding with China's economic opening to globalization and market, marked a change in its religious policies. Religious groups felt greater sense of freedom, and there was also an attempt to make good the past destruction and restore the confiscated properties and places of

---

[16] Cf. Kim-Kwong Chan and Eric R. Carlson, *Religious Freedom in China: Policy, Administration, and Regulation* (Santa Barbara: Institute for the Study of American Religion, 2005); Eric O. Hanson, *Catholic Politics in China and Korea* (Maryknoll, New York: Orbis Books, 1980); Donald E. MacInnis, *Religion in China Today: Policy and Practice* (Maryknoll, New York: Orbis Books, 1989); Daniel H. Bays, *Christianity in China: From the Eighteenth Century to the Present* (Stanford: Stanford University Press, 1996); Philip L. Wickeri, *Seeking The Common Ground: Protestant Christianity, and Three-Self Movement and China's United Front* (Maryknoll, New York: Orbis Books, 1988); David A. Palmer, et al., *Chinese Religious Life* (New York: Oxford University Press, 2011); Shawn Arthur, *Contemporary Religions in China*, 1st ed. (Leiden: Brill, 2019); Zhongjian Mou, Zhang Jian, *General History of Religions in China*, Part I & II, translated by Chi Zen (China: Paths International Ltd., 2017).

worship. The 1982 Constitution of China came out with a statement on the freedom of religion. Though admitted in theory, however, in practice, religious freedom is stifled by highly restrictive measures.[17] In China, it is the state which determines what is religious orthodoxy and what is heterodoxy. The criterion is simple: Those religions and religious practices that conform to the state and its policies are orthodox; and those showing any resistance are heterodox and become objects of persecution. Here we have a case of the state itself becoming a kind of religion subsuming under it all other religious expressions. What is happening, in short, is "Sinization" of all religions in the name of patriotism.

> The 'Rise of China' has been fanatically propelled by a state religion called 'Chinese patriotism'. 1 An 'imagined community' of 'China' serves as the supreme God to be worshipped by all Chinese. 2 The core catechism of this state religion is a political Trinity: patriotism, socialism, and the rule by the Chinese Communist Party (CCP). All other religions should be submissive to this state religion and integrate the Trinitarian political theology into their respective theologies. Freedom of religion, although in incremental progress, remains confined within the glass ceiling of Chinese patriotism and is meticulously restricted to pre-approved clergy, time, and place.[18]

Since religion could turn into a destabilizing force—a fear heightened since the collapse of state socialism in Eastern Europe—the Communist Party of China has intensified its policy of *penetration, regulation,* and *control.* Far from allowing autonomy to religious communities, the state has tried to penetrate them, divide them through various strategies, and set one group against the other, for example by creating a group of Catholics loyal to the state and its nationalist policies and programs, in opposition to a group of Catholics who tried to take on the state in their loyalty to the pope.[19] This latter group could not act in public but only clandestinely, and so came to be called "Underground Church." To ensure

---

[17] Cf. Jason Kindopp, and Carol Lee Hamrin, eds., *God and Caesar in China: Policy Implications of Church-State Tensions* (Washington D.C.: Brookings Institution Press, 2004).

[18] Cheng-tian Kuo, ed., *Religion and Nationalism in Chinese Societies* (Amsterdam: Amsterdam University Press, 2017), 13–14.

[19] Cf. Paul Philip Mariani, *Church Militant: Bishop Kung and Catholic Resistance in Communist Shanghai* (Cambridge, Massachusetts: Harvard University Press, 2011); Daniel Bays, *A New History of Christianity in China* (New York: Wiley-Blackwell, 2011); Fenggang Yang, *Religion in China: Survival and Revival under Communist Rule* (New York: Oxford University Press, 2011).

the loyalty to the state, a Chinese Catholic Patriotic Association was formed, which wields effective power over the church and controls its affairs. With provisional agreement between the Vatican and the Chinese government in September 2018, the rift between the "official" and the "Underground Church" has been somewhat bridged. More about this below in this chapter.

In China, religions are regulated by recognizing officially only five of them: Buddhism, Catholicism, Protestantism, Islam, and Daoism.[20] Only these have official sanction for pursuing religious activities. This restriction is meant to exclude many "sects," "superstitions," and popular cults. Throughout Chinese history, it is these marginal religious groups and cults with their base in rural areas and hinterland that represented a force of resistance to the empire, and now to the Chinese Communist Party. To have an idea of the deep insecurity of the Communist rulers vis-à-vis marginal religious groups, we may recall here the case of *Falun Gong*, which stands up to the state, but is being continuously persecuted.[21] Another example is the Tibetan-Buddhism, which has its distinct flavor and followed by a different ethnic community. But the Tibetan people have been ruthlessly suppressed and its religious leader Dalai Lama fled into exile. The Uyghur people, which due to heavy immigration by Han-Chinese, has become a Muslim minority in the province of Xinjiang is yet another case of denial of religious and cultural freedom in China.[22]

The officially recognized religions in China are controlled by a state apparatus called the Religious Affairs Bureau recently renamed as State Administration for Religious Affairs and placed directly under Communist Party control whose permission is required for all sorts of activities. The Constitution says that citizens have religious freedom for "normal religious activities." "Normal" is an ambiguous term. It is an euphemism to say that any activity that goes against the interests of the ruling power will

---

[20] Similarly, in Indonesia, only the following religions are officially recognized: Islam, Protestantism, Catholicism, Hinduism, Buddhism, and Confucianism. For any group to enjoy civil rights, it must be registered with the state.

[21] Cf. Marion Wyse, "Fa Lun Gong and Religious Freedom," *Cross Currents* 50, no. 1/2 (2000): 277–83.

[22] Cf. Carolyn Evans, "Chinese Law and the International Protection of Religious Freedom," *Journal of Church and State* 44, no. 4 (2002): 749–74. There seemed to be a slight improvement in the situation of religious freedom in China. However, looking at the development in recent years under Xi Jingping, there has been a massive deterioration of religious freedom in the PR China. See Kuo Cheng-tian, "Chinese Religious Reform," *Asian Survey* 51, no. 6 (2011): 1042–064; Peter Dziedzic, "Religion Under Fire: A Report and Policy Paper on Religious Freedom in Tibet," *The Tibet Journal* 38, no. 3–4 (2013): 87–113.

be viewed as "abnormal" or "superstitious," therefore could invite punishment. When authoritarian and centralized states like China and Vietnam proclaim religious freedom in their Constitutions, but in practice deny it through excessive controls, the seriousness of this proclamation is to be gauged on the basis of whether there are public measures and institutional mechanisms to protect this freedom. One such measure would be an independent judiciary. Unfortunately, the judiciary at the local and the national level—handpicked and controlled by the state—falls in line with state policies and cannot come to the defense of the religious communities. The state is very vigilant with foreign religions, especially Islam and Christianity. The colonial inheritance makes the Chinese state suspicious that foreign powers may use Christian churches to destabilize state power and cause social unrest. All religions, are to follow the Three Self-Movements, namely that they should be self-governing, self-supporting, and self-propagating. This explains why any foreign interventions are stoutly resisted as illustrated by the long Vatican-China stand-off in the appointment of bishops. In sum, to say of China and Vietnam that the state controls religious freedom is to say too little. What is happening is that the state is trying to redefine and reshape religions according to its own goals and policies.[23]

It is in this very complex situation that the Vatican has come to some understanding with the Chinese state, with an agreed statement to which I referred earlier. In the past, denial of freedom to Catholics and refusal to accept Vatican-appointed bishops have soured the relationships. The claim of the Vatican to appoint bishops has been viewed by the Chinese Communist Party as an unwarranted interference of a foreign state, namely the Holy See, undermining its autonomy and independence. The new agreement was met with enthusiasm on the one side and with a lot of skepticism on the other.[24] The reason for the skepticism is based on whether the Chinese government will abide by the agreement, and whether the Vatican was trapped by the Chinese Communist Party which

[23] Cf. Beatrice Leung, "China's Religious Freedom Policy: The Art of Managing Religious Activity," *The China Quarterly*, no. 184 (2005): 894–913.

[24] Cf. Agostino Giovagnoli and Elisa Giunipero, eds., *The Agreement between the Holy See and China. Chinese Catholics between past and future* (Rome: Urbaniana University Press, 2019). Cf. Paul J. Farrelly, "Rapprochement with The Vatican," in *Power*, edited by Farrelly Paul J., Golley Jane, Jaivin Linda, and Strange Sharon (Acton ACT, Australia: ANU Press, 2019), 123–28.

can use it for promoting its own diplomatic and political interests.[25] Cardinal Joseph Zen, former Archbishop of Hong Kong, denounced the accord saying, "They're [sending] the flock into the mouths of the wolves. It's an incredible betrayal."[26]

## Religious Freedom and Constitutional Democracy

The third situation of religious freedom is represented by countries with secular and democratic Constitutional base. For many Asian countries where religious minorities continue to suffer, democracy may appear a distant dream. However, at least three countries—India, the Philippines, and South Korea—found religious freedom on secular and democratic principles. However, there is a difference in understanding both these concepts. *Procedural* aspects of democracy are central to liberal thought. Instead, in Asia, with its bewildering diversity and plurality, what matters most is *substantive* democracy. Any attempt at the democratization of society and governance in Asia has to come to terms with identities—religious, regional, subnational, linguistic, and so on—whose concerns need to be represented justly and fairly. Hence, the concept and practice of democracy need to be reworked to suit this pluralist situation.

Contrary to most of its South Asian neighbors, India does not have a state religion or state-sponsored religion, even though the Hindus constitute the majority of the population. India defines itself as a secular state in its Constitution. However, the secular here does not mean any wall of separation between the state and religion, nor indifference to religion or animosity against it. The secular stands to signify the equidistance of the state from all religions, meaning that all of them are considered equal, and no religion is privileged. The Constitution grants the right and freedom "to profess, practice, and propagate religion" (Art. 25). A restriction could be placed on religion only when it goes against public order, morality, or hygiene.

Korea passed on to democracy after a lot of struggles against authoritarianism, and the state guarantees religious freedom. In the case of the Philippines, though Christians are the overwhelming majority, the

---

[25] Cardinal Joseph Zen, former Archbishop of Hong Kong, was one who vehemently raised this issue, given the low credibility of the Chinese state.

[26] Cf. https://www.theguardian.com/world/2018/sep/22/vatican-pope-francis-agreement-with-china-nominating-bishops [accessed on December 18, 2019].

country does not define itself according to the faith of its majority population. There is a considerable Muslim population which lives mostly in Mindanao or in other territories in the South of the country.[27] The 1987 Constitution of the Republic of the Philippines, despite its overwhelming Christian population, states that "the separation of church and State shall be inviolable" (Art. 26).[28]

For India and the Philippines, there are a number of practical difficulties in carrying out what is acknowledged in their Constitutions. In the case of India, there is a small but quite powerful and vociferous rightwing Hindu group which claims that India should be religiously defined as a Hindu nation. It is these extremist groups of *Hindutva*, which sporadically attack Christian places of worship, institutions, and destroy Christian symbols. They also enter into conflict with Muslims in the country. Ordinarily, within the democratic setup of the country, the minority religious communities should—in theory—be able to appeal to an independent judiciary and get redress based on the rights guaranteed to them in the Constitution. If anything, it is the proactive commitment of civil society groups and individuals who swear by the secular Constitution who now appears to be at the forefront of defending the religious freedom of minorities against the excesses of radical right-wing Hindu groups. In the case of the Philippines, though, as we noted, Christianity is not officially privileged, nevertheless, the minority Muslim population feels neglected and discriminated against. Added to this is the fact that the migration of Christians in the traditional Muslim territories raises a feeling of insecurity in the minds of the Muslim community. There has been armed resistance by the Moro National Liberation Front (MNLF) against discrimination and inequality of development in Muslim areas.

## Crisis Situations

The typology of situations in Asia we made above needs to undergo further fine-tuning in the face of critical political situations. Those who stand for religious freedom in India invoke the preamble of the Indian

[27] Cf. Michael C. Hawkins, *Making Moros: Imperial Historicism and American Military Rule in the Philippines' Muslim South* (Illinois: Illinois University Press, 2012); Jeffrey Ayala Milligan, *Islamic Identity, Postcoloniality, and Educational Policy: Schooling and Ethno-religious Conflict in the Southern Philippines* (Oxford: Palgrave Macmillan, 2005).

[28] Cf. David Buckley, *Faithful to Secularism: The Religious Politics of Democracy in Ireland, Senegal, and the Philippines* (New York: Columbia University Press, 2017), 133–182.

Constitution, which defines the country as "secular."[29] As we noted earlier, the secular in the context of India is to be understood that the state is equidistant from all religions. This is important to hold in mind against any attempt to give privileged treatment to Hinduism as if it were the religion of the nation. However, the right-wing political group—the Sangh Parivar—counters the argument saying that "secularism" is a Western concept. This sounds like the argument of "Asian values" by some Asian states which claim to use this in their critique and opposition to colonialism and imperialism, but in fact it is often a camouflage by centralized states for the violation of fundamental human rights of their citizens.[30]

The cause of religious freedom and equal treatment of all religions seems to rest on a weak foundation if it relies on the much-contested concept of *secularism*. Hence, Neera Chandhoke has rightly suggested that religious freedom of the minorities need to be based on a principle that cannot be contested because it is self-evident.[31] She speaks for the need of basing religious freedom in India, especially for its minorities, on the principle of *equality* and *democracy*. In recent times, the state policy followed in the country seems to be diametrically opposed to democracy and the principle of equality. The introduction of the "Citizens Amendment Bill" (CAB) in Parliament, passed into a law on December 11, 2019, and now called Citizenship Amendment Act (CAA), bases citizenship on religion, whereas the spirit and letter of the Constitution of the country would not allow this. It is the case of a political majority ruling the country with the Hindutva ideology discriminating against the minority Muslim community. The above-mentioned Citizens Amendment Bill accords citizenship to the Hindus who migrated or sought asylum from Pakistan, Bangladesh, and Afghanistan, whereas the same citizenship right is denied to the Muslim migrants and refugees from the same countries. Understandably, the passing of such a discriminatory law provoked stiff resistance from the

---

[29] Cf. Gary J. Jacobsohn, *The Wheel of Law: India's Secularism in Comparative Constitutional Context* (Princeton and Oxford: Princeton University Press, 2005). See also Alev Cinar, et al., *Visualizing Secularism and Religion: Egypt, Lebanon, Turkey, India* (Ann Arbor: University of Michigan Press, 2012); see also Rajeev Dhavan, "Religious Freedom in India," *The American Journal of Comparative Law* 35, no. 1 (1987): 209–54.

[30] Cf. Joanne R. Bauer, and Daniel Bell, eds., *The East Asian Challenge for Human Rights* (Cambridge: Cambridge University Press, 1999).

[31] Cf. Neera Chandoke, *Beyond Secularism: The Rights of Religious Minorities* (Delhi: Oxford University Press, 1999).

various segments of the society, including student groups and a large number of fair-minded Hindu citizens, all over the country.

The above case illustrates the twists and turns of religious freedom in a country manifestly secular and democratic. What is to be noted is that the ruling Bharatiya Janata Party (BJP) claims that it does not violate the religious freedom of Muslims or any other religious community. If so, it is well worth understanding what the party means by religious freedom. To hold that India is a Hindu country and to favor the Hindu refugees and migrants need not, according to them, amount to infringement of religious freedom of other religious groups. This reveals a typical pattern which could also be identified in other situations, for example, in several countries where Islam is the religion of the majority. The point to note is that any unequal treatment of citizens based on religion does seriously impair the concept and practice of religious freedom, despite the claims to the contrary.

The complexity of religious freedom in Asia could be illustrated with another case—the community of Rohingyas in Myanmar, which became a matter of great international concern.[32] In the state of Myanmar, which has been for many decades under martial law, with the suppression of civil rights, Aung San Suu Kyi, an awardee of the Nobel Peace Prize, signaled the dawn of a new era. The hope reposed on the change was short-lived, however. The Rohingyas are part and parcel of the multicultural Myanmar. This group which does not belong to the Buddhist majority is ethnically different, and suffered ill-treatment and expulsion from the country. In 2019, the matter came to the International Court for hearing where Aung San Suu Kyi tried to defend her regime appearing in person.[33]

## BORDERLINE ISSUES AND CRITICAL QUESTIONS

After having analyzed the typology of different situations of religious freedom and their nuances, we now turn to consider some of the areas that are ambiguous and present several difficulties in practice. Does religious

---

[32] Cf. Azeem Ibrahim, *The Rohingyas: Inside Myanmar's Genocide*, Revised and Updated ed. 2018 (London: Hurst & Company 2018); Mahfuzul Haque, Abdur Razzak, and Center for Human Rights, *A Tale of Refugees: Rohingyas in Bangladesh* (Dhaka: Center for Human Rights, 1995); Maung Zarni, and Natalie Brinham, *Essays on Genocide of Rohingyas (2012–2018)* (Dhaka: C.R. Akbar, 2019).

[33] https://www.theguardian.com/world/2019/dec/10/aung-san-suu-kyi-court-hague-genocide-hearing-myanmar-rohingya [accessed on December 22, 2019].

freedom extend, besides beliefs, also to the freedom to convert others to one's faith? To what extent can people exhibit the symbols, costumes, insignia, and so on that belong to their life as believers of a particular religion? This became a hot issue with the headscarf controversy in France.[34] Does religious freedom also imply the freedom to be governed by the personal laws specific to one's religious community? Could a minority religious community legitimately play a public role and participate in what concerns the common good of the society, or is it reserved only to the majority community? Does the state violate freedom of religion if it intervenes in the name of equality to protect minorities and weaker sections? What happens when Dalits ("the Untouchables") are prohibited from entering the *sanctum sanctorum* (Holy of Holies) of Hindu temples, or when women are discriminated and banned from ordination justified by religious beliefs? Can female circumcision be allowed if it is part of religious belief as it is the case in some countries? Is religious freedom violated if the state were to intervene in these situations? Asia is grappling with such issues of enormous social and political consequences. By way of example, let me elaborate one issue here—personal or customary laws.

## RELIGIOUS FREEDOM AND LEGAL PLURALISM

The intersection between religion and law is too evident, the former serving as the basis for the development of many legal systems and jurisprudence. In Asia, different religious communities were governed by their personal or customary laws.[35] Thus, we have Islamic laws binding Muslims, the Hindu legal system for Hindus, and the Canon law system for Roman Catholics. Many of these traditional laws have to do with issues of marriage, inheritance, the position of women, and so on. The ticklish question is whether one would be infringing the right of religious freedom if these were to be abolished and people were asked to follow a common civil code

---

[34] Nicky Jones, "Religious Freedom in a Secular Society: The Case of the Islamic Headscarf in France," in *Freedom of Religion under Bills of Rights*, edited by Babie Paul, and Rochow Neville (South Australia: University of Adelaide Press, 2012), 216–38; Cf. also, Katherine Pratt Ewing, "Legislating Religious Freedom: Muslim Challenges to the Relationship between 'Church' and 'State' in Germany and France," *Daedalus* 129, no. 4 (2000): 31–54; Melanie Adrian, *Religious Freedom at Risk: The EU, French Schools, and Why the Veil Was Banned* (Cham Heidelberg: Springer, 2015).

[35] Cf. D. K. Srivastava, "Personal Laws and Religious Freedom," *Journal of the Indian Law Institute* 18, no. 4 (1976): 551–86.

on civil issues, independent of their religious background. We are at the intriguing intersection of legal pluralism and legal universalism. It involves, on the one hand, the legitimate autonomy of religious communities, and, on the other, it carries with it also the danger of violation of some universal human rights, for example, relating to women and minorities. How does the state respond when a religious community claims its legal system as essential to its religion? How does that reconcile with claims of universal rights? During the colonial period, the British allowed personal and customary laws, some of which are still in vogue. They are also provided a space in the Constitution, for example in India.[36] However, the contradiction continues to persist.

The issue of legal pluralism is also of great concern in European countries with the advent of immigrants from other cultures and traditions, especially with Muslim immigrants. The question is hotly debated. A scholar like Christian Giordano would think of the possibility of legal pluralism within the European nations in today's circumstances. On the other hand, Elham M. Manea, in her recent work *Women and Shari'a Law: The Impact of Legal Pluralism in the UK*, has argued that if one were to uphold universal human rights, one should not compromise with Muslim personal laws since there is an incompatibility between them.[37] She argues how the legal pluralism in Britain has failed. The arguments Manea presents seem to me to be from the perspective of the liberals. I do not hear the voice of the communitarians of the West, who may argue differently. I would have liked to hear their arguments, instead of her taking one author, Christian Giordano, and dismissing him easily as a cultural essentialist. In this sense, the book lacks a dispassionate approach, and seems to be partisan and more like advocacy for the liberal school. I think the issue is much more complicated than what the author has tried to work out. The complexity could be illustrated with reference to the situation in India.

In India, for the last seventy years, this discussion of uniform civil code or legal pluralism is going on, and it is not merely a question of which position is legally correct. We need to place the issue also in the political

---

[36] Cf. Gerald James Larson, ed., *Religion and Personal Law in Secular India: A Call to Judgment* (Bloomington: Indiana University Press, 2001); Marc Galanter, *Law and Society in Modern India* (Oxford: Oxford University Press, 1989).

[37] Elham Manea, *Women and Shari'a Law: The Impact of Legal Pluralism in the UK* (London and New York: I.B. Tauris, 2016).

context. I wonder whether Manea has taken sufficiently into account the political context of the migrants in Europe. The argument of Manea is that we need to judge the ethical character of any action, not simply on the basis of *intention*, but from the *consequences* resulting from it. If so, Muslim personal laws affect the dignity and right of Muslim women and children. In India, those who are vehemently opposed to Muslim personal laws are not the secularists or the liberals, rather the right-wing Hindu radicals and extremists! That the liberals in the West and the fundamentalists in India converge in calling for the abolition of personal law and creation of uniform civil code only reveals how complex the question is. At issue is something more than a matter of essentialization of religious identities.

What is the agenda of the fundamentalists? Are they really concerned about the human rights of Muslim women and children? Is it a case of the wolf shedding tears for the lamb that is getting wet in the rain? Ground experience shows the truth is far from it! To understand this, one has to go deep into the history of Hindu-Muslim relationships of the past centuries. I am afraid a formal legal argument—the Kantian universal type—may not be most helpful on issues which have political and social implications. I am not advocating the establishment of Shariah law in the European and American societies; what I am arguing is for the need to go into the question taking into account the social and political aspects of the issue of immigration. In this discussion both in the West and in India, we need to take into account, besides the liberal arguments of infringement of personal freedom, the views of nationalists, concerns of feminists, and the cultural claims of minorities.[38] How one goes about personal laws of religious groups will depend a lot also on the way the public role of religion is seen and practiced in different societies.

## RELIGIOUS FREEDOM AND DEMOCRATIC MEDIATION

Religions have played and continue to play an intermediary role which is very crucial for the exercise of democracy. It is religion around which many human bonds and relationships were built up and this continues to be so in the societies of the South. Like many intermediary institutions

[38] Cf. Farrah Ahmed, *Religious Freedom under the Personal Law System* (Delhi: Oxford University Press, 2016); see also Rajeev Dhavan, "Religious Freedom in India," *The American Journal of Comparative Law* 35, no. 1 (1987): 209–54.

such as nongovernmental organizations, labor unions, and charitable and other associations, religion is amid social interactions and exchanges.

> It is a simple empirical fact that, in many parts of the world the most important mediating structures are religious in nature. Local churches, synagogues, mosques, shrine associations play a mediating role. So do larger organizations in which the individual has a sense of participation—such as denominations, caste associations, tribal and ethnic organizations built around religious symbols, and the like. These religious institutions create networks of meaning. One could also call them communities of meaning—which are, as it were, double faced: One face is turned toward the life of the individual, giving meaning to his private life and concerns; the other face is turned toward public life, linking the individual to the broad economic and political concerns of the overall society.[39]

Given this fact, the scope of religious freedom becomes much more extensive. The freedom enjoyed by religions ultimately goes to strengthen the fabric of society and make it vibrant. To deny the participation of a religious group (within a broader community) in what concerns the common good (without of course unwarranted intervention in the autonomy of other systems—political, economic, social, and cultural) is to deprive the community of the contribution a particular religious group could make to its own (community's) flourishing. To be able to play its human intermediary role effectively for the benefit of the common good, the religious freedom of different communities making up the polity needs to be guaranteed. This is a very different outlook from viewing religious freedom as a private matter of conscience or as a matter of unrestrained choice of the individual. In India and most other societies in the Global South, one needs to be committed both to *communities* whose freedom in matters religious is to be ensured, as well to *citizenship* which is based on the principle of equality.[40]

Of course, there is the danger of an intra-religious constraint on the freedom of the individuals. For example, one could think of inner-religious

---

[39] Peter L. Berger, Firuz Kazemzadeh, and Michael Bourdeaux, "The State of Religious Freedom," *World Affairs* 147, no. 4 (1985): 238–53 at 241.

[40] Rudolph sees Some would see in this a *contradiction* in the Indian conception of secularism. To my mind, it is not a contradiction (which would be the case if one departs from a standard Western view of secularism) but rather a unique way of relating the different dimensions of life and governance which (unique way) needs to be considered on its own and not in relation to a particular understanding of the secular.

dissent and freedom of expression. Legitimate expressions of these cannot be suppressed in the name of the community. However, this argument should not be so overriding as to blot out the benefits that accrue to the common good through recognizing and putting into practice the religious freedom of communities qua communities. Religious liberty of a community involves other rights such as to be able to run educational institutions and to do charitable services for the wellbeing of its own members as well as of the broader community. This expansion of religious freedom is particularly important when religious communities are also minorities. This more comprehensive recognition of communitarian religious freedom means affirming the dignity of this community. A religious community is not a group to be simply *tolerated*, but accorded larger space enabling its interlinking with other aspects of societal life and enabling its contribution to the common good. The Indian Constitution allows a range of freedoms for the minority religious communities. This has helped through the years toward the goal of creating a cohesive and harmonious society. With only freedom of conscience confined to the individuals, Christians, Muslims, and other minorities would not be enjoying real religious freedom. The situation is similar in many other multireligious countries of Asia and in the Global South at large.

## RELIGIOUS FREEDOM: THE STRUGGLES OF THE NORTH

For those familiar with religious freedom as part of universal human rights, and with the Declaration of Religious Freedom (*Dignitatis Humanae*) of Vatican II, it may sound strange to speak of struggles of religious freedom in the North, since this freedom is taken for granted. Even more, the Global North is supposed to be the guardian of religious freedom. But I think it is important to take note of some aspects of history to be able to understand the situation of the plurality of religions and their freedom today in the context of globalization.

One will do well to remember that the liberal approach to religious freedom is a matter of relatively recent history in the West. There are deep wounds that have been caused in Western Christian history by *denying* religious freedom, resulting in the alienation of other religious groups other than Christians, especially the Jews. Though thinkers like John Locke (*Letter on Toleration*) and John Stuart Mill (*On Liberty*) argued for religious freedom,[41] what should not be forgotten is the fact that through many centuries mainline Christianity had serious difficulty with the theory and practice of religious freedom. Just to recall some facts, the Inquisition, the Protestant, and Catholic religious wars, the exclusion of any other religion other than Anglicanism in England, not to speak of Medieval crusades stand out against any holier-than-thou attitude by Christian churches vis-à-vis Muslims and other non-Christian religions. There is also a darker and less known side of suppression of religious freedom in the Americas, which is now documented.[42] The forces outside the mainline Christian fold were the first ones to clamor for religious freedom and right for dissent. Here we may refer to a less-known group of French thinkers around the time of the Edict of Nantes (1598), which legislated for religious freedom.[43]

Christianity was not only too slow to recognize religious freedom, but it even maintained the claim of religious freedom as heretic and unorthodox.[44] Today, as we know, religious freedom is founded on human dignity. Are we to assume that the church denied human dignity when it expressed itself against religious freedom? The fact of the matter is that the church maintained that it held on to human dignity precisely by saving souls.[45] The traditional arguments against religious freedom were vehemently fielded during the discussions at Vatican II on the Declaration on Religious Freedom (*Dignitatis Humanae*), which made the document perhaps the most fiercely opposed one.[46] Many traditional objections were voiced as

---

[41] Cf. Sanford Kessler, "John Locke's Legacy of Religious Freedom," *Polity* 17, no. 3 (1985): 484–503.

[42] John Corrigan, and Lynn S. Neal, eds., *Religious Intolerance in America: A Documentary History* (Chapel Hill: University of North Carolina Press, 2010).

[43] Cf. Malcolm C. Smith, "Early French Advocates of Religious Freedom," *The Sixteenth Century Journal* 25, no. 1 (1994): 29–51. We also need to recall here the contribution of Roger Williams.

[44] In the Western tradition, the political philosophy of *cuius regio eius religio* (i.e., the principle that the religion of the ruler was to dictate the religion of those ruled) stifled religious freedom. Meant as a means to settle religious wars in Europe, ironically, it only contributed to suppressing freedom of religion.

[45] Cf. Michael J. Perry, "Liberal Democracy and the Right to Religious Freedom," *The Review of Politics* 71, no. 4 (2009): 621–35.

[46] Cf. John Coleman, "The Achievement of Religious Freedom," *U.S. Catholic Historian* 24, no. 1 (2006): 21–32.

*Dignitatis Humanae* was struggling to be born.[47] For example, to allow religious freedom is to claim that error has a right to exist, while truth can be the one and the unique way to salvation, with no choice. The Christian faith is the only true and final revelation of God, and the church is the only way to salvation, ruling out any alternative in the matter. The Roman Catholic Church declared itself against religious freedom in the nineteenth century. Pope Piux IX included religious freedom among his Syllabus of Errors (1864), and this position was maintained practically by all the subsequent popes. John XXIII apparently broke with this tradition in his encyclical *Pacem in Terris* (1963) and spoke of the freedom of conscience in the matter of religion.[48] But the break was decisive with Vatican II when with a resounding vote of 2308 against 70 the Council affirmed the right to religious freedom.

> The fact is that men of the present day want to be able freely to profess their religion in private and in public. Indeed, religious freedom has already been declared to be a civil right in most constitutions, and it is solemnly recognized in international documents. ... This council [Vatican II] greets with joy [this fact] as among the signs of the times.[49]

Despite such unambiguous teaching, there are still loud voices in the church maintaining that religious liberty is manifestly an error and contrary to the teachings of the church. So, a bishop in the USA could write in his pastoral letter about the "doctrinal errors" (*sic*) of *Dignitatis Humanae*.

> The reason this decree was the most controversial and the most destructive is that it explicitly taught doctrines previously condemned by past Popes. And this was so blatant that many conservative Council Fathers opposed it to the very end; while even the liberal cardinals, bishops and theologians who promoted the teachings of *Dignitatis Humanae* had to confess their inability to reconcile this decree with the past condemnations of Popes. Let

---

[47] See Columba Ryan, "The Second Vatican Council and Religious Freedom," *Blackfriars* 45, no. 531 (1964): 355–67; see also John Courtney Murray, *The Problem of Religious Freedom* (Westminster: The Newman Press, 1965).

[48] Cf. *Pacem in Terris*, no. 14. "Every human being has the right to honor God according to the dictates of an upright conscience, and right to profess his religion privately and publicly."

[49] *Dignitatis Humanae* section 15.

us examine the doctrinal errors of this decree on Religious Liberty to see what caused all this controversy during the Second Vatican Council.[50]

The claim of superiority and uniqueness of truth for one's own religion has been, perhaps, the most powerful aggression on religious freedom, and it refuses to die. Even today, this mindset of possession of absolute truth gets expressed in different ways and can be observed in the struggle Europe is going through to come to terms with migrants from another world of religions. We need a veritable "religious disarmament." From an Asian perspective, much of the Western grandiloquent discourse on the secular appears to be skin-deep rococo elaboration.

While the Roman Catholic Church has got out of its traditional opposition to religious freedom and affirmed it very positively as a fundamental right in *Dignitatis Humanae*, we are experiencing, ironically, among the secularists and liberals of North-Western Europe a new onslaught on religious freedom. They seem to think that human and community wellbeing is guaranteed if religions are kept as a private issue of an individual—for the choice of which he or she has freedom—whereas religion has no role to play in presenting its own vision of life, values, and ideals. The secularists and the liberals seem to claim that their vision of the world and values are the best and the ultimate. Thus, they deny the right of freedom to religions to present an alternative view of the world and life. In this way, paradoxically, the secularists and liberals *deny to religion* what they *claim for themselves* as their fundamental right. We shall go deeper into this question in Chap. 12 on religion and public life. The secular and liberal values are equated with the values of Western culture. Here Erik Borgmann finds duplicity. As he notes:

> Western culture is caught up in a strange contradiction. It considers itself to be the incarnation of the respect for human rights. At the same time, when the classical human rights ask something, people living within the Western culture find difficult to agree with; they tend to think that not our cultural habits but the human rights have to change.[51]

---

[50] Pastoral Letter of Bishop Mark A. Pivarunas, "The Doctrinal Errors of Dignitatis Humanae," see http://www.cmri.org/95prog2.htm [accessed on December 18, 2019].

[51] Erik Borgmann, "The Enduring Importance of the Freedom of Religion," *Concilium* *2016/4,* 97.

Religious freedom is not only a legal issue; it has to do with human coexistence, understanding and solidarity amid a plurality of views and ways of life. The concrete exercise of religious freedom would require a culture of interdependence and trust. Failing this, in practice, freedom of religion would mean the freedom for the people of the majority religion, and there will always be ways to exercise coercion on other religions in the name of protecting human rights. I think such reflections are essential to come to terms with the problematic question of legal pluralism among various religious identities.

New contexts have amplified the scope of religious freedom also in the Global North.[52] For example, the right to intervene in public life by religions or religious agents—something which the secularists would challenge—gets a fillip in the post-secular society where there is not only increasing recognition of the role of religion in public life but also a need for it being voiced. Thinkers like Jürgen Habermas have acknowledged a new and redefined role of religion.[53] Further empirical studies show how religions can transform public life, politics, and governance. New thoughts, orientations, and practices in the context of immigrants have raised new questions leading to rethink the traditional understanding of religious freedom in the West. There seems to be a convergence of the post-secular thought in the West on the public role of religion, and the relationship of religion and society in Asian history.

[52] See Craig Calhoun, Eduardo Mendieta, and Jonathan Van Antwerpen, eds., *Habermas and Religion* (Cambridge: Polity Press, 2013); Maureen Junker-Kenny, *Habermas and Theology* (London: T&T Clark, 2011); Jacques Derrida and Gianni Vattimo, eds., *Religion: Cultural Memory in the Present* (Stanford: Stanford University Press, 1996).

[53] William J. Meyer, "Private Faith or Public Religion? An Assessment of Habermas's Changing View of Religion," *The Journal of Religion* 75, no. 3 (1995): 371–91; Martin Laube, "Christentum und 'postsäkulare' Gesellschaft: Theologische Anmerkungen zu Einer Aktuellen Debatte," *Zeitschrift Für Theologie Und Kirche* 106, no. 4 (2009): 458–76; Kenneth G. MacKendrick, and Matt Sheedy. "The Future of Religious History in Habermas's Critical Theory of Religion," *Method & Theory in the Study of Religion* 27, no. 2 (2015): 151–74; Inger Furseth, "The Return of Religion in the Public Sphere?: The Public Role of Nordic Faith Communities," in *Institutional Change in the Public Sphere: Views on the Nordic Model*, edited by Engelstad Fredrik, et al. (Berlin/Boston: De Gruyter, 2017).

## CONCLUSION

Religion is an identity marker, which is so very evident in the South, especially in Asian societies. Hence, religious freedom has to do with recognition of religious identities and with establishing the necessary sociopolitical conditions for peaceful and harmonious coexistence. As such, the creation of space for religious freedom is a common task of all communities involved. This fundamental freedom may not be reduced to a merely legal matter. It can thrive only where there is an environment of tolerance and harmony. Where there is a fear of the other and xenophobia, this freedom cannot flourish.[54]

Religious freedoms has to do also with the balance of power in sociopolitical fields, and especially with the protection of minorities wherever religious and minority ethnic identities overlap. If religious freedom is, on the one hand, *immunity* of a religious community from unwarranted intervention by the state or other social and political actors or by the majority religious community,[55] on the other hand, it is also an issue of *protection* of the identity of minority groups. This is quite a different approach from understanding religious freedom as a right of the "unencumbered" individual or as a matter of conscience. In fact, neither liberal theory nor Marxism have any plausible theory about minorities, much less about religious minorities and their freedom. For liberal individualism, the two poles of relationship are the individual and the state. The intermediary group unity or identity are not given due place but rather are absorbed within the horizon of the individual.[56] Marxism supports the formation of great nations, but neglects and is even hostile to subnationalities.

In the South, especially in Asia, religious freedom is often a matter of subnationalities, given the overlap of religion and ethnicity.[57] In Asia, the

---

[54] Cf. Martha C. Nussbaum, *The New Religious Intolerance: Overcoming the Politics of Fear in an Anxious Age* (Cambridge, Massachusetts and London: Harvard University Press, 2012).

[55] In Malaysia, Christians are forbidden to use the term "Allah" to refer to God in their worship or in Bible translations. It is claimed exclusively by the majority Muslim community.

[56] Will Kymlicka in his theorizing has tried to create a space for community rights, by negotiating between liberalism and communitarianism. See Will Kymlicka, ed., *The Rights of Minority Cultures* (Oxford: Oxford University Press, 1995); ID., *Contemporary Political Philosophy: An Introduction* II edition (Oxford: Oxford University Press, 2002).

[57] Satish Saberwal and Mushirul Hasan, eds., *Assertive Religious Identities: India and Europe* (New Delhi: Manohar Publications, 2006).

recognition[58] and acceptance of every religious community and its freedom create the precondition for the discourse on religious freedom of the individual.[59] There is, however, also an intra-religious dimension to religious freedom in the sense that the individual is not constrained by diktats of his or her community in matters of doctrine, ethical issues (abortion, for example), or gender issues, but has the right to dissent and hold other views without being penalized for nonconformity. Thus, religious freedom remains a project that needs to be constantly negotiated in interreligious and intra-religious spheres. A formal invocation of religious freedom as a universal right in the abstract may not be very helpful unless it is read and interpreted through issues of conversion, personal laws pertaining to religious communities, public manifestation of religious symbols, and so on. These are integral parts in a holistic understanding of religious freedom in Asia. Asia's millennial experience of respect and tolerance for the religiously other is an invaluable heritage which can stand in good stead as the continent struggles to grapple with religious freedom in contemporary times.

Asian approach to religious freedom is undergirded by a broad theoretical perspective. This perspective admits that "truth is one, the sages speak of it variously."[60] This is vastly different from the theological position that error has no right to exist. In Asia, the admission that truth has many channels and none of them may be reduced to the other has fostered an atmosphere where religious plurality became not only a matter of tolerance but also part of spiritual and mystical experience and quest. It has fostered an attitude of deep reverence and respect for the religiously other which served also as the civilizational bedrock of substantive religious freedom. Besides, in Asia, the religious boundaries have been viewed as fluid and porous, and hence the mutual exchange and fecundation have been spontaneously taking place, and this can be observed even today in everyday practices of Asian peoples, despite religious conflicts fomented by economic and political forces and by identity politics. The substantive religious

---

[58] Cf. Axel Honneth, *The Struggle for Recognition: The Moral Grammar of Social Conflicts* (Cambridge: Polity Press, 1995).

[59] This is parallel to the political realm in Asia where democratic participation often involves the polity as a conglomeration of a plurality of communities, and not as the sum total of individuals.

[60] *Rig Veda* Book I, Hymn 164, Verse 46.

freedom, which allows other beliefs, conceptions of the good life, practices, and symbols to coexist with one's own in a spirit of harmony,[61] can be viewed as Asia's, and broadly Global South's, contribution to the entire human family in these times of deep crisis.

[61] In Hinduism for example, there is no concept of heterodoxy as generally understood. For, it allows immense scope for the plurality of beliefs and practices. At the one end is the high *advaitic* mysticism of non-dual unity with the Absolute, and on the other end of the spectrum, sexuality as a means of spiritual elevation, practiced in the tradition of *tantra*.

# CHAPTER 10

# Religious Identities by Choice and the Politics of Conversion

History is full of instances of people undergoing unique experiences to turn from their past ways of life to follow a new religious path. The foremost Christian saint here is St. Augustine (354–430).[1] There are other instances of a person following a particular religious tradition, turning his or her back on it, because of some extraordinary experience, like St. Paul on his way to Damascus to persecute the Christians.[2] Emperor Ashoka (BCE 304–232) of the Maurya dynasty was on a war spree with other kingdoms to expand the frontiers of his empire, but then deeply moved by the sight of the massive number of deaths and the flow of blood at the Kalinga War, completely changed (*ātmaparivartan*) to become a nonviolent ruler by following the path of Shakyamuni, the Buddha.[3] He became a messenger of peace and nonviolence.

---

[1] Augustine, *Confessions* 8. 6. 13–12. 30. See Jason David BeDuhn, *Augustine's Manichaean Dilemma: Conversion and Apostasy, 373–388 C. E.* Chapter 7 (Philadelphia: University of Pennsylvania Press, 2009); Allan Fitzgerald, "Arise! Scriptural Model for Augustine's Conversion," *Angelicum* 64, no. 3 (1987): 359–75.

[2] Cf. Richard N. Longenecker, ed., *The Road from Damascus: The Impact of Paul's Conversion on His Life, Thought, and Ministry* (Grand Rapids, Mich.: W.B. Eerdmans Pub, 1997).

[3] Cf. Bruce Rich, *To Uphold the World: A Call for a New Global Ethic from Ancient India* (Boston: Beacon Press, 2010).

© The Author(s), under exclusive license to Springer Nature Switzerland AG 2021
F. Wilfred, *Religious Identities and the Global South*,
New Approaches to Religion and Power,
https://doi.org/10.1007/978-3-030-60738-8_10

In the case of personal conversion through one's free choice, the new religious identity to which one moves could be viewed by the convert as a further stage in her spiritual experience, and, in this case, elements of the old religious identity are assimilated into the new one. But the changeover could also be an oppositional experience: The new is embraced following a rejection of the old. Further, in the case of conversion of individuals, studies and researches have focused on personal factors like crisis or critical moments in life, social, cultural, and institutional factors. Such scholars as Tom Beidelman, Kenelm Burridge, Jean and John Comaroff, James Fernandez, Clifford Geertz, Robin Horton, Rita Kipp, and Jane Schneider[4] have investigated conversion from the perspectives of sociology and psychology.[5] To what extent do these analyses fit into today's conditions of globalization? Do they correspond to the experiences in the Global South? This is something which needs to be explored. A discussion on conversion in the context of globalization provides an opportunity to think of religious identity and "the perennial having to do with agency" in new ways. It is also an issue which opens up discussion on cross-cultural dialogue and indigeneity.[6]

## CONVERSION AND COMMUNITY

In a liberal society of today, one may profess the religion one is most attracted to. Like in many other areas of personal life, this will be looked at as pertaining to the inalienable right of an individual. But this is not always the case. In most parts of the world, professing a religion is not only a personal matter but also part of one's social identity. One is bound to a family and has ties with a community. Though conversion may be personal, it implies negotiating a relationship with one's family, one's

---

[4] Cf. Andrew Buckser, and Stephen D. Glazier, eds., *The Anthropology of Religious Conversion* (Lanham Maryland: Rowman & Littlefield Publishers, 2003).

[5] Cf. Giuseppe Giordan, *Conversion in the Age of Pluralism* (Leiden: BRILL, 2009); Lewis R. Rambo, and Charles Farhadian, eds., *The Oxford Handbook of Religious Conversion* (New York: Oxford University Press, 2014).

[6] Richard Fox Young and Jonathan Seitz, *Asia in the Making of Christianity: Conversion, Agency, and Indigeneity, 1600s to the Present* (Leiden: BRILL, 2013). See also Richard Fox Young, "Christianity and Conversion: Conceptualization and Critique, Past and Present, with Special Reference to South Asia," in Felix Wilfred, ed., *Oxford Handbook of Christianity in Asia* (New York: Oxford University Press, 2014), 444–457.

caste, community, and so on. There is the social consequence of individual conversion when a converted person gets uprooted from the family and excluded from the community to which she belongs. Converts have been socially ostracized, and their businesses have been boycotted.[7] During the colonial period, individual conversions in India became a legal issue, when converts to Christianity were deprived of their community rights and inheritance. Parents and relatives of a convert went to court against such conversions of their wards and denied them social rights that they had earlier enjoyed within the fold of Hinduism.[8]

The history of conversion in Asia shows that except in sporadic cases, conversion was a community decision. Groups of people, or a people belonging to the same caste en masse converted to Christianity, for example, to gain a new identity and Christianity served as a new stamp of their ethnicity and a distinguishing mark from the rest of the population. Then, there is something like conversion by affiliation. Siding with the religion of ruling powers—during colonial times, to convert to Christianity— added prestige besides giving several advantages. This became a powerful motive for conversion. We have numerous such instances in China and Sri Lanka. In Sri Lanka today, many people have Christian names but are in fact Buddhists. They probably hail from those families during colonial times who changed to Christianity to draw benefit from the ruling colonial powers, but later reverted to Buddhism. To be part of the religion of the rulers gave them a better social standing and negotiating power. In the case of mass conversion of the Paravars to Christianity in the Coromandel Coast of South India in the sixteenth century, it was a matter of protection from the competing Muslims in fishing and trading pearls.

These are examples of change and conversion and the issues connected with it in the past. But today our world finds itself in a very different mood and situation, not only about the place of religion in the lives of people but also with regard to changing over to a new religious universe. The processes of globalization and fast communication have given opportunities to know more about other religious traditions than one's own, thus widening religious choices. But globalization has also inherited a history of Christian mission expansion under the aegis of colonial powers, turning

[7] Cf. John C. B. Webster, *A Social History of Christianity: North-west India since 1800* (New Delhi; Oxford: Oxford University Press, 2007), 62–67.

[8] Cf. Chandra Mallampalli, *Race, Religion, and Law in Colonial India: Trials of an Interracial Family* (Cambridge; New York: Cambridge University Press, 2011).

conversion into a political issue. This *political aspect* has come to relief today as a matter of numbers—majority or minority—with all its power implications. In this context, propagating one's religion to enlist new members has become highly contentious, even reaching the point of violence. This is all the more so when community identity overlaps with religious and ethnic identity. Choice of another religious path implicitly would mean the rejection of one's deeper identities. Small wonder that conversion of individuals has been perceived as a threat to the community, its tradition, and its ethnic identity. This is an argument used in the case of tribals converting to Christianity. Conversion makes them lose their cultural identity and transports them to the Western cultural world. A Western anthropologist Verrier Elwin maintained such a view in the immediate post-independence era in India and his views were invoked approvingly even today by radical Hindu groups and organizations.[9]

The community dimension acquires greater relevance when the nation is identified with religion. Conversion is viewed, then, as disloyalty to the nation, its tradition and culture. Loyalty to the nation is equal to being or becoming Hindu. Hence in India, for example, there is a whole move to *reconversion*. This means that efforts are made to convert Christians and Muslims to Hinduism. The assumption behind such a move is that those who are Christians or Muslims now were initially Hindus, and reconversion means "home-coming" (*garvapsi*). This concept of "home-coming" goes back to the Arya Samaj—a reformist Hindu organization that was started by Swami Dayananda Saraswati (1824–1883).[10]

Today's conversion of Dalits and tribals is seen as a betrayal of national identity, and efforts are on to prevent such conversions.[11] There are states in India which passed laws prohibiting conversion and making it a punishable offence.[12] Another strategy is to deprive Christian Dalits of the privi-

---

[9] Cf. Ramachandra Guha, *Savaging the Civilized: Verrier Elwin, His Tribals, and India* (Chicago, Ill: University of Chicago Press, 1999).

[10] Cf. Lajpat Rai, *A History of the Arya Samaj*, rev. ed. (Bombay: Orient Longmans, 1967).

[11] Cf. Sumit Sarkar, "Conversions and Politics of Hindu Right," *Economic and Political Weekly* 34, no. 26 (1999): 1691–700.

[12] Cf. South Asia Human Rights Documentation Center, "Anti-Conversion Laws: Challenges to Secularism and Fundamental Rights," *Economic and Political Weekly* 43, no. 2 (2008): 63–73; Laura Dudley Jenkins, "Legal Limits on Religious Conversion in India," *Law and Contemporary Problems* 71, no. 2 (2008): 109–27; Sarah Claerhout, and Jakob De Roover, "The Question of Conversion in India," *Economic and Political Weekly* 40, no. 28 (2005): 3048–055.

leged educational and job opportunities (called "reservation" or "affirmative action") enjoyed by their Hindu counterparts. Dalit Christians and Hindu Dalits are more or less at the same level in their economic condition and suffer the same kind of social and economic disabilities and discrimination. Yet, a presidential order enacted in 1950 deprived Christians of the benefits enjoyed by Hindu Dalits.[13] Christian missionary engagement resulted in the educational and economic upliftment of many Dalit and tribal groups. Often this is interpreted as a bait or material lure to the poor for the goal of proselytization. To counter this, Hindu organizations have taken to social and educational work among these underprivileged groups. One such well-known initiative is *Vanavasi Kalyan Ashram* (VKA).

Though there is a general welcome to globalization among the upper castes and classes of society for its advantages, there is also a sense of fear and feeling of threat regarding it. As Chad Bauman has noted, Christianity represents symbolically all those negative things feared about globalization.[14] For example, while the traditional society is based on ascriptive identity (a pregiven identity), under globalization identity is created through what one makes of one's life and not by birth as is the case with ascriptive identities like caste. On their part, many Dalits and tribals counter the claim of the right-wing radical Hindutva that they (Dalits and tribals) are Hindus. Most tribals see themselves belonging to primaeval religious traditions bound up with nature and its rhythm. Similarly, the Dalits claim that their religion and religious practices are different and may not be co-opted into the Hindu fold.

## CONVERSION AND GEOPOLITICAL FACTORS

We need to also go beyond micro-level factors in explaining conversion. There are macro-level and geopolitical reasons at play—something which theories of conversion have not taken into account. We are led to macro and geopolitical factors of conversion when we analyze the case of a large

---

[13] Prakash Louis, "Dalit Christians: Betrayed by State and Church," *Economic and Political Weekly* 42, no. 16 (2007): 1410–1414; Felix Wilfred, *Dalit Empowerment* (Delhi: ISPCK, 2007); John C. B. Webster, *The Dalit Christians: A History*. ISPCK Contextual Theological Education Series; no. 4 (Delhi: ISPCK, 2009).

[14] Chad M. Bauman, "Hindu-Christian Conflict in India: Globalization, Conversion, and the Coterminal Castes and Tribes," *The Journal of Asian Studies* 72, no. 3 (August 2013), 633–653, at 650.

scale of conversion of Koreans to Protestantism. Statistics show that Christians form one-third of the population in South Korea, which is also one of the largest missionary-sending countries in the world.[15] This is puzzling considering the fact that Christians are so small in number in Asia, and Korea shares a lot of cultural affinity with its Chinese and Japanese neighbors. Some scholars explain this fact saying that the Koreans who suffered under the Japanese imperialism and militarism turned away from its neighbors and turned to the West to embrace Christianity. Unlike China and Japan, where Christianity as the religion of the Westerners was viewed as a threat to the nation, in Korea, where Japan was the greatest threat since the nineteenth century, people turned to Western Protestant Christianity. It was associated with their national cause and independence from the Japanese, and a large number of conversions followed due to this geopolitical situation. Danielle Kane and Jung Mee Park make the following observation in this connection:

> The March First Movement, a major watershed in the history of Korean nationalism, was pivotal in identifying Christianity with nationalism, both by demonstrating Korean Christians' willingness to suffer for nationalism and by turning Western missionaries' neutrality into active support. As a measure of the significance of this ritual, Lee writes that "it was in this that the Korean Protestant Church contributed some of the most potent symbols of Korean nationalism, symbols that are still celebrated in (South) Korea and bespeak the positive association between Protestantism and Korean nationalism.[16]

---

[15] Cf. Sebastian Kim, "Inter-Asia Mission and Global Missionary Movements from Asia," in Felix Wilfred, ed., *The Oxford Handbook of Christianity in Asia* (New York: Oxford University Press, 2014), 145–157; Rebecca Y. Kim, *The Spirit Moves West: Korean Missionaries in America* (New York: Oxford University Press, 2015); Pyong Gap Min, "The Structure and Social Functions of Korean Immigrant Churches in the United States," *The International Migration Review* 26, no. 4 (1992): 1370–394.

[16] Danielle Kane and Jung Mee Park, "The Puzzle of Korean Christianity: Geopolitical Networks and Religious Conversion in Early Twentieth-Century East Asia," *American Journal of Sociology* 115, no. 2 (September 2009): 365–404, at 395.

## CONVERSION AND PHYSICAL VIOLENCE
## UNDER GLOBALIZATION

Globalization as a transnational movement of capital, goods, services, cultural products, labor, and human resources had its repercussion also on how religious conversion is welcomed on the one hand and how it is resisted on the other. On the Christian side, the globalization process has encouraged many evangelical missionary institutions and individuals to undertake a worldwide new movement of conversion. It is alleged that this new wave of mission and conversion is encouraged by the Western nations and financially supported by them. The availability of wealth and fast means of transportation has led Saudi Arabia and other West Asian (Middle Eastern) countries to make financial sources available for the work of conversion to Islam in other parts of the world. We can note contradictions here. In the case of the West, while Christianity seems to be waning as a result of dwindling number of members and loss of influence on the society, it wants to thrive in Asia and Africa, especially in competition with Islam. Whereas conversion is made illegal in most of the Middle Eastern countries, these very countries are investing many resources for the conversion of Westerners and people in other parts of the world to Islam. For example, Islam in Indonesia, known traditionally as a liberal and tolerant Islam, has undergone a change due to the influence of Wahhabism. Islam has made a conservative turn by promoting conversion, which has affected the traditional interreligious harmony in that country. Further, the effort to spread Islam among the Hispanics in the USA seems to be on the increase, thanks to such organization as American Dawah organization.[17] In Latin America, the evangelicals are struggling to stem the Islamic influence in that continent as people are attracted to Islam.

Resistance to conversion reveals the emergence of new phenomena under globalizing conditions. Let me illustrate this point with the case of India. India entered into globalization in a big way in the early 1990s with a new economic policy of liberalization. For the traditional elites—the upper castes, entrepreneurs, and industrialists—it was an ambiguous process. On the one hand, it helped them boost their economic conditions

---

[17] Cf. Maria del Mar, Logroño Narbona, Paulo G. Pinto, John Tofik Karam, eds., *Crescent over Another Horizon: Islam in Latin America, the Caribbean, and Latino USA* (Austin: University of Texas Press, 2015); Larry Poston, *Islamic Da'wah in the West: Muslim Missionary Activity and the Dynamics of Conversion to Islam* (New York; Oxford: Oxford University Press, 1992).

and accumulate wealth. On the other hand, it also brought new ideas and practices which were felt by these classes as threatening the traditional culture. Further, the process of globalization was also a new opportunity for suppressed groups to enter the field of education with many job opportunities. In other words, globalization meant awakening of suppressed castes and groups, which in turn threatened the hierarchical understanding of society. Christian churches and institutions played an important role in the education of lower castes and classes who could also advance their material conditions. Some of them were also able to compete with upper castes and classes who were their traditional oppressors. These developments triggered a violent reaction by radical Hindu groups to the educational and social involvement of Christians who were suspected to use it to convert the Dalits, lower castes and tribals. Hence, Christians, their churches, and their institutions became the target of attacks for the alleged conversion work they were doing. The number of attacks against Christians and Christian institutions increased significantly since the 1990s, the beginning of globalization and market-economy in India. The attacks happened in the state of Gujarat in 1998 and in Kandhamal area in the state of Odisha (then called Orissa) in 2008.[18] There is the gruesome case of an Australian missionary Graham S Staines and his two children, who, on January 23, 1999, were burnt to death in the car they were sleeping, by those who were suspicious of his activities of conversion. As for Kandhamal, according to one report,

> 93 people were killed, over 350 churches and worship places which belonged to the Adivasi Christians and Dalit Christians were destroyed, around 6500 houses were burnt or demolished, over forty women were subjected to rape, molestation and humiliation, and several educational, social service and health institutions were destroyed and looted. More than 56,000 people were displaced.[19]

[18] Cf. https://www.indiatoday.in/magazine/cover-story/story/19990208-staines-killing-murder-of-australian- [accessed on December 29, 2019]; See also Pralay Kanungo, "Hindutva's Fury against Christians in Orissa," *Economic and Political Weekly* 43, no. 37 (2008): 16–19.

[19] Cf. Angam P. Chatterji, Thomas Blom Hansen, and Christophe Jaffrelot, eds., *Majoritarian State. How Hindu Nationalism Is Changing India* (London: Harper Collins Publishers, 2019), 255; see also Biswamoy Pati, "Identity, Hegemony, Resistance: Conversions in Orissa, 1800–2000," *Economic and Political Weekly* 36, no. 44 (2001): 4204–212; Sumit Sarkar, "Conversions and Politics of Hindu Right," *Economic and Political Weekly* 34, no. 26 (1999): 1691–700.

Another intriguing factor of violence related to conversion is that the non-Christian Dalits and tribals, though sharing the same conditions of lower castes and classes, also joined with the upper castes and classes targeting Christians and their conversion activities. I have referred to the case of India as an example of conversion activities resulting in violence under globalization. A similar analysis could also be made in other parts of the world.

We need to pay attention today to another facet of conversion and violence. Sporadic cases of conversions of Westerners to Hinduism and Buddhism have been taking place for past several decades, thanks to many transnational religious movements. However, in recent times, we observe an increasing number of Europeans and Americans turning to Islam.

According to statistics, 4% of Muslims in the UK are people born and brought up locally. It is observed that high percentage among Muslims involved in violent and terrorist activities are not Muslim migrants, but rather the "home-grown" who converted to Islam. They exhibit the zeal characterisitc of new converts and are involved in several acts of terrorism, as for example, Khalid Masood, the perpetrator of the London Bridge terror attack killing and injuring many.

The perpetrator of attack near the British parliament building, in London on March 22, 2017, was someone born and brought up in the UK and was known as Adrian Russel Ajao before his conversion. It may be recalled here that there has been a tradition of the British people converting to Islam.[20] The neo-converts of today from the West are also the ones who went in significant numbers to join the ISIS to fight in Syria and Iraq. A deeper study needs to be done on this phenomenon. The rejection and marginalization these new converts experience could be a reason for their radicalization and their proclivity for perpetrating violence.[21]

---

[20] Cf. Jamie Gilham, *Loyal Enemies: British Converts to Islam 1850–1950* (Oxford University Press, 2014).

[21] *The Economist* 1 April 2017, 29.

## SOME ARGUMENTS CHALLENGING CONVERSION

There are serious difficulties regarding the right to conversion[22] in different regions of Asia. Even though secular and democratic countries like India and the Philippines accept the right to conversion, the issue has got highly politicized. There are historical, practical, and theoretical reasons for challenging conversion as part of religious freedom. For a dehistoricized liberal, thinking in the abstract, freedom to convert may look like something natural, something taken for granted; not so for Asians with their much-resented colonial legacy in this regard.

Many Asians feel that Christian proselytizing mission, bolstered by the support of ruling powers made aggressive inroads into their religions by converting people and luring them with material benefits. Conversion may appear as *a right*. For those who challenge this view maintain that they too have the *right to protect* their religious identity from intruding proselytizers. In colonial times, the converts were viewed as traitors entering the camps of the ruling foreign powers—Portuguese, Spanish, Dutch, French and British. This unfortunate colonial experience has led most Asian nations to come out with stringent laws at the local and national levels against conversion, *ironically* as an expression of freedom! Further, given the close familial, caste, and clan bonds, for an individual to convert to another religion has enormous social consequences as he or she could be cut off from these primordial ties with implications in terms of property, inheritance, marriage, status, and so on.

There is also another critical argument against conversion. Though at an abstract level conversion may appear as an expression of freedom, in concrete circumstances conversion could be the fruit of manipulation. A person may be enticed through material benefits to moving into another religious group. This is often the case with the poor and those at the lower rungs of society. This is what Christian missions have been accused of. In such a case, conversion is seen as an imposition of one's own religious conception by which the dignity and right of the other person is infringed.

---

[22] Cf. Rudolf C. Heredia, "Religious Disarmament: Rethinking Religious Conversion in Asia," in Felix Wilfred, ed., *The Oxford Handbook of Christianity in Asia* (New York: Oxford University Press, 2014): 257–272; Richard Fox Young, "Christianity and Conversion: Conceptualization and Critique, Past and Present, with Special Reference to South Asia," in Felix Wilfred, *The Oxford Handbook of Christianity in Asia*, 444–457; Sebastian C. H. Kim, *In Search of Identity: Debates on Religious Conversion in India* (Delhi: Oxford University Press, 2003).

Hence, the same argument advanced for religious freedom is turned around: conversion is viewed as an infringement of the freedom of the individuals through fraudulent means and manipulation.

From a theoretical perspective, the difficulty with conversion also stems from the fact that religious belonging is not seen as a matter of human agency and choice. One may not shop around, so to say, and choose the religion one likes. Instead, like geography and parentage, religious belonging pertains to the realm of the given; it is a primordial vocation. Changing one's religion would be tantamount to a betrayal. To phrase it in Christian terms, it would be going against one's vocation and the will of God. There is also a further argument against the right to conversion. It is the claim that for many people religion is an integral part of culture. Protection of one's religion from zealous proselytizers is to affirm one's cultural rights. With all his openness, the spirit of tolerance and promotion of interreligious understanding, Gandhi was one who came out with a very harsh critique on religious conversion. More about it later in this chapter.

Looking from a historical perspective, a connection is made between colonial violence and religious violence through conversion to Christianity. The same argument is advanced also concerning the contemporary situation. Reacting to the call for evangelization and conversion of Asia to Christianity by Pope John Paul II, during his visit to India, November, 5–7 1999, when he promoted the synodal document *"Ecclesia in Asia,"* a Hindu writer observed:

> Religions that are committed by their theologies to convert ...are necessarily aggressive, since conversion implies a conscious intrusion into the religious life of a person, in fact, into the religious person. This is a very deep intrusion, as the religious person is the deepest, the most basic in any individual...Thus, conversion is not merely violence against people; it is violence against people who are committed to non-violence.[23]

## ASIAN INHERENT OPENNESS TO CONVERSION

Interestingly within Asian traditions there are enough arguments that support positively conversion. We shall go into some of them here. As is well known, the word "religion" does not have an equivalent in

---

[23] Swami Dayananda Saraswati, as quoted in Sebastian Kim, *In Search of Identity,* 166.

Asian languages, and certainly not in Chinese or Indian languages. Such being the case, how conversion is viewed from a theological point of view will differ. To those who claim that their religion offers the ultimate truth and salvation for all, shifting to another religion cannot but mean apostasy and as a consequence, damnation. On the other hand, if religion is understood as "*marga*" or path as in Indian, or as "the way of Buddha" in Buddhism, and as "the way of the gods" in Shintoism, conversion is a change of path. One need not be worried if the paths never meet—quite the contrary. In fact, there is the belief that the paths may differ, but we reach the goal of ultimate bliss and salvation by more than only "one" way, because all the rivers meet in the same ocean. In this case, conversion may not appear as tragic as it is made out to be.

A second argument stems from the priority of the inner spiritual development Asian religious traditions have given in matters religious over externalities like the institutions surrounding a religion. There is an inner journey and evolution of a person that does not happen according to set patterns or as dictated by external factors and forces. Traditionally, the unique path each one chooses has been highly respected. Hence, a shifting from one religious path (*marga, dharma*) to another as happens in religious conversion (which word may not express precisely the change of *marga or dharma*) gets respected without any antagonism. In this vision, what we call religions are like scaffoldings in the spiritual construction of the self, and they are not ends in themselves, but rather a *means* for the inner spiritual development of a person. The spiritual quest gets priority over religion, its beliefs, institutions, and practices. Hence, a person could adopt another means, another pathway on her path to higher goals.

The arguments against conversion mostly do not take into account the agency of the persons or groups converted. They are looked at as objects which are manipulated by the proselytizers. This is to assume that those who convert do not have a will and understanding of their own. Such an assumption can be very humiliating for the converts whose freedom those who oppose conversion claim to defend. Gandhi also seems to have been of the same mindset when he expressed his anguish that the poor are converted by exploiting their ignorance and gullibility. If Dalits and tribals of India have converted to Christianity and Islam, it is their own decision coming out of their concrete social, political, and economic conditions and experiences of discrimination. It is an integral part of the larger movement of liberation they were involved in. In the case of Dalits, the discrimination and humiliation they experienced within the Hindu fold served as the trigger for their decision to convert.[24] This is also the reason why they could not equate Hinduism with nationalism which was the grand agenda of the Hindu Right at work since the nineteenth century.

In the case of Dalits and tribals, it is essential to pay attention to the collective or group character which has been rightly referred to as "mass conversion movements." A false picture of conversion would emerge if one studies only the subjective motivations of converts for their conversion without attending to socio-cultural factors. This movement of mass conversion during 1870–1930 was studied from an empirical point of view by J. Waskom Pickett. It is striking that 70% of Christians today could trace back their origin to this conversion movement, which speaks for its paramount importance in the history of Christianity in India as well as of national history.[25] It also would explain the alarm it created among radical Hindus and the insecurity these conversions caused for the understanding of national identity.

On their part, strangely, many earlier high-caste converts to Christianity discouraged such conversion movements and began to look down on the new converts because of their low-caste origin, and for what they considered as lack of maturity in faith. Dalit Christians were derided as "rice Christians" meaning that they became Christians for material benefits.[26] This is not only history but also an enduring problem in contemporary Indian Christianity in which despite their strong numerical presence, Dalits are prevented from occupying leadership positions in the churches. I think the phenomenon of mass conversions in India shows the complexity of conversion and its dynamics in interaction with social, cultural, economic, and political forces.

Gandhi, who was in the thick of politics, was seriously troubled by en masse conversion of Dalits to Christianity and did his own analysis of it, set in the context of the national struggle for independence. He was not able to see the vibrant agency of Dalits, tribals, and their leaders who sought the missionaries and expressed their willingness to change over to Christianity. Attributing conversion to the proselytizing work of the missionaries through the supply of material means, Gandhi presents the issue

[24] Cf. Jose Maliekal, *Stillstand Utopias. Dalits Encountering Christianity* (Delhi: ISPCK, 2017).

[25] Cf. Lalsangkima Pachuau, "A Clash of 'Mass Movements'? Christian Missions and the Gandhian Nationalist Movement in India," *Transformation* 31, no. 3 (2014): 157–74.

[26] Cf. Felix Wilfred, "What is Wrong with Rice Christians? Wellbeing of Salvation: A Subaltern Perspective," *Third Millennium IV* (2001): 6–8.

of conversion as an opportunity for the internal reform of Hinduism. For, according to him, in mass conversions, there are hardly any religious motives to be detected. He acknowledges that the impoverished material condition and discriminated social situation of Dalits force them to seek greener pastures in Christianity, and hence the way to arrest conversion is to better the economic and social conditions of the Dalits whom he called "Harijans" that is "children of Vishnu or God." Secondly, removal of religious discrimination against them expressed in innumerable forms as for example prohibition of temple entry will arrest their conversion.[27] Gandhi rarely had kind words for missionaries in whom he saw those who exploit the naive simplicity of the poor for the cause of proselytization. No wonder that he is invoked today by the Hindu Right against conversions and Christianity in general. He was seriously concerned that converts were denationalized and made to conform to the ways of the Christian colonizers of the British Raj.

Let me now put together some of Gandhi's argument against conversion. The first argument is that of spiritual self-sufficiency. In his words, "every nation's religion is as good as any other. Certainly, India's religions are adequate for her people. We need no converting spirituality."[28] This chimes with his political ideology of *swadeshi*, namely relying more on Indian cultural and traditional resources than allowing oneself to be overwhelmed by Western culture and values. The second argument of Gandhi stems from his understanding of the quintessence of religion to consist in ethics or morality. In fact, Gandhi is not known to have visited temples and participated in worships held there. If the essence of religion is morality, then Gandhi finds that "goodness" could be found in any religion and therefore does not require any conversion from one to the other. For him, "religion is no matter for words; it is the path of the brave. And my humble intelligence refuses to believe that a man becomes good when he renounces one religion and embraces another."[29] A third argument is the underlying conviction of Gandhi that all religions are equal. Consequently, it makes changing from one religion to another meaningless in terms of their worth. A fourth and final argument is his unfortunate conviction

[27] Cf. M. K. Gandhi, *Christian Missions. Their Place in India* (Navajivan Press: Ahmedabad, 1941),108–112.

[28] *The Collected Works of Mahatma Gandhi* vol. 45 (Delhi: The Publications Division. Government of India 1971), 320.

[29] *The Collected Works of Mahatma Gandhi* vol. 27 (Delhi: The Publications Division. Government of India, 1968), 204.

that Christianity is too complicated for the simple and poor Dalits to understand, and hence if conversion takes place, it cannot but be for material motives. As the Dalits leaders would react, Gandhi's view on the intellectual poverty of the Dalits to understand Christian faith is but a blatant insult to the Dalit community. In fact, Gandhi in a conversation with John Mott (1865–1955), then the president of the World Student Christian Federation, compared the understanding of the Dalits to that of cows.

> In my conversation with Dr Mott, at one stage of it I said, "Would you preach the Gospel to a cow? Well, some of the untouchables are worse than cows in understanding. I mean they can no more distinguish between the relative merits of Islam and Hinduism and Christianity than a cow". Some missionary friends have taken exception to the analogy. I have no remorse about the propriety of the analogy. [30]

As I noted earlier, the Hindutva Right has adopted many of the arguments of Gandhi and uses them in today's context. On the other hand, the most persuasive argument for conversion is the fact that Dalits and tribals have viewed it as a means for their liberation from many forms of oppression. Moreover, in conversion, they saw an opening to modernity.[31] Conversion is not so much a matter of accepting the truths religion speaks about, but, as Gauri Viswanathan has said, it is about a "conversion to equality." Its political nature is borne out by the fact that Ambedkar, at that time minister of law and justice, in a public ceremony converted together with a hundred thousand of his followers to Buddhism.

Referring to the extended interview with Gandhi, Mott, on his part, would remark about Gandhi's "evasion and gross ignorance of these untouchables."[32] At bottom, Gandhi and another highly regarded politician of the time C. Rajagopalachari failed to see conversion through the lens of the "Untouchables," who viewed it as a matter of liberation.

---

[30] M. K. Gandhi, *Christian Missions. Their Place in India*, 98.

[31] It is interesting to note that while there has been resistance to Western medicine in India by upper castes and classes, it would appear that it is the Dalits and lower castes who welcomed the medical facilities provided by the missionaries and which contributed to the modernization of medicine in the country. See Ashok Kumar, "We Called Her *Peddamma*: Caste, Gender, and Missionary Medicine in Guntur: 1880–1930," in *International Journal of Asian Christianity* 3, no.1 (March 2020): 69–84.

[32] Susan Billington Harper, *In the Shadow of the Mahatma. Bishop V.S. Azariah and the Travails of Christianity in British India* (Grand Rapids: William B. Eerdmans, 2000), at 336.

Conversion as a means of liberation could be observed in many cases across the globe.[33] It is a different question which needs to be enquired critically, whether the conversion undergone out of the motive of liberation did really fulfill the expectations of the converts.[34]

## IDENTITY OF RELIGIOUS COMMUNITY VS. FREEDOM OF THE INDIVIDUAL

The issue of conversion, viewed from a global perspective, brings into confrontation two indispensable rights, none of which could be given up—the freedom of the individual and the identity of the community. How are we going to reconcile both these poles? It is a constant dilemma and needs to be approached with a lot of tact and care.

The theoretical arguments against conversion could be countered, interestingly from Asian history itself. This is something many scholars have not taken into account. Buddhism, perhaps, was the earliest religion—from fifth century BCE onward—committed to mission and conversion and at the same time was a social movement of liberation, because the historical Gautama Siddhartha, himself belonging not to the Brahmin caste but to the Kshatriya caste, preached a religion which opened the way to enlightenment for everyone irrespective of his or her caste affiliation. Through its preachers of the path of righteousness (*dhamma*) and enterprising monks, Buddhism spread from India to every region, among peoples, civilizations, and cultures of Asia. It is said that Francis Xavier when he arrived in Kagoshima in Japan in 1549, he was taken for a Buddhist missionary preacher! Maybe drawing on the country's Buddhist roots, the Constitution of India affirms not only the freedom to profess religion but

---

[33] A glaring instance is that of the conversion of African Americans to Islam Cf. Rosanna Hertz, and Shereman A. Jackson, *Islam and the Blackamerican: Looking Toward the Third Resurrection* (Oxford and New York: Oxford University Press, 2005); Adele Reinhartz and Robert Dannin, *Black Pilgrimage to Islam* (Oxford and New York: Oxford University Press, 2005); See also Akbar Ahmed, *Journey into America: The Challenge of Islam* (Washington DC: Brooking Institution Press, 2010).

[34] In an exciting study on the movement of conversion among the Madigas (the Dalits of Andhra Pradesh), Jose Maliekal has concluded that the aspiration for liberation has remained a "standstill utopia." See Jose Maliekal, *Standstill Utopias: Dalits Encountering Christianity* (Delhi: ISPCK, 2017).

also "to propagate" it.[35] Further, Asian peoples have taken the freedom to change their religious affiliation when they felt discriminated against and oppressed in a particular religious system.

Those opposing conversions are not always motivated by any concern to protect individual freedom from being infringed upon. As we noted, there are today many political motives of power and control. Letting some members or a group from one's religious fold to convert to another religion weakens the religious identity of the community, and is perceived as a threat. Hence, various strategies are used to prevent any such thing happening. One of them is the enactment of laws preventing conversion by fraud or manipulation. For example, Indian Constitution upholds the propagation of one's faith as part of religious freedom. However, for fear of this freedom being exploited to swell the numbers of Muslims and Christians, as many as eight states in the country have enacted laws against conversion. The argument here again is to protect the poor and the marginalized, who may become victims of religious proselytization.

## CONVERSION IN A WORLD OF FLUID RELIGIOUS IDENTITIES

When religious identities are essentialized, conversion from one religion to another brings with it a host of problems, including violence. But in our global world, as we saw in an earlier chapter (Chap. 2), religious identities are becoming fluid and borders porous. Religious pluralism offers the possibility of exploring the mystery all the religions speak about in multiple ways. We are not confronted with many truths of religions and we have not to decide which is the correct one to convert to. Religious pluralism is the recognition of human limits and contingency vis-à-vis the ultimate mystery. Hence, the inexhaustible nature of the mystery after which the religions are in quest, on the one hand, and the human contingency and limits in approaching it, on the other, are apprehended when we look at religious pluralism as a theological reality, and not merely as religious consumer good. Viewed from this perspective, it is important that we respect the approach to the divine our neighbors take; to the expressions, they give to their faith; to the means they take in their pilgrimage to the shrine of truth. The fluidity of borders and boundaries calls for dialogue among

---

[35] Constitution of India, Art. 25. (1): "Subject to public order, morality and health and to the other provisions of this Part, all persons are equally entitled to freedom of conscience and the right freely to profess, practice and propagate religion."

religions as a *permanent* feature. It would allow a sincere seeker to navigate in different religious worlds which need not be interpreted as betrayal or disloyalty to what one has been believing as inherited faith. Dialogue puts people in a mood of exploring.

A few decades ago, I used to live in the town of Tiruchirapalli, Tamilnadu, on the banks of River Kaveri. Not far away in a small village, Tanneerpalli, Bede Griffiths, a British Benedictine, lived in the Saccidananda Ashram Shantivanam, involved deeply in dialogue and conversation with Hinduism. I had the privilege of his friendship in the final years of his life and know closely his experimentation with inculturation. I could sense the glow of the divine in his sparkling eyes turned ecstatically toward the earth, caring for the wellbeing of the villagers around. He narrated to me that many Westerners who visited his Ashram and spent some time in the utter simplicity of life were among those who lost contact with Christianity and the church. The experience in the ashram and encounter with the Hindu view and way of life led many of these seekers to rediscover anew the Christianity they thought they left behind. The experience of Hindu worship with all the primal elements—fire, water, earth, air, and ether— helped them to reconnect anew with the Christian sacramentality. How does one define conversion here? Here is a journey to the religious world of the other, crossing conventional boundaries and essentialist understanding of religious identity. There is, of course, a conversion, but then it is a turning toward, where borders become quite insignificant.

## Conversion and Emerging Theology of Religions

We need to take into account, besides the porousness of religious traditions, also developments in the theology of religions that provide yet another perspective to the understanding of conversion in these globalizing times. At the risk of simplification, we could trace, for example, the Christian theology of religions in recent centuries in different phases. From the time of the Church Fathers during the first centuries and during the high time of Christian missions in later centuries, it was the common position that all other religions were to be rejected as idol worship. After long centuries of mission, at the dawn of the twentieth century, some Christian theologians, harking back to early Christian writers like Saint Justin the Martyr (c.100–160) and Cement of Alexandria (c.150–215), realized that there are seeds of God's Word in other religions. This was followed by a theology of fulfillment. It meant to say that other religions, though they have some elements of truth, are deficient, and Christianity is presented as the fulfillment. This paved the way for a theology of inclusivism as we find in the *Nostra Aetate*, the document ex professo dealing with the relationship of the church to other religions in Vatican II. One could trace parallel developments in the Protestant Churches, primarily through the initiatives of the World Council of Churches. In the Roman Catholic Church, the theology of religions reached a new depth when in the encyclical *Redemptoris Missio* (1990) Pope John Paul stated that the Spirit is present and operative in other religious traditions too.[36] One would recognize the influence of Asian theologies, especially that of the Federation of Asian Bishops' Conferences (FABC) on such papal statements.[37] Yet another high point in the understanding of other religions was reached in the encounter of Pope Francis with the Grand Iman of Al-Azhar Ahmad Al-Tayyeb in February 2019. In the joint statement made regarding world peace and living together, it is stated that *all* religions are willed by God.

> God wills the pluralism and the diversity of religions, color, sex, race and language in His wisdom, through which He created human beings. This divine wisdom is the source from which the right to freedom and the freedom to be different derives. Therefore, the fact that people are forced to adhere to a particular religion or culture must be rejected, as too the imposition of a cultural way of life that others do not accept.[38]

## Two Examples of New Types of Religious Transition

Khrist Bhakta is a movement spread in the North of India which brings together people who are attracted by the person and teachings of Jesus, who read the Bible and interpret it for their lives, and who experience a certain mystical intimacy with Jesus, however without belonging to any Christian Church or group. They have evolved their own rituals. Most of these devotees are Hindus and they are not, and do not want to be,

---

[36] Pope John Paul II, *Redemptoris Missio* (1990), no. 28.

[37] Cf. Felix Wilfred, "Nostra Aetate of Vatican II: An Asian Re-reading after Fifty Years and the Way Forward," *FABC Papers no.152* (Hong Kong: FABC Secretariat, 2017). An expanded version in Felix Wilfred, *Theology for an Inclusive World* (Delhi: ISPCK, 2019), 333–354.

[38] A Document on Human Fraternity. For World Peace and Living Together, signed by Pope Francis and the Grand Imam of Al-Azhar, 4 February 2019. For the text, see http://www.vatican.va/content/francesco/en/travels/2019/outside/documents/papa-francesco_20190204_documento-fratellanza-umana.html [accessed on December 30, 2019].

baptized and made part of official or formal Christianity. Groups of Khrist Bhaktas exist in different parts of North India, especially in and around the holy city of Varanasi, or Banares.[39] It is difficult to name such a phenomenon as conversion. Khrist Bhaktas would not fit into the traditional definition of conversion which involves shifting from one religion to another. For, on the one hand, the Hindu tradition they practice is something fluid and porous, and on the other hand, their way of practicing discipleship of Jesus may not fall into the normativity and canons of Christian belonging.

A second unique phenomenon is found in the People's Republic of China. After the suppression of all religions as superstition and as anti-modern force during the Cultural Revolution (1966–1976), China allowed the practicing of religion under strict state control. There are reports of a newly awakened interest in the Christian tradition, history, and doctrines in China. Some speak of "Christian fever" in China. Other authors predict that within the next couple of decades, China would be a country with one of the largest Christian populations. Aikman thinks that within the next few decades, one-third of China could become Christian.[40] These predictions and the figures they quote may be exaggerated. However, what is undeniable is a renewed interest in and conversion to Christianity in a China deep into market economy and globalization. This presents a unique situation of conversion very different from the factors and forces that were at work for conversion, as we find in the history of Christianity. Most significant is the fact that this movement of conversion to Christianity is "home-made," that is, without foreign missionaries or agencies. As Bays notes, "Today, on any given Sunday there are almost certainly more Protestants in church in China than in all of Europe."[41]

The new turn to Christianity has brought about the phenomenon of the so-called "cultural Christians," mostly intellectuals who, in a search for an alternative to the Communist ideology, find in Christian tradition inspiration in their endeavor to work for change in Chinese society. They are attracted to a Christian worldview, values, and teachings and who

---

[39] Cf. Jerome Sylvester, *Khristbhakta Movement. Hermeneutics of a Religio-Cultural Phenomenon* (Delhi: ISPCK, 2013).

[40] David Aikman, *Jesus in Beijing: How Christianity is Transforming China and Changing the Global Balance of Power* (Oxford: Monarch, 2005); see also Tony Lambert, *China's Christian Millions* (Oxford: Monarch, 2006).

[41] D. H. Bays, "Chinese Protestant Christianity today," in *China Quarterly* 174, no. 2 (2013): 488–504, at 488.

connect these with the modernization of China, even though they may not profess themselves as Christians in public. Here again, it is difficult to name it as conversion. However, there is a shift from their previous athe-istic or religious affiliation to a new kind of religious existence.

Many reasons explain this kind of "conversion" to Christianity. One is the ideological and spiritual void that was left behind by the cultural revo-lution, something similar to what happened in Eastern Europe with the fall of socialist regimes. There are then other reasons like personal crisis, and individual choice in religious matters, as a mark of modernity. However, some other deeper factors and forces at work which also explain the present process of conversion to Christianity in China with "cultural Christians." In China, we have a modern flourishing market economy under a politically repressive regime. This situation creates new sets of problems and issues and the recourse to Christianity could be explained under such unique conditions. Christianity appears to Cultural Christians and others as a symbol of modernity, a force of liberation under repressive political conditions, cosmopolitan in its vision and as a religion that could offer peace and contentment under stressful market conditions and politi-cal repression. In concluding the analysis of such macro-conditions con-ducive to conversion to Christianity, a Chinese scholar notes:

> In today's China, religious seekers often seek out Christian churches to learn about this non-traditional religion. In line with the Chinese pursuit of mod-ernization and global integration throughout the 20th century, many edu-cated Chinese tend to prefer a meaning system that is universal instead of particularly Chinese. In the context of a globalizing market under political repression, many Chinese perceive Christianity as liberating, democratic, modern, cosmopolitan, or universal. They regard Buddhism, Daoism, and Confucianism as backwards-looking and traditionalistic, and thus incompat-ible with the market economy and increasingly globalizing world.[42]

Conversion is not limited only to mainland China. Many of the migrant communities of Chinese, especially in the USA and Canada, have con-verted to Evangelical Protestantism. Analysis shows that this is not due solely to personal or institutional factors, but also because of the social and cultural changes taking place in China from where migration takes place. As Fenggang Yang observes:

---

[42] Fenggang Yang, "Lost in the Market, Saved at McDonald's: Conversion to Christianity in Urban China," *Journal for the Scientific Study of Religion* 44, no. 4 (December 2005): 423–441 at 439.

My extensive ethnographic data and interviews show that the most crucial factors for the recent wave of Chinese conversions to Christianity are social and cultural changes in China. China began its process of modernization passively, having had it forced upon the nation by Western powers. Modern Chinese history is full of wars with imperialist powers, civil wars, political storms, and social turmoil. Chinese cultural traditions have been severely interrupted or lost. Coming from such a society, Chinese immigrants are both free and bound to seek alternate meaning system.[43]

Such being the situation, the Chinese immigrants more easily change over to the religion dominant in their new environment, which also responds to their quest for meaning.

## CONCLUSION

When religion was an important marker of identity, conversion had great significance at a personal level and also socially. This is especially so when religions were at loggerheads with each other, and were competing for loyalties. Hence, when Henry Newman converted from Anglicanism to Catholicism, it was a critical moment for both the religious groups involved, even though in the case of Newman personally conversion was not deserting of an earlier identity but a coming home. In India, when Ambedkar converted to Buddhism, it was a social and religious revolution, since it was to signify the rejection of a religion—Hinduism—in which "the Untouchables" of India found themselves trapped into a highly hierarchical system of exclusion. In converting they experienced liberation and hoped for the future. Further, the conversion had a tremendous psychological dimension. As Eleanor Zeliot has pointed out, the conversion freed the erstwhile Untouchables "from the sense of being a polluting person," and provided a sense of unity among them, and they acquired self-confidence.[44] Some contemporary Dalit Christian thinkers have also explored the theological dimension of conversion.[45]

In today's world of globalization, when religious identities are conceived and practiced in multiple ways, the approach to conversion is also

---

[43] Fenggang Yang, in *Sociology of Religion* 59, no. 3 (Autumn, 1998): 237–257, at 253.

[44] Cf. Eleanor Zelliot, *From Untouchable to Dalit. Essays on Ambedkar Movement* (Delhi: Manohar, 2005), 218–221.

[45] Cf. Sathiananthan Clarke, et al., *Dalit Theology in the Twenty-first Century. Discordant Voices, Discerning Pathways* (Delhi: Oxford University Press, 2010).

bound to change. We realize the polysemous character of the conception of conversion. Today's milieu of religious pluralism allows voyages and negotiation across the various religious traditions. Conversion becomes a *bridge* to the religious banks of the other rather than a *wall* of separation. However, often religious traditions continue to create and maintain walls to keep the flock on their side and conversion becomes anathema. Besides the fluidity of religious borders, the phenomenon of religious diaspora adds to relativizing the conventional understanding of conversion and turns the religious world of the other into a field of exciting encounter.

Finally, religious conversion is an explosive issue in these times, and it affects deeply the relationship among religious traditions which can turn antagonistic to each other, and the extremists can unleash communal conflicts and violence. No wonder conversion has also become a significant issue in international politics.

# CHAPTER 11

# Changing Ethical Discourses and Religious Identities

Time was when religions were the unquestioned authority on morals and there was a functional overlap of being religious and being moral. Some religions enunciated moral laws and prescribed injunctions for its followers to abide by, and others chartered the moral path (*dharma*) for its believers to walk. The decalogue summed up the innumerable rules and regulations for good moral conduct among the ancient Israelites. Each religion developed its moral traditions over the centuries so much so that certain ethical stances came to characterize religious identities. For example, nonviolence as a moral principle became the core of Jainism going back to the sixth century BCE.

Analysis of the contemporary world situation shows that globalization has pushed to the foreground three very crucial issues which are moral in nature: the question of inequality at all levels; the subtle and open exercise of power and domination; and the issue of identity and recognition.[1] The mishandling of these issues has been a source of violence. All the three are weighty issues, and the ways religions respond to them will also attest to their ethical potential. There are very many moral theories and ethical discourses. Their validity too will depend upon their adeptness to respond to these three major issues of our times. In this context, religions need to

---

[1] Cf. Michael Sohn, *The Good of Recognition: Phenomenology, Ethics, and Religion in the Thought of Levinas and Ricoeur* (Texas: Baylor University Press, 2014).

© The Author(s), under exclusive license to Springer Nature Switzerland AG 2021
F. Wilfred, *Religious Identities and the Global South*,
New Approaches to Religion and Power,
https://doi.org/10.1007/978-3-030-60738-8_11

revise their traditional ethical conceptions, priorities, and frames of reference. Since religions draw moral principles from their belief systems, they too require to be critically rethought and formulated, taking into account the contemporary exigencies.

This chapter argues that religions under conditions of globalization need to revise their practice of drawing moral conclusions from universalistic principles nurtured in their own traditions or from some abstract and abstruse ethical theories. Religions can support the moral quest of our times for justice, for check on power, and for identity and recognition by adopting more innovative and context-sensitive approaches. The new moral pluralism may not be fitted into conventional frameworks such as the theory of natural law.

## EXILING RELIGION AND ENTHRONING ETHICS?

Does the practice of ethics necessarily involve theism or religious beliefs? In what sense could agnostics and atheists be considered practitioners of morality? These have been questions heatedly debated in the past. Entering into this issue may take us afar from the focus of our reflections. Instead, we will direct our attention to more recent developments in relating religion and morality. Here is not a matter of belief in God or not, but instead whether religion could be replaced by morality. It may be interesting to study in this regard the position of Richard Rorty from the Global North.[2] Later in the chapter, we will discuss the position of Mahatma Gandhi from the Global South, for whom religion is practically synonymous with ethics. We could see some convergence of Rorty and Gandhi, albeit with different starting points and premises.

From a pragmatic point of view, for Rorty, religion is a "conversation stopper."[3] It is understandable in the context of controversial issues like abortion and homosexuality. Conflicting religiously backed ethical positions on such issues could disquiet society and hence religion is often considered a risky matter of conversation. In another equally important sense religion becomes a conversation stopper in that it does not allow argumentation since the believer tries to overwhelm others invoking the

---

[2] Later in the chapter, we will discuss the position of Mahatma Gandhi from the Global South, for whom religion is practically synonymous to ethics. We could see some convergence of Rorty and Gandhi, albeit with different starting points and premises.

[3] Richard Rorty, "Religion as a Conversation Stopper," in *Philosophy and Social Hope* (New York: Penguin, 1999): 168–174; see also Stuart Rosenbaum, "Must Religion Be a Conversation-Stopper?," *The Harvard Theological Review* 102, no. 4 (2009): 393–409.

authority and the will of God for his or her position. It ends all discussions. The conversation cannot proceed because no argument is offered except the stamp of divine will and revelation. This is the case when pro-life groups use the language of "sacredness of life" and deploy arguments culled out from the scriptures—the authority of God—for their public display of opposition to abortion.

Sidelining of religion for Rorty, however, has deeper roots. He considers any philosophical enterprise after the essence of things, metaphysics, and epistemology as of little significance and even futile. Similar is his disdain to such philosophically sacrosanct concepts like rationality, truth, and objectivity. In this, he is on the same page as Gianni Vattimo with his call for the dissolution of metaphysics.[4]

Rorty pulls together the best of John Dewey, William James, Charles Peirce, Hegel, and Darwin for his project of pragmatism and historicism, denying any need to deck them with philosophical conceptions or fit them into an epistemology that claims to mirror and represent reality.[5] He also rejects any essentialist conception of a universal human nature. With no metaphysical and philosophical foundation, the colossus—religion—falls on its face. Rorty's views on ethics flow from his pragmatic and metaphilosophical position. Like religion, ethics too has no foundation. Hence, unlike the classical approach, which draws from theoretical principles of *what* we *believe* to conclude *how* we should *act*, Rorty's ethics remains at the level of realism and pragmatism.

> As I read the history of philosophy, Kant is a transitional figure—somebody who helped us get away from the idea that morality is a matter of divine command, but who unfortunately retained the idea that morality is a matter of unconditional obligations. I would accept Elizabeth Anscombe's suggestion that if you do not believe in God, you would do well to drop notions like "law" and "obligation" from the vocabulary you use when deciding what to do.[6]

---

[4] Gianni Vattimo, "The Christian Message and the Dissolution of Metaphysics," in *After Christianity*, Chapter 8 (New York: Columbia University Press, 2002), 103–112; Gianni Vattimo, "The Trace of the Trace," in Jacques Derrida and Gianni Vattimo, eds., *Religion* (Stanford: Stanford University Press, 1998), 79–94.

[5] Cf. Richard Rorty, *Philosophy and the Mirror of Nature* (Princeton, Oxford: Princeton University Press, 1979); see also Rorty, *Consequences of Pragmatism* (Minneapolis: University of Minnesota Press, 1982).

[6] Richard Rorty, *Philosophy as Cultural Politics: Philosophical Papers*, vol. 4 (Cambridge: Cambridge University Press, 2007), 187.

In fact, Rorty is very much influenced by John Dewey and the pragmatism of Darwin. For Rorty, norms and rationality are nothing but what is generally believed in a particular context in society, enjoying consensus, at least, on the part of the elites. Norms keep changing. Moral judgments change according to times and difference of societies. Rorty views ethics as something oriented to the contingent and pluralist situation of the world and society. It is to be defined not with reference to absolute principles like in Kant or external authority as in religious belief, but rather with reference to habits and social practices by which humans communicate intersubjectively for realizing cooperative projects. He calls for expanding freedom (understood in the liberal sense), solidarity, and cultivating the ability to think of others. The concept of solidarity occupies a central place in Rorty's view. It confers a social character to ethics in contrast to the morality of individual behavior. His ethics is one which cares for the suffering and attends to the pain of others. For him, solidarity is the "imaginative ability to see strange people as fellow sufferers."[7]

## THEORIES OF ETHICS IN GLOBAL TIMES

Notwithstanding the critique of pragmatists like Rorty, Immanuel Kant's universalistic ethical orientation and his categorical imperatives have found many followers and representatives today. There are different variations of this model of ethics. At the core of this ethical orientation is liberal individualism, a philosophy that has dominated the West for the past two centuries. The autonomous self here as a moral subject is abstracted from the concrete situation and deprived of any social mediation. In other words, this type of ethics presupposes an autonomous subject de-situated from the community and intersubjective interactions. But the reality is different. For, just like the identity of the self is embedded in the community and culture of one's context, so too the ethical actions. These cannot be divorced from society and concrete history. Especially in the context of today when issues of environment and sustainability have become critical ethical issues, we need a moral vision that goes beyond the anthropocentrism embedded in the Enlightenment tradition and its categorical imperatives on how we ought to deal with other human persons. Alsdair MacIntyre in his well-known work *After Virtue* has shown with many

---

[7] Richard Rorty, "Responses," in *Deconstruction and Pragmatism,* edited by Chantal Mouffe (London and New York: Routledge, 1996), xvi.

examples the limits of universal normative ethics and the difficulties encountered today in resolving crucial contemporary questions touching upon politics, society, and the world. MacIntyre characterizes moral individualism as follows:

> To be a moral agent [as understood by modern moral philosophy] is … precisely to be able to stand back from any and every situation in which one is involved, from any and every characteristic that one may possess, and to pass judgment on it from a purely universal and abstract point of view that is totally detached from all social particularity—it is in the self and not in social roles or practices that moral agency has to be located.[8]

What happened with the European Enlightenment was that morality became an issue of an autonomous individual subject dissociated from the society and community. MacIntyre notes, "The price paid for liberation from what appeared to be the external authority of traditional morality was the loss of any authoritative context from the would-be moral utterances of the newly autonomous agent."[9] Over against the abstract and formal Kantian "morality of law," MacIntyre highlights the importance of a "morality of virtue" which needs to be fostered in society, so that people could act for the achievement of the common good. [10] In religious traditions, we will find laws and regulations which prevent us from harming others and society, namely "morality of law."

---

[8] Quoted in Lewis P. Hinchman, "Virtue or Autonomy: Alasdair MacIntyre's Critique of Liberal Individualism," *Polity* 21, no. 4 (Summer, 1989): 635–654, at 644.

[9] Alasdair MacIntyre, *After Virtue: A Study in Moral Theology* (Notre Dame, Indiana: University of Notre Dame Press, 1981), 68.

[10] Cf. Shannon Dunn, "Myth or Method: Religious Ethics, MacIntyre's Modernity, and the Question of Power," *Soundings: An Interdisciplinary Journal* 98, no. 3 (2015): 233–59; see also Richard J. Mouw, "Alasdair MacIntyre on Reformation Ethics," *The Journal of Religious Ethics* 13, no. 2 (1985): 243–57; David Humbert, "After Macintyre: Kierkegaard, Kant, and Classical Virtue," *The Journal of Religious Ethics* 42, no. 2 (2014): 310–33; Hugo Meynell, "MacIntyre on Morality," *New Blackfriars* 82, no. 961, (2001): 138–50.

## COMMON GROUND APPROACH: GLOBAL ETHICS

Global ethics is an attempt to formulate a set of universal ethical principles commonly agreed upon and applicable in every part of the globe and across national, cultural, ethnic, and religious divisions. [11] This, indeed, was done by the World Parliament of Religions gathered in 1993 in Chicago, where representatives of various religions converged from all over the world and came out with a "Declaration Toward a Global Ethic." [12]

What is highly positive and significant about the global ethics project is the acknowledgment of the role of religion today in providing inspiration and guidance to the contemporary world. It invites religions to come together to face the moral challenges in our global world. Hans Küng, a great promoter of global ethics, [13] has been critical of deriving inspiration and principles solely from the consideration of human rights as has been done by the various global bodies such as International Commission on Global Governance (1995), and the World Commission on Culture and Development (1995). The legal instruments of human rights may not instill ethical sensitivity as long as there is no reference to responsibilities. With responsibilities, we can speak of ethical obligations. For Hans Küng, the language of rights gives us "social and political postulates" rather than

---

[11] Cf. Darrel Moellendorf, and Heather Widdows, eds., *The Routledge Handbook of Global Ethics* (London and New York: Routledge, 2015); Heather Widdows, *Global Ethics: An Introduction* (London and New York: Routledge, 2014); Robert Bruce McLaren, *Religious Foundations for Global Ethics* (London and New York: Routledge, 2016); Frederick B, Bird, Sumner B. Twiss, et al., *The Practices of Global Ethics: Historical Backgrounds, Current Issues and Future Prospects* (Edinburgh: Edinburgh University Press, 2016); Mark J. Cherry, *Natural Law and the Possibility of a Global Ethics*, Philosophical Studies in Contemporary Culture; vol.11 (Dordrecht; London: Kluwer Academic Publishers, 2004); Darrell J. Fasching, Dell DeChant, and David M. Lantigua, *Comparative Religious Ethics: A Narrative Approach to Global Ethics*, 2nd ed. (Oxford: Wiley-Blackwell, 2011); J. Drydyk, "Foundational Issues: How Must Global Ethics Be Global?" *Journal of Global Ethics* 10, no. 1 (2014): 16–25.

[12] https://parliamentofreligions.org/pwr_resources/_includes/FCKcontent/File/TowardAGlobalEthic.pdf [accessed on February 28, 2020].

[13] Cf. Hans Küng, *Yes, to a Global Ethic* (New York: Continuum, 1996); Hans Kung and Helmut Schmidt, *A Global Ethic and Global Responsibilities: Two Declarations* (London: SCM Press, 1998); Hans Kung, *Global Responsibility: In Search of a New World Ethic* (New York: Crossroad Publisher, 1991); Rabbi Walter Homolka and Hans Kung, *How to Do Good and Avoid Evil: A Global Ethic from the Sources of Judaism* (US: SkyLight Paths Publishing, 2009).

principles of ethics. Moreover, the regime of human rights is viewed differently in different cultures and different parts of the world. At this juncture, he highlights the importance of religion and the need for religions to come together to give direction to the future of our global world—something which ethics *alone* cannot do. More needs to be done to enhance the quality of human life—individual and collective—than believe that the upholding of human rights is the supreme end of morality. Since the moral universe is much larger, we need to turn to religion and go *beyond* human rights for the life of society and of the world. Since we cannot hope for peace in the world with conflicting ethical views, it is necessary to develop a common ethical platform to which religions need to contribute significantly.

The intention of the project of global ethics and involvement of religions in it are laudable, and there can be no second opinion about it. However, there are some considerable difficulties about this common ground approach to global ethics. First, Patricia Walsh, while reviewing a book on the theme, points out that there is an ambiguity in the use of the term "global ethic."

> There [is] the difficulty of pinning down in any precise way the two key terms of this discourse, 'globalization' and 'global ethics'. To take just one of these terms: does 'global ethics' refer to 'a set of universally applicable and agreed moral values' or, quite differently, to 'ethics directed at problems resulting from the processes of globalization'? ... Because how we use a term determines how we theorize and what we theorize about, this ambiguity in meaning tends to muddy answers to the second question of whether global ethics is possible.[14]

Assuming the above first sense, from an ethical point of view, it is not clear how the problems and challenges thrown open by globalization such as the increase of inequality, migration, domination, human trafficking, exploitation of all kinds, racial, caste, and ethnic discriminations are going to be addressed by the proclamation of a list of commonly agreed-upon moral values and ideals. It cannot but give the impression of a moral discourse that passes by the burning issues of our times instead of coming to terms with them. It is said that hunger of every human being on earth can be eliminated and health care provided for all those who lack it if only $13

---

[14] Patricia Walsh, "Ethics in an Era of Globalization," in *International Affairs* 85, no. 4 (Jul. 2009): 875–876, at 875.

billion are available, and yet it is said that people in the United States and Europe spend $17 billion on food for pets per year.[15] Why do we have such an unequal and unethical world? Is it due to lack of global ethics to which everybody will consent to? We do not have solutions to these deeper structural questions by gathering people to sign a joint Declaration toward a Global Ethic as Hans Küng seems to have done.

What we require is more significant interaction and dialogue among religions. Even if leaders of various religions come together and agree to draft a joint statement of ethics, this act may not have the same validity for the followers of all religions. It would be a delusion to believe that we would have an ethically sound world if only we had something to agree upon. It presupposes contractual thinking, and contracts of this kind do not touch the people of all religions in the same way. Further, ethics is never a finished product. It is always in the process of construction, redesigning, and restructuring. In everyday practice, global ethics may mean very little. It may be right for international relationships. But people at the grassroots are not doing everyday international relationships. No wonder, global ethics has not reached the grassroots level. Like universal normative ethics, it is ethics from above, divorced from the complexity of life at the bottom.

What we require today is a multipronged approach that would include continuous dialogue among religious groups in particular contexts. If at all, there is room for global ethics, it needs to revise its approach completely. Instead of starting apparently from a Christian tradition to speak of global ethics, every religious tradition could draft *its own global ethics* of what they consider are crucial for our world today, and the conversations could be held on these different versions and expressions of global ethics which would also reveal *different starting points* for ethics.[16] Peace and tranquility do not come as a package but in small doses. What religiously committed people could and ought to do is to move from situations of *less* justice to *more* justice, from situations of brutality, inhumanity, and domination to a little more humanization, a little more peace. This involves sustained dialogue, promotion of understanding and efforts to collabo-

---

[15] Ronald Commers, Wim Vandekerckhove, and an Verlinden, eds., *Ethics in an Era of Globalization* (Aldershot: Ashgate, 2008), 55; see also the incisive analysis of the shocking and scandalous situation resulting from the current economic policies, Naomi Klein, *The Shock Doctrine* (New York: Penguin Books, 2007).

[16] Nicole Melara, "Global Ethic at The Grassroots: A Research Proposal Based on The Work of Leonard Swidler," *Journal of Ecumenical Studies*, 50, no.1 (Winter 2015): 18–20, at.19.

rate. Moreover, there is a need to look for new approaches to ethics itself which will vibrate with the ethos, culture, and tradition of the people.

## RELIGION AND THE TURN TO NARRATIVE ETHICS

The *universalistic* a priori ethics of the Kantian type and common ground ethics like that of global ethics are challenged by the *plurality* of cultures, histories, traditions, and contexts. This has led to a false dichotomy. The contextual and cultural aspects which call for a pluralist approach in ethics is stigmatized as moral relativism. The whole ethical discourse is then pushed into the straitjacket of moral universalism versus moral relativism. I think this contrast does not contribute much to take the ethical discourse forward.

Narrative ethics[17] seems to break the dichotomy between universal ethics and what is named as cultural relativism. If in the universalistic and common ground approach there is the concern about *impartiality* in ethics, namely what is universal applies to everybody, it fails to give enough room to the moral agent, subject who is expected to act ethically. Narrative ethics opens up a new horizon beyond the dichotomy of universal ethics and moral relativism.

Narrative ethics is based on an understanding of the self and the other mediated through narrations and stories. The continuity of the self takes place through the stories remembered and narrated at present, and they pave the way for the future. The self is not an abstract essence. If essentialism is to be challenged, it should happen first with the identity of the self. Abstract definitions of the self in universal terms falter in answering the question, Who are you? It is best answered by narrating one's past and

---

[17] Cf. Jakob Lothe, and Jeremy Hawthorn, eds., "Introduction The Narrative Ethics (Re) turn," in *Narrative Ethics*, vol. 267 (The Netherlands: Brill, 2013); William J. Ellos, *Narrative Ethics*, Avebury Series in Philosophy (Aldershot: Avebury, 1994); B. A. Dixon, *Food Justice and Narrative Ethics: Reading Stories for Ethical Awareness and Activism* (London and New York, Bloomsbury Academic, 2018); Katherine Saunders Nash, *Feminist Narrative Ethics: Tacit Persuasion in Modernist Form*, Theory and Interpretation of Narrative Series (Ohio State University Press, 2014); Idelber Avelar, *The Letter of Violence: Essays on Narrative, Ethics, and Politics* (New York: Palgrave Macmillan, 2004); Adams, T.E. "A Review of Narrative Ethics," *Qualitative Inquiry: QI.* 14, no. 2 (2008): 175–94; D. B. Morris, "Narrative, Ethics, and Pain: Thinking with Stories," *Narrative.* 9, no. 1 (2001): 55–77; Christopher T. Fleming, "Critical Legal Studies and Narrative Ethics in Contemporary Indian 'Epic' Fiction," *South Asian Studies: Journal of the Society for South Asian Studies (incorporating the Society for Afghan Studies)* 34 (2018), 81–92.

present and sharing with others how one envisages the future. Psychoanalysis and psychotherapy give us a clue to a better understanding of the self. A person does not define the self in the abstract; she does it by gathering together the scattered pieces of the self, making it into a narration and communicating it to the therapist. Thus, the narrative approach to the self implies intersubjectivity. For the self, if it does not understand its identity in relation to the other, would be a narcissistically reified entity. In other words, the narratively perceived self can exist only if it is open to the narrations of the other selves. Such is not the case when the individual is defined in contradistinction to the other. In the narrative mode, the bond of the self and the other comes out clearly. Paul Ricoeur expressed it succinctly when he spoke of "*soi meme comme un autre*" (Oneself as Another).[18]

While deontological and universalistic ethics seem to be out of touch with the developing culture and ethos, in the present globalized situation with its specific moral questions and dilemmas, narrative ethics offers new possibilities and openings. To suppose and claim that the entire world will follow a rule-bound morality derived from universally normative principles is to entertain an illusion. The narrative approach, on the other hand, is grounded and close to experiences of life. The challenge to religious traditions is to examine their own moral discourses and check to what extent they respond to the transformed conditions of the world and society.

More than *general moral principles*, Asian religious traditions have imparted morality through the *narration of stories*, presenting ideal figures for the exercise of different virtues.[19] The narratives have an element of moral persuasion and an impact on the fashioning of the self. Foremost among them are the two great epics—*Ramayana* and

---

[18] Paul Ricoeur, *Soi-meme comme un autre* (Paris: Seuil, 1990). On the narrative ethics of Paul Ricoeur, see Tara Flanagan, *Narrative Medicine in Hospice Care: Identity, Practice, and Ethics Through the Lens of Paul Ricoeur,* Studies in the Thought of Paul Ricoeur (Lanham: Lexington Books, 2019); Theo L. Hettema, *Reading for Good: Narrative Theology and Ethics in the Joseph Story from the Perspective of Ricoeur's Hermeneutics,* Studies in Philosophical Theology; 18 (Kampen: Kok Pharos, 1996); Alain Thomasset, *Paul Ricœur, Une Poétique de la Morale: Aux Fondements d'une Éthique Herméneutique et Narrative dans Une Perspective Chrétienne,* Bibliotheca Ephemeridum Theologicarum Lovaniensium; 124 (Leuven: Leuven University Press, 1996);

[19] Cf. Darrell J. Fasching, Dell DeChant, and David M. Lantigua, *Comparative Religious Ethics: A Narrative Approach to Global Ethics,* 2nd ed. (Oxford: Wiley-Blackwell, 2011).

*Mahabharata*—which, besides the main plot, have innumerable side stories and tales. The characters in these epics continue to inspire the good to be done and the evil to be avoided in daily life. These stories have become popular through serialized episodes in television programs in South Asia. Buddhist jataka stories composed between 300 BCE and 500 CE are indeed a treasure of wisdom for the practical conduct of life.

In the Indian subcontinent and in Greece, there has been a long tradition of storytelling. One may recall here the Greek fables of Aesop and the Indic *Panchatantra*. We could surmise mutual influence in the tradition of storytelling for moral education. It is important to note that Buddhist and Hindu traditions do not lack general principles for ethical conduct. We may refer here to the Noble Eightfold Path in Buddhism. It gives general direction for rightful conduct. So too dharma in Hinduism.[20] These principles work synergistically with the narratives and stories. With all their concrete grounding, narrations become illustrations of the ethical principles and turn them into practicable propositions. If the principles give conviction to the satisfaction of reason, the stories give practical *motivation* to ethical action. Surprisingly, we find recognition of narrative ethics in Richard Rorty when he says, "detailed descriptions of particular varieties of pain and humiliation (in, e.g., novels or ethnographies), rather than philosophical or religious treatises, were the modern intellectual's principal contributions to moral progress."[21] Narrative ethics would also echo with the Scottish philosopher David Hume for whom morality is a matter of sentiment rather than reason. Obviously, sentiments are best expressed through narrations, stories, and novels. Who would not be moved by *Les Miserables* of Victor Hugo and *David Copperfield* of Charles Dickens?

Though there are more systematic ethical works explicitly dealing with *dharma* (righteousness), and the fulfillment of one's duties, in practice, however, what captures the imagination of the people and leads them to ethical practice are ideals portrayed through the long tradition of moral stories. Millions of South Asians, for example, would be strongly motivated to act truthfully and abstain from lying by listening to the story of King *Harishchandra*. This classical story narrates the suffering this legendary character had to undergo for adhering to truth. This figure has been

---

[20] Cf. Roderick Hindery, *Comparative Ethics in Hindu and Buddhist Traditions* (Delhi: Motilal Banarsidass Publishers, 1996).

[21] Richard Rorty, *Contingency, Irony, and solidarity* (Cambridge: Cambridge University Press, 1989), 192.

the subject of many popular Indian films, dramas, and other cultural per-formances. Gandhi, too in his adherence to the truth principle was inspired by the story of Harishchandra. In the Roman Catholic tradition, the lives of saints were often used as inspiring examples for "doing the right thing," and often Catholics brought up by these narrations would quote a saint's life as the trigger for a moral act or decision.

There are two critical questions raised against narrative ethics. If ethics is related to narrative, is there not the danger of it ending in moral relativism? To what extent could one formulate general principles of ethics out of narrations? These are important questions, also from a religious point of view. For the traditional approach to religion tied to eternal truths, moral principles, and natural law, anything like narrative ethics could become suspicious.

On the other hand, if we examine religious scriptures and literature, we find not only moral teachings ex-professo, but in no less measure also narrations of stories, events that are pregnant with ethical significance. Narrative ethics would be misunderstood if it were interpreted to mean that every single person could determine, on his or her own, moral choices—"anything goes"—and every one of those decisions are of equal moral import. No, it is not moral relativism or the case of considering all moral choices as equal; rather, every choice is given due attention.[22] As for the question to what extent the morality coming of out of narrations are generalizable, we should admit that individual choices do not lend themselves for generalization. On the other hand, this limitation is made good by the ability of the narrative ethics to be closer to life and its greater capacity to resolve moral dilemmas compared to universalistic and propositional ethics. Arvind Sharma has attempted to relate human rights today to the Indic narrative ethics. According to him, in the stories guiding ethical decisions and choices one can find the interlocking of the particular and the universal. He finds in these stories the key to human rights in the Indic tradition, which shows the way for a fruitful interaction with the global discourse on human rights.[23]

---

[22] Tom Wilks, "Social Work and Narrative Ethics," *The British Journal of Social Work* 35, no. 8 (December 2005), 1249–1264, at 1259.

[23] Cf. Arvind Sharma, *Hindu Narratives on Human Rights* (Santa Barbara, Calif.: Praeger, 2010); see also Roderick Hindery, *Comparative Ethics in Hindu and Buddhist Traditions* (Delhi: Motilal Banarsidass Publishers, 1996).

## COMPLIANCE-BASED ETHICS AND ETHICS
## OF SELF-CULTIVATION AND COMPASSION

Generally speaking, we could identify two models of ethics—one is centered on compliance with ethical norms or legal provisions. Most universalistic and normative ethics with their categorical imperative fall into this category. This model has its own presuppositions such as the "sacredness" of the given law, principles, contracts, and so on. The ethical behavior is judged according to how one complies with these given. There are cultures where this works since it convinces the people of the imperative need to adhere to laws and principles. Any deviance here is viewed as unethical. What is worse is that in this compliance-based approach, one may devise sophisticated argumentation to circumvent the principles and still claim to act morally by a formal and theoretical justification of what one does, even if it is manifestly unjust. For example, the use of torture by governments across the world while universally regarded as wrong was sanctioned with the justification that information extracted from terrorist suspects could save lives. The invasion of privacy by several governments uses the same justification.

In our complex world of today, the lasting foundation for moral behavior and action are to be laid much more in depth than normativity which could foster simply a heteronomous morality without touching the inner self of individuals and communities as moral agents. Self-cultivation is a highly valuable moral tradition of ancient civilizations and very much fostered also by Asian religions. In modern times, some of the Western thinkers like Michael Foucault have taken up the approach of self-cultivation—*le souci de soi*—care of the self.[24] For Foucault, the self is not the knowing subject mirroring reality as in the European Enlightenment tradition. The self for him is the ethical self which can be shaped and transformed. In the Asian religious and ethical traditions, there has been an effort to season the self and infuse into it a moral sense in such a way that it acts morally in every situation with a certain spontaneity. Let me illustrate the point with two contrasting contemporary examples.

We have two different cases—Kevin Carter and Nick Ut—both of them Pulitzer Prize winners. Kevin Carter, a South African photojournalist,

---

[24] Cf. F. Gros, "Le souci de soi chez Michel Foucault: A review of The Hermeneutics of the Subject: Lectures at the Collège de France, 1981–1982," *Philosophy & Social Criticism* 31, no. 5/6 (2005): 697–708.

photographed in 1993 in South Sudan a child. This child was a famine victim, emaciated and reduced to a skeleton. The child was crawling to reach a feeding center. Behind the child was a huge vulture eagerly waiting for its prey. Carter too waited for the vulture to stretch its wings, so that he could have the best shot, but it did not. Nevertheless, he took the photograph of this scene. For that picture, he did win the Pulitzer prize to universal acclaim. Accolades came pouring forth. He was feted everywhere. However, Carter was apparently confronted by a friend who asked him, "What did you do for the dying child?" At this point, he was completely shattered and convulsed with the sense of guilt. This led him to commit suicide.[25] In his suicide note, he had this to say: "The pain of life overrides the joy to the point that joy does not exist."[26]

In the other case, Nick Ut too won a Pulitzer prize for a photo during the Vietnam War. He is a Vietnamese American, who was twenty-one-year old at that time. He served then as a photographer for the Associated Press. He took the photo of a nine-year-old terrified girl fleeing naked from the napalm bomb attack during the Vietnam War. He did take the iconic photo, which brought him laurels. It was one of the most horrendous images of the Vietnam war. But he did not stop with taking a photo. He rushed to the rescue of the child; carried her in his arms to the hospital for emergency medical treatment, and took care of her. The girl survived those horrific burns of the bomb after almost a dozen surgeries. The rescued girl Phan Thị Kim Phúc lives today in Canada to narrate the story.

These two different moral responses cannot be explained adequately by any amount of theorizing. It is not as if the one did not follow a universal ethical principle, and the other followed it. A more plausible explanation would be the difference in moral sensitivity which cannot be ensured by any amount of laws and principles cast in regulative rationality. The moral action was the result of an inner moral impulse than a deduction from a rationally justified principle. The crux of the question is the cultivation of this sensitivity. In the words of Zygmunt Bauman:

> Morality is endemically and irredeemably non-rational—in the sense of not being calculable, hence not being presentable as following impersonal rules, hence not being describable as following rules that are in principle

[25] The story of Kevin Carter is depicted in the film *The Bang Bang Club*.

[26] http://content.time.com/time/magazine/article/0,9171,165071,00.html [accessed on January 25, 2020].

universalizable. The moral call is thoroughly personal; it appeals to my responsibility ... As a moral person, I am alone, though as a social person I am always with others. Being with others can be regulated by codifiable rules. 'Being for the Other' conspicuously cannot. In Durkheim's terms, though in defiance of Durkheim's intuitions, we could say that morality is the condition of perpetual and irreparable anomie. Being moral means being abandoned to my own freedom.[27]

In the case of Nick Ut, there was, so to say, an "inner voice" saying that here and now this child needs care and the child should not die. It is this kind of ethics which we find in the Chinese Confucian sage Mencius in his analogy of a child at the brink of an open well and at the point of tumbling down. Someone grabs the child from the fatal fall and saves it. It is not done because the person who saved the child was convinced of moral categorical imperative or was motivated by what that action would bring him—praise from everyone and the gratitude of the parents. This act is motivated simply by the deeper moral sense within. Buddhism would characterize this as *compassion (karuna)*. Moral acts flow from a person overflowing in compassion. Referring to the analogy of the child at the well, Mencius says:

> Judging by this, without a heart-mind that sympathizes one is not human; without a heart-mind aware of shame, one is not human; without a heart-mind that defers to others, one is not human; and without a heart-mind that approves and condemns, one is not human.[28]

When many Germans during the Hitler regime hid and saved numerous individual Jews and families from the sight of the Nazis, they did it out of pure compassion. The ordinary people who did this did not think of themselves as heroes or as extraordinary men and women. Nor did they need global ethics and discourse ethics as premises for their morally laudable actions which involved risks for their own lives. In the face of moral dilemmas of today, individuals and communities need to take steps to cultivate the moral self. It is a great challenge to all religious traditions to open the springs of compassion within so that noble moral acts may flow and make life in the world and society blossom. To this end, Asian religious traditions had devised different means.

---

[27] Bauman Zigmunt, *Postmodern Ethics* (Oxford: Blackwell, 1993), 60.
[28] https://www.iep.utm.edu/mencius/ [accessed on January 25, 2020].

Instead of theoretical arguments, concrete instances like the ones I cited will show the feasibility or not of the various theoretical approaches and proposals in the field of ethics. In the one case, the ethical potential within did not develop, and in the other case there was an acute ethical sensitivity. The resistance of Dietrich Bonhöffer to an evil regime did not start from universalistic principles. It started at the micro level when he was confronted with the real experience of exclusion of his fellow ministers in the church because they were of Jewish origin. His moral empathy with such ministers widened to include other circles and eventually to any victim.

The ethics of self-cultivation appears to be very important in the context of today's "liquid modernity," globalization and consumerism. The self needs to be cultivated in such a way that it can contain and restrain itself and self-regulate, which is truly the mark of autonomy in contrast to heteronomy. The self today can dissolve itself in the endless and insatiable desires triggered by the continuous production of goods and services.[29] The identity of the self then becomes what it consumes. The ethics of self-limitation, on the other hand, shapes the moral person and makes her capable of responding to the face of the other. Without self-limitation, the inner ethical impulse for the care for the other and for the suffering of the other could be suppressed and eliminated. That would be most fearsome moral darkness. That the inner ethical impulse cannot be rooted out is borne out by the fact that even the Nazi regime did not succeed in this. Numerous examples of heroic care for the other, right in the midst of inhumanity and brutality, reveals a lot of hope for humanity. This hope of moral triumph needs to be upheld by religions in our modern times.

## RELIGION AND ETHICS OF TRUTH AND NONVIOLENCE

The personality of Gandhi and some of his significant actions in his political and public life may suggest that he was a person following a deontological morality. True as it may, it does not characterize the religious and moral landscape of Gandhi entirely. His ethical vision and practice had deeper religious roots, without any attachment to external manifestations of religion. In fact, Gandhi was someone who was hardly interested in visiting temples or someone who associated himself with religious ritual

---

[29] Cf. Zygmunt Bauman, *Does Ethics Have a Chance in a World of Consumers?* (Cambridge, Mass; London: Harvard University Press, 2008).

practices. And yet his moral universe was nurtured by religious roots that went deep.[30]

Gandhi's principles did not derive from any deontological, universalistic, and dehistoricized ethic, but rather from the experiences of his life in quest for truth. Truth for him was not something given, which one could take for granted. It was something one needed to seek and experiment. In fact, Gandhi titled his autobiography as *My Experiments with Truth*.[31]

> Instead of saying that God is Truth, I say that Truth is God. I did not always think thus. I realized this only four years ago. But without knowing it I always acted as if it was so. I have always known God as Truth. There was a time when I doubted the existence of God, but even at that time I did not doubt the existence of Truth. This Truth is not material quality but is pure consciousness. That alone holds the universe together. It is God because it rules the whole universe. ...For me this is almost a matter of direct experience. I say 'almost' because I have not seen face to face God Who is Truth. I have had only a glimpse of Him. But my faith is unshakeable.[32]

Ethical vision and practice was for him a sequel to the quest for truth which sets a person in a dynamic and interactive process with the world and society around.

Was Gandhi a moral relativist? I think one would misjudge him if he were to be viewed through the dyadic frame of moral absolute and relative. His firmness and absoluteness were not so much based on an a priori given principle, but rather an unshakable determination to seek truth at all costs. There was a sense of progress, dynamism, search, and movement in the ethical realm which would not qualify him as a moral absolutist for whom moral judgments are independent of the concrete situation and experiences. His determination to hold on to truth came to expression in his insistence on vows (*vrata*). In fact, the inmates of his ashram in Ahmedabad had to take vows of commitment to truth, to nonviolence, to the eradication of untouchability, and to free themselves from the greed of

---

[30] Cf. Raghavan Iyer, *The Essential Writings of Mahatma Gandhi* (Delhi: Oxford University Press, 2018)—Twenty-seventh impression; Margaret Chatterjee, *Gandhi's Religious Thought* (London: Macmillan Press, 1983); Ramachandra Guha, *Gandhi: The Years That Changed the World, 1915–1948* (Delhi: Penguin Books, 2018).

[31] M. K. Gandhi, *Gandhi, An Autobiography, Or, The Story of My Experiments with Truth.* Translated from the Original Gujarati by Mahadev Desai (Delhi: Penguin Books, 2007).

[32] Raghavan Iyer, *The Essential Writings of Mahatma Gandhi*, 233–234.

possession, and practice temperance in food. These vows for Gandhi were not an end in themselves, but an effective means for the ethical and spiritual transformation of the person who takes the vow.

To be able to understand Gandhi's approach, we need to hold in mind that for him religion meant primarily not doctrines and beliefs, but moral being and conduct. In this sense, religion is pervasive.

> I do not conceive religion as one of the many activities of mankind. The same activity may be either governed by the spirit of religion or irreligion. There is no such thing for me therefore as leaving politics for religion. For me every, the tiniest, activity is governed by what I consider to be my religion.[33]

Hence, for Gandhi, politics that is *divorced* from religion in this sense would end up in power politics devoid of any value orientation. He was also very critical of the separation of private and public in the realm of morality. Gandhi considered a religion which does not interpret itself in terms of public morality, as a sectarian religion. This is a very different approach to the relationship of religion, politics, and morality from the one which links religion and politics by creating state religion or official religion. In other words, for Gandhi, religion and politics are to be bound together by the cords of morality. It is important to note that Gandhi saw politics as a consequence of morality, since it is supposed to seek the good of the community and its flourishing. He did not think so much of an independent political realm which operates on pragmatic expediency and which needs to be checked through morality. For him, there should be a meeting of *personal* morality and *political* morality.

This presents a significant challenge to religions in these times of globalization. For some, such views of Gandhi may sound utopian. Gandhi was undoubtedly a great thinker, but not an armchair academic. He was a person down to earth and deeply immersed in the political cauldron, and he was someone who tried to practice what others may view as utopian. Hence, Gandhi's view of the interconnection between morality and politics cannot be easily dismissed. On the contrary, the political developments in our contemporary world only confirm the relevance of the vision of Gandhi on the need for a *new* conception of religion and a *new* discourse on the interconnection between politics and morality moving

---

[33] Raghavan Iyer, *The Essential Writings of Mahatma Gandhi*, 125.

beyond the dichotomy of private and public morality. The core of morality, according to Gandhi is the search for truth and the practice of nonviolence, or *ahimsa*. He even thought that nonviolence is the highest form of religion, since there is a practical overlap in life between truthfulness and no injury to others.

On the one hand, by considering truth and nonviolence (*ahimsa*) as indissolubly intertwined, Gandhi has given a concrete and practical interpretation of truth and has freed it from the realm of abstraction. On the other hand, he exposed violence (*himsa*) as falsehood and lie. *Ahimsa* was a power. He expressed nonviolence as a weapon, not of the weak but of the strong ones.

> My study and experience of non-violence have proved to me that it is the greatest force in the world. It is the surest method of discovering truth and it is the quickest because there is no other. It works silently, almost imperceptibly, nonetheless surely. It is the one constructive process of Nature in the midst of incessant destruction going on about us. I hold it to be a superstition to believe that it can work only in private life.[34]

Nonviolence does not amount to giving up one's rightful claims for fear of confrontation. As a matter of fact, *ahimsa* served as a powerful political and, at the same time, as a moral weapon in the struggles of Gandhi against the machinations of the British colonial government. Gandhi viewed the future of humanity, not in terms of its technological feats, but its steady progress toward nonviolence, freed from conditions of domination and violence. Here is for him the real contribution of religion.

Ahimsa or nonviolence is related not only to interhuman relationships, but also to nature, creation. A moral person practices truth by making his or her own the suffering of others including the harm done to nature, and by being compassionate toward everyone and every creature. In this sense, the religious and moral vision of Gandhi has great significance today also for an environmental ethics. Unlike many forms of environmental ethics which view it segmentally, in Gandhi's vision, the attitude and practice toward nature is part of a moral continuum which comprises the humans and the nature. Vinay Lal brings out succinctly the core of Gandhi's ecology:

---

[34] Raghavan Iyer, *The Essential Writings of Mahatma Gandhi*, 240.

Gandhi's entire life functioned much like an ecosystem. This is one life in which every minute act, emotion, or thought was not without its place: the brevity of Gandhi's enormous writings, his small meals of nuts and fruits, his morning ablutions and everyday bodily practices, his periodic observances of silence, his morning walks, his cultivation of the small as much as of the big, his abhorrence of waste, his resort to fasting—all these point to the manner in which the symphony was orchestrated.[35]

## DIALOGUE ON ETHICS BETWEEN ASIAN RELIGIOUS TRADITIONS AND POSTMODERNITY

Liberal modernity bases itself on universalistic principles for ethical choices. One claims to liberate the individual from the constraints of tradition and beliefs. Whereas modernity placed emphasis on the responsible action of the moral self, according to the canons of reason, postmodernity, on its part, has drawn our attention to the *responsibility of the subject to the other.* What governs the moral order is not the absoluteness of the principles, rather the unconditional responsibility toward the other, regardless of the response of the other. These are two different universes of ethical discourse and practice. Postmodern thought has deconstructed the "grand narratives" and has considerably weakened the kind of universalism whose claim it is to serve as an explanatory framework divested of time and context.

Further, history demonstrates that in critical times universal ethical norms have been of little help, as, for example, during the period of National Socialism in Germany. Ethics couched in universal principles were thrown to the winds and got crushed under the weight of an ideology. Enlightenment principles of universal morality based on reason inspire little credibility, when reason itself was wanting at critical times. By narrating their own stories, the stories of their community, its suffering and survival, the victims of the holocaust represent what should not befall any person or humankind. Most human behavior is driven by emotion. Our brains are hardwired to respond to emotion over reason. Ethics and religious principles that purely attempt to use codes and laws, and

---

[35] Vinay Lal, "Too Deep for Ecology: Gandhi and the Ecological Vision of Life," in Christopher Key Chapple, and Mary Evelyn Tucker, eds., *Hinduism and Ecology: The Intersection of Earth, Sky, and Water* (Cambridge, MA: Harvard University Center for the Study of World Religions, 2000), 206.

appeal to reason ultimately end up having a loose hold on people's behavior.

By its deconstruction of grand narratives and challenge to hegemonic universals, postmodernity has opened the doors for a fruitful dialogue with Asian ethical traditions. Asian religious traditions, as I noted earlier, have always emphasized the cultivation of the self as the moral agent rather than focus on principles and laws of morality. Therefore, when Foucault says, "I think there is only one practical consequence: we have to create ourselves as a work of art,"[36] we are reminded of our long Asian tradition. And he makes the point concrete by a question: "Why should the lamp or the house be an art object, but not our life?"[37] In Foucault, we could hear the echo of the age-old Asian tradition of self-cultivation.

The self-cultivation is not a process of isolation. It takes place in a dialogical mode in which the other is involved. Here we are very close to Hinduism, Buddhism, Jainism, and Confucianism, which have given rise to the practice of self-cultivation that reaches out to *the other*, *the different* with true concern and compassion.

Suffering, weakness, and vulnerability become the points of reference for ethical action, as can be seen in Buddhism and its path of *karuna* or compassion. Ethics of care, compassion, and self-cultivation is invariably directed to the other. Compassion goes beyond any expectations from the other as it focuses on the vulnerability and helplessness of the other. It is open to the difference the other represents. Openness to pluralism is an intrinsic element in self-fashioning. As is evident, there are many points of intersection between postmodern ethics and the ethics of Asian religious traditions. Both of them have an ethics relevant to these times of globalization—an ethics challenging all kinds of discrimination, exclusion, racism, and exploitation of the other.

---

[36] Michel Foucault, "Afterword: On the Genealogy of Ethics," in Hubert Dreyfus, Paul Rabinow, and Michel Foucault, eds., *Beyond Structuralism and Hermeneutics* (Chicago: University of Chicago Press, 1983), 237.

[37] Hubert Dreyfus, Paul Rabinow, eds, *Beyond Structuralism and Hermeneutics*, at, 236; See also Sergery S. Horujy., ed., *Practices of the Self and Spiritual Practices. Michel Foucault and the Eastern Christian Discourse* (Grand Rapids: William Eerdmans Publishing Company, 2010).

## RELIGIONS AND ETHICS OF RESISTANCE

Increasing number of protests is something we observe today practically all over the world. These protests reveal the darker side of globalization. They are expressions that the existing order of things is not just, and the present system is not able to cater equitably to the wellbeing of individuals, communities, and societies. The voices of protest and acts of resistance relate to many negations people suffer, and they invite us to consider a different kind of ethics. There has been a long tradition of civil resistance and disobedience inspired by moral values and ideals, and most well-known are the civil resistance by Mahatma Gandhi and Martin Luther King. Recent history shows that in many countries the change of regimes was effected thanks to the civil resistance movement. Such has been the case, for example, in the Philippines (1986), which overthrew the dictatorial regime of Ferdinand Marcos, in Chile (1988), Poland (1989), South Africa (1994), Tunisia (2010), and Egypt (2011).

In the Gandhian tradition, public fasting goes along with nonviolent civil resistance aimed at creating a new social and political ethics of the powerless. Gandhi used public fasting as a means to challenge the powers to desist from unethical means and action. He used it also for social reform. In 1931, he undertook a fast against the practice of untouchability. Meant as a sacrifice and a means of self-purification, fasting provoked those who practice untouchability to reform their ways and become respectful of the dignity of others. In his view, the taking on suffering on oneself through fasting could move the heart of others and bring out the just and positive energies inherent in them.

It is interesting to note how around the same time as Gandhi, Dietrich Bonhoeffer during the Nationalist Socialism in Germany represented an exceptional figure of resistance to the malevolent regime. When most of the institutional churches failed to speak out, individuals like Dietrich Bonhoeffer stood out to defend human dignity and resisted a too powerful and oppressive regime and ideology. I was very excited to note a connection between Bonheoeffer and Gandhi recently. In his voluminous work on Gandhi, Ramachandra Guha brings to light the fact that Bonhoeffer was keen to visit Gandhi, stay with him in his ashram, and learn more about *ahimsa*.[38] In a letter to his grandmother, Bonhoeffer

---

[38] Cf. Ramachandra Guha, *Gandhi. The Years That Changed the World 1914–1948* (Delhi: Penguin Books, 2018).

wrote that Gandhi's "heathenism has more of the Christian spirit than our State Church."[39] His plan to visit Gandhi did not materialize. In a letter to Gandhi, Bonhoeffer shared his thoughts. Among other things he told Gandhi, "we Western Christians should try to learn from you what realization of faith means, what life devoted to political and racial peace means."[40]

Bonhoeffer's example in the political, moral complexities of his time inspires many people who are engaged in challenging oppressive forces of today's world of globalization. Totalitarianism remains a reality in different parts of the world, even as much-flaunted liberal democracy has entered into a severe crisis exposing many lacunae in its functioning. People around the world find themselves in situations of having to resist populist dictators of right and left, authoritarian regimes and brutal suppression. In many cases, religious resources continue to inspire individuals and groups in their engagement of resistance. These individuals and groups have to often fight against the apathy of their own religious institutions. They stand in the line of the prophets of the Semitic religious traditions—Judaism, Christianity and Islam. The prophetic figures were not bearers of religious beliefs and doctrines, but the moral conscience of the religious groups to which they belonged.

## NEW SOCIAL MOVEMENTS: ETHICAL SPRINGS IN GLOBAL SPACES

The new social movements that have sprung up in the last few decades are not only politically and socially but also ethically very significant.[41] Each one of these movements is focused on a particular question—issue of

---

[39] Ramachandra Guha, *Gandhi.*, 488.

[40] Ramachandra Guha, *Gandhi.*, 489.

[41] Cf. Gail Omvedt, *Reinventing Revolution: New Social Movements and the Socialist Tradition in India*, Socialism and Social Movements (London and New York; Routledge, 2020); Ponna Wignaraja, ed., *New Social Movements in the South: Empowering the People* (London: Zed, 1993); Paul Almeida, ed., "Pushing the Limits: Social Movements in the Global South," in *Social Movements: The Structure of Collective Mobilization* (Oakland: University of California Press, 2019), 147–72; Malcolm J, Todd, and Gary Taylor, eds., with a Foreword by Frank Furedi, *Democracy and Participation: Popular Protest and New Social Movements* (London: Merlin Press, 2004); Hanspeter Kriesi, et al., *New Social Movements in Western Europe: A Comparative Analysis*, Social Movements, Protest, and Contention, v.5 (Minneapolis, Minn.: University of Minnesota Press, 1995); Mario Diani, and Donatella della Porta, *Social Movements: An Introduction*, 2nd ed. (Malden, MA and Oxford: Wiley-Balckwell, 2006); Neil Stammers, *Human Rights and Social Movements* (London and

women, environment, migrants and refugees, minorities, alienation of land, and so on. These movements are, so to say, collective ethical actors in our global times challenging dominations, inequality, and injustice of all kinds. These movements do not act based on any prepared ethical script but find their sources from the actual experiences on the ground of oppression and exploitation. Despite the utilitarian calculus the liberal economy tries to inject into the life of today, those actively engaged in these movements manifest altruism, empathy, and solidarity for the weak and the marginalized who are not in a position to reciprocate. They create great ethical sensibility, provoke responses from the people, and draw them to participate in protests and demonstrations against situations of oppression and negations.

Any religion that is sensitive to contemporary political, social, cultural, and economic context will find in these movements a very appropriate channel to give concrete moral expression to its beliefs and convictions. These movements also challenge societies and communities to rethink and rework the moral identity of religions. Association with them will help religions to come down from universalistic heights of general principles to encounter the concrete political, social, economic, and cultural scenarios on the ground. Since new social movements have a more in-depth analysis of the way power functions, they could help in evolving concrete strategies for the practical realization of moral ideals. Religions tend to avoid social and political conflicts, whereas experience shows that conflicts and confrontations are essential for the flourishing of democracy, justice, equality, and peace especially in highly unequal societies as is the case in the Global South. Social movements, in short, are a school for religions to learn from as how to come to terms with conflicts and thus make their own contributions to create a world and society with sharper ethical sensitivity.

## CONCLUSION

In broad terms, the process of globalization has brought about some radical changes in the conception, approach, and practice of ethics. Most obvious is the shift from objective norms and precepts on which ethics was focused in the past to the moral subject or agent in ethical decisions. The turn to the subject in morality, though in great part due to development of historical consciousness, namely the realization of the situated nature of

New York: Pluto Press, 2009); Paul D'Anieri, Claire Ernst, and Elizabeth Kier, "New Social Movements in Historical Perspective," *Comparative Politics* 22, no. 4 (1990): 445–58.

human beings and communities in definite time and space, globalization has contributed to make this consciousness planetary with its consequences in the moral field. The historical consciousness and globalization with local roots have led, on their part, to adopt an inductive methodology or methodology from below in morals. The Global South presents a rich field in experiments with morality from bottom-up.

All the above developments challenge religions to rethink their traditional moral universe and interrogate themselves about their ethical potential to contribute to the fast-changing world and society. How do religions under these changing conditions contribute to the transformation of the world? What is the shape of their social ethics? These are very momentous questions. Issues of peace, social justice, human rights, inclusion, nature, issues of women, minorities, and indigenous peoples need to gain greater attention of religions and the way their mission is defined today.[42] When religions face and try to respond to these issues, they have to come into dialogue with many intriguing ethical issues.

On the other hand, we note that there is a lot of reluctance to draw moral stimulus from religious sources. There is even a tendency to keep away from any reference to religion. The developments in the contemporary world and the increasing realization of the role of religion in different areas of human life, especially in the field of societal life prompt us to go more deeply into religious resources for ethical direction needed for our times. The increasing influence religions continue to acquire in our globalized world offer opportunities to them to bring to the fore their often-hidden or ignored ethical resources. In this way, religions also will get a new face as promoters of responsible and humanistic ethics, moving beyond the narrow confines of their identity construction in terms of creeds and rituals.

---

[42] The Roman Catholic Church, which started the tradition of social teachings, addressed its Catholic faithful on social issues, as the early papal social encyclicals show. But realizing that an issue of peace is that of the entire world across religions and nations, Pope John XXIII directed his encyclical *Pacem in Terris* (Peace on Earth) to all people of good will, and Pope Francis addressing the critical issue of ecology in his *Laudato Si* directs it to the entire world.

# CHAPTER 12

# Religion and Public Life: Continuing Debate

In the last few decades, a shift has taken place in the perception of the relationship between religion and public life. For the liberal secularists, religion is simply something that needs to be tolerated, and has nothing to contribute to public life. However, with the downturn of the secularization thesis and the progressive rejection of the view of religion as private, new equations between religion and public life are in the offing. Instead of going into an analysis of how this has come about, I shall try to examine some significant voices in the West whose positions on the relationship of religion to public life have become the core issue in public theology today, and at the same time most vigorously discussed and debated. Then we shall examine how the role of religion looks like viewed from the experience world of the Global South, especially Asia.

## FROM DENIAL TO THE RECOGNITION
## OF PUBLIC ROLE FOR RELIGIONS

Many liberal thinkers and secularists disqualify religion from participating in any public debate or from bringing arguments in favor of the common cause from the perspective of faith. The presupposition is that faith-based arguments for public cause invoke divine revelation, holy scripture and tradition, and these very often go against the demands of reason and logic.

273
F. Wilfred, *Religious Identities and the Global South*,
New Approaches to Religion and Power,
https://doi.org/10.1007/978-3-030-60738-8_12

Against this general mood, two highly significant Western thinkers—Jürgen Habermas and John Rawls—have come to theorize that religions could indeed contribute to enlighten and transform matters of common and civil concerns.

Whereas in his work the *Structural Transformation of the Public Sphere: An Inquiry into a Category of Bourgeois Society*, Habermas kept religion out of his theorizing in line with liberal secularists, there has been a development in his thinking on this issue. We could identify three phases in the thinking of Habermas about religion: (a) suppression of religion through communicative reason, (b) coexistence of religion and reason, and (c) cooperation of both for upholding the gains of modernity. The new turn to the third phase can be discerned in his works since 2001: *The Future of Human Nature, On Faith and Knowledge, Between Naturalism and Religion*. In the third phase of his thinking, Habermas shows his openness to the contribution of religion to the public sphere, challenging the claims of narrow secularity. He notes:

> [S]ecularized citizens may neither fundamentally deny that religious convictions may be true nor reject the right of their devout fellow citizens to couch their contributions to public discussions in religious language.[1]

By way of example, I may add here how Habermas shows the importance of Christian doctrine of creation for the strengthening of human dignity and rights. He also sees its importance in addressing biomedical technological issues such as genetic enhancement. Theological beliefs could throw light on these tricky questions and contribute to the present and future wellbeing of humankind. José Casanova speaks of deprivatization of religion after examining a few cases which include Spain, Brazil, Evangelical Christianity, and American Catholicism.[2]

However, there are other interesting points of view which relate religion in the West in a very different way to public life. Blumberg, for example, does not see any antagonism between religion and secularity as is the case in most other theorists of secularization. According to him, the secular world and its institutions, far from abandoning religions, have, in fact,

---

[1] As quoted in Maureen Junker-Kenny, *Habermas and Theology* (London: T&T Clark, 2011), 137; see also William Outhwaite, *Habermas* (Cambridge: Polity, 2007), 157 ff.

[2] Cf. José Casanova, *Public Religions in the Modern World* (Chicago and London: University of Chicago Press, 1994).

succeeded in promoting the humanistic ideals for the realization of which they also created the necessary structures and institutions. The medieval Christianity zealously engaged itself in caring for the poor, the orphans, the sick, and those at the margins of the society. One saw in them Christ himself. A poor person was considered as *alter Christus*.[3] The church and its religious orders created hospices, hospitals, orphanages, and homes for the abandoned. Now, according to Blumberg, the secular realm and the secular state have replaced the church in these works, and hence one speaks of welfare state today. In other words, what we experience is not a break of the secular with the religious, but a continuity in taking inspiration from the religious sphere. Blumberg uses an element of the Hegelian dialectic—*Aufhebung*—and thinks that religion is not lost but elevated to another plane and preserved through the secular.[4]

The Italian thinker Gianni Vattimo on his part reconnects religion and the "signs of the times" in the contemporary world through a complex process of thinking. As a postmodernist, he is highly critical of fixed centers, rigid definitions of things, and belief in continual human progress. The modernist process, by its inner logic, leads to emptying of religion and its marginalization. Vattimo's conception of "weak thought" (*pensiero debole*), characteristic of postmodernity, allows him to see in a reinterpreted religiosity (rooted in his own Christian tradition) a process of secularization—a secularization that is not at the expense of religion, but rather a secularization that proceeds from within it. The Christian belief in the incarnation of the divinity is a downward movement of self-abasement toward the world and its realities, which Vattimo calls "secularizing kenosis."[5] Hegelian thought sees the ultimate fulfillment and apogee of all human strivings in Christianity, while other religious traditions are thought to be on the way in an evolutionary scheme. Vattimo, instead, reverses the process and sees the core of religion in the downward movement of kenosis which, freed from a rigid frame of thinking and decentered, would be in a flexible and fluid position to relate with multiple other religious experiences. The rigidity of doctrine and dogmas go through a process of secularization. In the words of Vattimo:

---

[3] Cf. Michel Mollat, *Les pauvres au moyen âge* (Paris: Hachette, 1978).

[4] Cf. Hans Blumberg, *Säkularisierung und Selbstbehauptung* (Frankfurt a. M.: Suhrkamp, 1974).

[5] Cf. Gianni Vattimo, *Belief* (Stanford: Stanford University Press, 1996), 62.

Secularization as a 'positive' fact signifying the dissolution of the sacral structures of Christian society, the transition to an ethics of autonomy, to a lay state, to a more flexible literalism in the interpretation of dogmas and precepts, should be understood not as the failure of or departure from Christianity, but as a fuller realization of its truth.[6]

The other religions are also expected to practice the downward movement of self-emptying. Vattimo operates with the Christian scheme of incarnation and self-emptying. He is aware of this limitation, but cannot escape his own tradition. He attempts to understand the secular starting from the world of his religious belief. He invites others to enter a similar process. Such a process of downward movement will open up vast spaces for every religion to involve itself in the world and enter into cooperation with other religious traditions. Such a downward movement of self-emptying could be thought of as a precondition for any public role for religion today. It is a movement that coincides with the "dissolution of metaphysics" and indeed of a metaphysical God.

## THE QUESTION OF "COMPREHENSIVE DOCTRINES" AND PUBLIC REASON

In the context of today, a question of paramount importance is the relationship of religion to public reason.[7] Here is an issue that allows a wide range of interpretations but also raises many intricate questions. John Rawls speaks of "comprehensive doctrines" and "overlapping consensus."[8] By comprehensive doctrines he means articulated systems of thought or explanations that claim to give a full range of ultimate explanation of the world, nature, society, bearing upon their origin, value, their future, and so on. And this is done by philosophy, religion, moral beliefs, and so on. In simple terms, comprehensive doctrine means a theory of everything. Religions are habituated to present such a theory of everything—about

[6] Vattimo, *Belief*, 47.

[7] Cf. John Rawls, *The Law of the Peoples Revisited* (Cambridge MA: Harvard University Press, 2001), 129–180 ("The Idea of Public Reason Revisited"); see also Miguel Vatter, "The Idea of Public Reason and the Reason of State: Schmitt and Rawls on the Political," *Political Theory* 36, no. 2 (2008): 239–71.

[8] Cf. John Rawls, *Political Liberalism* (New York: Columbia University Press, 1993); see also Sonia Sikka, "On Translating Religious Reasons: Rawls, Habermas, and the Quest for a Neutral Public Sphere," *The Review of Politics* 78, no. 1 (2016): 91–116.

God, the humans, and the world. These comprehensive doctrines shape the way we look at the world, others, and ourselves.

To be able to understand Rawl's political theory and his conception of the role of religion vis-à-vis public life, we need to grasp how he transforms Kant's ideal of moral autonomy (*Critique of Practical Reason*) in an intersubjective manner. Here is a question of abiding by those laws and arrangements that find acceptance among all concerned in a polity based on their public use of reason, which, of course, is not the same as the opinion of the majority. Moral autonomy is not merely a matter of freedom from coercion; it has a necessary reference to the other and the public. This moral autonomy is linked to political autonomy. A religious group is politically autonomous not alone when it is free from any coercion in the profession and practice of its beliefs, but when it can abide by what the common good requires and what finds approval among all concerned in a particular society. In this sense, religious freedom today needs to be defined not in isolation from the other, but with the other, and what concerns the general good of all concerned. That is what we tried to do in Chap. 9.

However, one serious difficulty with religions is the fact that historically they have tended to claim absolute truth for their beliefs and impose themselves arguing that "error has no right to exist." That explains the reluctance to accept its comprehensive doctrines. Nevertheless, when a religion frees itself from this tendency and enters into conversation with others; when it becomes ready to accept that other comprehensive doctrines have an equal right to be listened to in deliberating on and shaping of the common good, then there can be no persuasive reason why it should be kept out in public matters. In contemporary discussions, some streams of thought, for reasons of the questionable historical role religions have played, continue to argue for the exclusion of religion from matters public, and relegate it to the realm of the private. Rawls, on the other hand, seems to create some space for religions when he states:

> Reasonable comprehensive doctrines, religious or nonreligious, may be introduced in public political discussion at any time, provided that in due course proper political reasons—and not reasons given solely by

comprehensive doctrines—are presented that are sufficient to support whatever the comprehensive doctrines introduced are said to support.[9]

On the other hand, contribution to public reason means that religious traditions do not get bogged down by their internal convictions and belief systems but raise their heads above and hold before their eyes the general interest of the people. It would also involve a kind of translation into the secular language of those beliefs that have public significance. The beliefs and convictions held by religious groups require to be supported by public reason if they are to have any role in public life. The creation narrative of the Bible, for example, can support the equality of woman, which is a secular issue in the polity. The same creation story can be deployed to support the cause of human rights. According to Christian belief, human beings are endowed with dignity since they have been created in the image of God.

Should religions be stripped of their beliefs to reach a common ground of neutrality—characterized as "freestanding" and "post-metaphysical"—to be able to enter conversation with other constituents in the polity, both nonreligious and religious? Is this denouement of religious beliefs a condition *sine qua non* for inclusion in the deliberation and participation in public life? Don't we lose, in this way, the richness that religious beliefs, myths, and symbols contain? Why not allow religions to carry their worldviews with them and enter into conversation with others, and thus through a mutuality that touches deeper chords reach consensus, and understanding? What happens to religious discourse when it is translated into rational language for public acceptance?

This is a point which some Western theologians like Linda Hogan, Nigel Biggar, Michael Perry, Robin Lovin, David Hollenbach, and Sonia Sikka contend when responding to the position of Rawls and Habermas concerning public reason or overlapping consensus. Linda Hogan notes, for example: "Fundamental flaw in the idea of the public reason lies in the manner in which it requires the speaker and listener to believe both the self and the other to be, or to act as though he or she is *rootless*."[10] Though legitimacy and stability are indispensable for the functioning of substantive

---

[9] John Rawls, "The Idea of Public Reason Revisited," *University of Chicago Law Review* 64 (1997): 783–784.

[10] Nigel Biggar and Linda Hogan, eds., *Religious Voices in Public Places* (Oxford: Oxford University Press, 2009): 223.

democracy and enforcement of laws, these need not be sought independently of religions the exclusion of which from the public realm would mean the loss of the moral resources these traditions enshrine. Sikka, on her part, argues for the untenability of dissection between public reason and religious reason when it comes to moral issues.[11]

We know that, after a heated debate, Vatican II came to accept religious freedom. It can be justified based on public reason as well as on theological foundations. Hence, we could consider it as a case of "overlapping consensus" in which other religious and secular ideologies could play a part. On the other hand, the same document on religious freedom cautions against any outright rejection of any role for religious doctrine in shaping public life.

> It comes within the meaning of religious freedom that religious bodies should not be prohibited from freely undertaking to show the special value of their doctrine in what concerns the organization of society and the inspiration of the whole of human activity.[12]

If public reason were to keep religion completely out of its purview, it could trigger a dangerous fundamentalist counter-public less reasonable and more dangerous than what is feared of religion. In an earlier chapter (chapter 5) we discussed deterritorialization of religion as part of the analysis of fundamentalism. What the fundamentalists imagine is an ideal religion in the abstract, cut off from culture, context, and sociopolitical situation.[13] It is an irony that the proposal of public reasoning by the secular and liberal stream too seems to evoke the same kind of deterritorialization or decontextualization of religion divested of meaning and purpose in context.

Further, Rawls and Habermas seem to follow a normative and procedural reasoning in determining the relationship between religion and the public sphere without reference to how things are at bottom and de facto.

---

[11] Cf. Sonia Sikka, "On Translating Religious Reasons: Rawls, Habermas, and the Quest for a Neutral Public Sphere," *The Review of Politics* 78, no. 1 (2016): 91–116.

[12] Vatican II: *Dignitatis Humanae,* no. 5.

[13] It is striking that another form of deterritorialization is taking place today in the field of communication. As Neil Postman notes, "The milieu in which Technopoly flourishes is one in which the tie between information and human purpose has been severed, i.e., information appears indiscriminately, directed at no one in particular, in enormous volume and at high speeds, and disconnected from meaning, or purpose." Neil Postman, *Technopoly: The Surrender of Culture to Technology* (New York: Vintage Books, 1993), 70.

In reality, there seems to be not so much public reasoning as a negotiation between religion and public life, and each case seems to be different, depending on the context and history of particular societies. Facts even in the Global North, not to speak of the South, illustrate this point. In many European countries, there are the so-called established religions. The clearest example is that of the UK, where the bishops form part of the House of Lords.[14] Similarly, in some Scandinavian countries, Lutheranism has been the established State Church—in Sweden till 2000, and in Norway till 2012. In these cases, as well as in Germany, Belgium, and the Netherlands, we find a kind of accommodation of religion in order to play a role in the public sphere in the changed circumstances. It finds its expression in different forms, such as availing state funding for educational institutions managed by Catholics, Protestants, Calvinists, and collection of tax for the church by the state.[15]

Further, there are differences in understanding what is meant by reason, and it is not clear which understanding of reason underlies when Rawls speaks of "public reason" or "justificatory reason" concerning religion in public life. This is important when reason is given a normative character in contrast to religion. The issue becomes critical in the case of supporting or rejecting disputed laws and ordinances. On what basis does one do that? Should the acceptance and rejection happen based on public reason alone? Can religious convictions be invoked? If so, to what extent? Christopher J. Eberle goes into such intricate questions and presents arguments that religious convictions can often provide a very persuasive basis for supporting or repudiating laws, no less than public reason.[16]

## ASIAN RELIGIONS AND THE LIMITS OF THE SECULAR

In June 2019, I had the privilege of participating in an international conference organized by the government of Singapore on "Cohesive Societies," and the focus of the conference was on the role of religions in creating cohesive societies. There were participants from over forty

---

[14] Cf. Peter Sedgwick, "The Public Presence of Religion in England: Anglican Religious Leaders and Public Culture," in Nigel Biggar, and Linda Hogan, eds., *Religious Voices in Public Places* (Oxford: Oxford University Press, 2009), 235–259

[15] Cf. José Casanova, *Public Religions in the Modern World* (Chicago: The University of Chicago Press, 1994).

[16] Cf. Christopher J. Eberle, *Religious Conviction in Liberal Politics* (Cambridge: Cambridge University Press, 2002).

countries, and I never heard anyone discussing, even mentioning, the word "secularism." I imagine that it is impossible to think of any conference on religion in the West without discussion on the secular. Singapore is, of course, a secular state that does not allow itself to be governed by religions. In fact, Singapore is one of the most religiously plural countries in the world. The conference was addressed by the president of the country and by the deputy prime minister. That is an indication of the importance of religion for harmony and peace in the world.[17]

At the global level, even before the advent of the welfare state, many public works of philanthropy were done by religious bodies and institutions, which continue even today to a large extent. The Catholic Church, for example, has an extensive network of hospitals and health centers in all the states of USA, and "one in six patients in the U.S. is cared for in a Catholic hospital."[18] Further, the role of religion in international politics could not but draw the attention of the United Nations. [19]

From these reflections as well as from the arguments presented in the previous chapters, it should be clear by now why the theory of secularization and its analysis may not be universalized. Very often the general thesis of secularization is built around the experience of a particular religion—Christianity and its relationship to public life. This gives the impression of a Christianity that is getting secularized, whereas other religions are not. How true or fair is that?

Setting up a contrast between a secular Christianity and an anti-secular Islam, Hinduism, Buddhism, and so on does not reflect the actual state of things. Given the globalization of Christianity and its axis shifting more and more to the South, as expressed by many scholars,[20] the claim of an association between the secular and the Christian can apply only to a small segment of Christian population, living in a rather small territory of the Northern and Western side of Europe comprising very few countries. For

---

[17] It may be pointed out here that the UN has for a long time presented itself as a secular body, distancing itself from anything to do with religion and its place in the world. However, since 2004 the UN seemed persuaded enough by arguments for it to address the issue of religion worldwide

[18] http://www.usccb.org/about/public-affairs/backgrounders/health-care-social-service-humanitarian-aid.cfm [accessed on January 20, 2020].

[19] Cf. Eric O. Hanson, *Religion and Politics in the International System Today* (Cambridge: Cambridge University Press, 2006).

[20] Cf. Philip Jenkins, *The Next Christendom. The Coming of Global Christianity* (New York: Oxford, 2002)

the rest, Christianity, globalized as it is today is lived in so many different ways, and the European secularists cannot claim here any association of Christianity with the secular.[21]

Christianity is lived in the Global South like other religious traditions right amid all the struggles and experiences of which individual and collective life is made of. In these parts of the world, Christianity is very much part of politics, culture, economy, and so on, where hardly any distinction between the secular and the sacred is possible. Like other traditional religions, in the Global South, Christianity has adopted itself to the ways of other religions. It is not as though other religions live in an unsecularized world, whereas Christianity has a clear distinction between the two. The facts about the presence and praxis of Christianity in the South do not support any such view.

Some thinkers in the South, like T.N. Madan and Ashish Nandy of India, maintain that secularism is a product of Protestant Christianity. They show how the experiences in India and in the South at large may not be interpreted with secularism as an interpretative key or as an epistemological device. Regarding the relevance of traditionally understood secularism, Madan notes the growth in religious vibrancy in India, today in the context of globalization and opening to market economy.

> The point to stress, then, is that, despite ongoing processes of secularization and deliberate efforts to promote it, secularism as a widely shared worldview has failed to make headway in India. Obviously, what exists empirically but not also ideologically exists only weakly. Acute observers of socio-cultural and political scenes contend that signs of weakening secularism are in evidence, particularly among the Hindus. Religious books...continue to outsell all the others in India and, one can be sure, in all the other South Asian countries. Religious pilgrimages attract ever larger congregations. Buildings of religious worship or prayer dot the urban landscape. God-men and gurus sit in seminars and roam the streets.[22]

In many regions of the Global South, we note that democratic governance is done in such a way that religion becomes an integral part of it. Whatever view one may hold about religion in terms of its beliefs, the fact is that innumerable people have religious beliefs and practice religion, and

---

[21] Felix Wilfred, "Asian Christianities and Theologies through the Lens of Postcolonialism," in *Concilium* 2018/1: 26.

[22] Cf. Rajeev Bhargava, ed., *Secularism and Its Critics* (Delhi: Oxford University Press, 1999), 300.

it would be a colossal failure to simply ignore this fact and still claim to practice democracy in the best way. The case of Indonesia illustrates the point. After many decades of dictatorial and despotic rule, Indonesia changed over to democracy in 1998. The exercise of democracy did not warrant exclusion of religion; rather it is integrated *within* the frame of democratic governance. The case is also an illustration that the conception of democracy and its practice is to be pluralistic. Dealing with the case of South Asia, one study observes:

> The strength of the practice of democracy in South Asia lies in its capacity to move away from the received model of democracy. Every aspect of democracy in South Asia is marked by a disjunction between the script and the practice of democracy that can take various forms...Rather than being merely a source of slippage and failure, and thus as distortion and deviation, this disjunction is also a source of innovation. Clearly not all kinds of deviations are necessarily sources of strength, but most sources of strength arise out of a capacity to deviate from practice.[23]

Secular democracy is one, but not the only one, nor does it need to be the best one. For the attainment of the common good in a particular society, both democratic practice and a contributory role of religion for public life can coexist. Undoubtedly, religion needs to be restrained. How this restraint is to be exercised cannot be dictated a priori but will depend upon the particular configuration of sociopolitical conditions and history in a particular society.

## RELIGION AND THE PUBLIC/PRIVATE DISTINCTION

The discussion around religion and the secular, and the debate on the role of religion in public life hinge on one of the characteristic divisions of modernity, namely the division of the private and the public. In the context of modernity, religion is seen as private. Interpreted in a positive sense, it would fall within the right to privacy. The state has no role to play in the private realm of the conscience of the individual. Thus understood, claiming religion to be private amounts to protecting the freedom of religion from the imposition of the state or its unwarranted intervention in the religious beliefs of people. However, the statement that religion is

---

[23] Cf. Harsh Sethi, ed., *State of Democracy in South Asia. A Report* (Delhi: Oxford University Press, 2008).

private today is interpreted in the sense that religion does not have any role to play in public life. This is based on presuppositions and prejudices going back to the European Enlightenment that considered religion as a *remnant* of the premodern era. It was associated with superstition, which needed to be overcome through the use of reason. Hence, religion is relegated to be a matter of *private* belief having no impact on *public* life.

The distinction of private and public is problematized today. Feminist theorizing has debunked such a distinction and shown its untenability. Issues of family and the relationship between husband and wife assume public nature when there are violations of basic human rights. There is no cover over the "private." Present-day social media too lead us to question radically the distinction between what is private and what is public. Private narratives, events, and personal choices assume a public character in the digital world and become an object of discussion, debate, and sharing. Internet and online groups are not private. Facebook becomes a public book. In the case of religion, the distinction between public and private was based on the experience with one particular religion—Christianity—and one does not seem to take into account the history, tradition, and worldview of other peoples and cultures in this matter where religion has been viewed and lived as a public matter. The private/public, in short, is a dehistoricized distinction that does not respect the gray areas of real life.

Moreover, we need to be also conscious of the way "public" is understood and defined. This has important consequence for the role of religion in general, and Christianity in particular, vis-à-vis the Asian societies. Here is something which distinguishes the Asian approach in its understanding of public and public theology. Hence, not only is the history of the relationship of religion to state different from the West, but different also is the way public is understood by peoples of the Asian continent. Everyday experience shows that what the cultural world of the Global North would consider private is seen to be blatantly public by Asians, and the reverse is also true. Cultural determination explodes the conventional demarcation between the public and the private. Without going into the details of the cultural determination, we may say that religion in Asia is *both public and private*. In a certain sense it is private; in another sense it is public. The intermingling and crisscrossing of the two in a particular way is something uniquely Asian.

There is another important reason why the private/public distinction is hard to sustain in the Asian context. The concept of religion in Asian traditions, as we noted earlier, has been quite different from the dominant conception of it in the Global North. To cite an example, religion is not viewed in Asia as a set of beliefs or doctrines, but as a way of life—a path (*marga*), a journey. Religion is embedded in the culture and daily life of the people as the folk traditions of Asia manifest. This makes it already extremely difficult to create any "wall of separation" between religion and public life.

## RELIGIONS AND ASIAN BRAND OF SECULARISM

It would be more appropriate to say that Asia, instead of replicating secularism of the Global North, has developed its *own* brand of secularism with momentous consequences for its social and political life. The Asian conception of secularism is not against religion, or indifferent toward it. It is a defense against authoritarianism and totalitarianism of all kinds. Secularism in the multireligious context of Asia means that no religion is privileged by the state and the state keeps equidistance from all religions, and there is no discrimination against any one of them. In India, this secular policy is known as "*sarva samaya samabhava.*" This secularism is meant to protect the society from the authoritarianism that could result if any particular religion were to be privileged or favored. No serious-minded people in Asia would object to religion playing a useful role to the general public as long as its beliefs and practices do not go against public order, morality, or hygiene—as the Indian Constitution puts it. This brand of secularism has historical roots in the tradition of tolerance in Asia. Today too political struggles in Asia are taking place in the name of this brand of secularism against attempts to create state religion, or impose any one particular religion, or legitimize state policies manifestly invoking religious beliefs. Secularism is also meant to be a *protection* against any religion that presents or understands its identity in terms of national identity *to the exclusion of* others. As we noted earlier with reference to Neera Chadhoke, in present-day Asian sociopolitical conditions, secularism needs to be inspired and sustained by the spirit of *equality.*[24]

Due to historical and political reasons, there is an asymmetry among religions. Often the majority religions get privileged, which goes against the principle of equal treatment of all religions. On the other hand, minority religious groups suffer discrimination, exclusion, and even suppression.

---

[24] Cf. Neera Chandhoke, *Beyond Secularism: The Rights of Religious Minorities* (New Delhi: Oxford: Oxford University Press, 1999).

Unlike *political* majorities and minorities which are *transient* and can be changed in a democracy through the electoral process, in the case of religious or ethnic groups we have *permanent minorities*. In such an odd religious situation, it is *equality* that calls for the protection of the minority or weaker groups. Hence, for the sake of democracy, secularism, and equality, minority religious groups need special protection.[25] Such a protection for minority religious groups exists, for example, in the Indian Constitution which has provisions that ensure that a brute majority does not hamper the identity of minorities, their public engagement, and growth. If we were to stick to the principle that in an unequal society the weaker ones and discriminated groups need protection to sustain equality, does not many European countries require to enact *specific* laws to protect their religious and ethnic minorities today? This protection may not be covered by a *general* regime of individual civil rights of the citizens. Strangely, what is happening is that the majority—ethnically, religiously and linguistically—wants to protect itself with all possible means against the minorities under the pretext of laïcité.

### RELIGIONS IN THE SOUTH VIS-À-VIS PUBLIC CONCERNS

The place of religion in public life in Asia does not derive from a deduction of presumed universal principles but from concrete exigencies and requirements of everyday life at the political, economic, social, and cultural realms. What are the challenges that call for a public role of religions in Asia, and the South at large?

In the first place, people of the Global South need *defense of freedom against state despotism of various kinds and grades*.[26] It is a fact that in many Asian countries, despotism, populism, political authoritarianism,

---

[25] Michael Walzer speaks of regimes of tolerance. One of those regimes is the empire which provided a flexible ambience for many identities—ethnic, linguistic, regional, and religious—to coexist. It would appear that the postcolonial nation-states, on the other hand, operate today with nation and majority as reference points which insecure the plight of minorities more than the period of empires. Cf. Michael Walzer, *On Toleration. The Castle Lectures in Ethics, Politics, and Economics* (New Haven; London: Yale University Press, 1997).

[26] Cf. Stephen C. Angle, *Human Rights and Chinese Thought. A Cross-Cultural Study* (Cambridge: Cambridge University Press 2002); Joanne R. Bauer and Daniel A. Bell, eds., *The East Asian Challenge for Human Rights* (Cambridge University Press, 1999); Charles F. Keyes, et al., eds., *Asian Visions of Authority. Religion and the Modern States of East and Southeast Asia* (Honolulu: University of Hawaii Press, 1994); Michael Jacobsen and Ole Bruun, eds., *Human Rights and Asian Values. Contesting national Identities and Cultural Representations in Asia* (Richmond: Cruzon, 2000).

and militarism continue to affect the lives of the people. China, for example, has become second largest economy in the world. However, its economic achievements rest on political feet of clay. The liberal economy coexists with traditional socialist political centralization and autocracy.[27] The situation is very similar in North Korea, Myanmar, and Vietnam. Even in countries where democracy is the form of government, in practice, there is a lack of true freedom. Expressions of dissent and protest by the marginalized and subaltern groups are suppressed. Religious freedom is heavily controlled in the socialist countries of Asia and in countries where a particular religion is the state religion or state-favored religion. Even in a democratic country like India with the constitutional guarantee of religious freedom, there are cases of serious violations of human rights.

The second area of public concern is the *defense of the poor from the tyranny of the market*.[28] The penetration of the liberal market has resulted in an unprecedented gulf of inequality between the poor and the rich, growing unemployment, pauperization of the peasantry, suppression of the rights of workers, starvation deaths—all these coexisting with a growing culture of middle-class consumerism and commercialization of every realm of life. When market economy seriously compromises the cause of the poor, Asia needs the contribution of religions in defense of the last and the least. It is required to play no less active role than what it did for emancipation of Asian nations from the colonial yoke.

The third crucial public concern is the *creation of harmonious and non-exclusive communities*. Two related issues are implied here. It is well known that in Asia there has been increasing violence and conflict among various

---

[27] Cf. Willy Lam, "China's Political Feet of Clay," *Far Eastern Economic Review* 172, no. 8 (2009): 10–14; Ching Kwan Lee and Mark Selden, "Inequality and Its Enemies in Revolutionary and Reform China," *Economic and Political Weekly* 43, no. 52 (December 27, 2008): 27–35; Robert Weil, "A House Divided: China after 30 Years if 'Reforms'," *Economic and Political Weekly* 43, no. 52 (December 27, 2008): 61–69; MinQi Li, "Socialism, Capitalism, and Class Struggle: The Political Economy of Modern China," *Economic and Political Weekly* 43, no. 52 (December 27, 2008): 77–85; Dic Lo and Yu Zhang, "Globalisation Meets Its Match: Lessons from China's Economic Transformation," *Economic and Political Weekly* 43, no. 52 (December 27, 2008): 97–102.

[28] Cf. Jon Sobrino and Felix Wilfred, eds., "Globalization and its Victims," *Concilium* 2001/5; see also Joseph Stiglitz, *Globalization and Its Discontents* (London: Penguin Books, 2002); Joseph Stiglitz, *The Roaring Nineties* (London: Penguin Books, 2003); Ajay Gudavarthy, "Human Rights Movement in India: State, Civil Society and Beyond," in *Contributions to Indian Sociology* (NS) 42, no.1 (2008): 29–57; Saskia Sassen, *Globalization and Its Discontents* (New York: The New Press, 1998).

ethnic and religious groups and among linguistic and regional communi-ties.[29] One may recall here the situation in Pakistan, Sri Lanka, India, China, Malaysia, Myanmar, and so on. In this regard, we need to pay attention to growing religious fundamentalism in many Asian countries. In recent times, India has witnessed the effects of Hindu fascism in the states of Gujarat where Muslims and Christians were targeted and in Odisha where Christian Tribals have been victimized. Well known are the manifestations of Islamic fundamentalism operative in Pakistan, Indonesia, Malaysia, and Thailand. Conflictual situations often arise because certain groups, for example, Dalits ("the Untouchables") and tribals, are excluded from equal participation in the affairs of the community. We need to also recall here the exclusion of women in which both traditional and modern forces converge. Therefore, the creation of a *communion* of communities among the various groups remains one of the critical public issues in the continent.

The fourth concern is that of *protecting the environment*. Asia is the home of bewildering biodiversity. The accelerated mode of development propelled by technology and market has created an environmental crisis in Asian countries. Natural resources are exploited, stretching them beyond their regenerative capacity. Commercial interests denude forests, depriving the indigenous people of their land and livelihood. States encourage the setting up of many hazardous industries by multinationals putting into serious peril the lives of the poor who work in these industries and who live in the immediate vicinity. In Asia, it is becoming clear that the defense of natural resources is to defend the poor, and defending the poor is the most effective way of protecting the continent from environmental degra-dation and crisis.[30] These four major areas which are manifestly public issues need to become the object of concern for Asian religions.

[29] Cf. Amartya Sen, *Identity and Violence. The Illusion of Destiny* (London: Penguin Books, 2006); Mark Juergensmeyer, *Terror in the Mind of God. The Global Rise of Religious Violence* (Delhi: Oxford University Press, 2000); T.N. Madan, *Modern Myths, Locked Minds: Secularism and Fundamentalism in India* (Delhi: Oxford University Press, 1998); R. Puniyani, *Communal Politics. Facts Versus Myths* (New Delhi: Sage Publications, 2003); L. Stanislaus and Alwyn D'Souza, eds., *Prophetic Dialogue. Challenges and Prospects in India* (Pune/Delhi: Ishvani Kendra/ISPCK, 2003).

[30] Cf. Vandana Shiva, "Farmers' Rights, Biodiversity and International Treatises," *Economic and Political Weekly* 28, no.4 (April 3, 1993): 555–560; Vandana Shiva and Holla Bhar R., "Intellectual Piracy and the Neem Tree," *The Ecologist* 23, no.6 (1993): 223–227; Ignacy Sachs, "From Poverty Trap to Inclusive Development in LDC'S," *Economic and Political Weekly* 39, no.18 (May 1, 2004):1802–1811.

In Asia, religions have been a rich source of inspiration and motivation for social and public commitment. Buddhism, for example, has not only been a set of doctrines and practices but became a way of life affecting every segment of the life of the people. Emperor Ashoka, who converted to Buddhism a couple of centuries before our present era, was inspired to dedicate himself to a life of service for the wellbeing of the people. Buddhism, Hinduism, Sikhism, and Daoism have all tried to reinterpret themselves vis-à-vis the social, economic, and cultural challenges of modern times. Gandhi and Vivekananda interpreted Hinduism as *karma marga*—way of action and involvement. Arya Samaj and other Hindu organizations were involved in transforming the Indian society of the nineteenth century by infusing social consciousness. In more recent times, the group of "Engaged Buddhists" has been very active reinterpreting Buddhism in the context of contemporary political, social and cultural situations of the world.[31] In this context, it would sound bizarre if one were to tell the followers of these religions that they should confine themselves to the private realm and should not involve themselves in public matters because that would hurt secularism! If at all, Asia needs more of religious involvement in service of common good. Hence, we begin to realize the importance of developing public theologies in Asia and in other parts of the Global South where conditions and contexts are similar.

## THEOLOGY FOR PUBLIC LIFE AND PUBLIC THEOLOGY

Most theologies define themselves as an explication of beliefs of a religious group to its adherents. They, at the same time, claim universal validity for their beliefs. These theologies generally operate through a method of internal analogy—the *analogy of faith*. That is to say, one belief is explained with the help of another belief, but within the same system. It is a closed system. Public theology provokes the self-insulation of this theology to come out in the open from behind the curtain where its religious group is stuck. It interrogates the public significance of what one holds in the name of faith.

---

[31] Cf. Arnold Kotler, ed., *Engaged Buddhist Reader: Ten Years of Engaged Buddhist Publishing* (Berkeley, Calif.: Parallax Press, 1996); Christopher S. Queen, and Sallie B. King, eds., *Engaged Buddhism: Buddhist Liberation Movements in Asia* (Albany: State University of New York Press, 1996).

Public theology is different from another kind of approach which can be characterized as *theology for public life*. This latter kind of theology does not begin from context, from the experiences; rather, it is keen on interpreting the truths of the Scriptures and dogmas of belief in their normative and moral implications for the life of society and its various systems. It is concerned about how a believer could be a good citizen and a patriot. Here one follows a unilateral method, namely from the religious sources to the reality with no dynamics of interaction.

A variant of this kind of theology for public life is pursued in Protestant neo-orthodoxy by authors like Max Stackhouse and John Milbank.[32] The above authors and their like remain fixed to an essentialist conception of faith and church, and they see the mission of public theology as that of making the world and society conform to the standards and normativity of the scriptures and Christian doctrines, rather than faith reaching out to the world. Theology is to be practiced and lived in such a manner as to be a *critique* of modernity. For Milbank, ecclesiology would be the model and norm for sociology, and the "secular" would be a heresy.[33] In short, the public theology of Stackhouse and Milbank aims at shaping through the power of Christian faith the structures and policies of public life, including economics.

## CIVIL RELIGION AND PUBLIC THEOLOGY

Public theology is not the same as "civil religion" used today, especially in the context of the USA. Though Jean-Jacques Rousseau coined the expression "civil religion" and used it in a different sense,[34] today it is being deployed to refer to the practice of using religious symbols and myths to uphold the spirit of a nation or state. Robert Bellah developed

---

[32] Max Stackhouse, *Public Theology and Political Economy* (Grand Rapids, MI: Eerdman's, 1987); L., Hainsworth et al., eds., *Public Theology for a Global Society: Essays in Honor of Max L. Stackhouse* (Grand Rapids, Mich.—Edinburgh: William B. Eerdmans, 2010); Max L. Stackhouse and Peter Paris, eds., *God and Globalization* (New York: T & T Clark, 2007); John Milbank, *Theology and Social Theory. Beyond Secular Reason* (Oxford and Cambridge: Blackwell, 1990); Simon Oliver and John Milbank, *The Radical Orthodoxy Reader* (London: Routledge, 2009).

[33] Cf. Georges De Schrijver, *Recent Theological Debates in Europe and Their Impact on Interreligious Dialogue* (Bangalore: Dharmaram Publications, 2004), 37.

[34] Jean-Jacques Rousseau, *Social Contract and Other Later Political Writings* (Cambridge: Cambridge University Press, 1998).

his sociology of religion in America with reference to an assumed public or civil religion in that country. According to him, civil religion is "that religious dimension found… in the life of every people, through which it interprets its historical experience in the light of transcendent."[35]

Civil religion does not make much sense in the Global South, for example in India; nor is it helpful. It will only add fuel to the right-wing Hindutva. On the other hand, public theology, while being sensitive to contextual issues such as the ones experienced in a particular nation or state, also plays a critical role vis-à-vis nation or state. It does not fall in line with the status quo or any uncritical nationalist chauvinism. And this is highly significant for South Asia which, unlike civil religion, is struggling to free the public sphere and civic life of the nation from being undergirded by religious symbols and myths. [36]

## Public Theology
### from an Interdisciplinary Perspective

Let me clarify public theology with reference to what is happening today in some of the other disciplines.

The appeal to public issues can be observed not only in the field of theology. A similar movement can also be identified in the field of philosophy. One speaks about *public philosophy*.[37] Abstruse explanation from a high pedestal have characterized philosophy in the past. Today, it is called upon to respond to the plight of humanity and nature. Philosophy is challenged to focus on these questions and cease to do decontextualized philosophizing. When students listen to philosophy, it is not uncommon that they fall asleep. Not so when Jean-Paul Sartre did philosophy. When he

---

[35] Robert Bellah, *The Broken Covenant: American Civil Religion in Time of Trial* (New York: Seabury, 1975), 3; see also Gail Gehrig, "The American Civil Religion Debate: A Source for Theory Construction," *Journal for the Scientific Study of Religion* 20, no.1 (1981): 51–63; Martin E. Marty, *A Nation of Behavers* (Chicago, IL: University of Chicago Press, 1980); Linell Elizabeth Cady, *Religion, Theology and American Public Life* (Albany: SUN Y Press 1993).

[36] See the enlightening article of J. Santiago on the connection between civil religion and nationalism which is very helpful to understand the current Indian situation: J. Santiago, "From 'Civil Religion' to Nationalism as the Religion of Modern Times: Rethinking a Complex Relationship," *Journal for the Scientific Study of Religion* 48 (2009): 394–401.

[37] Cf. Michael Sandel, *Public Philosophy. Essays on Morality in Politics* (Harvard: Harvard University Press, 2005).

did philosophy, students did not sleep, but were on the streets! It is the same Jean-Paul Sartre who made history by declining to accept the Nobel Prize (1964) awarded to him—the first person in the history of this prize to do so fully and freely. Sartre had a philosophy of refusal to accept this kind of acknowledgment. In his words:

> My refusal is not an impulsive gesture, I have always declined official honours... This attitude is based on my conception of the writer's enterprise. A writer who adopts political, social, or literary positions must act only with the means that are his own—that is, the written word. All the honors he may receive expose his readers to a pressure I do not consider desirable. If I sign myself *Jean-Paul Sartre* it is not the same thing as if I sign myself *Jean-Paul Sartre, Nobel Prizewinner*.[38]

A similar trend we also find in sociology, economics, and so on. For many sociologists, statistics, tables, and figures make up sociology. What marks off public sociology is that, unlike traditional sociology which observes and interprets society, it is engaged as an *actor* in society, and brings the professional knowledge to bear upon the goal of transformation. It is a "reflexive" and critical enterprise, and is the "conscience of professional sociology."[39] Public sociology does not get drowned in technical aspects of the issues of society but comes on board in dialogue with people premised on certain *fundamental* values. Thus, it can serve as the *conscience* of society rather than a *spectator* of social realities. Economics is also fond of dealing with statistics and figures. Public economics, on the other hand, is directed toward *transformation*. Welfare economics is public economics. What makes Amartya Sen different from thousands of his colleagues in the field is that his economics does not stop with explanations and projections. *Values* are built into explanations without distorting facts—values calling for change and transformation, for social and economic equity—and an alternative approach is envisioned.[40] Public

---

[38] https://www.nybooks.com/articles/1964/12/17/sartre-on-the-nobel-prize/ [accessed on May 27, 2019].

[39] See Dan Clawson et al., eds., *Public Sociology. Fifteen Eminent Sociologists Debate Politics and the Profession in the Twenty-first Century* (Berkeley: University of California Press, 2007); see also Philip Nyden, et al., *Public Sociology. Research, Action, and Change* (Delhi: Sage, 2012).

[40] For a different and holistic approach to the Indian economy, see Amartya Sen and Jean Dreze, *An Uncertain Glory. India and Its Contradictions* (London: Allan Lane, 2013).

economics involves itself in dialogue not only with professional economists but with *everyone* concerned.

## INSTANCES OF PUBLIC THEOLOGY

What is meant by public theology becomes concrete when we associate it with some instances of doing it. I think of Martin Luther King Jr—An African American pastor from the periphery of Montgomery, Alabama. He was faced with the stark reality of denial of civil rights, and practice of racial discrimination against the African Americans, segregation in buses, and various forms of negation. His faith took him to the path of civil rights movement of which he became an articulate and most visible spokesperson. His stirring public speech in 1963 addressed to over 250,000 people at the Washington DC march, began with those historic words, "I have a dream...." It was public theology in action and performance. The same pastor when he addressed his congregation did liberation theology, by drawing from biblical motives of liberation. Through his public theology, Martin Luther King could galvanize the energies of the public across race and religion in service of liberation, and create a "coalition of conscience." He played a leading role in the Selma to Montgomery March of 1965 to attain voting rights for the discriminated and oppressed black people. Joshua Heschel, a Jewish Rabbi and a great Biblical scholar, who participated in the Selma march, said of his experience, "For many of us the march from Selma to Montgomery was about protest and prayer. Legs are not lips and walking is not kneeling. And yet our legs uttered songs. Even without words, our march was worship. I felt my legs were praying."[41]

In East and Central Africa, Wangari Maathai, a Christian woman brought up and inspired by the Benedictines, was doing public theology when she created "The Green Belt Movement"—a massive ecological movement. Under her inspiration, fifty-one million trees were planted by women. Her public theology brought her into conflict with those grabbing common lands that belonged to the people, and she dared to speak *truth to power*. The environmental movement she initiated and sustained became in effect also a movement empowering women and cultivating their agency. Her local initiative blossomed into a global force for democracy, defense of human rights, and environmentalism. Her vision for

---

[41] https://blogs.library.duke.edu/rubenstein/2015/01/14/jewish-voices-selma-montgomery-march/ [accessed on May 28, 2019].

public life was shot through humanistic and environmental values and by her Christian faith.

## PUBLIC THEOLOGY FROM AN INTERRELIGIOUS PERSPECTIVE

Public theology is not a Christian invention to be imposed on others. Christian public theology will be in the comity of other such theologies from different religious traditions—Hindu, Buddhist, Jewish, Islamic, and so on.[42] Given the undeniable fact of religions playing a role in the life of societies and international relations today,[43] it is to be expected that there be convergence among the various theologies of public life which will be in conversation with each other in a way that mutually strengthens. Jointly they will try to respond to the burning questions of the world and society like human dignity, upholding of fundamental human rights, protection of the environment, the dignity of women, protection of children and minors, and so on. This kind of public theology will be different from comparative religion which tries to find similarities in doctrines and practices across religious tradition; it is different also from comparative theology which seeks to read the sacred texts of one religion through the textual world of another religion. Both comparative religion and comparative theology remain within the *symbolic* religious system. On the other hand, public theology challenges the religions about their *real* public significance.

In the past, interreligious dialogue has been mostly focused on creating understanding among religious groups by referring to communalities in doctrines, traditions, practices, and so on. The understanding of God as *Satchitananda*, for example, could vibrate with the Christian understanding of the Trinity, the theology of grace in Christian tradition with the Saivite, and the Vaishnavite understanding of *"arul."* Public theology is different. It does not focus on commonalities of *beliefs*, but on commonalities of *experiences* in society, economy, politics, and culture—a shared environment in which religion is practiced.

---

[42] In the context of globalization and migration, religions like Hinduism are in a challenging situation regarding its public presentation, giving rise to conflicts. There is a debate on how Hinduism is to be presented to diverse publics which entails a rethinking of its own theologies of the past. Cf. John Zavos, Pralay Kanungo, Deepa S. Reddy, Maya Warrier, Raymond Williams, eds., *Public Hinduism* (Delhi: Sage Publications, 2012).

[43] Cf. Eric O. Hanson, *Religion and Politics in the International System Today* (Cambridge: Cambridge University Press, 2006).

## FROM THEOLOGY OF NATION-BUILDING TO PUBLIC THEOLOGY: THE CASE OF INDIA

What is the need for a Christian public theology? There is no universal public theology.[44] The historical point of time and the context in which believers relate to public issues make much difference. Hence, it is proper that in the Indian context, for example, one develops a public theology bearing upon the present historical context. Besides the reason adduced on the importance of a movement of convergence among religious traditions, there is also a historical reason that prompts the believers to move to the realm of public theology.

In the immediate postindependence period, a *theology for nation-building* became programmatic and was promoted in South Asia by M.M. Thomas and others.[45] In the political environment where Christianity was viewed as "foreign," like Christians elsewhere in Asia, it was important for Indian Christians to affirm their belonging to the new nation and to seek ways to contribute to its building. The premises on which this theology was built are vastly different today in the context of a chauvinistic preprogrammed nationalism promoted for power and control. The result of many elections in Indian "democracy" today—as elsewhere, perhaps—are a triumph of myth over reason. The need of the hour is a public theology that will sustain the vision of the Constitution and its spirit, and apply it to real issues. The results of the 2019 election in India has confirmed fears about those in power tampering with the Constitution of the country. The forces behind this move operate with a particular idea of freedom. Public theology could make an impact on the society by strengthening the deeper humanistic values enshrined in the Constitution and by helping to create a society increasingly just, free, and equal.

Another critical contribution public theology could make is to strengthen the secular fabric of society. Christian faith and secularism in India can go together—unlike the way they are opposed in the West,

---

[44]We distinguish the "universal" from transnational public theologies which, like in the case of civil society initiatives, bring together many local public theological initiatives in different parts of the world. Thus, there could be transnational public theologies relating to environmental issues, issues of justice and peace, and so on.

[45] M.M. Thomas, *Christian Participation in Nation-Building* (Bangalore: Institute for the Study of Religion and Society, 1960). Indian Theological Association (ITA) went into this theme as recently as early twenty-first century (2002) in its twenty-fifth annual meeting held at Dharmaram Vidya Kshetram in Bangalore.

especially in the French understanding of *laicité*. As Sanjay Subrahmanyan has observed, when the French oppose wearing veils by Muslim women (the *hijab*), they unconsciously think of the veils of nuns and oppose it as a symbol of the church establishment. Secularism is the enemy of faith in Europe. In India, secularism is a friend of faith. For, in India, secularism is a matter of "mediating between different communities."[46] In short, by living Christian faith in service of secularism, Christians could make an impact on the society and contribute to overcome communalism and enable a life of tolerance and harmony.

Public theology presupposes a distinction between the state and society. The goals of the state are not identical with that of the society, which is something larger.[47] Authoritarian and populist regimes make the mistake of identifying both. This larger space of society is where critical corrective to the state and its policies need to take place. It is at this space that public theology turns out to be, along with other civil actors, promoter and advocate of the dignity of human beings and their fundamental human rights—civil, political, cultural, and economic. Public theology will contribute to foster social equity and to the overcoming of discrimination and exclusion of all kinds.

Public theology is highly important in pluralist societies like the Global South with multiple minorities—religious, ethnic, linguistic, and so on—to intervene and contribute for the common good through dialogue and exchange, and discussion and debate. It is an important mode of actively participating in the shaping of society as well as nation and its policies affecting everybody, and seeking shared solutions for common issues.

## THEOLOGIAN AS A PUBLIC INTELLECTUAL

Our above discussions on the nature and role of public theology are bound to transform the image of theologians along new lines. It is difficult to reconcile the classical profile of theologians with what public theology calls for. Theology is a critical enquiry both in understanding one's faith as

---

[46] Interview of Sanjay Subramaniyan, https://www.thehindu.com/opinion/interview/indian-secularism-is-about-mediating-between-different-communities/article5405669.ece [accessed on May 21, 2019].

[47] Cf. David Hollenbach, *The Common Good and Christian Ethics* (Cambridge: Cambridge University Press, 2002); David Hollenbach, *The Global Face of Public Faith: Politics, Human Rights, and Christian Ethics* (Washington, DC Georgetown University Press, 2003).

well as in bringing out its implications in praxis. The praxis in its turn leads to theory and reflection. Public theology cannot but be a critical theology. In broader terms, a theologian is called to be a public intellectual planted on the ground of praxis and contributing to transformation. Could we say this of today's religious studies?

Critical knowledge has an indispensable public role. In a highly illuminating work *"The Public Intellectual in India,"*[48] Romila Thapar makes an important contribution to the theme with an arresting title: "Question or not to Question? That is the question." The innovative intellectuals have alternative narratives to the dominant ones, and these they seek to bring to the foreground. A theology that helps to conform to the status quo is not critical. Theologian becomes a public intellectual when she raises critical question on what is taken for granted.

In fact, modernity begins when tradition ceases to be the ultimate criterion or norm of truth. If we accept multiple modernities, Siddhartha Gautama, the prince of Kapilavastu, adopted a reasoned approach to issues instead of appealing to tradition, myths, and astrology for legitimation; so too the *shamans, charvakas, Ajivakas,* who challenged the dominant narratives of the time. In Western history, Socrates, for example, was a great public intellectual deeply concerned about the welfare of the city and common good, continuously in dialogue (Socratic dialogues) with the people, and situations that could influence people, especially the youth.

More than ever, in these critical times, politically, economically, socially, and culturally, theologians need to play the role of public intellectuals drawing from multiple sources—both religious and secular. As a public intellectual, a theologian jointly with those from other professions will call for public accountability from those in power. For a theologian to be a public intellectual requires sharing in the same mission of other public intellectuals; it means to be uncorrupted by power and its lure, and to be critical vis-à-vis the absence of moral integrity and intellectual competence of the presiding deity of power in responding to the issues of the people.

[48] Romila Thapar, Abdul Gafoor Abdul Majeed Noorani, Sadanand Menon, eds., *Public Intellectual in India* (Delhi: Aleph, 2015).

## CONCLUSION

On October 31, 1517, as legend has it, when Martin Luther posted ninety-five theses of his opinions on the door of the Castle Church in Wittenberg, he was doing not merely a religious act. It was an act with far-reaching public and historical significance. By availing the public space, he challenged the preserve of knowledge and concentration of power in the hands of few—be it religious or political authorities. His faith took on a public character which had a great impact on the society of his times.

Some years ago, the center of the debate about religion was the theory of secularization which accorded nothing but private space to religion. It is an irony that some of the very scholars like Peter Berger and Harvey Cox, who were ardent advocates of secularism, revised their views and interpretations and even spoke of *de-secularization*.[49] Today, with the increasing realization of the failure of this theory, one has started speaking about post-secular societies. The case of Europe is seen more as an exception than the norm.[50] The question is reversed today. It is not a matter of finding the reason why North America and other parts of the world are not secular, but rather why most Europeans believe that anybody can be modern only if he or she is secular.[51] Today in our global world, the debate has shifted to the question of what kind of role and in which circumstances religion could play a role in the public sphere. In the post-secular Western societies, this question needs to be posed once again, especially in the context of them becoming increasingly multireligious and multicultural due to increasing migration.

Secularism is a polysemous concept. It is also open to bricolage. In some regions of the world, like in India, the traditional concept of secularism is reworked and reinterpreted to respond to the actual situation and experiences. In many parts of the Global South, secularism applied to the political sphere refers to the impartiality of the state versus the various religions represented in the polity. Secularism is seen then as a platform to accommodate a plurality of visions about life, and ways of life, fostering tolerance. Secularism, when interpreted as having its base in equality,

---

[49] Cf. Peter L. Berger, ed., *The Desecularization of the World: Resurgent Religion and World Politics* (Washington, DC: Ethics and Public Policy Center, 1999).

[50] Grace Davie, *Europe: The Exceptional Case: Parameters of Faith in the Modern World* (London: Darton, Longman & Todd, 2002).

[51] Cf. Peter Berger, Grace Davie, and Effie Fokas, *Religious America, Secular Europe? A Theme and Variations* (Hampshire and Burlington: Ashgate Publishing Limited, 2008).

serves as an essential means to protect the rights of the minorities. This understanding of secularism as a framework for pluralism could be an interesting point of reference for the West which has been for long home of one predominant and majority religion—Christianity. The pluralist situation in the world could benefit from the model of secularism interpreted with reference to minorities in many parts of the Global South.

The secularization thesis in the West made religion insecure. Religions were forced to think about themselves in a meaningful way for their survival. Public role of religion and public theology are not about making religion meaningful. Instead, the accent is on what religion in conditions of modernity and globalization, could contribute to overcome the crisis that has gripped humankind and nature. In doing so, the understanding of religion itself begins to change. Public theology is an enterprise with no walls, open on all sides. A persistently practiced public theology will also lead to more excellent illumination on the shape of the religion of the future.

# CHAPTER 13

# From Porous Borders to Cosmopolitan Horizons: Beyond Interreligious Dialogue and Multiple Belonging

Our previous chapters have shown with many examples the porous nature of religious experience in the Global South. Further, while dealing with issues such as new ways of being religious, new religious movements, the religious experience in the diaspora, and public character of religion, we noted how this fluid nature of religiosity in the South is becoming widespread, thanks to the process of globalization. From these premises, we could project the ideal of a cosmopolitan religious existence as the future of the world. In this inclusive world, religions will exist without walls of separation, and to be religious would mean to be cosmopolitan in spirit and practice. Could this become a collective project in which the Global North and South could meet and dialogue? Cosmopolitanism goes beyond interreligious dialogue, multiple religious belonging, and syncretism.[1]

---

[1] We are not going into the issue of syncretism in this chapter. The following literature could be usefully consulted. Anita M. Leopold, and Jeppe Sinding Jensen, *Syncretism in Religion: A Reader*. Critical Categories in the Study of Religion (New York; London: Routledge, 2016); Charles Stewart, Rosalind Shaw, eds., and European Association of Social Anthropologists, *Syncretism/anti-syncretism: The Politics of Religious Synthesis* (London: Routledge, 1994); Patrik Fridlund, and Mika Vähäkangas, ed., *Theological and Philosophical Responses to Syncretism: Beyond the Mirage of Pure Religion* vol. 7 (Boston: Brill, 2017); William H. Harrison, *In Praise of Mixed Religion: The Syncretism Solution in a Multifaith World* (Montreal: McGill-Queen's University Press, 2014).

© The Author(s), under exclusive license to Springer Nature Switzerland AG 2021
F. Wilfred, *Religious Identities and the Global South*,
New Approaches to Religion and Power,
https://doi.org/10.1007/978-3-030-60738-8_13

## MORE THAN INTERRELIGIOUS DIALOGUE AND MULTIPLE RELIGIOUS BELONGING

The last few decades have witnessed widespread interest in interreligious dialogue all over the world, something salutary compared to attitudes and practices of past many centuries when other religions than one's own were viewed as of little worth, even totally erroneous and inimical. Against this dark background, the practice of interreligious dialogue has contributed significantly to greater understanding among religions and to demolish walls of prejudice and exclusion. When I speak of religious cosmopolitanism, I do not mean to undermine the contributions of the project and practice of interreligious dialogue. Its continued contribution is required for the foreseeable future. I mean to say instead that we go beyond interreligious dialogue.

In more recent times, among scholars, there is also much discussion about what is called multiple religious belonging. It means that a person can have a hyphenated identity as Christian-Buddhist, or Hindu-Muslim, Buddhist-Shinto.[2] Such a project does not seem to capture the religious experience of Asia—and Global South at large—which tends toward religious cosmopolitanism rather than multiple religious belonging. Comparative theology which is gaining momentum appears to be a project between interreligious dialogue and multiple belonging. In the words of Francis Clooney, "the comparative theologian ventures to learn deeply in another tradition, and brings that learning back, to include it in some way in a refashioning of her or his home identity."[3]

Identity is what the above three share. In *interreligious dialogue*, one is firmly rooted in one's identity of scriptures, tradition, beliefs, laws, and rituals, but then seeks how this identity could be positively related to other religious identities and practices. In the case of *multiple religious belonging* as a project, two identities are conjoined (hyphenated) not to create something new and different but to be loyal to both identities and to live in two religious worlds simultaneously. But the multiple identities remain fixed and unintegrated. The discourse on multiple religious belonging seems to

---

[2] Cf Catherine Cornille, *Many Mansions? Multiple Religious Belonging and Christian Identity* (New York: Orbis, 2002); Peter C. Phan, "Multiple Religious Belonging: Opportunities and Challenges for Theology and Church," in *Theological Studies* 64 (2003): 71–76.

[3] Francis X Clooney, "Introduction to Comparative Theology in Australia and Asia," in *International Journal of Asian Christianity* 3, no. 2 (2020): 129–138.

be even "elitist" and "overly individualistic."[4] The proposal fails to capture the inextricable connection between culture and religion in Asia, and in the Global South at large. In the Global South, the various religions are, in a way, projections on the familiar screen of a shared culture which binds them all together. Commenting upon the project of multiple religious belonging, the Indonesian scholar Bagus Laksana has this to say:

> One can say that these ordinary Asians, for the most part, did not really pursue the negotiation of identity in such a dramatic and self-conscious manner, but rather through complex religio-cultural avenues that have become part and parcel of their natural identity. For them, the term "multiple religious belonging" and the self-proclaimed hyphenated religious identity might sound either foreign, too "academic," or simply confusing, if not failing to capture the concrete dynamics of their complex religio-cultural identity.[5]

*Comparative theology* too has the problem of identity in as much as one does not leave one's identity behind while entering into a comparative theological reading of other religious texts or relating to other religious traditions. There is a going out toward the other religions, but then one comes back home to one's own religious identity, and again to enter into the identity world of the other religions to learn more.[6] In this back-and-forth movement, one does not want to risk one's religious belonging much less to leave it behind in quest of something more, which is not yet there. Religious cosmopolitanism points to something beyond. Why this is so will be evident in the course of our reflections in the following pages.

## Religions Beyond Their Followers

Bhagavad Gita, Dhammapada, Tao Te Ching, Bible, Qur'an, and Adi Granth are for the entire humankind. Religious fundamentalism has thrived on the idea of exclusive possession of one's religion which one feels obliged to defend at all costs, even if it means inflicting violence. Our

---

[4] Cf. Bagus Lakshana, in *The Oxford Hand Book of Christianity in Asia*, 494.

[5] Bagus Laksana, *op, cit.*, 494.

[6] For a detailed discussion on comparative theology in Asia and Australia, see the special issue of *International Journal of Asian Christianity* 3, no. 2 (2020), with an introduction by Francis Clooney. This issue provides elaborate literature on comparative theology in general, and, more specifically, concerning Asia and Australia.

perception about religions begins to change when we look at them, not as the exclusive possession of any one particular group. Hinduism, Buddhism, Daoism, Christianity, Islam, Judaism, and many other primaeval religions belong to the human family. There is an inherent universalism in every religious tradition. It is crucial to open up the spring of this universalism which is often clogged by a narrow conception of religious identity.

If we were to speak from the perspective of Jewish and Christian resources, we could refer to narrations of the fall in the account of Genesis (Gen 3:1–24), the depiction of the times of Noah (Gen 6:11–13), the construction of the Tower of Babel (Gen 11:3ff.)—they all refer to the collective experience of humankind across nations and races. We would understand this better by invoking the Christian tradition regarding the universal destiny of resources of nature or earthly goods. The goods and resources of nature belong to the humankind in a primary sense.[7] The individual possession of goods or private property is subservient to this primordial right of possession of God's gifts by all God's children. If so, every religion needs to consider itself as being addressed to the entire humankind, and, consequently, every human being could draw on the heritage of humanity to the extent that it enhances his or her quest for life and spirituality.

Hinduism speaks of the world as a single family of God (*vasudhaiva kutumbakam*) to whose welfare everyone across religious boundaries is invited to contribute. The Tamil classical antiquity with more than 2000 years of history expressed the cosmopolitan universalism succinctly, saying "*Yādum ūre, yāvarum kelir*," which means, "every village is my home; every person my kin."

Qu'ran speaks of the unity of the entire humankind in these words:

[7] This we find in the scriptures in connection with the injunctions on the Year of Jubilee. All are to get back their original possessions and lands (Leviticus 25: 8–55). Several Fathers of the Church like Basel, Ambrose, and Chrysostom were critical of the rich who amassed wealth at the expense of the poor. In this context, they reminded the rich that the goods of creation are the gifts of God to be shared among God's children equitably. Drawing on the scriptures and the patristic tradition, Catholic social teaching has underlined the social mortgage on private property. There is no absolute right for private property. *Gaudium et Spes* continues this tradition when it speaks about the universal destination of earthly goods (no. 69), and the same is to be also found in the recent encyclical of Pope Francis, *Laudato Si*. See Julio de Santa Ana, *Good News to the Poor* (Geneva: WCC, 1977); Donal Dorr, *Option for the Poor: A Hundred Years of Catholic Social Teaching* (New York: Orbis Books, 2002); Felix Wilfred, "Theological Significance of *Laudato Si*: An Asian Reading," in *Theology for an Inclusive World* (Delhi: ISPCK, 2019), chapter 8, 152–173.

O mankind! Indeed, We have created you male and female, and have made you nations and tribes that you may know one another. Indeed, the noblest of you, in the sight of Allah, is the best in conduct.[8]

Precisely because the various religions and their scriptures belong to humankind, they are open to a broad spectrum of interpretations. Let me refer here to an analogy from the classical Indian hermeneutical tradition which compares texts to the beauty of a woman. The father of a girl, because he generated her, need not be the best judge about her beauty. The best judge could be her lover, husband, or her admirer.[9] So, is the case with the authors of texts. The fact of producing a text need not mean that the meaning of the text is exhausted by what the author intended and produced, or within the particular religious tradition which claims it as its own. Even more, the beauty of a religious text may be best admired by someone from another religious tradition. The modern hermeneutics on the autonomy of texts[10] could be profitably applied to religious traditions. Let me cite an example from my own experience. I was invited by a Hindu scholar to contribute to a collective volume by reading and commenting upon *Śakuntalā*, a classical play of Kālidāsa (late fourth century–early fifth century) from a Christian perspective. This exercise opened up a new horizon for me. I commented upon *Śakuntalā*—the Cinderella of the story and arguably the most famous heroine of India—through the narrative of Hagar in the Bible. There is an amazing convergence and beauty in the narratives of Hagar and that of *Śakuntalā*, both depicting similar human predicament.[11]

---

[8] *Qur'an*, 49:13.

[9] Cf. Felix Wilfred, "Navigating Cross-Hermeneutical Currents: A Subaltern Perspective," in Nishant Alphonse Irudayadasan, ed., *Musings and Meanings. Hermeneutical Ripples* (Delhi: Christian World Imprints, 2016), 1–14; see also, Anand Amaladass, *Indian Exegesis. Hindu-Buddhist Hermeneutics* (Chennai: Satya Nilayam Publications, 2003).

[10] Cf. Werner Jeanrond, *Theological Hermeneutics: Development and Significance* (New York: Crossroad, 1991).

[11] Cf. Felix Wilfred, "*Śakuntalā* and the Bible: Parallels and Resonances," in Namrata Chaturvedi, *Memory, Metaphor and Mysticism in Kālidāsa's AbhijñānaŚākuntalam* (London: Anthem Press, 2020), 85–105.

## SENSE OF MYSTERY

There is a sense of sacred in every religious tradition. It is the reflection of the inexhaustible mystery they try to express in words, symbols, rituals, and so on. Now, this mystery is not the possession of any one religious group. No religion can claim to exhaust that mystery, much less to possess it. Belonging to a religious group does not entitle one to claim possession of that particular religion, because believing is, in point of fact, a witnessing to what one has experienced. It follows that what is experienced by a witness is only a scintilla or spark. The infinite and radiant light it points to surpasses the limited realm of one's community or religious group in which this witnessing takes place. In the Christian tradition, Paul expressed the inexhaustibility of the mystery, when he stated, "For now we see in a mirror, dimly, but then we will see face to face. Now I know only in part; then I will know fully, even as I have been fully known" (I Cor 13:12).

Moreover, religions are in the realm of means and not that of ends. Beliefs, rituals, traditions, laws, and injunctions—these are not end in themselves. Saint Augustin considered even the Christian scriptures as a means. He makes an important distinction between *use* and *enjoyment*—the latter identified ultimately with the experience of God.[12] We use something to attain something else. It is an instrumental approach. Enjoyment, on the other hand, is when something is loved for its own sake, and which can confer us true happiness.[13] Scripture is an effective means as long as it could lead us to God, and the enjoyment of the divine mystery. Religion is a penultimate reality, and not the ultimate one. It is simply a scaffolding, meant for something greater—and this "greater" is the mystery that envelops us all. This something all theologies—in whichever religion—needs to hold in mind.

> In theological knowledge, expression always falls short of reality, precisely because we are dealing with a mystery which cannot be fully comprehended. Since no expression is perfect, additional expressions are not only possible but beneficial for a fuller understanding of the mystery.[14]

---

[12] Cf. Jeanrond, *Theological Hermeneutics*, 22–23.

[13] Cf. Eleanore Stump and Norman Kretzmann, eds., *The Cambridge Companion to Augustine* (Cambridge: Cambridge University Press, 2001), 235.

[14] Vimal Tirimanna, ed., *Sprouts of Theology from the Asian Soil. Collection of TAC and OTC Documents [1987–2007]* (Bangalore: Claretian Publications, 2007), 262.

The mystery is the point of convergence of all religions, and it is that which bestows meaning and provides sustenance to them. The experience of the ultimate mystery to the enjoyment of which the entire humankind is called is nourished with a wide variety of spiritual foods offered by the religions, and no one has full control of the spiritual metabolism of the experience and enjoyment the mystery causes.

## Interdependence: Indra's Net

The religious cosmopolitan approach could also be derived from the primordial fact of the interdependence of all that is. To illustrate it, both Hinduism and Buddhism use the analogy of Indra's net. In these traditions, one speaks of the world as a vast net woven by God Indra, and it is infinitely wide with nodes of jewels, each one of them reflecting the whole—a microcosm indeed. This analogy wants to convey the web of interconnection the world is. The environmental crisis has brought home the truth that the lives of humans is bound up with the survival and wellbeing of nature. Not only is everything connected to everything else, but there is life pulsating through the entire body of the world that exhibits marvelous beauty, harmony rhythm, and vibrancy in its interconnectedness. Seeing anything independently from the rest is both distortion and an illusion.

Such being the primordial nature of the world and universe, could religions act as disconnected fragments? The convergence of the visions (*darśana*) various religious represent—without diminishing the clarity and beauty of any one of them—is the goal toward which humanity needs to strive today. Each religion, like the node in Indra's net, would reflect the pluriverse of all other religions. This approach to religion through the lens of organic unity encapsulated in the ideal of religious cosmopolitanism is something to be promoted, especially for the mindset, attitudes, and values it would foster, and the contribution it would make for a peaceful human togetherness and harmony with nature.

## Religions with Universal Mission

Another important motivation for pursuing religious cosmopolitanism is the realization that there is a common and universal mission for all religions. Heated debates are taking place among the religions on the question of revelation, absoluteness, uniqueness, universality, and other similar issues. There is, however, little discussion, on the shared *mission* of all religions for the wellbeing of humanity and nature. The converging point of the mission of various religions should be the future shape of the human community and its flourishing. The awareness of being on a shared journey toward a shared future can help build up the community of humanity as one single family. Respect for other religions necessarily includes respect for the *mission* to which people of other religions feel called, especially when this mission has something to contribute to the unity of the human family and its wellbeing. In this context, the claim of absoluteness and monopolistic possession of truth is as much a question of the unity of the human community as it is a question of truth and epistemology.

## Universality from Below

In order to foster community, religions need to practice what I would call *reverse universality*. Religions require multilateral universality, which happens when a religion lets diverse peoples interpret its message through their conception of good life, their vision of the human family and its destiny. The cultivation of doctrinaire dogmatism and the fostering of stratified religious identity make it difficult to accept incoming universality. Incoming or reverse universality is the movement by which a religion receives from other religions and cultures.

One way in which reverse universality can be kept alive is to ask: What do religious doctrines have to say to humanity at large? This question frees religions from getting entangled in internal discussions and get lost in texts and exegesis. It provokes them all to get out of their doctrinal world and open their eyes to the broader issues of humanity and its future destiny. Let me illustrate this point with an example. Discerning the implications of polygenism or monogenism for humanity is more important than choosing among these two positions in order to uphold the authority of the Bible. Upholding polygenism and yet believing in the unity of the human family is more important than maintaining monogenism and practicing racism as if human beings were not of one single family, as if some peoples and races are somehow more equal than others. If monogenism could coexist with the practice of racism and polygenism could exist alongside the affirmation of the unity of the whole of the human family, this shows us the urgent need of a self-critique of religious beliefs—in this case,

Christian beliefs—regarding what they have to contribute to the creation of human community and its flourishing.

The great Thai Buddhist monk Buddhadasa realized this truth when he said:

> If an interpretation of any word in any religion leads to disharmony and does not positively further the welfare of the many, then such an interpretation is to be regarded as wrong; that is against the will of God, or as the working of Satan or Mara.[15]

No religious belief could claim to be above human dignity and rights. Religions cannot arrogate exception for themselves in this matter. If a belief contradicts the dignity and equality of all human beings, then it is not worth to be considered as a spiritual message which one would expect religions to deliver.

## COSMOPOLITANISM: ELITE AND VERNACULAR

We need to distinguish two streams of cosmopolitanism. There could be a bourgeois theory of cosmopolitanism[16] that is at home with transnational projects, Western classical antiquity[17] and of course, with capitalism. Today, under the capitalistic dispensation, cosmopolitanism has become the virtue of, so to speak, "frequent travelers" dealing with peoples across cultural and ethnic boundaries, involved in the same mode of production, distribution, and aggressive consumption of goods and services.

---

[15] As quoted in Kari Storstein Haug, "Christianity as a Religion of Wisdom and Kamma: A Thai Buddhist Interpretation of Selected Passages from the Gospels," in *Bulletin, The Council of Societies for the Study of Religion* 35, no. 2 (April 2006): 43.

[16] Today in political theory, one speaks of transnational world citizenship, drawing inspiration from Kant's theory of cosmopolitan right, something that has been reconstructed with new impetus and radicality in the work of Jürgen Habermas. Such theoretical exercises may confer legitimacy to the transnational European Union, but the extent to which they apply to other parts of the world remains a serious, and indeed unanswered, question. J. Habermas, *The Postcolonial Constellation* (Cambridge, MA: MIT Press, 2001); J. Habermas, "Kant's Idea of Perpetual Peace: At Two Hundred Years' at Historical Remove," chapter 7 in *Inclusion of the Other: Studies in Political Theory* (Cambridge, MA: MIT Press, 1998), 165–202.

[17] We are here reminded of Diogenes, who, when asked where he came from, replied, "I am a citizen of the world." As quoted in https://www.plato.stanford.edu/entries/cosmopolitanism [accessed on January 28, 2020].

There is another cosmopolitanism—the vernacular. It is a civilizational and humanistic one and is embedded in *the particular* and in solidarity with *the local*. The particular could be one's nation, ethnicity, culture, geographic region, or language, and these are not necessarily in opposition to cosmopolitanism as is often mistakenly assumed. Cosmopolitan transcendence does not consist in setting aside these primordial realities of human groups, but in searching for alternative modes of life along with other groups, other peoples, and other cultures. This humanistic and community-sensitive cosmopolitanism is not a political theory; it is a praxis that has civilizational roots; it provides the framework to understand and practice religious cosmopolitanism.

While we often hear of emperors and rulers whose support of a particular religion helped it thrive, we rarely hear of emperors who were inspired by the spirit of religious cosmopolitanism and coexistence. Among these are the Indian emperors Ashoka the Great (BCE 304–232) and Emperor Akbar (CE 1542–1605).[18] They represent a counter-paradigm to the *cuius regio eius religio* (religion of the ruler—the religion of the region). Though a Buddhist, Ashoka's breadth of vision was such that in one of his edicts he made it known that anyone harming another religion would be harming one's own.[19] It is the same cosmopolitan spirit that inspired Emperor Akbar, who fostered closer contacts and regular dialogues with Jesuit missionaries, Hindu representatives, Jews, Parsees, Jains, and even nonbelievers.[20]

---

[18] We already referred to Akbar, the philosopher-king and his cosmopolitan religious vision. Though he did not know to read or write, he surrounded himself with scholars across different religious traditions. He brought them together regularly. Remarkably, it happened at the same time when religious wars were tearing apart Europe. Among his religious partners were Hindus, Parsis, Jains, and Christian missionaries. As a report states, "And later that day the emperor came to Fathepur. There he used to spend much time in the Hall of Worship in the company of men and sheikhs...when he would sit up there the whole night continually occupied in discussing questions of religion, whether fundamental or collateral...Learned monks also from Europe, who are called *Padre*, and have an infallible head, called *Papa*... brought the Gospel, and advanced proofs for the Trinity. His majesty firmly believed in the truth of the Christian religion, and wishing to spread the doctrines of Jesus ordered Prince Murad to take a few lessons in Christianity under good auspices, and charged Abul Fazl to translate the Gospel." WM Theodore de Bary et al., eds., *Sources of Indian Tradition* (New Delhi: Motilal Banarsidass, 1988), 39–41.

[19] Emperor Ahoka, Rock Edict no. 12.

[20] Cf. Amartya Sen, *Identity and Violence: The Illusion of Destiny* (London: Penguin Books, 2006), 64.

## The Dialectics in Cosmopolitanism

Cosmopolitanism involves the dialectics of the particular and the universal, identity and transcendence, local and the global, nation and the larger world.[21] This could be expressed in the form of two metaphors—*root* and *journey*. To live is to strike roots, and it is equally true that all life is a journey. These two metaphors seem to contradict each other; but do not very often the most sublime truths irrupt into our horizons in the form of contradictions? One such contradiction is human existence, which is rooted, situated, and circumscribed and is also a journey. This quality of human existence needs to mirror also in our understanding of cosmopolitanism. Rightly then Kwame Anthony Appiah speaks of "rooted cosmopolitanism," something which Will Kymlicka has tried to elaborate with reference to the experience of his country, Canada.[22] Homi Bhabha proposes the concept of vernacular cosmopolitanism in the context of minorities and migration into the UK.[23] The different expressions bring out the nuances in relating the particular and the universal. There is no denial of the particularity of ones' religion, nation, civilization. Nevertheless, these could be lived in a cosmopolitan spirit when the religious, the civilizational or the national cease to be the sole point of reference. As Amartya Sen observes:

---

[21] Kwame Anthony Appiah's expression "cosmopolitan patriot" brings out the dialectics involved. If patriot recalls one's roots, cosmopolitanism points to the expansive earth on which nation is planted. See Kwame Anthony Appiah, "Cosmopolitan Patriots," in *For Love of Country*, edited by Joshua Cohen, 21–29 (Boston: Beacon Press, 1996). The Canadian political scientist Will Kymlicka speaks of "rooted cosmopolitanism." Will Kymlicka, and Kathryn Walker, *Rooted Cosmopolitanism: Canada and the World* (Vancouver: UBC Press, 2013).

[22] An interesting empirical study done in Quebec, Canada, reveals the spirit of cosmopolitanism pervading different religious communities in Montreal city and Quebec at large without experiencing any contradiction between rootedness and cosmopolitan way of believing and practicing religion. Cf. Meintel, Deirdre, and Mossière, Géraldine. "In the Wake of the Quiet Revolution: From Secularization to Religious Cosmopolitanism." *Anthropologica* 55, no. 1 (2013): 57–71.

[23] Cf. Homi K. Bhabha, "The Vernacular Cosmopolitan," in Ferdinand Dennis and Naseem Khan, eds., *Voices of the Crossing: The Impact of Britain on Writers from Asia, the Caribbean, and Africa*, 133–42 (London: Serpent's Tail, 2000). "It is this double life of British minorities that makes them "vernacular cosmopolitans," translating between cultures, renegotiating traditions from a position where "locality" insists on its own terms while entering into broader national and societal conversations," at 139.

Our religious or civilizational identity may well be very important, but it is one membership among many. The question we need to ask is not whether Islam (or Hinduism or Christianity) is a peace-loving religion or a combative one ("tell us which it is really?"), but how a religious Muslim (or Hindu or Christian) may combine his or her religious beliefs or practices with other features of personal identity and other commitments and values (such as attitude to peace and war). To see ones' religious—or "civilizational"—affiliation as an all-engulfing identity would be a deeply problematic diagnosis.[24]

Cosmopolitanism is not to be an amorphous universal or a "colorless cosmopolitanism" in the words of Sugata Bose,[25] pursued at the expense of the particular. History amply bears witness how the universal was invoked by the powerful to suppress the particular and the indigenous. The clearest example is the colonial practice and epistemology. The rootedness saves cosmopolitanism from being treated as an abstraction. One may find oneself in the landlocked Bhutan, Nepal, or the heart of Amazon forests, and nevertheless, be a true cosmopolitan. On the other hand, a person may find himself or herself in the most modern metropolis or "megacities" of New York, Rio de Janeiro, Mumbai or Paris, and still, be parochial. Indigenous peoples practicing *cosmic religion* come across as cosmopolitan in spirit in contrast to many who belong to the so-called *world-religions.* In other words, cosmopolitanism springs forth from *mind and heart*; external spatiality is not a criterion to measure it. Rooted cosmopolitanism is no oxymoron since the two poles of the particular and the universal are mutually enriching.

*Having* a religious identity and *being rooted in* it need to go hand in hand with a *journey toward* the religious world of the other. Creating an enclave to shore up one's identity is to insulate oneself from the stream of life, and this is as much undesirable as the dissolution of one's identity in the waters of misconceived cosmopolitanism.

All religions speak in one way or other about detachment or *kenosis.* But the point is that this detachment should also apply to one's religion. Many people assume it natural to be rooted in one's religion and its tradition. It rarely occurs to believers that one also needs, at the same time, to

---

[24] Amartya Sen, *Identity and Violence. The Illusion of Destiny* (London: Allen Lane, 2006), 66–67.

[25] Sugata Bose, and Ira Pande, "Tagorean Universalism and Cosmopolitanism," *India International Centre Quarterly* 38, no. 1 (2011): 2–17.

transcend one's own religion. Religious cosmopolitanism precisely takes place in this dialectic between rootedness and detachment; it is an attempt to construct a collective nontribal self of a particular religious group. Christianity, like other religions, also has a soil to strike roots and times of journey. To the extent a religious tradition can maintain this tension between rootedness and journey, it will be in a position to commune and share itself with other religious traditions and experiences.

The sense of obligation to one's religion at all costs could be a stumbling block to cosmopolitanism. Here I would like to recall my conversation with Bagus Laksana from Indonesia, who referred to a dialogue he had with a taxi driver at the time of the heated campaign for the mayor election of Jakarta in 2017. In every respect, the Christian candidate stood head and shoulders above the Muslim candidate. The campaign became a matter of Islam versus Christianity, especially after the accusation that the Christian candidate was guilty of blasphemy against the Qur'an. At the height of the campaign when Bagus Laksana asked a Muslim taxi driver whom he would vote for, he replied that he thought, undoubtedly the Christian candidate had more merits than the Muslim candidate. Nevertheless, he was going to vote for the Muslim candidate. When pressed why nevertheless he intended to give his vote to the Muslim candidate, he said: "After all, I am a Muslim" The same kind of attitude could be found with Christians or Hindus in other contexts.

Some Christians and church leaders in Europe did not think differently. Some of them maintained the view that they should admit into their country and the European Union only Christian migrants and refugees. They may have done so out of the conviction: "After all, we are Christians." In the case of India, the new policy of migration allows Hindu migrants from neighboring countries, but not Muslims. What these examples tell is that there is the inherent faith compulsion to favor one's own religious group. Hence, opening up to religious cosmopolitanism may not be easy. It needs to touch the chords of faith. The greatest challenge is to cross the internal borders of religion.

## CREATION OF COMMUNITY AND COSMOPOLITAN SOLIDARITY

If there are no common threads among religions and no strands of convergence, and if religions exist in a scattered way with no communication among themselves, then there is little likelihood of creating authentic communities. Religious postures of self-isolation will disrupt the vital goal of creating a shared community to which all religions are called. For example, if Christians and Christian leaders take offence in praying together with peoples of other faiths as it happened after the encounter in Assisi in 1986 of Pope John Paul II with leaders of other faiths,[26] what kind of community could we expect to foster? This can only discredit Christian efforts for the creation of community and cosmopolitan solidarity.

Fortunately, in the Christian tradition, there is a steady but less know stream of thought that views Christian life and existence as a cosmopolitan experience. To be a Christian is to be *at home* everywhere. This is the central thought that we find in one of the earliest Christian documents: *The Epistle to Diognetus*. Responding to the accusation that Christians take refuge in a narrow identity of a "spiritual" community, the anonymous author observes:

> The difference between Christians and the rest of mankind is not a matter of nationality, or language, or customs. Christians do not live apart in separate cities of their own, speak any special dialect, nor practice any eccentric way of life... [They] conform to ordinary local usage in their clothing, diet, and other habits... For them, any foreign country is a motherland, and any motherland is a foreign country.[27]

Claims of absolutism and monopoly of truth would go against the spirit of cosmopolitanism, divide the human community, and diminish the prospects of its unity to which all religions declare themselves to be

---

[26] The Assisi initiative of Pope John Paul became a matter of hot debate. Some Catholics found the pope's praying with other religious leaders as fostering relativism and syncretism. For them, his action compromised the position of Jesus Christ as the unique savior of the world. Ironically, Pope Benedict XVI, who fought against relativism, and even spoke of "dictatorship of relativism" at the funeral of John Paul II, himself came under critique when he called for a repetition of the Assisi event in 2011! To ward off the critique of the right-wing Catholics, who were scandalized at such prayer meetings, an argument smacking of sophistry was put forward. It claimed that the pope was not "praying together simultaneously"; rather, it was an event "to be together and pray." The argument by the neo-con Catholics is that pope and others cannot pray to the same God, as they do not have the same understanding of God. In this connection, the Indian theologian Michael Amaladoss tells us that, when people of different religious traditions are praying together, they "are experiencing the same God. But they are not having the same experience." See Michael Amaladoss, *Walking Together: The Practice of Interreligious Dialogue* (Anand: Gujarat Sahitya Prakash, 1992), 58.

[27] *The Epistle to Diognetus*, no. 5. For the text of the letter, see *Early Christian Writings: The Apostolic Fathers* (Aylesbury: Penguin Books, 1968), 176.

committed. Religions play a destructive role when they begin to compare themselves with each other in order to demonstrate their superiority over others. Each religious tradition is distinct and should be understood in its particular context, history, and background. As Kosuke Koyama notes, there is no point in the giraffe finding fault with the zebra because it (zebra) lacks a long neck![28]

As in the case of Christianity, in every religious tradition, we could observe two fundamental trends regarding community. The first one emphasizes the community of all those who share the same faith, way of life, religious rituals, laws, and traditions. According to Emile Durkheim, the sacred and the religious are identified here with a particular group or community.[29] In some religions, such as Hinduism, this community is loose, thereby creating ample space for diversity. In contrast, in Abrahamic religious traditions, the sense of the faith community is profoundly entrenched and robust. In the main, the concern is centered on fostering the growth of the particular community and its expansion. How mistaken it is for a religious tradition to think that the salvation of humanity is identical with the worldwide expansion of itself. We can see this kind of religious ideology at work, for example in the European missionary movement starting from the sixteenth century. This kind of perspective is also found in other religions. Every religion imagines that the future of humanity is reached when everybody else becomes like itself, when the entire world becomes Christian, Islamic, or Hindu.

There is a second trend in all religious traditions which considers the human community in an open and universalistic spirit. According to this trend, besides one's faith community, there is the broader community of the world and humanity. There is an obligation to foster and promote this universal human community that extends beyond the borders of one's faith community. We can characterize this as the cosmopolitan orientation. The spirit of religious cosmopolitanism tells us that it is by fostering the world community that one's own faith community grows. The relationship is not in inverse proportion; on the contrary, the more the world community grows, the more one's religious community will also grow.

---

[28] Cf. Kosuke Koyama, "Observation and Revelation. A Global Dialogue with Buddhism," in Max L. Stackhouse and Diane B. Obenchain, eds., *God and Globalization: Christ and the Dominions of Civilization* (Harrisburg: Trinity Press International, 2002), 270.

[29] Émile Durkheim, *Elementary Forms of Religious Life* (London: George Allen & Unwin Ltd., 1915).

Here, we can recall the words of prophet Jeremiah. "Seek the welfare of the city…for in its welfare you will find your welfare" (Jer. 29:7).

## CONCLUSION

It is a collective experience that despite globalization, divisions are deepening day by day. We observe escalation of conflicts, an increase of inequality, and new forms of exclusion. Added to them is the threat to humankind from the growing ecological imbalance and resultant climate change. The backlash of nature is beginning to take a heavy toll. The sudden outbreak of the new virus Covid-19 has stupefied and battered the humankind. The realization that the destiny of human family is bound together has come out more powerfully than ever, beckoning it to greater unity and solidarity.

Globalization that fails in inclusion will be a contradiction, a body without a soul. There are deeper reasons for an inclusive global world in religious terms. No single religion can determine humanity's destiny. All religions have their role in saving humankind, which is credibly done when they do this jointly. For this to happen, we need to cultivate religious cosmopolitanism which goes beyond interreligious dialogue.

Religious cosmopolitanism is a way of life, and it presupposes a different vision and set of values. As experience shows, interreligious dialogue has remained by and large an endeavor by religions as institutionalized entities to reach out to each other. There is often the preoccupation and even fear of losing one's identity by entering into dialogue. The points of reference in the interreligious dialogue are sacred writings, doctrinal tenets, symbolic codes, ethical injunctions, ritual practices, and so on. Instead, in religious cosmopolitanism, the point of reference is the *other*. Cosmopolitanism in this sense is a centrifugal or "eccentric" movement.[30] In interreligious dialogue, we acknowledge religious pluralism. But this pluralism could be merely aesthetic in the sense that we recognize and value plurality. Religious cosmopolitanism instead is a journey to the world of the other. It is to be at home in the religious universe of my neighbor.

The scope and moral concerns go beyond the confines of one's religious identity and affiliation. One is likely to limit the scope of it when he or she views it through the lens of syncretism or hybridity. Religious

---

[30] Cf. Marianna Papastephanou, *Thinking Differently about Cosmopolitanism: Theory, Eccentricity, and the Globalized World* (Boulder: Routledge, 2012).

cosmopolitanism is to be understood on its own terms and through a tinge of mysticism that sees everything in terms of unity. It also involves a continuous quest for truth that transcends borders and boundaries. This quest for truth inherent in the process of becoming religiously cosmopolitan does not negate the historically inherited or chosen religious identity and belonging. Instead, it allows one to see one's religious affiliation with new eyes and from a broader perspective, from the perspective of the entire humanity and the immense universe.

Mission has been often very narrowly defined. It often meant propagating and expanding one's religious borders. It has been controversial since it was seen as a play of power. Those with higher political power and material resources tended to impose their religion, and its tenets on others and hence mission have been a matter of serious controversy and contestation. Religious cosmopolitanism instead involves a joint mission for all the religions—the mission of saving humankind and nature.

# CHAPTER 14

# By Way of Conclusion: The Present Crisis and the Religions of the Future

In his widely acclaimed books *Sapiens* and *Homo Deus*, the historian Yuval Harari invites us to consider humankind from the broader perspective of the universe, whose origins go back to over thirteen billion years, and the appearance of life to four billion years.[1] Against this immensely large span of time and birth of life, human beings are latecomers in the universe and have a relatively short history. During this period, which scientists call "*Anthropocene*" (the age of humans) and which extends just about 70,000 years, humankind has developed from the ape and dominated the earth and exacted a heavy toll on its flora and fauna. In the words of Harari, "an insignificant ape became the ruler of the planet Earth."[2] The destruction of the biosphere caused by human beings has now come to threaten their own existence. To aggravate further the situation, some technologies—biotechnology, artificial intelligence, and so on—are turning into Frankenstein monsters.[3] Today the crisis is such that we cannot take for granted the

---

[1] Cf. Yuval Noah Harari, *Sapiens. A Brief History of Humankind* (London: Penguin Random House, 2015); Homo Deus, *A Brief History of Tomorrow* (London: Vintage, 2016).

[2] Yuval Noah Harari, *21 Lessons for 21st Century* (London: Jonathan Cape, 2018), ix.

[3] Today, we live in an age of "Technopoly." Cf. Neil Postman, *Technopoly* (New York: Knopf, 1992), in which technology is not merely a segment or dimension of life or having its own power, but something that has created a different way of being human. Life is taken over by technology as human minds are being mined and scanned to collect data and turned into raw materials for technological processes. Digital technology is widespread, surveillance

© The Author(s), under exclusive license to Springer Nature Switzerland AG 2021
F. Wilfred, *Religious Identities and the Global South*,
New Approaches to Religion and Power,
https://doi.org/10.1007/978-3-030-60738-8_14

survival and future of us as a human species. In fact, the history of the earth shows that numerous species that once inhabited it no longer do. Are we going to be one such species moving toward extinction?

## Tracking the Roots of the Crisis

The crisis that envelops humankind has multiple and interlocking aspects and dimensions. The source of destruction is not only from without but also from within. In nature, human beings are aggressive and fight with each other like wolves—*homo homini lupus*, so said Thomas Hobbes. Violence against each other could have caused the extermination of humanity. However, humankind found a way of survival by organizing themselves into societies with rights and duties. "Social Contract" became later the central organizing principle of human societies in political liberalism.[4] Relations are governed, and shared goals are achieved thanks to this contract in its manifold expressions.

But we know that not all human relationships can be subsumed under contract, nor contracts are effective in most critical times. We have come to realize the limits of contractual thinking more than ever before. For example, how does social contract work with the threat of a nuclear war? Unlike in other conventional wars where, despite the loss of precious human lives, rearrangement of relationships is possible, in a nuclear war all of humankind is in danger of being obliterated from the earth. The outbreak of Covid-19, which caught like wildfire across the entire globe, nations and borders brought to our awareness how vulnerable the humans are and how we could come in no time to the brink of colossal unforeseen disasters. Such critical predicaments go beyond the parameters of societal life shaped by contractual thinking.

Despite unprecedented technological progress and ability to predict future developments, our world is wobbling, woefully insecure, vulnerable, and imbalanced to sustain itself and move ahead. The digital and communication technology is disrupting the structures of human coexistence, the most important of which is democracy. Democracy has become a

---

technology (panopticon) is increasingly practiced, and artificial intelligence (AI) is being developed apace. All this has consequences in every field of life, including religions. It is no more the humans controlling technology, but technology determining the human.

[4] The idea of the social contract was initially proposed by Jean-Jacques Rousseau; see Victor Gourevitch, trans. and ed., *Social Contract and Other Later Political Writings*, originally published in 1762 (Cambridge: Cambridge University Press, 1998).

victim of digital communication with global spread of lies and fake news, and manipulation of electoral processes, leading increasingly to the emergence of authoritarianism and populism all over the globe.

Another source of crisis for humanity is the negative consequences of advanced capitalism. It is growing and visible in every part of the world, causing unprecedented inequality of wealth and income. The economist Thomas Piketty draws our attention to how the concentration of wealth and its unequal distribution produce social unrest and economic imbalance and threaten democratic order and human coexistence.[5] The disaffection with the market economy seems to be widespread in the Global North and the South. The exponential growth of economic inequality has left millions of people in disarray, with their dreams trampled upon and their aspirations shattered. Oxfam's 2018 report stated that 82 per cent of the wealth created in the world the previous year had gone to one per cent of the human population. The bottom 50 per cent received nothing.[6] When all doors are shut and a sense of nowhere to go pervades, "saviors" emerge for the folk. Gifted speakers and manipulators of symbols and media systems appear on the scene to exploit popular sentiments of fear and disempowerment and present themselves as alternatives to the prevailing situation.

No religion can be insensitive to these developments and the immense challenges of inequality embedded in economic, social, cultural, and political structures of our present times. Hence, the religion of the future will have its ears on the margins to hear the cry of the poor and its hands on the ground to feel the pulse of nature. The quality of religion will be tested by its commitment to shaping a different world of justice and peace, and its engagement to critically challenge any political and economic system and social mores that corrode human solidarity and togetherness.

## Perpetual Reminder

From the broader perspective of the universe, human beings are today reduced to consuming animals that rely on money and market for anything to happen. Every human relationship is viewed from the viewpoint

---

[5] Cf. Thomas Piketty, *Capital in the Twenty-First Century* (Cambridge; Massachusetts; London; England: The Belknap Press of Harvard University Press, 2017); see also Heather Boushey et al., eds., *After Piketty* (Cambridge: Harvard University Press, 2017).

[6] https://www.oxfam.org/en/press-releases/richest-1-percent-bagged-82-percent-wealth-created-last-year-poorest-half-humanity [accessed on March 3, 2020].

of the market, and the entire gamut of social life and interactions is judged by market reasoning and logic. There is nothing today which money cannot buy—acquiring citizenship, jumping queues, priority in boarding planes, priority appointment with doctors (concierge doctors), right to emit carbon, recruit mercenaries for war, buying kidneys, and getting surrogacy.[7] However, in reality, not all human problems can be solved by money, nor can money buy everything. It is an experience of daily life which humanity tends to forget.

The religion of the future will remind humankind of values that go beyond commodity and market relations and point to another world of love, compassion, solidarity, and cooperation. It will nurture necessary ethical impulses for the flourishing of the human and of nature. The forgetfulness of humans about the essentials will require a perpetual reminder in the form of religion, which will point to the best that is forgotten and hidden. Could our present religions reimagine their roles for the future?

## COMING TO TERMS

The scenarios of human extinction I mentioned are a wake-up call. Already now, radical measures and steps are to be taken. To start with, the foundation of the social contract on which human, intersocietal, and international relations are based is so thin that it is not able to hold any longer the increasing pressure of societal and interhuman problems and conflicts. Moreover, the social contract—the cornerstone of liberal philosophy—is highly individualistic and does not seem to give due importance to the community. In a true community, people feel bound together not simply because they are party to a contract, but because of another set of values like love, the search for common good, altruism, compassion, the spirit of cooperation, and solidarity. How could religions become nurseries where these values are nurtured?

At this juncture, we cannot but resist raising some critical questions about those disciplines concerned about the study of religion. Academically with what vision does the discipline of religious studies function? Are these studies immersed in fragments and lost in the minutiae of religious ethnography? What contributions do the scholars in this field think they could offer to a world and humanity in crisis? Are the kind of theologies

---

[7] Cf. Michael J. Sandel, *What Money Can't Buy. The Moral Limits of Market* (London: Penguin Books, 2012).

pursued today with heavy baggage of tradition and doctrine able to come to terms with a world on fire? Some forms of theology are so cut off from the real world that they appear as "selling words" in the "bazaar of loquacity."[8]

We need to take stock of the fact that we live today in a world of networking which offers endless possibilities. There are many players involved in expanding this network to an unimaginable extent. Despite all this, we find more walls around than bridges. It is an irony that in an age that promises massive connectivity, there should be heavy loss of human connectedness and solidarity. Those involved in building networks as the big conglomerates seem to be least interested and are indifferent to what passes through these portals of connectivity.[9] This kind of organized irresponsibility is in need of greater ethical concern and infusion of values that will promote all-round wellbeing of humanity and flourishing of nature.[10] For, the future of the world is likely to be determined by this connectivity rather than by isolated nations and borders. It is no more a situation in which we try to assess what is the impact of globalization on religion. Religions are today an important factor and a force for globalization. They contribute to networking and global culture. As a player in the process of globalization, the religion of the future needs to bring greater ethical concerns and sensitivity to the lives of communities and in the international order. It will speak truth to power, without counting the cost.

## RELIGIONS OF THE FUTURE

One speaks of "return of religion." This is quite ambiguous. There is no return of religion in the Global South because it never departed! It has remained an abiding element in the lives of the peoples of the South. That the ceaseless presence of religion should put the peoples of the South in a less-developed stage of human history is to invoke the Hegelian myth of "Philosophy of History". The return of religion is often spoken about from the perspective of the history of the Global North, and its

---

[8] St Augustine, *Confessions*. A New Translation by Henry Chardwick (Oxford: Oxford University Press, 2008), Introduction p. xi.

[9] Cf. Shoshana Zuboff, *The Age of Surveillance Capitalism. The Fight for a Human Future at the New Frontier of Power* (London: Profile Books, 2019).

[10] Cf. Felix Wilfred, ed., "Social Media," *Jeevadhara* 50, no. 295 (January 2020).

post-secular context, and in more recent times in relation to the tragic condition of human existence, the anomie, and the profound existential angst. It is too little if religion returns, after a failed interpretation of its seeming absence, only as a stopgap to a helpless human predicament.

Increasingly in the North as well as in the South, we need to speak about *the religion of the future, rather than the future* of religion. To speak of the future of religion would mean that religions are threatened of their survival and in need of defense. The religion of the future, on the other hand, will be one that will be concerned about the future of humanity and the future of creation. This religion will understand its beliefs, organization, values, morals, laws, practices, and worship as oriented to common good, wellbeing of humankind and flourishing of nature. As such, it will never worry about its own survival because it perceives its mission as a call to serve humanity and sustain nature.

## Facing Challenges

Hitherto, religions have served as bricks and mortar to build up identities, and hence they (religions) became sources of conflict. Warmed-up versions of nationalism and populism, on their part, invoke religion and religious symbols for political ends and for creating a social and political order that excludes peoples and communities. We know from history that the ideology of nationalism, very much like that of religion, pits nations one against the other, and kills millions as happened in the two world wars. Today, numerous armed conflicts are waged by subnationalities in different parts of the world against centralizing and oppressive state powers. State violence gets legitimized by invoking the ideology of nationalism and national security. Warmongering and feigned national security take precedence over the real issues of the people and their human security vis-à-vis the fundamental needs of life. I am appalled at the sight of country after country parading their most lethal weapons on national days or republic days. Through these senseless and mad exhibitions of weapons a nation is showing how effectively it can kill others, and this sight is applauded and celebrated by millions in the name of nationalism. A culture of death becomes a showpiece and a badge of honor.

The perils inherent in the ideology of nationalism were sensed with much prescience by two great thinkers—one from the Global North and the other from the South. The one from the North was Immanuel Kant, who in his work *Perpetual Peace*, proposed an arrangement for the life of humanity that goes beyond the division of nations.[11] It was a vision like that of the astronauts who from space can see just one earth, and not able to identify the borders of nations which are zealously but senselessly guarded at the cost of a lot of human lives. The other thinker from the South was Rabindranath Tagore, who was very universalistic in his outlook. Even before the outbreak of World War I, in his lectures delivered in the USA and Japan, he warned about the danger of nationalism and stated that the reality of humans is above the imagined nation.[12] If Kant maintained that "all politics must bend its knee before morality [right],"[13] Tagore taught us that the human has primacy over the nation. The contributions of these thinkers from the North and the South are fundamental lessons for today.

What they said is equally applicable to religion. Religion, like nationalism—both often intertwined—is to be tamed and cured from its instinct to violence. It will have to shed much deadwood that has accumulated in the name of tradition. What nationalism is to a country, tradition is to religion. But the deadwood of tradition is so thick and it has so covered religion that it is benumbed and no more able to sense the burning issues of humanity. It remains narcissistic, concerned all the time about itself. It is like nationalism clouding the mind and heart and instilling aggression.

Like the instinct for violence, religions have an innate proclivity to taboos. Taboos around beliefs and rituals, and social shibboleths are things that defy reason. They are believed and performed with a magical consciousness. The religion of the future will critically interrogate its own belief system, rituals, and practices as to what they could really signify for the wellbeing of humankind and of nature. I am not advocating the abolition of all existing religions, instead suggesting that they renounce many things—like snake shedding its skin—to be able to renew itself and rise up as religions of the future with a different focus and orientation. Symbols, worship, and rituals of a religion will not serve only its adherents and followers but will be open-ended to the larger goal of the wellbeing of the entire human family. In other words,

---

[11] Immanuel Kant, *Perpetual Peace and Other Essays*. Translated by Ted Humphrey (Indianapolis and Cambridge: Hackett Publishing Company, 1983).

[12] Cf. Rabindranath Tagore, *Nationalism*. Initially published in 1917 (Calcutta: Rup & Co, 1992).

[13] Immanuel Kant, *Perpetual Peace*, 135.

what I am advocating is that every religion becomes cosmopolitan in its vision, spirit, beliefs, rituals, worship, and so on.[14] This is what globalization should mean for religious identities.

## PUBLIC SIGNIFICANCE OF RELIGIOUS BELIEFS

There are many efforts at re-presenting religion, trying to remove deadwood, to refurbish it, reform, and renew it. Some would think that the sources of this renewal can be found in the forgotten germane tradition of the religions themselves, and that renewal would be envisaged as *ressourcement*—going back to the sources. This trend is there in all major religious traditions in their efforts to renew themselves and make themselves more meaningful. Surely these are laudable efforts. However, for a religion to reinvent itself as a religion of the future, much more needs to be done. It is crucial to bring out the *public significance* of what it believes and what it could contribute to the attainment of common good.

Certain radicality is inevitable if religions are to reinvent themselves and serve the future of humanity and nature. The ideal is not to create one single universal or planetary religion in the name of globalization. This will be only as successful as Esperanto—an experiment in a common language for humankind created artificially. I think such an ideal would do away with all the richness and plurality of the beautiful rainbow that religions really are. Humanity will be more impoverished with one single universal religion which cannot but also appear as utopian. What we need is that every single existing religion reimages and endows itself with the spirit of universality and open-endedness in such a way that everyone can feel at home and benefit from its riches. This vision of the future shape of religion calls for deploying the necessary means and measures now for the realization of the lofty goals it points to.

After all, religions are not ends in themselves but windows that open up to a new view of life and way of life. The religion of the future will have its feet on the "rough ground" of everyday life. It will help us see the reality around in a new light, with different eyes. It is not alienation, but an immersion into reality to dispel shadows as in the allegory of the cave of Plato. For the transforming vision and way of life to take place, there is the need to mold oneself and one's community of faith in a new direction. The more an individual or a community thinks and acts in a

[14] Cf. Chap. 13.

noninstrumental manner, they will have a mystical experience—a "mysticism with open eyes"—that is fully aware of the reality all around.

## ENGAGING NEW QUESTION

The dialectic between reason and religion has characterized the past. With rationality defined in a univocal manner by the dominant and held out as the measure of everything, religion was required to justify itself in the court of reason.[15] It is too evident from history that reason goes to slumber and that we need other forces to awaken it. The tragic wars of the twentieth century and gruesome instances of genocide give us little room to trust reason beyond a point, and hold it as the ultimate. I think the whole discussion in the Global North about secularism and secularization is, at bottom, a part of this dialectic of reason and religion. The future of religions needs to be set—beyond the North and the South polarity—in the context of today's stupendous and at the same time highly ambiguous developments which on the one hand condition human freedom as never before, and at the same time seem to offer immense and unprecedented opportunities and openings to reshape the destiny of humankind and nature.

---

[15] Cf. Felix Wilfred, "Christian Faith and Socio-Cultural Rationalities: Reflections from Asia," in *Concilium* 2017/1 (London: SCM Press, 2017), 101–110.

# BIBLIOGRAPHY

BOOKS & ARTICLES

Aarts, Olav, Need, Ariana, Te Grotenhuis, Manfred, and De Graaf, Nan Dirk. "Does Belonging Accompany Believing? Correlations and Trends in Western Europe and North America between 1981 and 2000." *Review of Religious Research* 50, no. 1 (September 2008): 16–34.

Acevedo, Deepa Das. "Pause for Thought. Supreme Court Judgment on Sabarimala." *Economic and Political Weekly of India* 53, no. 43 (October 27, 2018): 12–15.

Adams, T. "A Review of Narrative Ethics." *Qualitative Inquiry: QI*, 14, no. 2 (2008): 175–94.

Adrian, Melanie. *Religious Freedom at Risk: The EU, French Schools, and Why the Veil Was Banned*. Cham Heidelberg: Springer, 2015.

Agana, Wilfred Asampambila. *Succeed Here and in Eternity*. Bern: Peter Lang, 2016.

Aggarwal, Neil Krishan. *The Taliban's Virtual Emirate: The Culture and Psychology of an Online Militant Community*. New York: Columbia University Press, 2016.

Ahmad, Irfan. "The Secular State and the Geography of Radicalism." *Economic and Political Weekly* 44, no. 23 (June 6, 2009): 33–38.

Ahmed, Hilal. *Politics of Monuments and Memory in Postcolonial North India: A Study of Muslim Political Discourse on Jama Masjid and Babri Masjid*. London: University of London, 2007.

© The Author(s), under exclusive license to Springer Nature Switzerland AG 2021
F. Wilfred, *Religious Identities and the Global South*,
New Approaches to Religion and Power,
https://doi.org/10.1007/978-3-030-60738-8

329

Ahu Sandal, Nukhet. "Clash of Public Theologies? Rethinking the Concept of Religion in Global Politics." *Alternatives: Global, Local, Political* 37, no. 1 (February 2012): 66–83.

Aikman, David. *Jesus in Beijing: How Christianity is Transforming China and Changing the Global Balance of Power.* Oxford: Monarch, 2005.

Akkara, Anto. *Kandhamal A Blot to Indian Secularism.* Delhi: Media House, 2009.

Alan, E. *Pilgrimage in the Hindu Tradition: A Case Study of West Bengal.* New York: Oxford University Press, 1984.

Alles, Gregory, ed. *Religious Studies: A Global View.* New York: Routledge, 2008.

Al-Mohammad, Hayder. "Poverty beyond Disaster in Post-invasion Iraq Ethics and the 'Rough Ground' of the Everyday." *Current Anthropology* 56, no. 11 (October 2015): 108–115.

Altizer, Thomas J. J. "Hegel and the Christian God." *Journal of the American Academy of Religion* 59, no. 1 (Spring 1991): 71–91.

American Academy of Arts and Science. "Fundamentalism Observed. A Hypothetical Family." *Bulletin of the American Academy of Arts and Sciences* 45, no. 2 (November 1991): 10–40.

Andersen, Walter K, and Damle, Shridhar D. *The Brotherhood in Saffron. The Rashtriya Swayamsevak Sangh and Hindu Revivalism.* Delhi: Vistaar Publications, 1987.

Anderson, Pamela. "Having It Both Ways: Ricoeur's Hermeneutics of the Self." *Oxford Literary Review* 15, no. 1/2 (1993): 227–52.

Anderson, Benedict R. *Imagined Communities: Reflections on the Origin and Spread of Nationalism,* rev. ed. London and New York: Verso, 2016.

Ansari, Humayun, and Hafez, Farid, eds. *From the Far Right to the Mainstream: Islamophobia in Party Politics and the Media.* Frankfurt and New York: Campus, 2012.

Appadurai, Arjun, ed. "Disjuncture and Difference in the Global Cultural Economy." *Theory, Culture & Society* 7, no. 2–3 (1990): 295–310.

Appiah, Kwame Anthony. *The Lies That Bind: Rethinking Identity: Creed, Country, Colour, Class, Culture.* New York: Liveright Publishing Corporation, 2018.

Ariel, Yaakov. "Jews and New Religious Movements: An Introductory Essay." *Nova Religio, The Journal of Alternative and Emergent Religions* 15, no. 1 (2011): 5–21.

Arokianathan, A. "Vailankanni as Tourist and Pilgrimage Centre." Unpublished doctoral dissertation Bharathidhasan University, Tiruchirapalli, 2013.

Asamoah-Gyadu, J. Kwabena. "African Initiated Christianity in Eastern Europe: Church of the "Embassy of God" in Ukraine." *International Bulletin of Missionary Research* 30, no. 2 (2006): 73–75.

Assayag, Jackie, and Benei, Veronique, eds. *At Home in Diaspora. South Asian Scholars and the West.* Bloomington: Indiana University Press, 2003.

Attanasi, Katharine, and Yong, Amos. *Pentecostalism and Prosperity. The Socio-Economics of the Global Charismatic Movement.* New York: Palgrave Macmillan, 2012.

Avelar, Idelber. *The Letter of Violence: Essays on Narrative, Ethics, and Politics.* New York: Palgrave Macmillan, 2004.

Bachmann, Peter R. *Roberto Nobili 1577–1656: Ein Missionsgeschichtlicher Beitrag zum Christlichen Dialog mit Hinduismus.* Roma: Institutum Historicum S.I., 1972.

Badone, Ellen, and Roseman, Sharon R., eds. *Intersecting Journeys: The Anthropology of Pilgrimage and Tourism.* Urbana-Champaign, IL: University of Illinois Press, 2004.

Baird, Robert D., ed. *Religion in Modern India*, 3rd rev. ed. Delhi: Manohar, 1998.

Baldini, Simona Bonini. "Narrative Capability: Self-Recognition and Mutual Recognition in Refugees' Storytelling." *Journal of Information Policy* 9 (2019): 132–47.

Barboza, Francis Peter. *Christianity in Indian Dance Forms.* Delhi: Sri Satguru Publications, 1990.

Barr, M., and Govindasamy, A. R. "The Islamisation of Malaysia: Religious Nationalism in the Service of Ethnonationalism." *Australian Journal of International Affairs: The Journal of the Australian Institute of International Affairs* 64, no. 3 (2010): 293–311.

Bartkowski, John. "Beyond Biblical Literalism and Inerrancy: Conservative Protestants and the Hermeneutic Interpretation of Scripture." *Sociology of Religion* 57, no. 3 (1996): 259–72.

Batalden, Stephen K. *Seeking God: The Recovery of Religious Identity in Orthodox Russia, Ukraine, and Georgia.* DeKalb: Northern Illinois University Press, 1993.

Bates, Crispin. "Some Thoughts on the Representation and Misrepresentation of the Colonial South Asian Labor Diaspora." *South Asian Studies* 33, no. 1 (2017): 7–22

Bauer, Joanne R., and Bell, Daniel, eds. *The East Asian Challenge for Human Rights.* Cambridge: Cambridge University Press, 1999.

Bauman, Chad M. "Sathya Sai Baba: At Home Abroad in Midwestern America." In John Zavos, Pralay Kanungo, Deepa S. Reddy, Maya Warrier, Raymond Williams, eds., *Public Hinduism*, 141–159. Delhi: Sage, 2012.

Bauman, Zygmunt. *Does Ethics Have a Chance in a World of Consumers?;* Cambridge, MA and London: Harvard University Press, 2008.

Baumeister, Roy F. *Identity: Cultural Change and the Struggle for Self.* New York: Oxford University Press, 1986.

Bayly, Susan. "History and the Fundamentalists: India after the Ayodhya Crisis." *Bulletin of the American Academy of Arts and Sciences* 46, no. 7 (April 1993): 7–26.

Bays, Daniel H. *A New History of Christianity in China.* New York: Wiley-Blackwell, 2011.

Beaman, Lori G. "Reframing Understandings of Religion: Lessons from India." *India International Centre Quarterly* 40, no. 3/4 (Winter 2013–Spring 2014): 35–46.

Beckford, James. "The 'Cult Problems' in Five Countries. The Social Construction of Religious Controversy." In E. Barker, ed., *Of Gods and Men: New Religious Movements in the West*, 198–214. Macon, GA: Mercer Unity Press, 1983.

BeDuhn, Jason David. *Augustine's Manichaean Dilemma: Conversion and Apostasy, 373–388 C. E.* Chapter 7. Philadelphia: University of Pennsylvania Press, 2009.

Bell, Daniel. *The Coming of Post-Industrial Society*, 2nd ed. New York: Basic, 1999.

Benoit, Pierre. "La Plénitude de sens des Livres Saints." *Revue Biblique (1946-)* 67, no. 2 (1960): 161–96.

Berg, Travis Vande, and Kniss, Fred. "ISKCON and Immigrants: The Rise, Decline, and Rise Again of a New Religious Movement." *The Sociological Quarterly* 49, no. 1 (Winter 2008): 79–104.

Berger, Peter L. ed. "The Desecularization of the World: A Global Overview." In Peter Berger, ed., *The Desecularization of the World: Resurgent Religions and World Politics*, 1–18. Washington, DC: Ethics and Public Policy Center, 1999.

Berger, Peter, Davie, Grace, and Fokas, Effie. *Religious America, Secular Europe? A Theme and Variations.* Hampshire and Burlington: Ashgate Publishing Limited, 2008.

Bernstein, M. "Identity Politics." *Annual Review of Sociology* 31 (2005): 47–74.

Bert, Jean-François. *Michel Foucault: Regards croisés sur le corps: Histoire, Ethnologie, Sociologie [sous la direction de Jean-François Bert].* Strasbourg: Portique, 2007.

Bharadwaj, Surinder M., and Lochtefeld, James G. "Tirtha." In *The Hindu World*, edited by Sushil Mittal and Gener Thursby, 478–501. London: Routledge, 2004.

Bhargava, Rajeev. "Rehabilitating Secularism." In *Rethinking Secularism*, edited by Craig Calhoun, Mark Juergensmeyer, Jonathan VanAntwerpen, 92–113. New York: Oxford University Press, 2011.

Bhargava, Rajeev, ed. *Secularism and Its Critics;* Delhi and Oxford: Oxford University Press, 1999.

Bielefeldt, Heiner. *Freedom of Religion or Belief: Thematic Reports of the UN Special Rapporteur 2010–2013.* Bonn: Verlag Für Kultur Und Wissenschaft, 2014.

Binawan, Andang L. "The Case of a Christian Governor in Jakarta as a Sign of Times for Catholics (and Christians) in Indonesia." *International Journal of Asian Christianity* 1, no. 1 (2018): 135–142.

Birnbaum, Raoul. "Buddhist China at the Century's Turn." *The China Quarterly* 174 (2003): 428–450.

Bliss, Catherine. "The Marketization of Identity Politics." *Sociology* 47, no. 5 (2013): 1011–025.

Bloomer, Kristin C. *Possessed by the Virgin: Hinduism, Roman Catholicism, and Marian Possession in South India*. Oxford: Oxford University Press, 2018.

Bocken, Inigo, ed. *Conflict and Reconciliation Perspectives on Nicholas of Cusa*. Leiden and Boston: Brill, 2004.

Bordo, Susan. "Postmodern Subjects, Postmodern Bodies." *Feminist Studies* 18, no. 1 (1992): 159–75.

Bose, Purnima. "Hindutva Abroad: The California Textbook Controversy." *The Global South* 2, no. 1 (2008): 11–34.

Bourchier, David M. "Two Decades of Ideological Contestation in Indonesia: From Democratic Cosmopolitanism to Religious Nationalism." *Journal of Contemporary Asia*, 49 (2019): 713–33.

Boyle, Kevin, and Sheen, Juliet, eds. *Freedom of Religion and Belief: A World Report*. London and New York: Routledge, 1997.

Bräuchler, Brigit. "Religious Conflicts in Cyberage." *Citizenship Studies* 11, no. 4 (2007): 329–47.

Broadhead, Philip, and Keown, Damien, eds. *Can Faiths Make Peace? Holy Wars and the Resolution of Religious Conflicts*. London and New York: International Library of War Studies, 2007.

Brown, Judith M. *Global South Asians. Introducing the Modern Diaspora*. Cambridge: Cambridge University Press, 2007.

Bruckner, Pascal. "Samuel Huntington ou le retour de la fatalité en histoire." *Esprit* 237, no. 11 (November 1997): 53–67.

Brzuszkiewicz, Sara. "Radicalisation in Europe after the Fall of Islamic State: Trends and Risks." *European View*, 17 (2018): 145–54.

Buckser, Andrew, and Glazier, Stephen D., eds. *The Anthropology of Religious Conversion*. Lanham Maryland: Rowman & Littlefield Publishers, 2003.

Burke, Denis J. "Tibetans in Exile in a Changing Global Political Climate." *Economic and Political Weekly* 43, no. 15 (April 2008): 79–85.

Buterin, Damion. "Hegel, Recognition, and Religion." *The Review of Metaphysics* 64, no. 4 (2011): 789–821.

Byrd, Dustin J. "Professing Islam in a Post-Secular Society." In *Islam in a Post-Secular Society. Religion, Secularity and the Antagonism of Recalcitrant Faith*. Leiden: Brill, 2017.

Cady, Linell Elizabeth. *Religion, Theology and American Public Life*. Albany: SUN Press, 1993.

Calhoun, Craig, Juergensmeyer, Mark, and Van Antwerpen, Jonathan, eds., *Rethinking Secularism*. New York: Oxford University Press, 2011.

Calkins, Martin. "Recovering Religion's Prophetic Voice for Business Ethics." *Journal of Business Ethics* 23, no. 4 (February 2000): 339–352.

Campion, Kristy. "Blast through the Past: Terrorist Attacks on Art and Antiquities as a Reconquest of the Modern Jihadi Identity." *Perspectives on Terrorism* 11, no. 1 (2017): 26–39.

Candido, Mariana. *An African Slaving Port and the Atlantic World: Benguela and its Hinterland.* Cambridge and New York: Cambridge University Press, 2013.

Cartagenas, Aloysius Lopez. "Religion and Politics in the Philippines: The Public Role of the Roman Catholic Church in the Democratization of the Filipino Polity." *Political Theology* 11, no. 6 (2010): 846–872.

Casanova, José. "Religion, the New Millennium, and Globalization." *Sociology of Religion* 62, no. 4, (2001): 415–441.

Centre for Developing Societies. *State of Democracy in South Asia. A Report.* Delhi: Oxford University Press, 2008.

Chadwick, Owen. *The Secularization of the European Mind in the Nineteenth Century.* Cambridge: Cambridge University Press, 1975.

Chan, Kim-Kwong, and Carlson, Eric R. *Religious Freedom in China: Policy, Administration, and Regulation.* Santa Barbara: Institute for the Study of American Religion, 2005.

Chandhoke, Neera. *Beyond Secularism: The Rights of Religious Minorities.* Delhi: Oxford University Press, 1999.

Chandra, Bipan. *Communalism in Modern India.* New Delhi: Har-Anand Publication, 1984.

Chatterji, Angam P., Hansen, Thomas Blom, and Jaffrelot, Christophe, eds. *Majoritarian State. How Hindu Nationalism Is Changing India.* London: Harper Collins Publishers, 2019.

Chattopadhyaya, Debiprasad. *What is Living and What is Dead in Indian Philosophy,* 3rd ed. Delhi: Peoples' Publishing House, 1993.

Cheng-tian, Kuo. "Chinese Religious Reform." *Asian Survey* 51, no. 6 (2011): 1042–064.

Chidester, David, Tayob, Abdulkader, and Weisse, Wolfram, eds. *Religion, Politics, and Identity in a Changing South Africa,* vol. 6. Münster: Waxmann, 2004.

Chowdhury, Mehdi, and Irudaya Rajan, S., eds. *South Asian Migration in the Gulf: Causes and Consequences.* London: Palgrave Macmillan, 2018.

Christie, Kenneth, and Roy, Denny. *The Politics of Human Rights in East Asia.* London: Pluto Press, 2001.

Chryssides, George D. *The Advent of Sun Myung Moon: The Origins, Beliefs and Practices of the Unification Church.* London: Palgrave Macmillan, 1991.

Claerhout, Sarah, and De Roover, Jakob. "The Question of Conversion in India." *Economic and Political Weekly* 40, no. 28 (2005): 3048–055.

Clarke, Sathianathan, Manchala, Deenabandhu, and Peacock, Philip Vinod, eds. *Dalit Theology in the Twenty-first Century: Discordant Voices, Discerning Pathways,* New Delhi and Oxford: Oxford University Press, 2010.

Cobb, James C., and Stueck, William Whitney, eds. *Globalization and the American South.* Athens, Georgia: University of Georgia Press, 2005.

Coleman, John A. "The Achievement of Religious Freedom." *U.S. Catholic Historian* 24, no. 1 (2006): 21–32.

Coles, Romand. "Communicative Action & Dialogical Ethics: Habermas & Foucault." *Polity* 25, no. 1 (1992): 71–94.

Collins, Adela Yarbor. *Cosmology and Eschatology in Jewish and Christian Apocalypticism.* Leiden: Brill, 1996.

Conkle, Daniel O. "Secular Fundamentalism, Religious Fundamentalism, and the Search for Truth in Contemporary America." *Journal of Law and Religion* 12, no. 2 (1995): 337–70.

Corduan, Winfried. "Hegel in Rahner: A Study in Philosophical Hermeneutics." *The Harvard Theological Review* 71, no. 3/4 (July–October 1978): 285–298.

Cornille, Catherine. *Many Mansions? Multiple Religious Belonging and Christian Identity.* New York: Orbis, 2002.

Corrigan, John, and Neal, Lynn S., eds. *Religious Intolerance in America: A Documentary History.* Chapel Hill: University of North Carolina Press, 2010.

Costantini, Mariaconcetta. "Reconfiguring the Gothic Body in Postmodern Times: Angela Carter's Exposure of Flesh-Inscribed Stereotypes." *Gothic Studies* 4, no. 1 (2002): 14–27.

Courtine, Jean-Jacques. *Déchiffrer le corps: penser avec Foucault.* Grenoble: Milon, 2011.

Cox, Neville. "Understanding 'Je suis Charlie'." *Studies: An Irish Quarterly Review* 105, no. 418 (2016): 148–58.

Crites, Stephen D. "The Gospel According to Hegel." *The Journal of Religion* 46, no. 2 (April 1966): 246–263.

Cronin, Vincent. *The Wise Man from the West. Matteo Ricci and his Mission to China.* London: Harvill Press, 1984.

Cullmann, Oscar. *Salvation in History: New Testament Library*, S. 1. London: SCM Press, 1967.

Curran, Charles E., and Hunt, Robert E. *Dissent in and for the Church. Theologians and Humanae Vitae.* New York: Sheed and Ward, 1969.

Dallmayr, Fred. "Cosmopolitanism: Moral and Political. Political Theory." *Political Theory* 31, no. 3 (June 2003): 421–442.

D'Anieri, Paul, Ernst, Claire, and Kier, Elizabeth. "New Social Movements in Historical Perspective." *Comparative Politics* 22, no. 4 (1990): 445–58.

Dasgupta, Samir, and Kivisto, Peter, ed. *Postmodernism in a Global Perspective.* New Delhi: Sage Publication, 2014.

Davie, Grace. *Religion in Britain since 1945: Believing without Belonging.* Oxford: Blackwell, 1994.

Davie, Grace. *The Sociology of Religion.* London, Los Angeles, New Delhi and Singapore: Sage Publication, 2007.

Davis, Winston. "Heaven's Gate: A Study of Religious Obedience." *Nova Religio: The Journal of Alternative and Emergent Religions* 3, no. 2 (2000): 241–67.

Dawson, Lorne L. "The Cultural Significance of New Religious Movements and Globalization: A Theoretical Prolegomenon." *Journal for the Scientific Study of Religion* 37, no. 4 (December 1998): 580–595.

Dawson, Lorne L., and Cowan, Douglas E., eds. *Religion Online: Finding Faith on the Internet.* New York and London: Routledge, 2004.

Dayil, Plangsat Bitrus. *Ethno-religious Conflicts and Gender in Nigeria's Middle Belt.* Unpublished Thesis, Department of African Studies and Anthropology, University of Birmingham, 2015.

De La Torre, Carlos, ed. *The Routledge Handbook of Global Populism*, 1st ed. London and New York: Routledge, 2018.

De Schreijver, Georges. *Recent Theological Debates in Europe and Their Impact on Interreligious Dialogue.* Bangalore: Dharmaram Publications, 2004.

Delanty, Gerard, and Kumar, Krishan, eds. *The SAGE Handbook of Nations and Nationalism.* London and Thousand Oaks: SAGE, 2006.

Derrida, Jacques, and Vattimo, Gianni, eds. *Religion: Cultural Memory in the Present.* Stanford: Stanford University Press, 1996.

Devotta, Neil. "Sri Lanka at Sixty: A Legacy of Ethnocentrism and Degeneration." *Economic and Political Weekly* 44, no. 5 (31 January–6 February 2009): 46–53.

Dhavan, Rajeev. "Religious Freedom in India." *The American Journal of Comparative Law* 35, no. 1 (1987): 209–54.

Diehl, Claudia, and Koenig, Matthias. "Religiosität türkischer Migranten im Generationenverlauf: Ein Befund und einige Erklärungsversuche / Religiosity of First- and Second-Generation Turkish Migrants: A Phenomenon and Some Attempts at a Theoretical Explanation." *Zeitschrift für Soziologie* 38, no. 4 (August 2009): 300–319.

Dixon, B. A. *Food Justice and Narrative Ethics: Reading Stories for Ethical Awareness and Activism.* London and New York: Bloomsbury Academic, 2018.

Dodd, James. "Philosophy and Art in Schelling's 'System des transzendentalen Idealismus'." *The Review of Metaphysics* 52, no. 1 (September 1998): 51–85.

Dorsey, James. "Culture, Nationalism, and Sakaguchi Ango." *Journal of Japanese Studies* 27, no. 2 (2001): 347–79.

Dreyfus, Hubert L., and Rabinow, Paul. *Michel Foucault. Beyond Structuralism and Hermeneutics.* Chicago: The University of Chicago Press, 1983.

Drydyk, J. "Foundational Issues: How Must Global Ethics Be Global?." *Journal of Global Ethics* 10, no. 1 (2014): 16–25.

Dufoix, Stephane. *Diasporas.* Berkeley: University of California Press, 2008.

Duke, James T., and Johnson, Barry L. "The Stages of Religious Transformation: A Study of 200 Nations." *Review of Religious Research* 30, no. 3 (March 1989): 209–224.

Dunne, Nikki, and Jamieson, Lynn. *Who Cares? Indian Nurses 'on the Move' and How Their Transnational Migration for Care Work Shapes Their*

*Multigenerational Relationships of Familial Care over Time*. Ph.D. Thesis, Edinburgh: University of Edinburgh, 2018.

Dwyer, Rachel. "The Swaminarayan Movement." In *South Asians in the Diaspora. Histories and Religious Traditions*, edited by Jacobsen K. A. and Kumar, P. P. 180–202. Leiden and Boston: Brill, 2004.

Dziedzic, Peter. "Religion Under Fire: A Report and Policy Paper on Religious Freedom in Tibet." *The Tibet Journal* 38, no. 3–4 (2013): 87–113.

Eade, John, and Sallnow, Michael, eds. *In Contesting the Sacred: The Anthropology of Christian Pilgrimage*. Eugene, OR: Wipf & Stock, 1977.

Eberle, Christopher J. *Religious Conviction in Liberal Politics*. Cambridge: Cambridge University Press, 2002.

Eck, Diana. *India: A Sacred Geography*. New York: Harmony Books, 2012.

Éigeartaigh, Aoileann Ní, et al., eds. *Rethinking Diasporas: Hidden Narratives and Imagined Borders*. Cambridge: Cambridge Scholars Publisher, 2007.

Eisenstadt, S. N. "Heterodoxies and Dynamics of Civilizations." *Proceedings of the American Philosophical Society* 128, no. 2 (1984): 104–13.

Eliade, Mircea. *Yoga: Immortality and Freedom*. Translated from the French by Willard R. Trask. 2nd edn. Routledge & Kegan Paul, 1982.

Ellos, William J. *Narrative Ethics*. Aldershot: Avebury, 1994.

Eltis, David, and Richardson, David, eds. *Extending the Frontiers: Essays on the New Transatlantic Slave Trade Database*. New Haven: Yale University Press, 2008.

Engelhardt, Jr. H. Tristram. "Kant, Hegel, and Habermas: Reflections on 'Glauben und Wissen'." *The Review of Metaphysics* 63, no. 4 (2010): 871–903.

Engineer, Asghar Ali, ed. *Politics of Confrontation: The Babri-Masjid Ramjanmabhoomi Controversy Runs Riot*. Delhi: Ajanta Publications, 1992.

Eremina, Natalia, and Seredenko, Sergei. *Right Radicalism in Party and Political Systems in the Present-day European States*, Newcastle upon Tyne, UK: Cambridge Scholars Publishing, 2015.

Erikson, Erik H. *Childhood and Society*, rev. ed. New York and London: W. W. Norton & Company,1963.

Eslin, Jean-Claude. "Has France Renounced Its Own Identity?" *The Political Quarterly* 73, no. 3 (2002): 266–272.

Ewing, Katherine Pratt. "Legislating Religious Freedom: Muslim Challenges to the Relationship between 'Church' and 'State' in Germany and France." *Daedalus* 129, no. 4 (2000): 31–54.

Farrelly, Paul J. "'Rapprochement with The Vatican." In *Power*, edited by Farrelly Paul, J., Jane, Golley, Linda, Jaivin, and Sharon, Strange, 123–28. Acton, ACT: ANU Press, 2019.

Fernando, Jude Lal. "The Politics of Representations of Mass Atrocity in Sri Lanka and Human Rights Discourse: Challenge to Justice and Recovery." In *Loss and*

*Hope,* edited by Peter Admirand, 25–49. London and New York: Bloomsbury, 2014.

Finlayson, Caitlin C. "Performativity and the Art of Tai Chi: Understanding the Body as Transformative." *Southeastern Geographer* 55, no. 3 (2015): 362–76.

Fisher, M. *Counterflows to Colonialism. Indian Travellers and Settlers in Britain 1600–1857.* Delhi: Permanent Black, 2003.

Fitzi, Gregor, Mackert, Jürgen, and Turner, Bryan S., eds. *Populism and the Crisis of Democracy, vol.3, Migration, Gender and Religion,* 1st ed. London and New York: Routledge, 2018.

Flanigan, Shawn T. "For the Love of God: NGOs and Religious Identity in a Violent World Virginia." *Voluntas: International Journal of Voluntary and Non-profit Organizations* 23, no. 1 (March 2012): 279–280.

Fleming, Chris. *René Girard: Violence and Mimesis.* Cambridge: Polity, 2004.

Flynn, Gabriel, Murray, P. D., and Kelly, Patricia Hardcastle, eds. *Ressourcement: A Movement for Renewal in Twentieth-century Catholic Theology.* Oxford: Oxford University Press, 2012.

Foltz, F. "Religion on the Internet: Community and Virtual Existence." *Bulletin of Science, Technology & Society* 23, no. 4 (2003): 321–30.

Foret, F. "Political Roof and Sacred Canopy? Religion and the EU Constitution." *European Journal of Social Theory* 9, no. 1 (2006): 59–81.

Foucault, Michel. "Afterword: On the Genealogy of Ethics." In *Michel Foucault. Beyond Structuralism and Hermeneutics,* edited by Dreyfus Hubert, and Rabinow, Paul. Chicago: University of Chicago Press, 1983.

Fox Young, Richard. "Christianity and Conversion: Conceptualization and Critique, Past and Present, with Special Reference to South Asia." In *Oxford Handbook of Christianity in Asia,* edited by Felix Wilfred, 444–457. New York: Oxford University Press, 2014.

Fox, Jonathan, and Sander, Samuel. "Separation of Religion and State in the Twenty-First Century: Comparing the Middle East and Western Democracies." *Comparative Politics* 37, no. 3 (April 2005): 317–335.

Fox, Jonathan. "Religion as an Overlooked Element of International Relations." *International Studies Review* 3, no. 3 (2001): 53–73.

Freeman, Mark. "From Substance to Story: Narrative, Identity, and the Reconstruction of the Self." In *Narrative and Identity. Studies in Autobiography, Self and Culture,* edited by Jens Brockmeier, and Donal Carbaugh, 283–98. Amsterdam: John Benjamins Publishing Company, 2001.

French, Warren, and Weis, Alexander. "An Ethics of Care or an Ethics of Justice." *Journal of Business Ethics* 27, no. 1/2 (September 2000): 125–136.

Freud, Sigmund. *Civilization and Its Discontents.* New York: W.W. Norton & Company, 2010.

Frykenberg, Robert E., ed. *Christians and Missionaries in India. Cross-Cultural Communication Since 1500.* Grand Rapids: William B. Eerdmans, 2003.

Fukuyama, Francis. *The End of History and the Last Man*. New York: The Free Press, 1992.

Gagné, Isaac. "Religious Globalization and Reflexive Secularization in Japan." *Japan Review*, no. 30 (2017): 153–177.

Galanter, Marc. *Cults: Faith, Healing, and Coercion*, 2nd ed. New York: Oxford, 1999.

Gallagher, Eugene. "'Cults' and 'New Religious Movements.'" *History of Religions* 47, no. 2/3 (2007–2008): 205–220.

Gandhi, M. K. *Gandhi, An Autobiography, Or, The Story of My Experiments with Truth*. Translated from the Original Gujarati by Mahadev Desai. Delhi: Penguin Books, 2007.

Garraway, Doris L. "'What Is Mine': Césairean Negritude between the Particular and the Universal." *Research in African Literatures* 41, no. 1 (2010): 71–86.

Gautier, François. *The Guru of Joy: Sri Sri Ravi Shankar & the Art of Living*. New Delhi: Books Today, 2001.

Gehrig, Gail. "The American Civil Religion Debate: A Source for Theory Construction." *Journal for the Scientific Study of Religion* 20, no. 1 (1981): 51–63.

Gemzöe, Lena. "Ritual Creativity, Emotions and the Body." *Journal of Ritual Studies* 28, no. 2 (2014): 65–75.

Germond, Paul, and De Gruchy, Steve, eds. *Aliens in the Household of God: Homosexuality and Christian Faith in South Africa*. Cape Town: D. Philip, 1997.

Giddens, Anthony. *The Consequences of Modernity*. Stanford, CA: Stanford University Press, 1990.

Gilligan, James. *Violence: Reflection on a National Epidemic*. New York: Vintage Books, 1997.

Giovagnoli, Agostino, and Giunipero, Elisa, eds. *The Agreement between the Holy See and China. Chinese Catholics between Past and Future*. Rome: Urbaniana University Press, 2019.

Giri, Ananta Kumar. "Civil Society and the Limits of Identity Politics." *Sociological Bulletin* 50, no. 2 (September 2001): 266–285.

Glendinning, Tony, and Bruce, Steve. "Privatization or Deprivatization: British Attitudes About the Public Presence of Religion." *Journal for the Scientific Study of Religion* 50, no. 3 (September 2011): 503–516.

Gnanapragasam, Patrick. "Virtual Religion: Opening of Closures or Closing of Open Spaces?" *Asian Communication Research* 13, no. 2 (2016): 27–46.

Goldie, Peter. "Narrative Thinking, Emotion, and Planning." *The Journal of Aesthetics and Art Criticism* 67, no. 1 (2009): 97–106.

Goodson, Ivor F., and Gill, Scherto R. "The Concept of Narrative." *Counterpoints* 386 (2011): 3–16.

Gremillion, Joseph. *The Gospel of Peace and Justice. Catholic Social Teaching Since Pope John*. Maryknoll: Orbis, 1976.

Griffin, David Ray. *God and Religion in the Postmodern World*. New York: State University of New York Press, 1989.

Grimshaw, Mark, ed. *The Oxford Handbook of Virtuality*. Oxford and New York: Oxford University Press, 2014.

Gudavarthy, Ajay. "Human Rights Movement in India: State, Civil Society and Beyond." *Contributions to Indian Sociology (NS)* 42, no. 1 (2008): 29–57.

Gueneli, Berna. "Reframing Islam: The Decoupling of Ethnicity from Religion in Turkish-German Media." *Colloquia Germanica* 47, no. 1/2 (2014): 59–82.

Guha, Ramachandra. *Savaging the Civilized: Verrier Elwin, His Tribals, and India*. Chicago, Ill: University of Chicago Press, 1999.

Gunn, T. Jeremy. "Religion, Identity, and Morality in Public Schools." *Counterpoints* 374 (2009): 51–55.

Gutterman, David S., and Murphy, Andrew R. *Political Religion and Religious Politics: Navigating Identities in the United States*. New York and London: Routledge Series on Identity Politics, 2015.

Habito, Ruben. "International Conference on Religion and Globalization." *Buddhist-Christian Studies* 24 (2004): 241–243.

Haddad, Mahmoud. "Arab Religious Nationalism in the Colonial Era: Rereading Rashīd Riḍā's Ideas on the Caliphate." *Journal of the American Oriental Society* 117, no. 2 (April–June 1997): 253–277.

Haers, Jacques, Wilfred, Felix, Justaert, Kristien, and De Maeseneer, Yves. *Concilium 2013/1*. London: SCM Press, 2013.

Halbfass, Wilhelm. *Tradition and Reflection. Explorations in Indian Thought*. New York: State University of New York Press, 1991.

Hall, John R. "The Apocalypse at Jonestown." In *Cults and New Religious Movements: A Reader*, edited by Lorne L. Dawson, 186–207. Oxford: Wiley-Blackwell, 2003.

Hanna, Judith Lynne. "The Representation and Reality of Religion in Dance." *Journal of the American Academy of Religion* 56, no. 2 (Summer 1988): 281–306.

Hansen, Peter. "The Vietnamese State, the Catholic Church and the Law." In *Asian Socialism and Legal Change. The Dynamics of Vietnamese and Chinese Reform*, edited by Gillespie, John, Nicholson, Pip, 310–340. Canberra: ANU Press, 2005.

Hanson, Eric O. *Catholic Politics in China and Korea*. Maryknoll: Orbis Books, 1980.

Haque, Mahfuzul, Razzak, Abdur, and Centre for Human Rights. *A Tale of Refugees: Rohingyas in Bangladesh*. Dhaka: Centre for Human Rights, 1995.

Harper, Susan Billington. *In the Shadow of the Mahatma. Bishop V.S. Azariah and the Travails of Christianity in British India*. Grand Rapids: William B. Eerdmans, 2000.

Harris, Alana, ed. *The Schism of '68: Catholicism, Contraception and 'Humanae Vitae' in Europe, 1945–1975*. London: Palgrave Macmillan, 2018.

Hartman, Keith. *Congregations in Conflict: The Battle over Homosexuality in Nine Churches*. New Brunswick, NJ: Rutgers University Press, 1996.

Hawkins, Michael C. *Making Moros: Imperial Historicism and American Military Rule in the Philippines' Muslim South*. Illinois: Illinois University Press, 2012.

Haynes, J., ed. *Routledge Handbook of Religion and Politics*. New York: Routledge, 2009.

Hefner, Robert W. "Religious Resurgence in Contemporary Asia: Southeast Asian Perspectives on Capitalism, the State, and the New Piety." *The Journal of Asian Studies* 69, no. 4 (November 2010):1031–1047.

Heidegger, Martin. *Identity and Difference*, translated with an Introduction by Joan Stambaugh. Chicago, IL and London: University of Chicago Press, 2002.

Heiler, Friedrich, *Das Gebet. Eine Religionsgeschtliche und Religionspsychologische Untersuchung*, 5th ed. Munich: Nabu Press,1923.

Henn, Alexander. "Crossroads of Religions: Shrines, Mobility and Urban Space in Goa." *International Journal of Urban and Regional Research* 32 no. 3 (2008): 658–670.

Heredia, Rudolf C. "Religious Disarmament: Rethinking Religious Conversion in Asia." In *The Oxford Handbook of Christianity in Asia*, edited by Felix Wilfred, 257–272. New York: Oxford University Press, 2014.

Herzfeld, Noreen. "The Dangers of Religious Nationalism: Lessons from Srebrenica," *Dialog: A Journal of Theology*, no. 58 (2019): 16–21.

Heuser, Andreas, ed. *Pastures of Plenty. Tracing Religio-Scapes of Prosperity Gospel in Africa and Beyond*. Frankfurt a.M: Peter Lang, 2015.

Hexham, Irving, and Poewe, Karla O. *Understanding Cults and New Religions*. Grand Rapids: Eerdmans, 1986.

Hinchman, Lewis P. "Virtue or Autonomy: Alasdair MacIntyre's Critique of Liberal Individualism." *Polity* 21, no. 4 (Summer, 1989): 635–654.

Hinnellls, John. "South Asian Religions in Migration." In *The South Asian Religious Diaspora in Britain, Canada, and the United States*, edited by Coward, Harold, Hinnells, John R., and Williams, Raymond Brady, 1–12. Albany, NY: State University of New York Press, 2000.

Hinnenkamp, Volker, and Meng, Katharina, eds. *Sprachgrenzen überspringen: Sprachliche Hybridität Und Polykulturelles Selbstverständnis*. Tübingen: Narr, 2005.

Hirsch, Elisabeth Feist. "Martin Heidegger and the East." *Philosophy East and West* 20, no. 3 (1970): 247–63.

Hobbes, Thomas, "Of the Natural Condition of Mankind Concerning their Felicity and Misery." In *Leviathan*, edited by Richard Tuck, 86-90. Cambridge: Cambridge University Press, 1996.

Hoffmann, Gerhard, and Hornung, Alfred, eds. *Postmodernism and the fin de siè-cle*, vol. 81. Heidelberg: Universitätsverlag C. Winter, 2002.

Hoffmann, John P., and Bartkowski, John P. "Gender, Religious Tradition and Biblical Literalism." *Social Forces* 86, no. 3 (2008): 1245–72.

Hojsgaard, Morten T., and Warburg, Maargit, eds. *Religion and Cyberspace*. London: Routledge, 2005.

Hollenbach, David. *The Common Good and Christian Ethics*. Cambridge: Cambridge University Press, 2002.

Holmes, Nathaniel. "Lost in Translation? Multiple Religious Participation and Religious Fidelity." *The Journal of Religion* 94, no. 4 (2014): 425–435.

Homolka, Rabbi Walter, and Kung, Hans. *How to Do Good and Avoid Evil: A Global Ethic from the Sources of Judaism*. Vermont: SkyLight Paths Publishing, 2009.

Hoon, Shim Ja. "Doing God's Work for the Taliban, Korean Christian Missionaries End up Bolstering the Terrorists in Afghanistan." *Yale Global*, September 4, 2007.

Hopkins, Dwight N., Lorentzen, Lois Ann, Mendieta, Eduardo, and Batstone, David. "Religions/Globalizations: Theories and Cases." *African Studies Review* 45, no. 3 (December 2002): 57–62.

Horujy, Sergery S., ed., *Practices of the Self and Spiritual Practices. Michel Foucault and the Eastern Christian Discourse*. Grand Rapids: William Eerdmans Publishing Company, 2010.

Howell, J. Day, P. L. Nelson. "Structural Adaptation and 'Success' in the Transplantation of an Asian New Religious Movement: The Brahma Kumaris in the Western World, Part I." *Research in the Social Scientific Study of Religion: A Research Annual* 8 (1997): 1–34.

Huddy, Leonie. "From Social to Political Identity: A Critical Examination of Social Identity Theory." *Political Psychology* 22, no. 1 (2001): 127–156.

Huet, Michel, and Savary, Claude. *Africa Dances*. London: Thames & Hudson, 1995.

Human Rights Watch. *Dangerous Meditation. China's Campaign against Falungong*. New York: Human Rights Watch, 2002.

Huntington, Samuel P. *The Third Wave: Democratization in the Late Twentieth Century*. Oklahoma: University of Oklahoma Press, 1991.

Hurd, Elizabeth Shakman. *The Politics of Secularism in International Relations*. Princeton, NJ: Princeton University Press, 2008.

Ibry, David. *Exodus to Humanism: Jewish Identity without Religion*. Amherst, NY: Prometheus Books, 1999.

Inuzuka, Ako, and Fuchs, Thomas. "Memories of Japanese Militarism: The Yasukuni Shrine as a Commemorative Site." *The Journal of International Communication*, 20 (2014): 21–41.

Islamic Research Institute, International Islamic University, Islamabad. "Open Letter to His Holiness Pope Benedict XVI." *Islamic Studies* 45, no. 4 (Winter 2006): 604–613.

Issac, Jeffrey C. "Faith-Based Initiatives: A Civil Society Approach." *The Good Society* 12, no. 1 (2003): 1–10.

Jacobs, Alan, ed. *Osho: Living Dangerously: Ordinary Enlightenment for Extraordinary Times.* Watkins Masters of Wisdom. London: Watkins, 2011.

Jacobsen, Knut A., and Kumar, P. P., eds. *South Asians in the Diaspora. Histories and Religious Traditions.* Leiden and Boston: Brill, 2004.

Jacobsen, Knut A. "Hindu Processions, Diaspora, and Religious Pluralism." In *Religious Pluralism in the Diaspora,* edited by Kumar, P. Pratap, 163–174. Leiden: Brill Academic Publishers, 2005.

Jacobsen, Knut A., and Raj, Selva J., eds. *South Asian Christian Diaspora: Invisible Diaspora in Europe and North America.* Farnham: Ashgate, 2016.

Jacobsohn, Gary J. *The Wheel of Law: India's Secularism in Comparative Constitutional Context.* Princeton and Oxford: Princeton University Press, 2005.

Jaffrelot, Christophe. *The Hindu Nationalist Movement in India.* New York: Columbia University Press, 1996.

Jain, Prakash C., and Oommen, Ginu Zacharia, eds. *South Asian Migration to Gulf Countries: History, Policies, Development.* New York: Routledge, 2017.

Jameson, Fredric. *Postmodernism, or, The Cultural Logic of Late Capitalism.* London: Verso, 1991.

Janzen, R. "Reconsidering the Politics of Nature: Henri Lefebvre and The Production of Space." *Capitalism, Nature, Socialism* 13, no. 2 (2002): 96–116.

Jasper, James M. "Emotions and Social Movements: Twenty Years of Theory and Research." *Annual Review of Sociology* 37 (2011): 285–303.

Jeevanandam, S., and Pande, Rekha. *Devadasis in South India: A Journey from Sacred to Profane Spaces.* New Delhi: Kalpaz Publications, 2017.

Jenkins, Philip. *Mystics and Messiahs: Cults and New Religions in American History.* New York: Oxford University Press, 2000.

Johnson, Benton. "A Critical Appraisal of the Church-Sect Typology." *American Sociological Review* 22 (1957): 88–92.

Jones, Nicky. "Religious Freedom in a Secular Society: The Case of the Islamic Headscarf in France." In *Freedom of Religion under Bills of Rights,* edited by Paul, Babie, and Neville, Rochow, 216–38. South Australia: University of Adelaide Press, 2012.

Juergenmeyer, Mark. *The New Cold War? Religious Nationalism Confronts the Secular State.* Berkeley, LA and London: University of California Press, 1993.

Juergenmeyer, Mark. *Terror in the Mind of God. The Global Rise of Religious Violence.* Berkeley: University of California Press, 2000.

Junker-Kenny, Maureen. "Arguing for a Humanity of Equals: From Capabilities to Recognition." In *Negotiating Borders. Theological Explorations in the Global Era. Essays in Honor of Prof. Felix Wilfred,* edited by Patrick Gnanapragasam, and Elisabeth Schüssler Florenza, 242–257. Delhi: ISPCK, 2008.

Kakar, Sudhir, and Kakar, Katharina. *Indians: Portrait of a People.* Delhi: Penguin, 2009.

Kalam, Mohammed A. "Religious Conversions in Tamil Nadu: Can These Be Viewed as Protest Movements." *Indian Anthropologist* 20, no. 1/2 (1990): 39–48.

Kallestrup, Louise Nyholm, Toivo, Raisa Maria, eds. *Contesting Orthodoxy in Medieval and Early Modern Europe: Heresy, Magic and Witchcraft.* London: Palgrave Historical Studies in Witchcraft and Magic, 2017.

Kaltwasser, Cristóbal Rovira, Taggart, Paul A., and Ostiguy, Pierre, eds. *The Oxford Handbook of Populism,* 1st ed. New York: Oxford University Press, 2017.

Kane, Danielle, and Park, Jung Mee. "The Puzzle of Korean Christianity: Geopolitical Networks and Religious Conversion in Early Twentieth-Century East Asia." *American Journal of Sociology* 115, no. 2 (September 2009): 365–404.

Kanungo, Pralay. "Hindutva's Fury against Christians in Orissa." *Economic and Political Weekly* 43, no. 37 (2008): 16–19.

Kasper, Walter. *The Gospel of the Family.* New Jersey: Paulist, 2014.

Katz, Adam. *Postmodernism and the Politics of 'Culture'.* New York: Routledge, 2018.

Kaushik, Surendra Nath. *Ahmadiyya Community in Pakistan: Discrimination, Travail and Alienation.* New Delhi: South Asian Publishers, 1996.

Kearney, Richard, and Williams, James. "Narrative and Ethics." *Aristotelian Society, Supplementary* 70, no. 1 (1996): 29–62.

Ketchum, William C. *Simple Beauty: The Shakers in America (Art Movements).* New York: Todtri, 1996.

Khan, Mamnun, and Nizami, Shaykh Mohammed. "Writer of Supplementary Textual Content." In *Being British Muslims: Beyond Ethnocentric Religion and Identity Politics.* Bloomington: Author House, 2019.

Kim, Rebecca Y. *The Spirit Moves West: Korean Missionaries in America.* New York: Oxford University Press, 2015.

Kim, Sebastian. "Inter-Asia Mission and Global Missionary Movements from Asia." In *The Oxford Handbook of Christianity in Asia* edited by Felix Wilfred, 145–157. New York: Oxford University Press, 2014.

King, Ursula. *Turning Points in Religious Studies: Essays in Honour of Geoffrey Parrinder.* London: Bloomsbury Academic, 2016.

Kingston, Jeff. *The Politics of Religion, Nationalism, and Identity in Asia.* Lanham, MD: Rowman & Littlefield, 2019.

Kirkham, David M., ed. *State Responses to Minority Religions.* London and New York: Taylor & Francis Group, 2013.

Klaver, Miranda, and van de Kamp, Linda. "Embodied Temporalities in Global Pentecostal Conversion." *Ethnos* 76, no. 4 (2011): 421–425.

Klostermeier, Klaus. *Hinduism. A Short History.* Oxford: Oxford University Press, 2000.

Kobayashi, Hiroaki. "Religion in the Public Sphere: Challenges and Opportunities in Japan." *Brigham Young University Law Review* 3, no. 6 (2005): 683–710.

Koenig, Sarah. "Almighty God and the Almighty Dollar: The Study of Religion and Market Economies in the United States." *Religion Compass* 10 (2016): 83–97.

Koopmans, Ruud, and Statham, Paul. "Challenging the Liberal Nation-State? Postnationalism, Multiculturalism, and the Collective Claims Making of Migrants and Ethnic Minorities in Britain and Germany." *American Journal of Sociology* 105, no. 3 (November 1999): 652–696.

Kopf, David. *The Brahmosamaj and the Shaping of the Modern Indian Mind.* Princeton: Princeton University Press, 1979.

Kotler, Arnold, ed. *Engaged Buddhist Reader: Ten Years of Engaged Buddhist Publishing.* Berkeley: Parallax Press, 1996.

Kranenborg, R., and Rothstein, Mikael, eds. *New Religions in a Postmodern World.* Aarhus and Oxford: Aarhus University Press, 2003.

Kriesi, Hanspeter, et al. *New Social Movements in Western Europe: A Comparative Analysis,* Minneapolis: University of Minnesota Press, 1995.

Kubálková, Vendulka. "A 'Turn to Religion' in International Relations?" *Perspectives* 17, no. 2 (2009): 13–41.

Küng, Hans, and Schmidt, Helmut. *A Global Ethic and Global Responsibilities: Two Declarations.* London: SCM Press, 1998.

Küng, Hans. *Global Responsibility: In Search of a New World Ethic.* New York: Crossroad Publishers, 1991.

Kuru, Ahmet T. "Globalization and Diversification of Islamic Movements: Three Turkish Cases." *Political Science Quarterly* 120, no. 1 (Summer 2005): 253–274.

Kuzminski, Adrian. *Fixing the System: A History of Populism, Ancient and Modern.* New York and London: Bloomsbury Publishing, 2008.

Kymlicka, Will. *Contemporary Political Philosophy: An Introduction* 2nd ed. Oxford: Oxford University Press, 2002.

Laborde, Cécile, Norton, Anne, Downs, Donald, Sinno, Abdulkader, and Warner, Carolyn M. "The Danish Cartoon Controversy and the Challenges of Multicultural Politics: A Discussion of 'The Cartoons That Shook the World'." *Perspectives on Politics* 9, no. 3 (2011): 603–19.

Laksana, Albertus Bagus. "Multiple Religious Belonging or Complex Identity? An Asian Way of Being Religious." In *The Oxford Handbook of Christianity,* edited by Felix Wilfred, 493–509. New York: Oxford University Press, 2014.

Lal, Vinay. "Too Deep for Ecology: Gandhi and the Ecological Vision of Life." In *Hinduism and Ecology: The Intersection of Earth, Sky, and Water*, edited by Christopher Key Chapple and Mary Evelyn Tucker, 206. Cambridge, MA: Harvard University Center for the Study of World Religions, 2000.

Lambert, Tony. *China's Christian Millions*. Oxford: Monarch, 2006.

LaMothe, Kimerer L. "What Bodies Know about Religion and the Study of It." *Journal of the American Academy of Religion* 76, no. 3 (September 2008): 573–601.

Langer, Robert, and Simon, Udo. "The Dynamics of Orthodoxy and Heterodoxy: Dealing with Divergence in Muslim Discourses and Islamic Studies." *Die Welt des Islams* 48, no. 3/4 (2008): 273–88.

Larson, Gerald James, ed. *Religion and Personal Law in Secular India: A Call to Judgment*. Bloomington: Indiana University Press, 2001.

Laven, Mary. *Mission to China: Matteo Ricci and the Jesuit Encounter with the East*. London: Faber & Faber, Bloomsbury, 2011.

Lefebvre, Henri. *The Production of Space*. Oxford: Blackwell, 1991.

Lemert, Charles C. "Defining Non-Church Religion." *Review of Religious Research* 16, no. 3, (Spring, 1975): 186–197.

Leslie, Julia, and McGee, Mary, eds. *Invented Identities: The Interplay of Gender, Religion and Politics in India*. Delhi and Oxford: Oxford University Press, 2000.

Leve, Lauren. "Identity." *Current Anthropology* 52, no. 4 (August 2011): 513–535.

Lew, Seok-Choon, Choi, Woo-Young, and Wang, Hye Suk. "Confucian Ethics and the Spirit of Capitalism in Korea: The Significance of Filial Piety." *Journal of East Asian Studies* 11, no. 2 (2011): 171–96.

Lewis, James R., and Petersen, Jesper A. *Controversial New Religions*, 2nd ed. New York: Oxford University Press, 2014.

Li, MinQi. "Socialism, Capitalism, and Class Struggle: The Political Economy of Modern China." *Economic and Political Weekly* 43, no. 52 (December 27, 2008): 77–85.

Linden, Ian, and Thorp, Thomas. "Religious Conflicts and Peace Building in Nigeria." *Journal of Religion and Violence* 4, no. 1 (2016): 85–100.

Lo, Dic, and Zhang, Yu. "Globalisation Meets Its Match: Lessons from China's Economic Transformation." *Economic and Political Weekly* 43, no. 52 (December 27, 2008): 97–102.

Loh, Francis Kok-Wah, Öjendal, Joakim, eds., and Institute of Southeast Asian Studies. *Southeast Asian Responses to Globalization: Restructuring Governance and Deepening Democracy*. Copenhagen and Singapore: NIAS Press and Institute of Southeast Asian Studies, 2005.

Lothe, Jakob, and Hawthorn, Jeremy, eds. "The Ethical (Re)turn." In *Narrative Ethics*, vol. 267, 1–10. The Netherlands: Brill, 2013.

Lovelace, Douglas C. ed. *Terrorism: Commentary on Security Documents. The Evolution of the Islamic State*, vol. 143. New York: Oxford University Press, 2016.

Lowe, Scott. "Chinese and International Contexts for the Rise of Falun Gong." *Nova Religio: The Journal of Alternative and Emergent Religions* 6, no. 2 (2003): 263–76.

Lucas, Phillip Charles. "New Religious Movements and the 'Acids' of Postmodernity." *Nova Religio: The Journal of Alternative and Emergent Religions* 8, no. 2 (November 2004): 28–47.

Luo, Qiangqiang, and Andreas, Joel. "Using Religion to Resist Rural Dispossession: A Case Study of a Hui Muslim Community in North-west China." *The China Quarterly* 226 (2016): 477–498.

MacInnis, Donald E. *Religion in China Today: Policy and Practice*. Maryknoll: Orbis Books, 1989.

Madan, T. N. "Freedom of Religion." *Economic and Political Weekly* 38, no. 11 (March 15–21, 2003): 1034–1041.

Madan, T. N. *Modern Myths, Locked Minds: Secularism and Fundamentalism in India*. Delhi: Oxford University Press, 1998.

Mahajan, Gurpreet. *Identities and Rights: Aspects of Liberal Democracy in India*. New Delhi: Oxford University Press, 2001.

Malik, Sadia M. "Horizontal Inequalities and Violent Conflict in Pakistan: Is There a Link?." *Economic and Political Weekly* 44, no. 34 (August 22, 2009): 21–24.

Mallampalli, Chandra. *Race, Religion, and Law in Colonial India: Trials of an Interracial Family*. Cambridge and New York: Cambridge University Press, 2011.

Manea, Elham. *Women and Shari'a Law: The Impact of Legal Pluralism in the UK*. London and New York: I.B. Tauris, 2016.

Mar, Maria del, Logroño, Narbona, Pinto, Paulo G., Karam, John Tofik, eds. *Crescent over Another Horizon: Islam in Latin America, the Caribbean, and Latino USA*. Austin: University of Texas Press, 2015.

Margry, Peter Jan. "Memorialising Europe: Revitalising and Reframing a 'Christian' Continent." *Anthropological Journal of European Cultures* 17, no. 2 (2008): 6–33.

Marler, Penny Long, and Hadaway, C. Kirk. "'Being Religious' or 'Being Spiritual' in America: A Zero-Sum Proposition?." *Journal for the Scientific Study of Religion* 41, no. 2 (June 2002): 289–300.

Martin, Walter, Rische, Jill Martin, and Van Gorden, Kurt. *The Kingdom of the Occult*. Nashville, TN: Thomas Nelson, 2008.

Marty, Martin E. "Explaining the Rise of Fundamentalism." *Bulletin of the American Academy of Arts and Sciences* 46, no. 5 (February 1993): 5–9.

Marty, Martin E. "The Future of World Fundamentalisms." *American Philosophical Society* 142, no. 3 (September 1998): 367–377.

Marty, Martin E., and Appleby, R. Scott, eds. *Fundamentalism Observed*. Chicago: University of Chicago Press, 1991.

Mathew, George. "Politicisation of Religion: Conversions to Islam in Tamil Nadu." *Economic and Political Weekly* 17, no. 26 (1982): 1068–072.

Mathew, Sam P., and Martin, Chandran Paul, eds. *Waters of Life and Death. Ethical and Theological Responses to Contemporary Water Crisis*. Delhi: UELCI/ISPCK, 2005.

Mayrl, William W. "'Marx' Theory of Social Movements and The Church-Sect Typology." *Sociological Analysis* 37, no. 1 (1976): 19–31.

Mazumdar, Sucheta. "Women on the March: Right-Wing Mobilization in Contemporary India." *Feminist Review*, no. 49 (1995):1–28.

McAlister, Elizabeth. "Globalization and the Religious Production of Space." *Journal for the Scientific Study of Religion* 44, no. 3 (2005): 249–255.

McGaughey, Douglas R. "Ricoeur's Metaphor and Narrative Theories as a Foundation for a Theory of Symbol." *Religious Studies* 24, no. 4 (1988): 415–37.

McIntyre-Mills, Janet. "Challenging Economic and Religious Fundamentalisms: Implications for the State, the Market and 'the Enemies Within'." *International Journal of Applied Systemic Studies*, vol. 1 (2007): 49–67.

Mead, George Herbert, Huebner, Daniel R., and Joas, Hans. *Mind, Self, and Society: The Definitive Edition*, edited by Morris, Charles W. Chicago: University of Chicago Press, 2015.

Meintel, Deirdre, and Mossière, Géraldine. "In the Wake of the Quiet Revolution: From Secularization to Religious Cosmopolitanism." *Anthropologica* 55, no. 1 (2013): 57–71.

Melé, Domènec, and Sánchez-Runde, Carlos. "Introduction: Cultural Diversity and Universal Ethics in a Global World." *Journal of Business Ethics* 116, no. 4 (September 2013): 681–687.

Menashri, David. *The Iranian Revolution and The Muslim World*. London: Routledge, 2019.

Metz, Johann Baptist, Schillebeeckx, Edward, and Lefebvre, Marcus, eds. *Orthodoxy and Heterodoxy*. Edinburgh: T & T Clark, 1987.

Mickler, Michael L., and Lewis, James R. eds. *The Unification Church*. New York: London: Garland, 1990.

Miller, Robert A. "The Ethics Narrative and the Role of the Business School in Moral Development." *Journal of Business Ethics* 90, Supplement 3 (2009): 287–293.

Min, Pyong Gap. "The Structure and Social Functions of Korean Immigrant Churches in the United States." *The International Migration Review* 26, no. 4 (1992): 1370–394.

Mitchell, Claire. "The Religious Content of Ethnic Identities." *Sociology* 40, no. 6 (2006):1135–1152.

Mitrofanova, Anastasia. "Russian Ethnic Nationalism and Religion Today." In *The New Russian Nationalism: Imperialism, Ethnicity and Authoritarianism 2000–2015*, edited by Kolstø, Pål, 104–31. Edinburgh: Edinburgh University Press, 2016.

Mollat, Michel. *Les pauvres au moyen âge*. Paris: Hachette, 1978.

Morris, D. B. "Narrative, Ethics, and Pain: Thinking with Stories." *Narrative*. 9, no. 1 (2001): 55–77.

Mouw, Richard J. "Alasdair MacIntyre on Reformation Ethics." *The Journal of Religious Ethics* 13, no. 2 (1985): 243–57.

Mullins, Mark R. "Japanese Response to Imperialist Secularization: The Postwar Movement to Restore Shinto in the Public Sphere." In *Multiple Secularities Beyond the West: Religion and Modernity in the Global Age*, edited by Burchardt, Marian, et al., 141–167. Boston and Berlin and Munich: De Gruyter, 2015.

Murray, John Courtney. *The Problem of Religious Freedom*. Westminster: The Newman Press, 1965.

Nagel, Stephan. *Brahmas Geheime Schöpfung: Die Indische Reformbewegung Der "Brahma Kumaris": Quellen, Lehre, Raja Yoga*. Frankfurt Am Main: P. Lang, 1999.

Nakamaki, Hirochika. *Japanese Religions at Home and Abroad: Anthropological Perspectives*. London: Routledge, 2003.

Napoleoni, Loretta. *Merchants of Men: How Kidnapping, Ransom and Trafficking Funds Terrorism and ISIS*, Main ed. London: Atlantic Books, 2017.

Nelson, Geoffrey K. "The Spiritualist Movement and the Need for a Redefinition of 'Cult'." *Journal for the Scientific Study of 'Religion'* 8, no. 1 (Spring, 1969): 152–160.

Nietzsche, Friedrich. *On Truth and Untruth*. New York: Harperperennnial, 2010.

Noorani, A. G. "The Babri Masjid-Ram Janmabhoomi Question." *Economic and Political Weekly* 24, no. 44/45 (1989): 2461–466.

Nussbaum, Martha C. *The New Religious Intolerance: Overcoming the Politics of Fear in an Anxious Age*. Cambridge, MA and London: Harvard University Press, 2012.

O'Brien, David M., and Ohkoshi, Yasuo. *To Dream of Dreams: Religious Freedom and Constitutional Politics in Postwar Japan*. Honolulu: University of Hawaii Press, 1996.

O'Hanlon, Gerry. "Religious Freedom." *The Furrow* 64, no. 2 (February 2013): 67–77.

Olarinmoye, Omobolaji Ololade. "Faith-Based Organizations and Development Prospects and Constraints." *Transformation* 29, no. 1 (January 2012): 1–14.

Olson, Carl. *Religious Studies: The Key Concepts*. London and New York: Routledge, 2011.

Omvedt, Gail. *Dalits and the Democratic Revolution: Dr. Ambedkar and the Dalit Movement in Colonial India.* New Delhi and London: Sage, 1994.

Oonk, Gijsbert, ed. *Global Indian Diasporas: Exploring Trajectories of Migration and Theory.* Amsterdam: Amsterdam University Press, 2007.

Osho. *Returning to the Source,* 2nd ed. Shaftesbury: Element, 1995.

Otten, Cathy. *With Ash on Their Faces: Yezidi Women and the Islamic State.* New York and London: OR Books, 2017.

Owens, Timothy J., Robinson, Dawn T., and Smith-Lovin, Lynn. "Three Faces of Identity." *Annual Review of Sociology* 36 (2010): 477–499.

Pace, Stefano. "Does Religion Affect the Materialism of Consumers? An Empirical Investigation of Buddhist Ethics and the Resistance of the Self." *Journal of Business Ethics* 112, no. 1 (2013): 25–46.

Padmanabhan, Sudarsan. "Debate on Indian History: Revising Textbooks in California." *Economic and Political Weekly* 41, no. 18 (2006): 1761–763.

Pande, Anupa. *A Historical and Cultural Study of the Nāṭyśāstra of Bharata.* Jodhpur: Kusumanjali, 1991.

Panikkar, K.N., ed. *The Concerned Indian's Guide to Communalism.* New York: Viking, 1999.

Parish, Steven M. *Hierarchy and Its Discontents: Culture and the Politics of Consciousness in Caste Society.* Philadelphia: University of Pennsylvania Press, 1996.

Parvez, Z. Fareen. *Politicizing Islam. The Islamic Revival in France and India.* New Delhi: Oxford University Press, 2017.

Pathak, V. "Indian Diaspora in South Africa." *Africa Quarterly* 43, no. 1 (2003): 72–85.

Pauwels, Teun. *Populism in Western Europe: Comparing Belgium, Germany and the Netherlands.* London and New York: Routledge, 2014.

Peek, Lori. "Becoming Muslim: The Development of a Religious Identity." *Sociology of Religion* 66, no. 3 (2005): 215–242.

Penny, Benjamin. *The Religion of Falun Gong.* Chicago: Chicago University Press, 2012.

Pereira, Shane N. "A New Religious Movement in Singapore: Syncretism and Variation in the Sathya Sai Baba Movement." *Asian Journal of Social Science.* 36, no. 2 (2008): 250–270.

Perry, Michael J. "Liberal Democracy and the Right to Religious Freedom." *The Review of Politics* 71, no. 4 (2009): 621–35.

Phan, Peter. *Christianity with an Asian Face. Asian American Theology in the Making.* Maryknoll: Orbis Books, 2003.

Piirimäe, Pärtel. "The Explanation of Conflict in Hobbes's Leviathan." *Trames* 10, no. 60/55 (2006): 1–21.

Pilario, Franklin, Wilfred, Felix, and Po Ho, Huang, eds. "Asian Christianities." In *Concilium 2018/1.* London: SCM Press, 2018.

Podipara, Placid J. *The Thomas Christians*. London: Darton, Longman & Todd, 1966.

Pontoniere, Paolo. "Al Quaeda—Call it a Cult." *Asia Week*, November 22, 2001.

Postman, Neil. *Technopoly: The Surrender of Culture to Technology*. New York: Vintage Books, 1993.

Prabhu, Anjali. *Hybridity: Limits, Transformations, Prospects*. Albany: State University of New York Press, 2007.

Pridemore, W.A., and Freilich, J.D. "The Impact of State Laws Protecting Abortion Clinics and Reproductive Rights on Crimes Against Abortion Providers: Deterrence, Backlash, or Neither?" *Law and Human Behavior* 31, no. 6 (2007): 611–27.

Pui-lan, Kwok. "2011 Presidential Address: Empire and the Study of Religion." *Journal of the American Academy of Religion* 80, no. 2 (2012): 285–303.

Puri, Balraj. "Amartya Sen and Identities." *Economic and Political Weekly* 41, no. 26 (June 30–July 7, 2006): 2690–2944.

Purvis, Zachary. "Quiet War in Germany: Friedrich Schelling and Friedrich Schleiermacher." *Journal of the History of Ideas* 76, no. 3 (July 2015): 369–391.

Puttick, Elizabeth. "Women in New Religious Movements." In *Cults and New Religious Movements: A Reader*, edited by Dawson, Lorne L., 230–244. Oxford: Wiley-Blackwell, 2003.

Rai, Lajpat. *A History of the Arya Samaj*, rev. ed. Bombay: Orient Longmans, 1967.

Raj, Selva J. "New Land, New Challenges: The Role of Religion in the Acculturation of Syro-Malabar Catholics in Chicago." In *South Asian Christian Diaspora. Histories and Religious Traditions*, edited by Jacobsen, Knut A., and Raj, Selva J., 183–196. Leiden and Boston: Brill, 2004.

Rajamanickam, S., ed. *Adaptation*. Palayamkottai: De Nobili Research Institute, 1971.

Rajan, Gita, and Sharma, Shailja, eds. *New Cosmopolitanisms: South Asians in the US*. Stanford: Stanford University Press, 2006.

Rambo, Lewis R., and Farhadian, Charles, eds. *The Oxford Handbook of Religious Conversion*. New York: Oxford University Press, 2014.

Ravenscroft, Ruth Jackson. *An Analysis of Friedrich Schleiermacher's On Religion: Speeches to its Cultured Despisers*. London and New York: The Macat Library, 2018.

Rawls, John. *Political Liberalism*. New York: Columbia University Press, 1993.

Reader, Ian. "Imagined Persecution: Aum Shinrikyo, Millennialism and the Legitimation of Violence." In *Millennium, Persecution, and Violence: Historical Cases*, edited by Wessinger, Catherine, 138–152. Syracuse: Syracuse University Press, 2000.

Reinhartz, Adele, and Dannin, Robert. *Black Pilgrimage to Islam*. Oxford and New York: Oxford University Press, 2005.

Revelli, Marco. *The New Populism: Democracy Stares into the Abyss*, translated by David Broder. London and New York: Verso, 2019.

Richards, Patricia. "Decolonizing Globalization Studies." *The Global South* 8, no. 2 (2014): 139–154.

Ricoeur, Paul. *Soi-meme comme un autre*. Paris: Seuil, 1990.

Riera-Gil, Elvira. "The Communicative Value of Local Languages: An Underestimated Interest in Theories of Linguistic Justice." *Ethnicities* 19 (2019): 174–99.

Robbins, Thomas. "'Quo Vadis' the Scientific Study of New Religious Movements?" *Journal for the Scientific Study of Religion* 39, no. 4 (2000): 515–23.

Robinson, James M. "Scripture and Theological Method: A Protestant Study in 'Sensus Plenior'." *The Catholic Biblical Quarterly* 27, no. 1 (1965): 6–27.

Rochford, E. Burke. *Hare Krishna in America*. New Brunswick, NJ: Rutgers University Press, 1985.

Roger, Frère. *Communauté De Taizé*. Taizé: Les Presses De Taizé, 1980.

Roopesh, O.B. "Sabarimala Protest." *Economic and Political Weekly of India* 43, no. 53 (December 15, 2018).

Rorty, Richard. "Responses." In *Deconstruction and Pragmatism* edited by Chantal Mouffe. London and New York: Routledge, 1996.

Rorty, Richard. *Contingency, Irony, and Solidarity*. Cambridge: Cambridge University Press, 1989.

Rorty, Richard. *Philosophy as Cultural Politics: Philosophical Papers*, vol. 4. Cambridge: University Press, 2007.

Ross, Kenneth R., Jeyaraj, Daniel, and Johnson, Todd M., eds. *Christianity in South and Central Asia*. Edinburgh: Edinburgh Companions to Global Christianity, 2019.

Rowe, Paul S., ed. *The Routledge Handbook of Minorities in the Middle East*, London: Routledge, 2018.

Roy, Olivier. *Holy Ignorance. When Religion and Culture Part Ways*. London: Hurst & Company, 2010.

Rudnyckyj, Daromir, and Osella, Filippo, eds. *Religion and the Morality of the Market*. Cambridge: Cambridge University Press, 2017.

Ryan, Columba. "The Second Vatican Council and Religious Freedom." *Blackfriars* 45, no. 531 (1964): 355–67.

Sachs, Ignacy. "From Poverty Trap to Inclusive Development in LDC'S." *Economic and Political Weekly* 39, no. 18 (May 1, 2004): 1802–1811.

Sahoo, Ajaya Kumar, and De Kruijf, Johannes G. *Indian Transnationalism Online: New Perspectives on Diaspora*. London and New York: Routledge, 2014.

Said, Edward. *Orientalism. Western Conception of the Orient*. London: Penguin Books, 1978.

Salim, Arskal. *Challenging the Secular State: The Islamization of Law in Modern Indonesia.* Honolulu: University of Hawaii Press, 2008.

Sandal, Nukhet, and Fox, John. *Religion in International Relations Theory: Interactions and Possibilities.* London and New York: Routledge, 2013.

Sandel, Michael. *Public Philosophy. Essays on Morality in Politics.* Harvard: Harvard University Press, 2005.

Santiago, J. "From 'Civil Religion' to Nationalism as the Religion of Modern Times: Rethinking a Complex Relationship." *Journal for the Scientific Study of Religion* 48 (2009): 394–401.

Sarkar, Sumit. "Conversions and Politics of Hindu Right." *Economic and Political Weekly* 34, no. 26 (1999): 1691–700.

Sassen, Saskia. *Globalization and Its Discontents.* New York: The New Press, 1998.

Scharlemann, Robert P., ed. *Theology at the End of the Century: A Dialogue on the Postmodern.* Charlottesville: University Press of Virginia, 1990.

Schleiermacher, Friedrich. *On Religion. Speeches to Its Cultured Despisers: Introduction, Translation, and Notes.* Cambridge: Cambridge University Press, 1988.

Schneewind, J. B. "Virtue, Narrative, and Community: MacIntyre and Morality." *The Journal of Philosophy* 79, no. 11 (1982): 653–63.

Schumacher, E.F. *Small is Beautiful. A Study of Economics as if People Mattered.* New Delhi: Radha Krishna, 1977.

Sébastia, Brigitte. *Caste et christianisme à Vailankanni,* Pondicherry: CIDIF, 2008.

Selden, Mark. "Japan, the United States and Yasukuni Nationalism." *Economic and Political Weekly* 43, no. 45 (2008): 71–77.

Sen, Amartya, and Drèze, Jean. *An Uncertain Glory. India and Its Contradictions.* London: Allan Lane, 2013.

Seneviratne, H.L., ed. *Identity, Consciousness and the Past.* Delhi: Oxford University Press, 1999.

Shannon, Jonathan H. "The Aesthetics of Spiritual Practice and the Creation of Moral and Musical Subjectivities in Aleppo, Syria." *Ethnology* 43, no. 4 (Autumn, 2004): 381–391.

Sharma, Arvind. *Modern Hindu Thought. The Essential Texts.* Delhi: Oxford University Press, 2002.

Sharma, Satish Kumar. *Social Movements and Social Change: A Study of Arya Samaj and Untouchables in Punjab.* Delhi: B.R. Pub., 1985.

Sheedy, Matt, ed. *Identity, Politics and the Study of Islam: Current Dilemmas in the Study of Religions.* Indonesia: Equinox Publishing, 2018.

Shekhar, Vibhanshu. "Malay Majoritarianism and Marginalised Indians." *Economic and Political Weekly* 43, no. 8 (February 23, 2008): 22–25.

Shiva, Vandana, and Holla, R. "Intellectual Piracy and the Neem Tree." *The Ecologist* 23, no. 6 (1993): 223–227.

Shive, Glenn. "Refugees, Minorities and Religion: A Case Study of Hong Kong in 1945–1960." *International Journal of Asian Christianity* 3, no. 1 (March 2020): 107–120.

Sievers, Angelika, Bhardwaj, Surinder Mohan, and Rinschede, Gisbert, eds. "Pilgrimage in World Religions: Presented to Prof. Dr. Angelika Sievers on the Occasion of Her 75th Birthday." in *Geographia Religionum*, Bd. 4. Berlin: D. Reimer, 1988.

Singh, Baljit. "Politics of Identities: Global, South Asian and Indian Perspective." *The Indian Journal of Political Science* 67, no. 2 (2006): 205–20.

Singh, Pashaura, and Fenech, Louis E. eds. *The Oxford Handbook of Sikh Studies*. New Delhi: Oxford University Press, 2014.

Skultans, Vieda. "The Brahma Kumaris and the Role of Women." In *Women as Teachers and Disciples in Traditional and New Religions* edited by Elizabeth Puttick, and Peter B. Clarke, 47–62. Lewiston: The Edwin Mellen Press, 1993.

Slater, David. "Post-Colonial Questions for Global Times." *Review of International Political Economy* 5, no. 4 (1998): 647–678.

Smith, Anthony D. *Theories of Nationalism*. New York: Harper & Row, 1971.

Smith, Janet E. *Humanae Vitae, a Generation Later: A Generation Later.* Washington, DC: Catholic University of America Press, 1991a.

Smith, Malcolm C. "Early French Advocates of Religious Freedom." *The Sixteenth Century Journal* 25, no. 1 (1994): 29–51.

Smith, Wilfred Cantwell. *The Meaning and End of Religion*. Minneapolis: Fortress Press, 1991b.

Sobrino, Jon, and Wilfred, Felix, eds. "Globalization and its Victims." *Concilium* 2001/5. London: SCM Press, 2001.

Sökefeld, Martin. "Reconsidering Identity." *Anthropos* 96, no. 2. (2001): 527–544.

Somers, Margaret R. "The Narrative Constitution of Identity: A Relational and Network Approach." *Theory and Society* 23, no. 5 (October 1994): 605–649.

South Asia Human Rights Documentation Centre. "Anti-Conversion Laws: Challenges to Secularism and Fundamental Rights." *Economic and Political Weekly* 43, no. 2 (2008): 63–73.

Spivak, Gayatri Chakravorty. "Criticism, Feminism, and the Institution." *Sage Journal* 10-11, no. 1 (1985): 175–187.

Srinivas, Tulasi. "The Sathya Sai Baba Movement." In *The Cambridge Companion to New Religious Movements*, edited by Ola Hammaer and Mikael Rothstein, 184–197. Cambridge: Cambridge University Press, 2012.

Srivastava, D. K. "Personal Laws and Religious Freedom." *Journal of the Indian Law Institute* 18, no. 4 (1976): 551–86.

Stackhouse, Max L., and Paris, Peter, eds. *God and Globalization*. New York: T & T Clark, 2007.

BIBLIOGRAPHY 355

Stammers, Neil. *Human Rights and Social Movements*. London and New York: Pluto Press, 2009.

Stark, Rodney, and Bainbridge, William Sims. *A Theory of Religion* [with a New Foreword by Jeffrey K. Hadden]. New Brunswick, NJ: Rutgers University Press, 1996.

Stark, Rodney, and Bainbridge, William Sims. *The Future of Religion: Secularization, Revival and Cult Formation*. Berkeley: University of California Press, 1984.

Stein, Stephen J. *The Shaker Experience in America: A History of the United Society of Believers*. New Haven and London: Yale University Press, 1992.

Stepan, Alfred. "The Multiple Secularisms of Modern Democratic and Non-Democratic Regimes." In *Rethinking Secularism*, edited by Craig Calhoun, Mark Juergensmeyer, Jonathan VanAntwerpen. New York: Oxford University Press, 2011.

Stievano, Alessandro, Olsen, Douglas, Ymelda, Tolentino Diaz, Laura, Sabatino, and Rocco, Gennaro. "Indian Nurses in Italy: A Qualitative Study of Their Professional and Social Integration." *Journal of Clinical Nursing* 26 (2017): 4234–245.

Stiglitz, Joseph. *The Roaring Nineties*. London: Penguin Books, 2003.

Striblen, Cassie. "Collective Responsibility and the Narrative Self." *Social Theory and Practice* 39, no. 1 (2013): 147–65.

Sudesh, Sister. "Women as Spiritual Leaders in the Brahma Kumaris." In *Women as Teachers and Disciples in Traditional and New Religions*, edited by Elizabeth Puttick, and Peter B. Clarke, 39–46. Lewiston: The Edwin Mellen Press, 1993.

Sullivan, Winnifred Fallers. "We Are All Religious Now. Again." *Social Research* 76, no. 4 (Winter 2009): 1181–1198.

Swatos, William H. "Weber or Troeltsch? Methodology, Syndrome, and the Development of Church-Sect Theory." *Journal for the Scientific Study of Religion* 15, no. 2 (1976): 129–44.

Swatos, William H., and Kaelber, Lutz, eds. *The Protestant Ethic Turns 100: Essays on the Centenary of the Weber Thesis*. Colorado, USA and London: Paradigm, 2005.

Tagore, Rabindranath. *Nationalism* (1917). Calcutta: Rupa & Co 1992.

Tan, Jonathan. *Introducing Asian American Theologies*. New York: Orbis Books, 2009.

Taylor, Charles. "The Politics of Recognition." In *Multiculturalism: Examining the Politics of Recognition*, edited by Appiah, K Anthony, et al., 25–74. Princeton: Princeton University Press, 1994.

Taylor, Charles. *Sources of the Self. The Making of Modern Identity*. Cambridge: Cambridge University Press, 1989.

Tayob, Abdulkader. "Religion, Culture and Identity in a Democratic Society." *Journal for the Study of Religion* 15, no. 2 (2002): 5–13.

Temperman, Jeroen. *State-religion Relationships and Human Rights Law: Towards a Right to Religiously Neutral Governance.* Leiden: BRILL, 2010.

Thapar, Romila, Noorani, A. G., and Sadanand Menon. *On Nationalism.* Delhi: Aleph, 2016.

Thapar, Romila, Noorani, A. G., and Menon Sadanand. "Ethics, Religion, and Social Protest in the First Millennium B.C. in Northern India." *Daedalus* 104, no. 2, (Spring, 1975): 119–132.

Thomas, M.M. *Christian Participation in Nation-Building.* Bangalore: Institute for the Study of Religion and Society, 1960.

Thomas, Paul, and Sanderson, Pete. "Unwilling Citizens? Muslim Young People and National Identity." *Sociology* 45, no. 6 (December 2011): 1028–1044.

Thompson, William R, and Reuveny, Rafael. *Limits to Globalization: North-South Divergence.* London: Routledge, 2010.

Thottakkara, Augustine, ed. *Dialogical Dynamics of Religions.* Rome: CIIS, 1993.

Todd, Malcolm J., and Taylor, Gary, eds., with a Foreword by Frank Furedi. *Democracy and Participation: Popular Protest and New Social Movements.* London: Merlin Press, 2004.

Torri, Davide, and Riboli, Diana, eds. *Shamanism and Violence: Power, Repression and Suffering in Indigenous Religious Conflicts.* London: Routledge, 2013.

Trijono, Lambang, ed. *The Making of Ethnic and Religious Conflicts in Southeast Asia: Cases and Resolutions.* Yogyakarta: CSPS Books, 2004.

Troeltsch, Ernst. *The Social Teachings of the Christian Churches.* London: Allen & Unwin, 1931.

Ukiwo, Ukoha. "Politics, Ethno-Religious Conflicts and Democratic Consolidation in Nigeria." *The Journal of Modern African Studies* 41, no. 1 (2003): 115–138.

Urban, Hugh B. *Zorba the Buddha: Sex, Spirituality, and Capitalism in the Global Osho Movement.* Oakland: University of California Press, 2015.

Van Allen, Rodger. "John Cogley's Dissent from 'Humanae Vitae'." *U.S. Catholic Historian,* 26, no. 3 (2008): 69–83.

Van der Veer, Peter, and Vertovec, Steven, eds. *Aspects of South Asian Diaspora.* OUP, Delhi, 1991.

Van der Veer, Peter. *Religious Nationalism: Hindus and Muslims in India.* Berkeley and London: University of California Press, 1994.

Van Straelen, Henry, "The Religion of Divine Wisdom: Japan's Most Powerful Religious Movement." *Folklore Studies* 13 (1954): 1–166.

Vance, Laura Lee. *Women in New Religions.* NY: New York University Press, 2015.

Varga, I. "The Body—The New Sacred? The Body in Hypermodernity." *Current Sociology* 53, no. 2 (2005): 209–235.

Vatter, Miguel. "The Idea of Public Reason and the Reason of State: Schmitt and Rawls on the Political." *Political Theory* 36, no. 2 (2008): 239–71.

Vattimo, Gianni. *After Christianity.* New York: Columbia University Press, 2002.

Vertovec, Steven. "Hinduism in Diaspora: The Transformation of Tradition in Trinidad." In *Hinduism Reconsidered*, edited by Gunther D. Sontheimer and Herman Kulke, 157–186. Delhi: Manohar, 1991.

Vinolo, Stéphane. *René Girard: du mimétisme à l'hominisation: La violence différante.* Paris: Harmattan, 2005.

Viswanathan, Gauri. *Outside the Fold: Conversion, Modernity, and Belief.* Princeton, NJ and Chichester: Princeton University Press, 1998.

Von Stietencron, Heinrich. "Hinduism: On the Proper Use of a Deceptive Term." In *Hinduism Reconsidered,* edited by Günther D. Sontheimer and Herman Kulke, 11–27. Delhi: Manohar, 1991.

Wallerstein, Robert S. "Erikson's Concept of Ego Identity Reconsidered." *Journal of the American Psychoanalytic Association* 46, no. 1 (1998): 229–48.

Wallis, John. *The Brahma Kumaris as a 'Reflexive Tradition': Responding to Late Modernity,* 1st ed. London: Routledge, 2017.

Walvin, James. *Crossings: Africa, the Americas and the Atlantic Slave Trade.* London: Reaktion Books Limited, 2013.

Wani, Milind, and Kothari, Ashish. "Globalisation vs India's Forests." *Economic and Political Weekly* 43, no. 37 (September 13, 2008): 19–22.

Ward, Graham, ed. *The Blackwell Companion to Postmodern Theology.* Malden: Blackwell, 2001.

Warrick, Joby. *Black Flags: The Rise of ISIS.* New York: Anchor Books, 2015.

Weber, Max, and Kalberg, Stephen. *The Protestant Ethic and the Spirit of Capitalism,* New Introduction and Translation by Stephen Kalberg. Chicago and London: Fitzroy Dearborn, 2001.

Webster, John C. B. *A Social History of Christianity: North-west India since 1800.* New Delhi: Oxford University Press, 2007.

Weidinger, Bernhard. "Equal before God, and God Alone: Cultural Fundamentalism, (Anti) Egalitarianism, and Christian Rhetoric in Nativist Discourse from Austria and the United States." *Journal of Austrian-American History* 1, no. 1 (2017): 40–68.

Weiler, Joseph H. H. "A Christian Europe? Europe and Christianity: Rules of Commitment." *European View* 6, no. 1 (December, 2007):143–150.

Westoff, Charles F., and Ryder, Norman B. "United States: The Papal Encyclical and Catholic Practice and Attitudes, 1969." *Studies in Family Planning* 1, no. 50 (1970): 1–7.

White, Stephen K. "Heidegger and the Difficulties of a Postmodern Ethics and Politics." *Political Theory* 18, no. 1 (February 1990): 80–103.

Wickeri, Philip L. *Seeking The Common Ground: Protestant Christianity, and Three-Self Movement and China's United Front.* Maryknoll: Orbis Books, 1998.

Wiegele, Katharine L. *Investing in Miracles: El Shaddai and the Transformation of Popular Catholicism in the Philippines.* Honolulu: University of Hawai'i, 2005.

Wilfred, Felix. "Asian Christianities and Theologies through the Lens of Postcolonialism." In *Concilium* 2018/1, edited by Pilario, Daniel F, Hwang, Po Ho, and Wilfred, Felix. London: SCM Press, 2018.

Wilfred, Felix. "Christianity in Hindu Polytheistic Structural Mould. Converts in Southern Tamil Nadu Respond to an Alien Religion during 'the Vasco Da Gama Epoch'." *Archives de sciences sociales des religions* 43, no. 103 (1998): 67–86.

Wilfred, Felix. "Toward an Interreligious Eco-theology." *Concilium* 2009/3, edited by Elaine M. Wainwright, Luiz Carlos Susin and Felix Wilfred, 43-54. London: SCM Press, 2009a.

Wilfred, Felix. *Asian Public Theology. Critical Concerns in Challenging Times.* Delhi: ISPCK, 2010.

Wilfred, Felix. ed. *The Oxford Handbook of Christianity in Asia.* New York: Oxford University Press, 2014.

Wilfred, Felix. ed. *Transforming Religion. Prospects for a New Society.* Delhi: ISPCK, 2009b.

Wilke, Annette. "Tamil Hindu Life in Germany. Competing and Complementary Modes in Reproducing Cultural Identity, Globalized Ethnicity, and Expansion of Religious Markets." In *Religious Pluralism in the Diaspora*, edited by Kumar, P. Pratap, 235–268. Leiden: Brill Academic Publishers, 2005.

Willaime, Jean-Paul. "La sécularisation: Une exception européenne? Retour sur un concept et sa discussion en sociologie des religions." *Revue française de sociologie* 47, no. 4 (October–December 2006): 755–783.

Williams, Rowan. "The Prophetic and the Mystical: Heiler Revisited." *New Blackfriars* 64, no. 757 (1983): 330–47.

Wilson, Bryan R. *Religious Sects: A Sociological Study.* London: Weidenfeld & Nicolson, 1970.

Wittgenstein, Ludwig. *Philosophical Investigations.* Oxford: Basil Blackwell, 1976.

Wolf, Eric R. "The Virgin of Guadalupe: A Mexican National Symbol." *The Journal of American Folklore* 71, no. 279 (1958): 34–39.

World Council of Churches, Commission on the Program to Combat Racism. *Challenge to the Church: A Theological Comment on the Political Crisis in South Africa: The KAIROS Document and Commentaries.* Geneva: Program Unit on Justice and Service, Commission on the Program to Combat Racism, WCC, 1985.

Wyse, Marion. "Falun Gong and Religious Freedom." *Cross Currents* 50, no. 1/2 (2000): 277–83.

Yadav, Kripal Chandra, and Arya, Krishan Singh. *Arya Samaj and the Freedom Movement.* New Delhi: Manohar Publications, 1988.

Yamamoto, J. Isamu. *Hinduism, TM, and Hare Krishna.* Zondervan Guide to Cults & Religious Movements. Grand Rapids, MI: Zondervan Publishing House, 2016.

Yang, Fenggang. "Chinese Conversion to Evangelical Christianity: The Importance of Social and Cultural Contexts." *Sociology of Religion* 59, no. 3 (1998): 237–257.

Yang, Fenggang. *Religion in China: Survival and Revival under Communist Rule.* New York: Oxford University Press, 2011.

Yew-Foong, Hui, ed., and Institute of Southeast Asian Studies. *Encountering Islam: The Politics of Religious Identities in Southeast Asia.* Singapore: ISEAS, 2013.

Zarni, Maung, and Brinham, Natalie. *Essays on Genocide of Rohingyas (2012–2018).* Dhaka: C.R. Akbar, 2019.

Zavos, John, Pralay Kanungo, Deepa S. Reddy, Maya Warrier, Raymond Williams, eds. *Public Hinduism.* Delhi: Sage Publications, 2012.

Zelliot, Eleanor. *From Untouchable to Dalit: Essays on the Ambedkar Movement.* New Delhi: Manohar Publications, 1992.

Zima, P. V. *Subjectivity and Identity: Between Modernity and Postmodernity.* London: Bloomsbury, 2015.

## WEB SOURCES

https://international.la-croix.com/news/matteo-salvinis-rosary-stunt-angers-italian-church/10146 [accessed on February 10, 2020].

https://www.newindianexpress.com/nation/2020/jan/27/scribe-moves-supreme-court-seeking-entry-of-muslim-women-for-prayers-in-mosque-2095249.html [accessed on February 24, 2020]; https://www.indiatoday.in/india/story/supreme-court-plea-women-mosques-namaz-entry-1502775-2019-04-16 [accessed on February 24, 2020].

http://www.vatican.va/gpII/documents/homily-pro-eligendo-pontifice_20050418_en.html [accessed on February 11, 2020].

http://jurnal.uinbanten.ac.id/index.php/kwl/article/view/2043 [accessed on October 25, 2019].

https://www.orfonline.org/research/the-islamic-state-in-indias-kerala-a-primer-56634/; https://www.theguardian.com/world/2016/nov/29/isis-recruiters-fertile-ground-kerala-indias-tourist-gem [accessed on February 17, 2020].

https://www.europarl.europa.eu/RegData/etudes/BRIE/2019/635525/EPRS_BRI(2019)635525_EN.pdf [accessed on October 31, 2019].

https://catholicherald.co.uk/news/2016/11/14/full-text-cardinals-letter-to-pope-francis-on-amoris-laetitia/ [accessed on November 7, 2019].

https://www.indiatoday.in/magazine/cover-story/story/20001204-allegations-of-sexual-molestation-continue-to-dog-sai-baba-778528-2000-12-04 [accessed on February 19, 2020].

https://thediplomat.com/2017/12/has-caste-discrimination-followed-indians-overseas/ [accessed on December 12, 2019].

https://www.catholicsandcultures.org/norway/migration-immigration [accessed on December 12, 2019].

https://www.theguardian.com/world/2018/sep/22/vatican-pope-francis-agreement-with-china-nominating-bishops [accessed on December 18, 2019].

https://www.theguardian.com/world/2019/dec/10/aung-san-suu-kyi-court-hague-genocide-hearing-myanmar-rohingya [accessed on December 22, 2019].

http://www.cmri.org/95prog2.htm [accessed on December 18, 2019].

https://www.indiatoday.in/magazine/cover-story/story/19990208-staines-killing-murder-of-australian- [accessed on December 29, 2019].

http://www.vatican.va/content/francesco/en/travels/2019/outside/documents/papa-francesco_20190204_documento-fratellanza-umana.html [accessed on December 30, 2019].

https://parliamentofreligions.org/pwr_resources/_includes/FCKcontent/File/TowardAGlobalEthic.pdf [accessed on February 28, 2020].

http://content.time.com/time/magazine/article/0,9171,165071,00.html [accessed on January 25, 2020].

http://www.usccb.org/about/public-affairs/backgrounders/health-care-social-service-humanitarian-aid.cfm [accessed on January 20, 2020].

https://www.nybooks.com/articles/1964/12/17/sartre-on-the-nobel-prize/ [accessed on May 27, 2019].

https://blogs.library.duke.edu/rubenstein/2015/01/14/jewish-voices-selma-montgomery-march/ [accessed on May 28, 2019].

https://www.thehindu.com/opinion/interview/indian-secularism-is-about-mediating-between-different-communities/article5405669.ece [accessed on May 21, 2019].

www.viveksamity.org/user/doc/CHICAGO-SPEECH.pdf.

https://www.plato.stanford.edu/entries/cosmopolitanism [accessed on January 28, 2020].

https://www.oxfam.org/en/press-releases/richest-1-percent-bagged-82-percent-wealth-created-last-year-poorest-half-humanity [accessed on March 3, 2020].

# Index[1]

---

[1] Note: Page numbers followed by 'n' refer to notes.